Based on the 'O' and 'A' level DOEACC syllabus
(M1-R4/A1-R4, Module I)

IT TOOLS AND BUSINESS SYSTEMS

Based on the 'O' and 'A' level DOEACC syllabus

(M1-R4/A1-R4, Module I)

IT TOOLS AND BUSINESS SYSTEMS

Instructional Software Research and Development (ISRD) Group

Lucknow

Tata McGraw Hill Education Private Limited

NEW DELHI

McGraw-Hill Offices

New Delhi New York St Louis San Francisco Auckland Bogotá Caracas
Kuala Lumpur Lisbon London Madrid Mexico City Milan Montreal
San Juan Santiago Singapore Sydney Tokyo Toronto

Tata McGraw-Hill

Published by the Tata McGraw Hill Education Private Limited,
7 West Patel Nagar, New Delhi 110 008.

IT Tools and Business Systems

ISBN (13): 978-1-25-900313-4
ISBN (10): 1-25-900313-2

Vice President and Managing Director—McGraw-Hill Education, Asia Pacific Region: *Ajay Shukla*

Head—Higher Education Publishing and Marketing: *Vibha Mahajan*
Manager: Sponsoring—SEM & Tech Ed.: *Shalini Jha*
Assoc. Sponsoring Editor: *Suman Sen*
Development Editor: *Surbhi Suman*
Executive—Editorial Services: *Sohini Mukherjee*
Sr Production Manager: *Satinder Baveja*
Jr Manager—Production: *Anjali Razdan*
Dy Marketing Manager—SEM & Tech Ed.: *Biju Ganesan*
Sr Product Specialist—SEM & Tech Ed.: *John Mathews*

General Manager—Production: *Rajender P Ghansela*
Asst General Manager—Production: *B L Dogra*

Typeset at Tej Composers, WZ-391, Madipur, New Delhi 110063, and printed at Avon Printers, Plot No. 16, Main Loni Road, Jawahar Nagar Industrial Area, Shahdara, Delhi-11094.

Cover Printer: SDR Printers

RALLCRZCRQRCX

The McGraw-Hill Companies

The ISRD Group

The Instructional Software Research and Development (ISRD) Group has been established by UPTEC Computer Consultancy Ltd. for content development and has been awarded the latest prestigious ISO 9001:2008 Certification that further authenticates its focus on quality in all aspects. The Group is committed to develop and produce high-quality learning and instructional material to facilitate all-round professional development of students. The Group continuously strives to enrich their content repository by constantly researching and developing new learning and instructional material. The content thus developed is tailored to take various forms including textbooks, teaching aids, lecture notes, lab assignments and exercises, both in print as well as in electronic media (CDs, etc.). It is all set to launch *www.teachmate.in*. It's an innovative online service that shall offer top-of-the-line professional education programmes via the e-learning mode. Teachmate's portfolio will include DOEACC's 'O' and 'A' Levels, engineering and IT courses along with university and open university degree programmes such as BBA, BCA, MCA, and diploma courses.

Many professionals have helped in creating UPTEC series of 'O'/'A' Level text books, and each of their contributions have been valuable. This particular book has taken its final shape with the noteworthy contributions of the following:

Ms. Leenu Jain has more than 12 years of experience in academics and has been developing instructional material for UPTEC. Presently, she is working as Senior Systems Officer at UPTEC.

The work would not have been possible without the enriching guidance and support of the following key professionals:

Er. Alok Singhal is an Electronics and Telecommunication Engineer from Roorkee University (now IIT Roorkee), with a Master's degree in Systems Engineering. He has 35 years of experience in the areas of entertainment electronics, microcomputers and microprocessor-based products. In his last assignment he was General Manager and Head of Communication Division at UPTRON India Ltd and was handling manufacturing and marketing of EPABX, RAX, radio communication, office communication, data communication, and computer products. At present, he is associated with UPTEC as a Director.

Prof. K. K. Bhutani holds his Bachelor's, Master's and Doctoral degree from the University of Allahabad, and has more than 40 years of experience in academics and industry. He has been a professor of Electronics and Head of Computer Centre, University of Allahabad. He has also worked as General Manager (Computers), Computronics India. He is former Chairman, Computer Engineering Board, Institution of Engineers (India). At present, he is associated with UPTEC as a Director.

Er. K. N. Shukla is an Electronics Engineer from IIT Kanpur with more than 35 years of experience in electronics and computer industry. He started his career with J. K. Electronics, Kanpur and has held several managerial positions at UPTRON, HILTRON and other similar companies. He was Director (Technical) at UPTRON India Limited before joining UPTEC as wholetime Director.

Dr. R. K. Jaiswal holds a Doctoral degree from the University of Lucknow and has more than 20 years of experience in academics. He started his career with Lucknow University as a Lecturer, and has worked under College Science Improvement Programme (COSIP), a Government of India scheme. He has to his credit more than a dozen research papers in national and international journals. He is presently holding the position of General Manager at UPTEC.

Er. R.K. Lele holds a bachelor's degree in Electrical Engineering from IIT Kanpur. He has Design and Development experience in embedded software/firmware, system software, computer and telecommunication/data communication hardware and exposure to real-time software in the area of switching and communication protocols. At a managerial position, he has handled various design projects with engineers during all the phases of the product design cycle. He is presently holding the position of Sr. General Manager (Systems) at UPTEC.

Dr. Upendra Kumar is an Industrial Engineer and holds a Ph.D from IIT, Delhi and has more than 30 years of experience in industry, academics and research. Dr. Kumar has worked with BHEL Corporate Systems Group, Eicher, UPTRON, National Institute for Training in Industrial Engineering (NITIE) and Indian Institute of Management (IIM), Lucknow. Dr. Kumar had conceived, created and established UPTRON-ACL and Computer Consultancy and Services Division at UPTRON earlier, as General Manager and Divisional Incharge. He has been consultant to many national/international organizations and is presently working as the Managing Director of UPTEC Computer Consultancy Ltd.

Mr. Kirti Kumar Pant has more than 20 years of experience in academics and has been developing instructional material for UPTEC. He holds a Master's Degree in Physics and Post Graduate Diploma in Business Administration (Human Resource Management). At present, he is heading Instructional Software Research and Development (ISRD) Group at UPTEC.

We are also indebted to **Mr. Surya Prakash Sharma**, **Mr. Vikash Bajpayee** and **Mr. Rajan Awasthi** for their help with the DTP work — including data entry, formatting, making corrections, drawing and capturing figures, creating tables, and preparing the table of contents and index.

Contents at a Glance

Contents

Preface

The field of Information Technology is changing very rapidly and it has influenced nearly all dimensions of the modern society. It is related not only with computers but with a variety of similar forms such as the Internet, digital TV and cameras, DVD disks, wireless telephones, advanced fax machines, and other digital equipment.

The objective of this book is to help you understand the technology that lies beneath this IT revolution. This book is composed exactly as per syllabus (M1-R4/A1-R4) of the prescribed for Module-I - "IT Tools and Business System" of Revised "O"/"A" level course prescribed by DOEACC. It includes complete and easily understandable explanations of computer fundamentals, hardware and software concepts, operating systems, MS Office packages, and IT and society. The exercises at the end of each chapter are designed to match the DOEACC's question paper pattern. This book is divided into twenty-three chapters.

Chapter 1 provides information about application areas, generations, characteristics, and limitations of computers. It also gives you a clear understanding of different number systems like binary, decimal, hexadecimal and octal conversions from one system to another. Here you will also understand how data is internally represented in the computer.

In **Chapter 2,** You will get to know how each component is connected to the other and how they interact with each other during an operation. You will also learn about the importance of a computer's main memory and different types of memories that are available nowadays.

Chapter 3 deals with the peripheral devices that are attached to the computer system. In this chapter you will study in detail the different types of input and output devices and their usage.

Chapter 4 gives an insight into the secondary storage devices which are extensively used for input as well as output and are commonly termed auxilliary storage devices.

Chapter 5 discuss the concepts related to software. In this chapter you will study about different classification of softwares and a variety of programming languages with their uses that are available nowadays.

Chapter 6 talks about Multimedia which is a woven combination of text, graphic art, sound, animation, and video elements. It also discusses various animation techniques and multimedia applications.

Chapters 7, 8 and 9 give an overview of different operating systems like MS Windows, Linux and MS-DOS.

Chapter 10 explains the basics of working in the Word 2003 environment. It covers such fundamentals as starting and exiting, learning to perform various operations like creating, saving, opening, and printing your documents. It also explains how to perform essential word processing tasks such as entering text, navigating a document, copying, and moving text.

Chapter 11 describes Word's tools to check spelling and grammar in documents, including proofing with AutoComplete, AutoCorrect, and AutoText.

Chapter 12 covers formatting features and techniques to add a finishing touch to your documents. You will learn the fundamentals of formatting characters, lines, paragraphs, and sections.

Chapter 13 deals with Word's powerful mail merge feature which enables you to create and print form letters, envelopes and mailing labels by combining information from two different files.

Chapter 14 explains how to use Wizards, which are built-in programs supplied with Word and templates, that are frameworks of formatting that define a document's appearance.

Chapter 15 tells you how to create sophisticated tables in your Word documents to effectively present your information. It also talks about using Word to create and publish HTML documents on the World Wide Web.

Chapter 16 explains the elements of Excel workspace, features of Excel 2003, how to navigate the worksheet and basic functions. This chapter will teach you the essential workbook file operations.

In **Chapter 17**, you will learn how to enter formulae. An explanation on cell references and their types also forms part of this chapter.

Chapter 18 explains the details of creating a chart and covers the basic information required to start working with charts. You also learn about data sharing with other Office applications.

Chapter 19 gives an insight into one of the most powerful presentation packages—Microsoft PowerPoint. It will teach you about the presentation customization, i.e., how to apply a new design template, animation and transitional effects and finally how to set up a slide show.

Chapter 20 explains the details of a database management system. This chapter deals with the basic concepts of data and its organization along with its components and architecture.

In **Chapter 21** you receive background information on Microsoft Access. You learn how to create and change a database table. You will also learn how to enter, display, change, and delete data.

Chapter 22 teaches the basics of creating data-entry forms, queries, report creation.

Chapter 23 explore the issues related to IT and its applications.

Acknowledgements

We would like to take this opportunity to thank experts who took pains to provide us valuable feedback. Their names are given below.

Mr Satish Kandhary (Arora)
Sr Manager
Aztech Education Private Limited, New Delhi
Capt. R. K. Mittal
Director,

Mohan Institute of Technology, New Delhi

ISRD Group

Feedback

Constructive suggestions and criticism always go a long way in enhancing any endeavour. We request all readers to email us their valuable comments/views/feedback regarding the book at *tmh.csefeedback@gmail.com*, mentioning the title and author name in the subject line. Also, please feel free to report any piracy of the book spotted by you.

M1-R4/A1-R4 : IT TOOLS AND BUSINESS SYSTEMS

Syllabus

Objective Of The Course

The goal of this course is to present overview of IT tools used in day to day use of computers and data base operations. The Course has been designed to provide knowledge on various hardware and software components of computer, operating system, various packages used for different applications, data base concepts & operations and various issues related to IT and application of IT.

At the end of the course the students will be able to

- Acquire the foundation level knowledge required to understand computer and its operations
- Understand the hardware and software components of the computer
- Understand the basic concept of operating system and get knowledge about various different operating systems
- Understand to use the packages of word processing, spreadsheets and presentations in detail
- Understand various database concepts and operations
- Understand the issues related to IT and IT applications

Outline of Course

S.No	Topic		Minimum Hours
1.	Computer Appreciation		04
2.	Computer Organization		06
3.	Operating System		13
4.	Word Processing		06
5.	Spreadsheet Package		09
6.	Presentation Package		05
7.	DataBase Operations		13
8.	Information Technology and Society		04
	Lectures	=	**60**
	Practical/Tutorials	=	**60**
	Total	=	**120**

Detailed Syllabus

1. Computer Appreciation 4 Hrs.

Characteristics of Computers, Input, Output, Storage units, CPU, Computer System, Binary number system, Binary to Decimal Conversion, Decimal to Binary Conversion, ASCII Code, Unicode.

2. Computer Organization 6 Hrs.

Central Processing Unit - Processor Speed, Cache, Memory, RAM, ROM, Booting, Memory- Secondary Storage Devices: Floppy and Hard Disks, Optical Disks CD-ROM, DVD, Mass Storage Devices: USB thumb drive. Managing disk Partitions, File System Input Devices - Keyboard, Mouse, joystick, Scanner, web cam, Output Devices- Monitors, Printers – Dot matrix, inkjet, laser, Multimedia- What is Multimedia, Text, Graphics, Animation, Audio, Images, Video; Multimedia Application in Education, Entertainment, Marketing. Names of common multimedia file formats, Computer Software- Relationship between Hardware and Software; System Software, Application Software, Compiler, names of some high level languages, free domain software.

3. Operating System 13 Hrs.

Microsoft Windows- An overview of different versions of Windows, Basic Windows elements, File management through Windows. Using essential accessories: System tools – Disk cleanup, Disk defragmenter, Entertainment, Games, Calculator, Imaging – Fax, Notepad, Paint, WordPad. Command Prompt- Directory navigation, path setting, creating and using batch files. Drives, files, directories, directory structure. Application Management: Installing, uninstalling, Running applications. Linux- An overview of Linux, Basic Linux elements: System Features, Software Features, File Structure, File handling in Linux: H/W, S/W requirements, Preliminary steps before installation, specifics on Hard drive repartitioning and booting a Linux system.

4. Word Processing 6 Hrs.

Word processing concepts: saving, closing, Opening an existing document, Selecting text, Editing text, Finding and replacing text, printing documents, Creating and Printing Merged Documents, Character and Paragraph Formatting, Page Design and Layout. Editing and Profiling Tools: Checking and correcting spellings. Handling Graphics, Creating Tables and Charts, Document Templates and Wizards.

5. Spreadsheet Package 9 Hrs.

Spreadsheet Concepts, Creating, Saving and Editing a Workbook, Inserting, Deleting WorkSheets, entering data in a cell / formula Copying and Moving from selected cells, handling operators in Formulae, Functions: Mathematical, Logical, statistical, text, financial, Date and Time functions, Using Function Wizard.

Formatting a Worksheet: Formatting Cells – changing data alignment, changing date, number, character or currency format, changing font, adding borders and colors, Printing worksheets, Charts and Graphs – Creating, Previewing, Modifying Charts. Integrating word processor, spread sheets, web pages.

6. Presentation Package **5 Hrs.**

Creating, Opening and Saving Presentations, Creating the Look of Your Presentation, Working in Different Views, Working with Slides, Adding and Formatting Text, Formatting Paragraphs, Checking Spelling and Correcting Typing Mistakes, Making Notes Pages and Handouts, Drawing and Working with Objects, Adding Clip Art and other pictures, Designing Slide Shows, Running and Controlling a Slide Show, Printing Presentations.

7. Data Base Operations **13 Hrs.**

Data ManipulationConcept: Database, Relational Database, Integrity. Operations: Creating, dropping, manipulating table structure. Manipulation of Data: Query, Data Entry Form, Reports.

8. Information Technology and Society **4 Hrs.**

Indian IT Act, Intellectual Property Rights – issues. Application of information Technology in Railways, Airlines, Banking, Insurance, Inventory Control, Financial systems, Hotel management, Education, Video games, Telephone exchanges, Mobile phones, Information kiosks, special effects in Movies.

C H A P T E R 1

GETTING TO KNOW COMPUTERS

FEATURING

- Computers — An Introduction
- Characteristics of Computers
- Limitations of Computers
- Applications of Computers
- The Computer System
- Components of Computer System
- Number System — An Introduction
- Memory Addressing
- Coding Schemes
- Conversion of Numbers

The era of automation/mechanization and electronic applications has dawned. The electronic and mechanical equipments have been introduced in every field of life and have brought radical change in the way tasks are performed. All this has led to greater efficiency and reduced manual labour. Computers are the most popular electronic equipments which have revolutionized almost every conceivable sphere of life.

The chapter begins with the characteristics and applications of computers. The discussion also explores the basic computer units. The chapter concludes with an overview on various number systems along with the coding schemes.

Computers – An Introduction

A computer can be defined as an electronic device that accepts some kind of data, analyzes it, and performs specified operations on the same, to produce some output. In other words, a computer accepts the input, processes it, and generates output. For example, on a railway reservation counter, your request for a ticket is fed to the computer. The computer then analyzes the given input and makes a reservation. A ticket is finally printed for you. In this case, the ticket is the output which is generated after the processing is done on the input fed to the computer.

The computer is often compared with the human brain. Like the brain that designed it, a computer can take in data and process it. It can store the data either in raw form or as processed results and can deliver the raw or processed data on demand. We can call it a data processor, because it can receive, store, process and retrieve any kind of data. For example, you can store various details (names, addresses, fee status) pertaining to a student in a computer file. On a later date, you can easily access the details of all those students, of a particular class, who have not deposited their fees.

Characteristics of Computers

The ever increasing use of computers in all walks of life is due to its special characteristics. Some of the important characteristics are described below:

- **Speed** Modern computers operate at very high speed. Electrical pulses travel at incredible speed and because the computer is an electronic device, its internal speed is virtually instantaneous. Many of today's computers can execute several million instructions in just one second. The speed of a computer is calculated in MHz (Megahertz), that is, one million instructions per second. At present, a powerful computer can perform billions of operations in just one second.
- **Accuracy** The computer's physical processing circuits rarely make errors. If the correct data and instructions are fed in, the computer gives correct results. The errors, it ever makes, is due to the erroneous data fed into it.
- **Versatility** Computers can handle a variety of applications and jobs and can be used in various fields. From preparing the balance sheet of an organization to monitoring the patient in an ICU, it can be used in almost every conceivable area of operation.
- **Diligence** Computers can perform a given set of functions endlessly without getting tired or bored. It can keep on calculating the Net Salary of thousands of employees of a company without showing any signs of fatigue.
- **Automation** No human intervention is required, once the instructions and data are given. The CPU follows these instructions until it meets the last instruction which says — stop program execution.

- **Storage Capacity** Computers can store massive amount of information. Today's computers can be equipped with disks capable of storing almost any type of data, such as pictures, sound, graphics, etc. Data, once stored, can be retrieved in the same form even when recalled after several years.
- **Reliability** Reliability is the measurement of the performance of a computer, which is measured against some predetermined standard for operation without any failure. Computers have built-in diagnostic capabilities, which help in continuous monitoring of the system.

Limitations of Computers

Computers have no intelligence of their own. It is through the instructions that are given to a computer, that it carries out its task. Some of the limitations of computers are as follows:

- It is not possible to communicate with computers using normal conversational language.
- They possess limited intelligence.
- They cannot take unstructured decision because of programmed software limitation.
- For each step to be performed by the computer, instructions are required.
- They have extremely limited ability to learn by experience.

Applications of Computers

Computers have revolutionized almost every aspect of our life. Computers are being increasingly used and their impact on social, economic, education, and scientific systems is being widely recognized. Given below are some of the areas where computers are used:

Personnel

Computers are a boon for personnel administrators as it handles routine jobs automatically and with efficiency. For example, management of payroll operations and insurance claims can be left to the computer.

Education

Computer Aided Learning (CAL) has made computer popular amongst learners. From tiny toddlers to research scholars, every learner is accruing benefits from computers. Children are being taught to use computers in their schools. Today, students can fill their application forms and give their exams online that facilitates distance education. Computer-based learning and web-based learning are very popular amongst students.

Scientific Research

Computers are extensively being used in research centres and laboratories. With the help of computers, scientists are moving towards the possibility of predicting natural disasters, such as earthquake and tsunami. Scientific research has gained momentum ever since the usage of computers has started, leading to new inventions and discoveries.

Business

This is one of the important uses of the computer. It is used in different types of business to store a large amount of information in form of databases. Currently computer are mainly used for real time applications (like at the sales counter) that require immediate response from the computer. Buyers and sellers can conduct business online through the use of computer and internet.

Medicine

Computers are playing a vital role in the field of medicine. The doctors and physicians have been largely benefited as computers are being used to monitor the patients in ICUs. They are also being used for storing information about the symptoms of various diseases along with their remedial details to facilitate the doctors.

Communication

These days, computers are being used for railway booking, plane reservations and bus reservations. Computer that are connected with each other can be used to transfer data to and from other computers. E-mail is one of the communication media in which computer is used.

Law and Order

The lawyers are finding it easier to work with the use of computers. Their task requires them to refer to a whole lot of books and previous cases necessitating them to work amidst gigantic shelves stuffed with papers. Now they can resort to computers and store large volumes of judicial proceedings in the secondary storage of the computer. Police departments and investigation departments are also using computers to keep track of criminals. In addition to this, computers are also being used to match fingerprints and make sketches of the criminals based on their physical characteristics as specified by the witnesses.

Banking

Banks have largely been benefited by the use of computers. Through online banking, the users or customers can transfer and receive money by using computers and Internet. People can use the ATM (Automated Teller Machine) Services 24 hours of the day in order to deposit and withdraw cash. Some banks also provide the facility of online bill payment through their websites.

Animation and Graphics

It is easier to understand and retain information if it is represented graphically. For example, a simple graph can easily make you decipher the sale that has taken place in various regions of the country. On the contrary, if the same is given using text, it is incomprehensible. A number of video games have been developed for entertainment.

The Computer System

Computers are information processing machines. Computer is not a single machine but, it can be viewed as a system, which consists of number of interrelated components that work together with the aim of converting data into information. Computer processed data electronically, usually with little or no intervention from a human user.

A computer accepts input in different forms such as data, programs and user reply. Data refer to the raw details that need to be processed to generate some useful information. Programs refers to the set of instructions that can be executed by the computer in sequential or non sequential manner.

The physical parts that make up a computer (the central processing unit, input, output and storage) are called hardware. Any hardware device which is connected to a computer, any part of the computer system outside the CPU and working memory, all together called peripherals. Some example of peripheral are keyboard, mouse, and monitor.

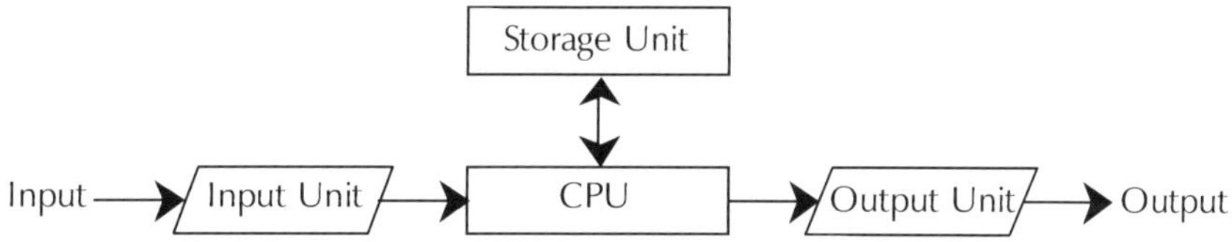

Figure 1.1 : Computer System

Components of Computer System

Even though the size, shape, performance, reliability, and cost of computer have been changing over the years, the basic logical structure, as proposed by Von Neumann, has not changed. No matter what shape and size of computer we are talking about, all computer systems comprise following four components:

1. **Input Unit** This unit accepts data and instructions.
2. **Output Unit** This unit supplies information to the user.
3. **Storage Unit** This unit stores temporary and final results.
4. **Central Processing Unit** This unit process raw data and instructions and generate meaningful information.

Input Unit

The input unit facilitates man to machine communication. Input of any form is converted into binary electronic signals which can be understood by the CPU. This process is called digitizing. Input data may be graphical, audio, visual, linguistic or mechanical. Some of the input services used for this purpose are keyboard, mouse, Voice Data Entry (VDE), Magnetic Ink Character Reader (MICR), bar code reader, magnetic tapes and disks, etc.

Output Unit

The job of an output unit is just the opposite of that of an input unit. It links the computer with the external environment. The output unit translates machine-readable codes into a form that can be used by humans. The output that comes from the CPU is in the form of binary signals which gets converted into a form that can be understood by humans, that is, graphical, audio visual or language form. Some of the popular output devices are Visual Display Unit (VDU), plotter, printer, speech synthesizer, magnetic disks, magnetic tapes, etc.

Storage Unit

The storage unit of a computer system is designed to store all the data and instructions that are entered into the system, and also the results produced after processing done by the computer. It also holds the intermediate results produced by the computer for ongoing processing. The storage unit of a computer consists of the following two types of storage:

1. **Primary storage or main memory** — It holds data and instructions, intermediate results of processing, and results of processing of the ongoing job(s). The information stored in the main memory can be directly accessed by the central processing unit at a very fast speed.
2. **Secondary storage or auxiliary storage** — It is used to supplement the limited storage capacity and the volatile characteristic of primary storage. It can store the data and instructions for processing at a later time. Magnetic disk is the most commonly used secondary storage medium.

Central Processing Unit (CPU)

The Central Processing Unit (CPU) is the brain of the computer system. All the actions performed by the computer system are initiated, performed and controlled by the CPU. The CPU works with binary signals only i.e., either 1 or 0. Every instruction that is executed first gets stored in the memory unit, then it gets processed by the CPU. Among other things, its configuration determines whether a computer is fast or slow.

Number System –An Introduction

A computer is a digital system that stores and processes different types of data in the form of 0s and 1s. The different types of data handled by a computer system include numbers, alphabets and some special characters. Therefore, there is a need to change the data entered by the users into a form that the computer system can understand and process. Different types of codes have been developed and used to represent the data entered by the users in the binary format. The binary system represents each type of data in terms of binary digits, 0s and 1s. Since these codes convert the data into the binary form, the computer codes are also referred as **binary codes**.

Computer professionals use different number systems according to their requirements to communicate with the computer system. All the number systems used by computer professionals to interact with computer systems come under the category of **positional number system**. In this system, numbers are represented using some symbols called digits and the values of these numbers can be determined by taking the position of digits into consideration. The different number systems, which come under the category of positional number system, are as follows:

- Decimal Number System
- Binary Number System
- Octal Number System
- Hexadecimal Number System

Decimal Number System

Our present number system with a base or radix of 10 is based on use of 10 different digits (0-9), known as Arabic numerals. The highest numerical symbol, that is, 9 has a value one less than the base for the decimal number system. This number system is most easily understandable and is most popular.

Binary Number System

Gotfried Wilhelm Von Leibnitz advocated use of binary number system in the 17th century. Binary number system uses only two digits, that is, 0 and 1 and has a base or radix of 2. All decimal numbers can be represented using the combination of these two digits only. Use of binary number system in computers simplifies the design, reduces the cost, and improves the reliability. It also simplifies the design of storage devices. All the modern computers use binary number (0 and 1) system. The binary number system is the most natural number system, requires a small amount of circuitry, and is more efficient.

Octal Number System

A number system with base or radix of 8 is known as octal number system. Digits used in this number system are 0 to 7. For the representation of an octal number in binary number system, 3 bits are required to represent each digit of octal number system.

Hexadecimal Number System

Hexadecimal number system is a number system with base or radix of 16. Digits used in this number system are 0 to 9 and A, B, C, D, E, F where decimal values of A to F are 10 to 15 respectively. A represents 10, B represents 11, and so on. In binary representation, 4 bits (1 nibble) are used to represent each digit of hexadecimal number. It is more compact than any other number system.

Memory Addressing

Memory consists of an array of storage units known as **cell** or **location** and each cell has a unique address. The smallest unit to store data in memory location is a single bit, and 8 bits form a byte. Byte is the basic unit to store data. Data can be stored as a single byte or multiples of 2 bytes (16 bits), 4 bytes (32 bits), 8 bytes (64 bits), according to the word size in the memory, where the identification code of each cell corresponding to a word in memory, is known as its address. If a memory has the size of eight words, 8 different combinations of bits will be required to uniquely address these locations. So, we can say that, in general, with n bits 2^n words of a memory can be addressed.

For random access capability, each memory location has to be assigned a unique address. Normally memory addresses are represented in *octal* and *hexadecimal* number systems. Memory addressing in binary number system would be too long and complex. Computer's memory size is represented in terms of octal and hexadecimal number systems, because these are more compact.

Coding Schemes

Computer represents information in coded form instead of pure binary numbers. To represent the names and other pertinent information it is necessary to formulate a binary code for letters of the alphabet so that we can have code in the form acceptable to the computer.

An alphanumeric code is a binary code of a group of elements. These elements may be decimal digits from 0-9, letters of alphabet (A,B,C,...Z) and certain number of special symbols such as +, -, *, /, $. There are lot of ways to represent numeric, alphabetic and special characters in computer's internal storage area. In computers, the code is made up of fixed size groups of binary position. Each binary position in a group is assigned a specific value; for example 8,4,2, or 1. In this way, every character can be represented by a combination of bits that is unique. Although there are many coding schemes available for representing characters. The most commonly used coding systems are ASCII and Unicode.

ASCII

The American Standard Code for Information Interchange (ASCII), was developed to standardize codes of various data processing equipment; it is primarily used by non-IBM computer systems. ASCII represents total 256 symbols as we can have only 256 different combinations out of 8 bits of binary system using only two symbols 0 and 1.

Decimal	Character	Hex	Decimal	Character	Hex	Decimal	Character	Hex
0	(null)	00	44	,	2C	88	X	58
1	(start of heading)	01	45	-	2D	89	Y	59
2	(start of text)	02	46	.	2E	90	Z	5A
3	(end of text)	03	47	/	2F	91	[	5B
4	(end of transmission)	04	48	0	30	92	\	5C
5	(enquiry)	05	49	1	31	93	]	5D
6	(acknowledge)	06	50	2	32	94	^	5E
7	(bell)	07	51	3	33	95	_	5F
8	(backspace)	08	52	4	34	96	`	60
9	(horizontal tab)	09	53	5	35	97	a	61
10	(line feed)	0A	54	6	36	98	b	62
11	(vertical tab)	0B	55	7	37	99	c	63
12	(form feed)	0C	56	8	38	100	d	64
13	(carriage return)	0D	57	9	39	101	e	65
14	(shift out)	0E	58	:	3A	102	f	66
15	(shift in)	0F	59	;	3B	103	g	67
16	(data link escape)	10	60	<	3C	104	h	68
17	(device ctrl 1)	11	61	=	3D	105	i	69
18	(device ctrl 2)	12	62	>	3E	106	j	6A
19	(device ctrl 3)	13	63	?	3F	107	k	6B
20	(device ctrl 4)	14	64	@	40	108	l	6C
21	(negative acknowledge)	15	65	A	41	109	m	6D
22	(synchronous idle)	16	66	B	42	110	n	6E
23	(end of transmission)	17	67	C	43	111	o	6F
24	(cancel)	18	68	D	44	112	p	70
25	(end of medium)	19	69	E	45	113	q	71
26	(substitute)	1A	70	F	46	114	r	72
27	(escape)	1B	71	G	47	115	s	73
28	(file separator)	1C	72	H	48	116	t	74
29	(group separator)	1D	73	I	49	117	u	75
30	(record separator)	1E	74	J	4A	118	v	76
31	(unit separator)	1F	75	K	4B	119	w	77
32	(space)	20	76	L	4C	120	x	78
33	!	21	77	M	4D	121	y	79
34	"	22	78	N	4E	122	z	7A
35	#	23	79	O	4F	123	{	7B
36	$	24	80	P	50	124	|	7C
37	%	25	81	Q	51	125	}	7D
38	&	26	82	R	52	126	~	7E
39	'	27	83	S	53	127	(delete)	7F
40	(	28	84	T	54			
41	)	29	85	U	55			
42	*	2A	86	V	56			
43	+	2B	87	W	57			

Table 1.1 : ASCII Code Chart

Almost all smaller computers, including minicomputers and personal computers use the ASCII. Originally, ASCII used a seven-bit system i.e., 128 (2^7) different characters, but those systems didn't allow computers, to represent enough characters. Today ASCII uses an eight-bit coding system, that can represent 256 (2^8) different characters. The codes of first 128 characters (symbols) are identical in ASCII-7 and ASCII-8. Table 1.1 of ASCII coding chart shows upper case and lower case alphabetic characters and numeric digits 0 to 9. The standard ASCII code define 128 character codes (0 to127) of which, the first 32 are control codes (non-printable), and other 96 are representable characters.

Unicode

Unicode provides a unique number for every character, no matter what the platform, no matter what the program, no matter what the language. Fundamentally, computers just deal with numbers. They store letters and other characters by assigning a number for each one. Before unicode was invented there were hundreds of different encoding systems for assigning these numbers. No single encoding could contain enough characters. For example, the European Union alone requires several different encodings to cover all its languages. Even for a single language like English no single encoding was adequate for all the letters, punctuation, and technical symbols in common use.

These encoding systems also conflict with one another. That is ,two encodings can use the same number for two different characters, or use different numbers for the same character. Any given computer (especially servers) needs to support many different encodings; yet whenever data is passed between different encodings or platforms, that data always runs the risk of corruption. The 16-bit unicode is an International 16-bit character set that contains a maximum of 2^{16} =65,536 different characters. The code assigned to each character of different languages, is universal and can be used on any platform without any modification.

Unicode is Changing all that !

The unicode standard has been adopted by such industry leaders as Apple, HP, IBM, JustSystems, Microsoft, Oracle, SAP, Sun, Sybase, Unisys and many others. It is supported in many operating systems, all modern browsers, and many other products. The emergence of the Unicode Standard, and the availability of tools supporting it, are among the most significant recent global software technology trends. Unicode enables a single software product or a single website to be targeted across multiple platforms, languages and countries without re-engineering.

Conversion of Numbers

The computer systems accept the data in decimal form, whereas they store and process the data in binary form. Therefore, it becomes necessary to convert the numbers represented in one system into the number represented in one system into the number represented in another system. Various techniques, which can be used to convert numbers from one base to another are:

Conversion from Decimal Number System to Other Number Systems

Integer/Whole Numbers

The decimal to binary conversion is performed by dividing the decimal number, by the base of the required number system, and record the remainder as the right most digit (least significant digit), then divide the quotient again by the base and record the remainder as the next significant digit. Repeat these steps until quotient becomes 0. The last remainder is the left most, that is, most significant digit of the required system.

For binary divide by 2, for octal divide by 8, and for hexadecimal divide by 16.

Examples:

i. Decimal to Binary

$(55)_{10} \longrightarrow (110111)_2$

2	55	Remainder (LSB)	
2	27	1	
2	13	1	
2	6	1	
2	3	0	
2	1	1	
	0	1	(MSB)

ii. Decimal to Octal

$(55)_{10} \longrightarrow (67)_8$

8	55	Remainder (LSB)	
8	6	7	
	0	6	(MSB)

iii) Decimal to Hexadecimal

$(55)_{10} \longrightarrow (37)_{16}$

16	55		Remainder (LSB)
16	3	7	↑
	0	3	(MSB)

Fractional Numbers

For fractional numbers, the system of conversion from decimal number system to other number systems is just the opposite. Multiply the fraction by the base of the required number system. Note the integer part of result as left most, that is, most significant digit of required result. Then multiply the fraction part of the result by the base again. Note the integer part of the result as the next digit of the result. Repeat these steps until fractional part of the result becomes 0.

Examples:

i. **Decimal to Binary**

$(55.127)_{10} \rightarrow (110111.00100)_2$ Approx.

$.127 \times 2 = 0.254$

$.254 \times 2 = 0.508$

$.508 \times 2 = 1.016$

$.016 \times 2 = 0.032$

$.032 \times 2 = 0.064$ . . .

ii. **Decimal to Octal**

$(55.24)_{10} \rightarrow (67.1727)_8$ Approx.

$.24 \times 8 = 1.92$

$.92 \times 8 = 7.36$

$.36 \times 8 = 2.88$

$.88 \times 8 = 7.04$ . . .

iii. **Decimal to Hexadecimal**

$(55.25)_{10} \rightarrow (37.4)_{16}$ Exact

$.25 \times 16 = 4.00$

Conversion from Other Number Systems to Decimal Number System

Integer/Whole Numbers

Each digit of the given number is multiplied by its base (2, 8 or 16) that has a power of position -1. The position is counted from the right most bit of the given number. Then all the products of multiplication are summed to get the decimal equivalent of the number of other number system.

Examples:

i. Binary to Decimal

$(1110111)_2 \rightarrow (119)_{10}$

$1 \times 2^6 + 1 \times 2^5 + 1 \times 2^4 + 0 \times 2^3 + 1 \times 2^2 + 1 \times 2^1 + 1 \times 2^0$
$= 64 + 32 + 16 + 0 + 4 + 2 + 1$

$= 119$

ii. Octal to Decimal

$(127)_8 \rightarrow (87)_{10}$

$1 \times 8^2 + 2 \times 8^1 + 7 \times 8^0$

$= 64 + 16 + 7$

$= 87$

iii. Hexadecimal to Decimal

$(12\ A)_{16} \rightarrow (298)_{10}$

$= 1 \times 16^2 + 2 \times 16^1 + A \times 16^0$

$= 298$

Fractional Numbers

Each digit of given number is multiplied by the base of required number that has a negative power equal to position of the digit. Position is counted from immediate right of the decimal. After multiplication all the products are summed to get decimal equivalent of the fraction.

Examples:

i. Binary to Decimal

$(.11)_2 \rightarrow (.75)_{10}$

$1 \times 2^{-1} + 1 \times 2^{-2}$

$= 1 \times 1/2 + 1/2^2$

$= 1/2 + 1/4$

$= .5 + .25 = .75$

ii. Octal to Decimal

$(.24)_8 \rightarrow (3124)_{10}$ Approx.

$2 \times 8^{-1} + 4 \times 8^{-2}$

$= 2 \times .125 + 4 \times .0156$

$= .250 + .0624 = (.3124)_{10}$

iii. Hexadecimal to Decimal

$(.A2)_{16} \rightarrow (.6328)_{10}$ Approx.

$A \times 16^{-1} + 2 \times 16^{-2}$

$= 10 \times 1/16 + 2 \times 1/16^2$

$= 10 \times .0625 + 2 \times .0039$

$= .625 + .0078$

$= .6328$

Summary

- A computer is a machine that stores, retrieves, sends, receives, analyses, and synthesizes the data to produce information.
- Some of the important characteristics of computers are: speed, accuracy, versatility, diligence, automation, storage capacity and programmability
- Computers are changing people's lives in areas as diverse as medicine, education, publishing, business, home, and transportation.
- Computer is an electronic machine that takes input from the user and stores and processes it to generate the output in the form of useful information to the user.
- Data are raw details that need to be processed to generate some useful information.
- CPU is referred to as the brain of the computer and is responsible for processing the data inside the computer system.
- Computer being an electronic machine can have all inputs and outputs in the form of electronic pulses.
- The different number systems are decimal, binary, octal and hexadecimal.

- The octal and hexadecimal numbers are used to represent the memory addressing and data representation in computers.
- ASCII systems are of two types, 7 bit and 8 bit, and are used to represent numbers and characters, in ASCII code system.
- Unicode provides a unique number for every character.

Review Exercise

Multiple choice questions

1. Which component of the computer is known as the brain of computer?
   a) Monitor
   b) CPU
   c) Memory
   d) None of the above
2. Which of the following is a characteristic of the modern digital computer?
   a) High speed
   b) Large storage capacity
   c) Greater accuracy
   d) All of the above
3. The program and instructions that help the computer in carrying out their processing are known as?
   a) Hardware
   b) Software
   c) Data
   d) None of the above
4. Hexadecimal number system has
   a) base of 10
   b) base of 8
   c) base of 16
   d) none of these
5. The octal equivalent of $(10110.0101)_2$ is
   a) 26.35
   b) 25.24
   c) 26.24
   d) 26.25

State whether true or false

1. The speed of computer is calculated in Kilohertz.
2. The processor only operates on binary data, that is, data composed of 1s and 0s.
3. The decimal equivalent of $(31)_{16}$ is $(63)_{10}$.
4. Hexadecimal number system uses digits from 0 to 9 and the letters A, B, C, D, E and F.
5. The decimal equivalent of $(110.1001)_2$ is $(6.7324)_{10}$.

Fill in the blanks

1. CPU stands for ______________.
2. The 16-bit ______________ is an international standard for representing characters from various languages.
3. The base of any number system depends upon the number of ______________ in the system.
4. Redix in Hexadecimal system is ______________.
5. ASCII represents total ____________ symbols.

Descriptive questions

1. Why do we use binary number system in computers? Is it feasible to use decimal number system?
2. What are the benefits of using hexadecimal code for memory addressing? What do you understand by memory addressing.?
3. Discuss briefly the various characteristics of a computer.
4. List, with example, five important areas of computers today.
5. What are the different components of a computer? Explain, each of them.
6. Write short notes on:
   a) ASCII
   b) Unicode

CHAPTER 2

PROCESSING AND MEMORY

FEATURING

- Introduction
- CPU
- Processor Speed
- Main Memory Unit
- Random Access Memory (RAM)
- Read Only Memory (ROM)
- Cache Memory

For most users, what's inside the system unit - the big box that contains the processing circuitry and storage devices — is a mystery. Yet a little knowledge of what's inside the box is essential for computer literacy. In this chapter, we will learn the role of Central Processing Unit (CPU) in a computer system and the working of various components of CPU. This chapter also explain the role played by the computer's internal memory and the different forms of memory.

Introduction

Computer represent data in digital form; computers treat everything, even text, numerically. The Central Processing Unit processes the data, and internal memory keeps program instructions and data readily available in an electronic scratch pad. Computers are used not only for processing of data for immediate use, but also for storing of large volume of data for future use. In order to meet these two specific requirements, computers use two types of storage locations — one, for storing the data that are being currently handled by the CPU and the other, for storing the results and the data for future use. These two storage locations are known as primary memory and secondary memory respectively.

CPU

The Central Processing Unit (CPU) is referred to as the "brain" of a computer system, which converts data (input) into meaningful information (output). It is the most complex computer system component, responsible for directing most of the computer system activities based on the instructions provided. The CPU circuitry of a microcomputer, called a **microprocessor**, fits on a chip about the size of your thumbnail, or even smaller. The main operations of the CPU include four phases:

- Fetching instructions from the memory.
- Decoding the instructions to decide what operations to be performed.
- Executing the instructions.
- Storing the results back in the memory.

The CPU consists of the three main subsystems, the Arithmetic/Logic Unit (ALU), the Control Unit (CU) and the Registers.

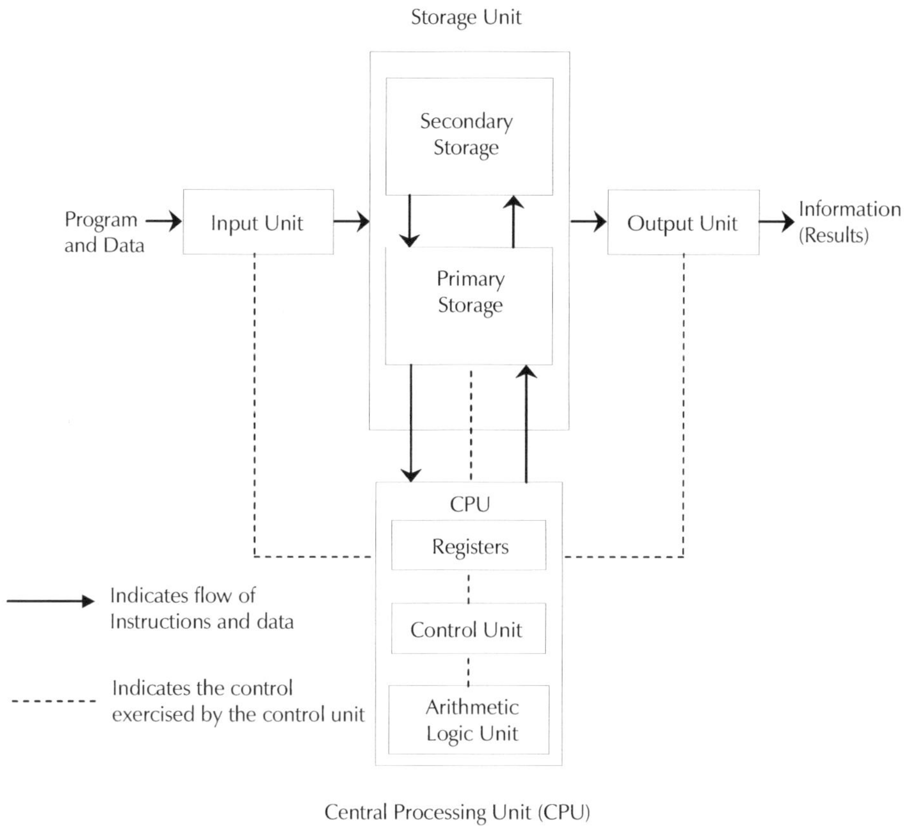

Figure 2.1 : Basic organization of a computer system

Control Unit

It is the most important component of the CPU. It manages and coordinates the entire computer system. In other words, it acts as a central nervous system for the other components of the computer. It is responsible for generating control signals to stream line the functioning of the CPU and other units. The control unit determines the sequence in which program instructions are interpreted and executed. It also controls the flow of data to and from secondary storage devices.

It has some special purpose registers and a decoder to perform these activities. The special purpose registers hold the current instruction and the next instruction to be executed and in this way help the control unit in instruction selection. On the other hand, the decoder has the necessary circuitry to decode and interpret the meaning of each and every instruction supported by the CPU.

Although the control unit does not perform any actual processing on the data, it acts as a central nervous system for the other components of the computer. It manages and coordinates the entire computer system including the input and output units. It obtains instructions from the program stored in the main memory, interprets the instructions, and issues signals that cause other units of the system to execute them.

Arithmetic and Logic Unit (ALU)

The ALU of the CPU is the place where the actual execution of the instructions take place during the data processing operation. The arithmetic unit performs number of calculations and computations. The logic unit is used to apply logic, that is, used to compare, certain types of tests and take decisions. All such logical operations are performed in this unit. This unit has a number of registers and accumulators for short-term storage of data while doing calculations and comparisons.

For example, the control unit might load two numbers into the registers in the ALU. Then, it might tell the ALU to add the two numbers (an arithmetic operation), or to check if the two numbers are equal. The ALU also controls the speed of calculations.

Registers

As the CPU interprets and executes the instructions, movement of information takes place between the various units of the computer system. In order to speed up the rate of information transfer, the computer uses a number of special purpose, high-speed temporary memory units called **registers**.

These registers are used to store the instructions as well as temporary results. The number and types of registers in a CPU vary according to the CPU's design. The length of a register equals the number of bits it can store. Thus, a register that can store 8 bits is normally referred to as an 8-bit register. Their size (capacity) and number can dramatically affect the processing power of a computer system. In general, the larger the register, the greater the processing power. Some of the common registers and their functions are given below:

- **Memory Data Register (MDR)** It is used for storing the operands and other data.
- **Memory Address Register (MAR)** It holds the address of the next location in memory to be accessed.
- **Accumulator (A)** It is a general-purpose register used for storing temporary results and results produced by arithmetic and logical unit.
- **Instruction Register (IR)** It holds instruction to be decoded by the control unit.
- **Program Counter (PC)** It holds the address of the next instruction to be executed.

Processor Speed

The operations of the ALU and the control unit are performed with incredible speed. These operations are usually synchronized by a built-in electronic clock (known as **system clock**) that emits millions of regularly spaced electric pulses per second (known as **clock**

cycles). Commands are interpreted and then executed at proper intervals, and the intervals are timed by a specific number of clock cycles. One cycle is the time it takes to perform one operation. Normally, several clock cycles are required to fetch, decode, and execute a single program instruction. The shorter the clock cycle, the faster the processor. Thus, the speed with which an instruction is executed is directly related to the computer's built-in clock speed, which is the number of pulses produced each second. The clock speed is measured in **megahertz**. The number of operations performed per clock cycle also affects CPU performance.

Main Memory Unit

The main memory, also known as the primary memory is an integral component of the CPU but physically it is a separate part placed on the computer's motherboard. It is also known as Random Access Memory (RAM). It is a temporary storage medium that holds the data and instructions for a short period of time. It is volatile in nature, which means the information stored in it remains as long as the power is switched on. As soon as the power is switched off, the information contained is lost. The data and instructions store in the primary memory can be directly accessed by the CPU using the data and address buses. However, the information stored in the secondary memory is not directly accessible to CPU. Firstly, the information has to be transferred to the primary memory using I/O channels and then, to the CPU. This technique is known as **swapping**.

Figure 2.2 : RAM Chip

In the memory, values are represented from by sequences of binary digits, known as **bits**. Most computers use a group of eight bits known as **byte**, to represent a character. Memory can be think of as a "bunch" of bytes or cells into which data is placed. Each cell, known as a data item, is assigned a unique number known as **address**, through which the CPU identify each cell. Each of these cells can store a fixed number of bits called **word length** of the memory.

You might have heard about 8-bit computers, 16-bit computers, 32-bit computers, etc. They refer to the word length of memory of a computer in terms of its total number of bits per memory word. More number of bits per word, means a more rapid flow of electronic signals, in other words, a faster computer can amount of data that an 8-bit computer can transfer to and from memory in one minute, a 32-bit computer may transfer in a few seconds.

Computer memories are often rated in terms of their capacity to store information. Typically, capacities are described using the unit of bytes as follows:

1 character = 1byte = 8 bits

1 Kilo byte (KB) = 1024 bytes or 2^{10} bytes

1 Mega byte (MB) = 1024 KB

= 1024×1024 bytes or 2^{20} bytes

1 Giga byte (GB) = 1024 MB

= $1024 \times 1024 \times 1024$ bytes or 2^{30} bytes

Thus if we say that the capacity of a primary memory is 16 MB it means it contains 16×2^{20} bytes or 2^{24} bytes.

Random Access Memory (RAM)

RAM stands for Random Access Memory and is a read-write memory of a computer. In a Random Access Memory, any location can be accessed in a random manner and the access time is same for each memory location. RAM is made up of different ICs, are mounted on a printed circuit board.

Files and programs are loaded into memory from external media like hard disk, RAM is a hardware location in the computer where the operating system, application programs, and data in current use are kept so that they can quickly reached by the computer's processor.

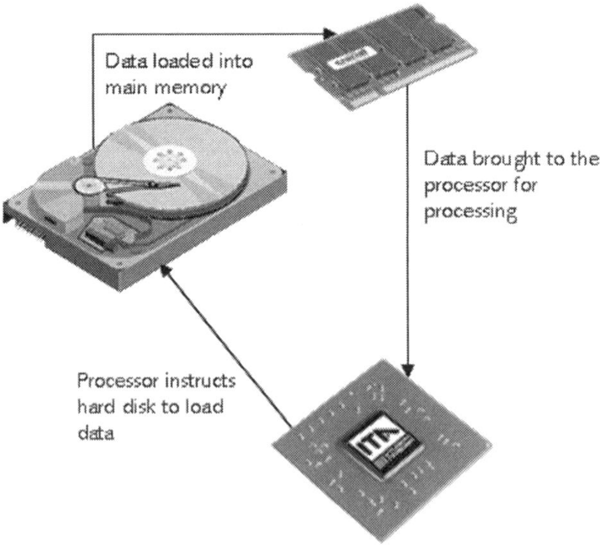

Figure 2.3 : Communication of Memory and Storage with CPU

Types of RAM

Random Access Memory is of two types :

- **Static RAM (SRAM)** Static RAM consists of internal flip-flops that store binary information. The stored information in the SRAM remains valid as long as power is applied to the unit. SRAM is easier to use and has shorter read and write cycles, that is, high speed. Static RAMs are costlier and consume more power. SRAM is often used as cache memory due to its high speed.
- **Dynamic RAM (DRAM)** Dynamic RAM stores binary information in the form of electric charges that are applied to capacitors. The stored charges on the capacitors tend to discharge with time. The capacitors must be periodically recharged by refreshing the dynamic memory. This refreshing is done by cycling through the words every few milliseconds to restore the decaying charge. DRAM has reduced power consumption and larger storage capacity in a single memory chip.

Read Only Memory (ROM)

ROM stands for Read Only Memory, that is, nothing can be written on it. ROM is a non-volatile memory; the information stored on it is not lost when power goes off. It is used for storing the bulk of the programs that are permanently resident in the computer. The contents of ROM are decided by the hardware manufacturer. The necessary programs are hardwired during the manufacture of computer. It also possesses random access property and stores information which is not subject to change.

ROM is used for storing an initial program called a "**Bootstrap loader**". This is a program whose function is to start the computer operating system when power is turned ON. Since RAM is volatile, its contents are destroyed when power is turned OFF. The contents of ROM remain unchanged after power is turned OFF and ON again. When power is turned ON, the hardware of the computer sets the program counter to the first address of the bootstrap loader. The bootstrap program loads a portion of the operating system from disk to main memory and control is then transferred to the operating system.

ROM is divided into four types. They are distinguished by the methods used to write new data to them and the number of times they can be rewritten. Common feature of these devices is their ability to retain data and programs, even during a power failure. ROM comes in following types:

1. **Programmable ROM** PROM has been programmed once, its contents can never be changed. As a result, PROM is also known as one-time programmable (OTP) device. To write the data on the PROM chip, a device known as PROM programmer or PROM burner is required. It is mostly used in video games and electronic dictionaries.
2. **Erasable PROM** EPROM is a type of ROM in which data can be erased or destroyed using Ultraviolet Light (UL). EPROMs are used to store programs which

are permanent but need updating. Note that an EPROM eraser is not selective; it will erase the entire EPROM. It is more expensive than PROM.

3. **Electrically Erasable PROM** EEPROM is a type of ROM in which data can be erased or destroyed by exposing it to an electric charge. The chip can be erased and reprogrammed on the board easily on a byte by byte basis, rather than erasing the entire chip with ultraviolet light. Hence, the process of re-programming is flexible, but slow.

4. **Flash ROM** Flash ROM is a type of EEPROM, that can be erased and re-programmed in blocks (rather than byte). Flash memory is often used to hold control code such as the BIOS in a personal computer. This memory is mainly used in the memory cards of mobile phones, digital cameras and ipods for storing data.

Cache Memory

The cache memory is placed between the CPU and main memory. It is a fast speed memory and is expensive and faster than the main memory. Cache memory is used to store the frequently accessed data of the main memory. The instructions that are frequently used by the CPU are stored in cache memory. It is used to reduce the average access time for address, instructions or data which are normally stored in the main memory. Thus the cache memory increases the operating speed of the system. But it is much costlier than the main memory. From economic considerations, the capacity of the cache memory is much less as compared to the main memory.

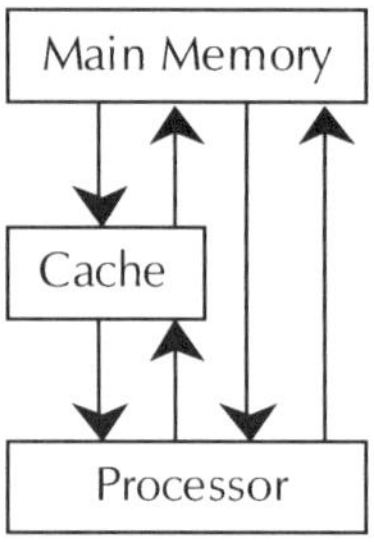

Figure 2.4 : Placement of cache memory

Most of the 32-bit microprocessors, nowadays, have the cache memory on a chip. Besides this, modern computers also provide external cache on the mother board.

Summary

- Computer is not a single machine but a combination of several working units: Input, Output, storage and central processing unit.
- The CPU is the brain of any computer system in which all calculations and comparisons performed by a computer are carried out.

- Registers are small, high-speed storage units, which are used to hold the information on a temporary basis when there is an interpretation and execution of instructions by the CPU.
- Cache memory is a small high speed memory, which is used to increase the speed of processing by making current programs and data available to the CPU at a rapid rate.

Review Exercise

Multiple choice questions

1. The cache memory enhances
   a) speed of input devices
   b) access speed of the CPU and the main memory
   c) speed of output devices
   d) none of the above
2. RAM is a
   a) permanent memory
   b) temporary memory
   c) both of the above
   d) none of the above
3. DRAM
   a) has reduced power consumption
   b) does not require periodic refreshing
   c) is costlier than SRAM
   d) none of the above
4. Which of the following is not a determining factor of computer speed?
   a) number of disk drives
   b) internal data bus width
   c) clock speed
   d) external data bus width

5. Which of the following is an example of volatile memory?
   a) ROM
   b) PROM
   c) EPROM
   d) RAM

State whether true or false

1. ALU is used to control operations of CPU.
2. Instruction Register contains 16 bits to store instructions.
3. DRAM consists of flip-flops that store binary information.
4. PROM can be erased.
5. Cache memory increases load on main memory.

Fill in the blanks

1. All the physical components of a computer system are called ___________ .
2. The ___________ unit acts as an interface between the CPU and the output devices.
3. The ___________ is the brain of a computer system.
4. The CPU needs ___________ for storing instructions as well as intermediate results.
5. An 8-bit unit used ot code data is called a ___________.

Descriptive questions

1. Explain the role of cache memory.
2. Distinguish between
   a) CPU and ALU
   b) Internal and External Memory
   c) Static RAM and Dynamic RAM
   d) Cache Memory and Main Memory
3. What is a register? Explain the role of different types of registers in processing.
4. What do the following stand for:
   RAM, EPROM, DRAM, EROM, PROM
5. What determines the time required to access the needed data?

CHAPTER

3 PERIPHERAL DEVICES

FEATURING

- Peripheral Devices — An Introduction
- Input Devices
- Output Devices

The peripheral devices of a computer, referred to as I/O (Input/Output) devices, provide an efficient mode of communication between the central system and the outside environment. Programs and data must be entered into the computer for processing and results obtained must be recorded or displayed. A computer serves no purpose without the ability to receive information from an outside source and transmit back the results in a meaningful form. The most familiar means of entering information into a computer is through the keyboard and mouse. Similarly, a number of output devices are available on which the computer system can give its processing results like printer, computer screen (VDU), plotter, and disks. In this chapter we will study, in detail, different types of input and output devices and their usage.

Peripheral Devices – An Introduction

Input/Output (I/O) devices attached to a computer are also called **peripherals**. Among the most common peripherals are keyboards, display units, and printers. Peripherals that provide auxiliary storage for the system are magnetic disks and tapes. Peripherals are electromechanical and electromagnetic devices. These devices are called peripherals because they are attached in the surroundings (periphery) of the computer systems. Peripheral devices are classified mainly into two types: input devices and output devices.

Input Devices

Input devices are used to enter the data and instructions into the computer system before any processing can be performed. They are electromechanical devices and act as an interface between the computer and the user. Input devices are used to take the input from the user, translate it into the machine readable form and then present it to the processing unit of the computer for execution. Computer accepts input in two ways, either manually through devices such as keyboard and mouse, or directly by transferring information automatically from a source document (like barcode) into the computer. Some of the commonly used input devices are keyboard, mouse, joystick and scanner.

Keyboard

The most widely used input device today is the keyboard. It is similar to a typewriter in that all the keys are arranged like those on a typewriter but there are some extra keys also (Figure 3.1). Every key and key combination passes a unique signal to the computer. It is generally used for typing text-based information. During typing, the keys get displayed on the VDU so that the user can see what is being typed. Control (Ctrl) and Alternate (Alt) keys in combination with other keys have special functions. The traditional format of a computer keyboard is called QWERTY keyboard because of the sequence of the six letters on the left hand corner of the upper row. Today wireless keyboards are also available that work with the help of batteries.

Figure 3.1 : Keyboard

Mouse

Mouse is a small hand-held pointing device, usually, a mouse contains two or three buttons, which can be used to input commands or information. It is basically controls the two-dimensional movement of the cursor on the displayed screen. The mouse may be classified as a mechanical mouse or an optical mouse, based on the technology it user. A mechanical mouse consists of two or three buttons. Inside the plastic coating of the mouse, there is a ball, which is rolled over a flat surface corresponding to which the cursor moves on the display screen.

An optical mouse uses a light beam instead of a rotating ball to detect movement across a specially patterned mouse pad. Pricies then their mechanical counterparts, modern optical mice are accurate and often do not need a mouse pad. The mouse cannot easily be used with laptop, notebook or palmtop computers. These types of computers need a track ball or a touch sensitive pad called a touch pad.

Figure 3.2 : Mouse

Joystick

Joystick is a pointing device that moves in all directions and controls the movement of the cursor. The basic design of a joystick consists of a stick that is attached to a plastic base with a flexible rubber sheath. It is commonly used for playing games on computers. It provides fast, controlled movement on the screen and allows movement of objects around the screen with ease. The movement is sensed by a vertical stick which is attached to a solid base. It is also used for applications, which includes flight simulators, training simulators, CAD/CAM Systems, and for controlling industrial robots.

Figure 3.3 : Joystick

Scanners

Scanners look and work somewhat like photo copiers. Scanners are optoelectric devices which convert any type of printed or written information into digital pulses, which can be manipulated by computer into any mode. Scanners are useful to store printed data electronically in the computer's memory. The scanned image is transferred to the system and saved in a graphic format generally as a paint package file or CorelDraw file. Scanners are of two types:

- Flat-bed Scanner
- Hand-held Scanner

Flat-bed Scanner

Flat-bed scanners look similar to a photocopies machine that consists of a box with a glass plate on its top and to cover the glass plate, a lid is there. To scan a document, the document is placed upside-down on the glass plate. Below the glass plate, the light source is situated that moves left to right horizontally, when activated. The light beam moves up a little and the next line is scanned after scanning the previous line. This process is repeated for all the lines. It takes about 20 seconds to scan a document of size 21 cm x 28 cm. Nowdays the flatbed scanners are widely used in almost every organization.

Figure 3.4 : A Flat-bed Scanner

Hand-held Scanner

In this type of scanner, a set of light emitting diodes are there that are encased in a small case which makes it convenient and easy to hold in hands. The hand-held scanner is slowly dragged from one end of the document to the other end with its light ON. The dragging has to be done carefully otherwise, the equivalent bit map conversion of the document is not proper. This is the reason, hand-held scanners are preferred only in the case where high accuracy is required. Hand-held is also preferred when the amount of documents to be scanned is low. These scanners are cheaper in comparison to flat bed scanner. The hand-held scanning devices are generally used for identifying the bar-code label of the products. The bar-code is a code comprising vertical bars of different widths that can be read only electronically. The code captured by the scanning device is stored permanently in the memory.

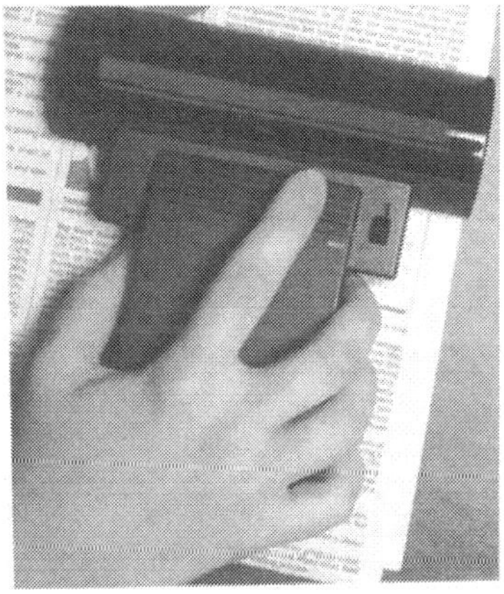

Figure 3.5 : Hand-Held Scanner

Web Cam

A webcam, or web camera is the loosely used term for any camera that generates images that can be accessed by and displayed on the world wide web through a server. A webcam is essentially just a camera that is connected to a computer, either directly or wirelessly, and gathers a series of images for remote display elsewhere. Webcam technology is widely used by all sorts of people for all sorts of different reasons.

Webcams are often used for personal use. The uses of webcam are limitless. Businesses often use webcams for video conferencing. Some schools and day care facilities use a webcam to allow parents to see what their children do at school.

Figure 3.6 : Webcam

Output Devices

Output devices are essential part of a computer system. They receive the processed data (information) from the CPU and present it to the user in a desired form. The output may be typed, printed or graphical, or may be of video or audio type. Output devices can be classified as soft copy devices and hard copy devices. All the output devices communicate with the CPU through an output unit. Some popular output devices are Printer, Plotter, Speaker, and CRT Monitor.

Printers

Printers are used to make "hard-copies" of documents and graphics. Hard copy means that the output is in an instantaneously usable form, that is, in printed or plotted form. Hard copy devices produce a permanent record on media such as paper or microfilm. Printers can be divided into two distinct categories on the basis of producing impression over the paper:

- Impact Printers
- Non-impact Printers

Impact Printers

In an impact printer, a character is printed on the paper through physical contact between the print head and paper. Either the needle or a character is struck on the paper through the ribbon. This creates a lot of noise when these printers work. Examples of impact printers are **Dot matrix printer, Daisy wheel printer** etc.

Dot Matrix Printer

Dot Matrix Printer is a character printer. The character is formed with closely packed dots. The printing head contains a vertical array of pins. Formation of character is done by the movement of head across the paper. Selected print needles strike the inked ribbon against paper to produce an image of the character. Dot matrix printer supports printing of graphics also. It is faster than daisy wheel printer and the printing speed lies between 30 to 600 cps (characters per second). It comes in two print head specifications, 9 pin and 24 pin.

Figure 3.7 : Dot Matrix Printer

Non-Impact Printers

In non-impact printers, the head does not come directly in contact with the paper. There is no impact or hitting of needles so non-impact printers do not make any noise while printing. Their printing speed is much faster than impact printers, because they are generally page printers, i.e., they print one page at a time. They come in many varieties such as: **Thermal Printer, Inkjet Printer, Laser Printer,** and **Electrostate Printer.**

Laser Printer

Laser printer works on the concept of using laser beams to create an image on a photosensitive surface (Figure 3.8). Initially the desired output image is written on a copier drum with a laser beam that operates under the control of the computer. The laser exposed drum areas attract a toner that attaches itself to the laser generated charges on the drum. The toner is permanently fused on paper with heat and/or pressure by rolling the drum over the blank paper. Laser printers are quiet and produce very high quality of output.

Figure 3.8 : Laser Printer

Ink-jet Printer

Ink-Jet printers use dot matrix approach to print text and graphics. Nozzles in the print head produce tiny ink droplets. These droplets are charged which are deflected and then directed to the desired spots on the paper to form the impression of a character. It has a speed of 40-300 *cps* with software controls on size and style of characters. These printers support color printing and are very quiet and noiseless in operation. The print quality of such printers is very near letter-quality.

Printer Name	Speed	Price	Technology
Dot Matrix Printer	25 to 450 Characters per second or 1 to 18 pages per minute	Least expensive	Works by impact
Inkjet Printer	0.5 to 4 pages per minute	Less expensive than colour	Sprays ink through holes
Laser Printer	4 to 24 pages per minute	Expensive	Uses a fine powdered ink, called toner

Table 3.1 : Characteristics of the commonly used printers

Figure 3.9 : Ink Jet Printer

The Monitor

The monitor is the most commonly used soft copy device. Soft copy devices do not produce a permanent record. Other soft copy devices are — Audio Response Unit (ARU), Multimedia Projectors, and Speech Synthesizers.

The monitor of a PC works like a television screen. It displays text characters and graphics in colour or in shades of grey. The monitor is sometimes also known as a screen, display or a CRT (Cathode Ray Tube). Images produced on a PC depend on the screen you use. An image is made up of tiny dots called **pixels**.

Anything typed on the keyboard is displayed on the monitor. When a program is executed, the information is displayed on the monitor. However, the results on the screen one shown only temporarily and are not permanent unless they are saved in the hard disk.

At present, various types of monitors available in the market - such as the monochrome (single colour) monitor, colour monitor etc. The monochrome monitor and the colour monitor differ in terms of their resolution (i.e. the sharpness of the images on the screen). Higher the resolution, higher the cost. Generally colour monitors have a higher resolution. High resolution monitors are used for specialised jobs, like creating graphics and images.

Through the cathode ray tube monitors are very common, recent times have seen an increased demand for LCD (Liquid Crystal Display) monitors. The screen of the LCD monitor is made up of a special substance (liquid crystals) stuffed between two specially treated sheets of glass. The images displayed on the LCD monitor offer clearer and sharper pictures as compared to the conventional one. Although more expensive than a CRT monitor; an LCD monitor is lighter, thinner and consumes lesser power.

Summary

- Input/Output devices and secondary storage devices attached to a computer are called "peripherals".
- Data and instructions are entered into a computer through input devices.
- The results and response of a computer system are communicated back to the user through output devices.
- The most common output devices are VDU and printer.
- On a VDU, soft copy is generated while printer gives a hard copy output.
- All the storage devices also come under I/O devices. These devices like magnetic tapes, magnetic disks, CD-ROMs are classified separately as storage devices.

Review Exercise

Multiple choice questions

1. The mouse is a
   a) pointing device
   b) data entry device
   c) output device
   d) none of the above
2. An impact printer
   a) is faster than a non-impact printer
   b) makes higher-quality copy than a non-impact printer
   c) can make carbon copies
   d) all of the above
3. Which of the following devices would likely be used by an instructor to grade exams?
   a) handheld scanner
   b) pointing device
   c) MICR system
   d) optical mark Reader
4. Which of the following is not a type of monitor?
   a) Cathode-ray-tube
   b) flatbed
   c) electronuminescent display
   d) Gas plasma
5. Which of the following is an impact printer?
   a) laser
   b) inkjet
   c) dot-matrix
   d) plotter

State whether true or false

1. I/O Interface is used to communicate with various types of devices.
2. Joystick is used to select a menu option displayed on screen.
3. The smaller the number of pixels, the better the resolution of monitor.
4. Images on monitors are created by configurations of dots.
5. QWERTY is the most popular keyboard layout.

Fill in the blanks

1. A computer __________ generally combines Input and Output functions.
2. __________ printer prints by spraying ink droplets on paper.
3. __________ are available to display your work onto big-screen surfaces.
4. An optical mouse basically consists of ________, ________, and ________ buttons.

Descriptive questions

1. Explain the difference between
   i) Soft copy and hard copy devices
   ii) Impact and non-impact printer
2. Explain how does the laser printer works.
3. What is meant by an input device? What is the importance of an input device in a computer system?
4. Explain the different technologies used in the touchscreens.
5. Write any five usage of web cam.

CHAPTER

4 SECONDARY STORAGE DEVICES

FEATURING

- Secondary Storage Devices — An Introduction
- Magnetic Disks
- Optical Disks
- Mass Storage Devices

Computer's main memory is volatile in nature i.e., whenever power supply is switched off, the data stored in it, if not saved, is completely washed off and lost forever. Computers provide various means for keeping the data intact. Magnetic storage devices are the most popular means of storing data permanently and are also the main source of transferring data between different computers. The most common storage devices are magnetic tapes and disks. These storage devices are extensively used for input as well as output and are commonly termed as auxiliary storage devices or secondary storage devices. In this chapter we will study about the auxiliary storage devices and their functioning.

Secondary Storage Devices – An Introduction

Secondary storage, also known as auxiliary memory or external memory is an additional memory which is used with most computer systems to supplement the primary memory. Secondary storage is used to store data/information permanently, but it generally has an operating speed far slower than that of the primary storage. Its storage capacity is virtually unlimited because a large database can be stored across number of floppy disks/tapes. Data cannot be processed directly from secondary devices hence we need the main memory also. Thus, a secondary storage device cannot, in any way, replace the primary memory of the computer system. Commonly used secondary storage devices are hard disks, magnetic disks, floppy disks, and optical disks.

Magnetic Disks

Magnetic disks are used as an input, output or external storage devices. They are a popular medium for direct access secondary storage. It is a thin, circular metal plate/platter coated on both sides with a magnetic oxide layer. It usually comes in the form of a disk pack, also known as hard disk. All the disks in the disk pack rotate at a very high speed of 700 or 3,600 rpm.

Information is stored on both the surfaces of each disk platter except the upper surface of the top platter and lower surface of the bottom platter. Each disk platter is divided into concentric circles known as **tracks**. A set of corresponding tracks in all the surfaces of a disk pack is called a **cylinder**. Data is stored in one cylinder first and then the head moves to the next cylinder, this saves time wasted in moving the head track by track for a particular disk. Information is recorded as a series of magnetized spots (signifying a 1-bit) or non-magnetized (signifying a 0-bit) spots. Each track contains equal number of characters. Information can be erased from anywhere on the disk and new data can be recorded on it. Normally there are 200 tracks on a disk surface numbered 0 to 199. Each track is divided into 8 or 12 equal sectors. Sectors are used to store the information — about 512 bytes can be stored per sector, as shown in Figure 4.1.

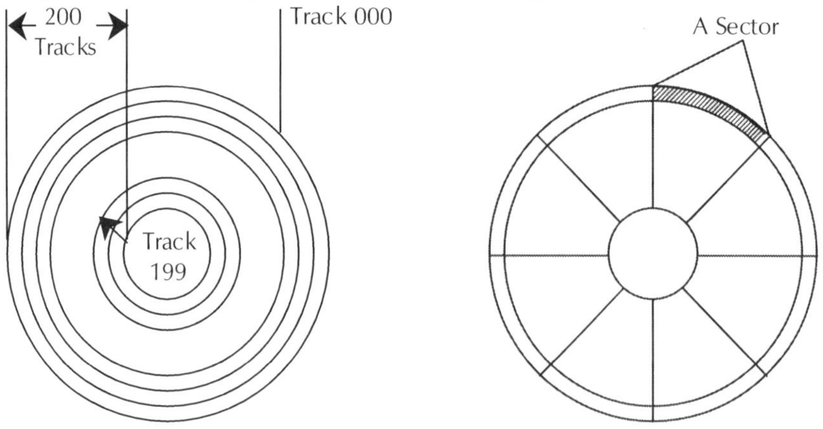

Tracks on a Disk **Sector of a Disk**

Figure 4.1 : Tracks and Sectors

These sectors can be accessed by one of the disk drive's read/write heads, in one rotation of the disk, without the head having to change its position. Frequently, multiple disks (Platters) are maintained and used together to create a larger disk storage system. Typically, two or more platters are stacked on top of each other with a common spindle, which turns the whole assembly.

Information is accessed from the disk by referencing the disk address. Disk address is specified in terms of surface number, track number, and sector number. Access time in any disk system is made up of three components — seek time, latency time and data transfer time.

- **Seek Time** It is the time required to position the head over the proper track, normally measured in milliseconds. For fixed head system, seek time is always zero.
- **Latency Time** Time required to rotate the disk pack to bring the correct sector under the read-write head is known as latency time. Average latency time is to the order of 8-10 minutes.
- **Data Transfer Time** Time required to read or write the actual data on the disk is called the data transfer time.

Types of Magnetic Disks

All magnetic disks are platters coated with a magnetic material and round in shape. They come in different sizes. They are either portable or permanently mounted on the computer system. The complete unit to read and write on these disks is called disk drive unit. Disks can also be differentiated on the basis of their size, sectors, number of sides, storage capacity and density. Two types of magnetic disks are described below:

Hard Disk

It is a group of large metal or plastic disks permanently sealed in a container. Read-write heads and access mechanisms are also built within the container. These sealed containers are not generally removed from their disk drives. In operation, the disk is rotated at a high speed on the spindle. There is one read-write head for each surface. The heads can move to and fro to select desired track position. During operation, heads do not touch the magnetic surface, a thin cushion of air is maintained between the rotating disk and read-write head. To store or retrieve data, the system finds the disk address used to contain the data by moving the read-write head to the appropriate track where it waits until the desired sector passes by. The capacity of hard disks is very high as compared to other disks. Nowadays hard disks of 320 GB capacity are available. Although hard disks are fixed in the PC, porting of disks from one place to another is more secure than before because all the disks are safely packed inside a protective covering, as shown in Figure 4.2.

Figure 4.2 : Hard Disk

Floppy Disks

Hard disks are costly and not suitable for transferring data from one place to another. Floppy disks are portable and can be used to transfer data easily from one computer to the other. These diskettes are economical and very flexible to use. The diskette can be frequently taken out and inserted in the disk drive unit. While in the operation, floppy disk drive heads actually touch the surface of magnetic disk. This results in quick wear and tear of the disks and the read-write heads. These diskettes are made up of plastic and have a magnetic coating. The disk is covered in a protective sheath with an opening for editing and writing.

Optical Disks

While magnetic tapes and magnetic disks are based on principle of magnetism, optical disks are secondary storage medium based on principle of light or laser beam technology. An optical disk is a flat, circular, plastic disk coated with a thin layer of metal (aluminium, gold or silver) that acts a reflective surface. It user laser beam technology for recording/ reading of data on disk surface.

Optical disk comes in various sizes and capacities. A Compact Disk (CD) holding 600-700 MB of information having 12 cm diameter is the most popular means of optical storage. In a single-track optical disk, storage capacity is calculated by the multiple of number of sectors and number of bytes per sector. It is directly proportional to the spot size and the geometrical dimensions of disk. Since the storage capacity of an optical disk is huge, the cost per bit of storage is very low.

An optical disk consists of one long spiral track starting at the outer edge and ending at the center. It is used for reading large sequential data. The random access time of an optical disk is slower than that of a magnetic disk as sectors in a magnetic disk can be located faster because they are found on a given track at a fixed distance from the center.

Access Mechanism

Optical disks use two laser beam sources in place of read/write head. The laser beam with greater intensity is used for writing by focussing it on the surface of the spinning disk and turning it ON and OFF so as to burn tiny pits into the metal coating of the disk along its tracks.

Laser beam of lesser intensity is focussed on the disk surface to read the stored data. This beam is strongly reflected by coated surface and weakly by burnt surface (pit) producing patterns of ON and OFF reflections that are converted into electronic signals of binary Is and Os by a sensor.

Types of Optical Disks

Optical disks come in several varieties, which are made in some what different ways for different purposes. The following are some of the examples of optical storage systems:

- Compact Disk - Read Only Memory (CD-ROM)
- Digital Video Disc (DVD)
- Compact Disk - Recordable (CD-R)
- Compact Disk - Rewritable (CD-RW)
- Digital Video Disc - Recordable (DVD-R)
- Digital Video Disc - ReWritable (DVD-RW)

Advantages of Optical Disks

- Possess large capacity to store data/information. They can store more data in less amount of space as compared to magnetic tapes and floppy or zip disks.
- Longer life span, about 10-20 years as compared to magnetic disks.
- Low cost per bit of storage.
- Easily portable and stored.

Disadvantages of Optical Disks

- They posses slow data access speed as compared to the magnetic disks.
- Copying data from optical disk is not easy. One needs to use both software and hardware for writing disks.
- Optical disk drive mechanism is more complicated than the magnetic and floppy disks.

Read-Only Optical Disks

Read-only optical disk stores data, such as audio, video, and text permanently and allows it to be accessed randomly, whenever required. They can store data in the range of 700 MB. As the name implies, it comes pre-recorded with the data, which cannot be altered. The most common type of optical disk the CD-ROM, and DVD-ROM.

A CD-ROM disk is a shiny, silver colour metal disk of 12 cm in diameter. It is made up of three layers : a **polycarbonate** base through which light can pass, a layer of **aluminum**, and a protective layer of **acrylic** on the top of that. A CD-ROM has one track that spirals from the center to the outside edge.

DVD-ROM is a high capacity data storage medium. In DVD, the tracks are placed closer together, thereby allowing more tracks per disc.

Write Once-Read Many

Write Once-Read Many (WORM) disks allow the end users to write the data on the disk only once. That is data can be written, but cannot be erased on an optical disk. To burn the data onto the WORM disk, a CD-Writer device is required. These disk are used for writing the data once and storing it for a long period of time. CD-R (Compact Disk - Recordable) is an example of this category.

Mass Storage Devices

Storage Devices that have a tremendously large amount of storage capacity (i.e., several trillions of bytes of data) are called **mass storage devices**. Features of both magnetic tapes and magnetic disks are incorporated in these devices. A magnetic tape which is in the form of strips is wrapped up on the plastic surface of these devices. The access time of mass storage devices is in seconds instead of milliseconds.

- **Disk Array** — In 1993, the disk array first appeared in the market. It is a set of hard disks and hard disk drives with a controller mounted in a single box. All the disks of a disk array form a single large storage unit. The commonly used term for Disk Array is RAID (Redundant Array of Inexpensive Disks). As each of the medium-sized hard disks in the disk array is less expensive than a single large hard disk, therefore the term **Inexpensive** is used.

  Originally, RAID systems were developed to provide large secondary storage capacity with enhanced performance, however, today they are also becoming popular due to enhanced reliability.

- **Automated Tape Library** — It is a set of magnetic tapes with a controller mounted in a single unit. The unit has one or more tape drives to read and write data on the tapes in the tape library. In case of units with multiple tape drives, it is possible to read/write data from/to multiple magnetic tapes simultaneously resulting in faster data transfer rates. Multiple drives result in improved reliability of the storage unit because if one of the drives fails, the unit can continue to function with other drives at a slower speed.

Data Arching is done by Automated tape libraries. It also acts as an on-line data backup device for automated backup. Automated tape libraries are mainly found in large computer centres.

- **CD-ROM Jukebox** — CD-ROM jukebox has similar principle of operation as of automated tape library except for the fact that it uses a set of CD-ROMs instead of magnetic tapes as the storage media. A CD-ROM jukebox is a set of CD-ROM disks with a controller mounted in a single unit. The unit has one or more CD ROM disks in the jukebox. In case of units with multiple CD-ROM drives, it is possible to read data from multiple CD-ROM drives, it is possible to read data from multiple CD-ROM disks simultaneously resulting in faster data transfer rates.
- **Thumb Drive** — A thumb drive is portable memory storage. It is re-writable and holds its memory without a power supply, unlike RAM. Thumb drives will fit into any USB port on a computer. They will also "hot swap", which means a user can plug the drive into a computer and will not have to restart it to access the thumb drive. The drive are small about the size of a human thumb-hence, their name and are very stable memory storage devices.

Summary

- Secondary storage devices are an essential part of a computer system.
- Magnetic media has been extensively used for storing the data.
- Generally, magnetic tapes are used for taking backups.
- The programs, data files and software are stored on magnetic disks.
- The access speed of magnetic disks and storage devices directly affects the overall throughput of the computer systems.
- With the invention of optical media, that is, CD-ROMs CD-RW ROMs and DVDs, a new revolution is taking place in secondary storage media.
- CD-ROMs are gaining popularity and are emerging as a cheaper media for permanent data storage.
- Storage Devices that have a tremendously large amount of storage capacity (i.e., several trillions of bytes of data) are called mass storage devices. Commonly used mass storage devices are disk array, automated tape library and CD-ROM jukebox.

Review Exercise

Multiple choice questions

1. A laser beam is used to read data from
   a) Magnetic disk
   b) Optical disk
   c) Magnetic tape
   d) None of the above
2. A floppy disk is
   a) A first generation computer invention
   b) Smaller and lighter than a disk in a fixed disk pack
   c) Most commonly used with very large computer systems
   d) None of the above
3. Data stored on a magnetic disk
   a) Can be read more quickly than data stored on a magnetic tape
   b) Are less likely to be destroyed than data stored on a magnetic tape
   c) Can be directly accessed
   d) All of the above
4. A spiral shape track formatting is present in:
   a) Floppy disk
   b) Hard disk
   c) Optical disk
   d) Tape cartridge
5. In which kind of disk does the read/write head physically touches the surface?
   a) Hard disk
   b) Floppy disk
   c) Compact disk
   d) None of these

State whether true or false

1. The secondary storage of a computer system is volatile and has low cost per bit stored.
2. The surface of a magnetic disk is divided into a number of invisible concentric circles called tracks. Each track is further subdivided into sectors.
3. Magneto-optical disks integrate optical and magnetic disk technologies to enable rewritable storage with laser-beam technology.
4. The CD-ROM has a storage capacity of about 650 KB.
5. Music CDs can be played on a computer having a CD-ROM drive along with a sound board and speakers.

Fill in the blanks

1. ________ time is the time required to bring the correct sector under the read-write head.
2. ________ have special tracks for recording the data.
3. A ________ in a magnetic hard disk is a set of tracks.
4. Data stored on a disk can be accessed in either a direct or ________ way.
5. ________ reads/writes the data by making use of laser and optical technologies.

Descriptive questions

1. What is a CD-ROM ? How does it store data ? What are its advantages over hard disks.
2. How does a floppy diskette differ from a magnetic disk pack? What is the significance of index hole?
3. Discuss advantages and disadvantages of :
   a) Magnetic disks
   b) Optical disks
4. What do you understand by tracks and sectors on the surface of a magnetic disk?
5. What is meant by storage systems? What is the advantage of having storage system in a computer system?

C H A P T E R

5 SOFTWARE CONCEPTS

FEATURING

- **Introduction**
- **Relationship between Hardware and Software**
- **Categories of Software**
- **Public Domain Software**
- **Software Licensing**
- **Computer Languages**
- **Generations of Programming Languages**
- **Types of Programming Languages**
- **Introduction to Some High-Level Languages**

The software is the backbone of the computer industry. It provides the facility to manipulate data, maintain integrity within the system components and set the course of communication with other systems. The hardware without software is like a human without a brain. The software development is the most critical area of industry and it contributes to the national economy to a very large extent. In earlier systems, computer software was very task oriented and not interactive. But today we have very sophisticated interactive softwares which can be used for a variety of tasks.

In this chapter, we will study about the types of software, their usage and their implementation. This will not only give a better understanding of various software technologies but will also talk about their use in our daily lives.

Introduction

Computer hardware on its own cannot do anything until it is supplemented with software. For a computer to function properly, both the hardware and software must work together. Software is a set of computer programs, procedures, and associated documents (flowcharts, manuals, etc.) that describe the programs and how they are to be used to make a computer usable in terms of accomplishing the user's tasks. We will study software in detail in this chapter. More specifically, software means a collection of program whose objective is to enhance the capabilities of the hardware. A software package is a group of programs that solve a specific problem or perform a specific type of job. For example, word processing software package provides functionality to the computer so that it can be used to create text documents like letters and mailing lists.

Relationship between Hardware and Software

Hardware and software are two basic elements of a computer system complementary to each other that work together to produce useful output. Entire computer hardware is driven by software. Software is responsible for optimum utilization of hardware resources. Different software are used with the same hardware to make a computer system perform different types of jobs. For example, same cassette player (hardware) is used to play different songs (software). Software makes use of hardware resources like printer, scanner, VDU, processor and memory. Job scheduling for each and every hardware is done by the software.

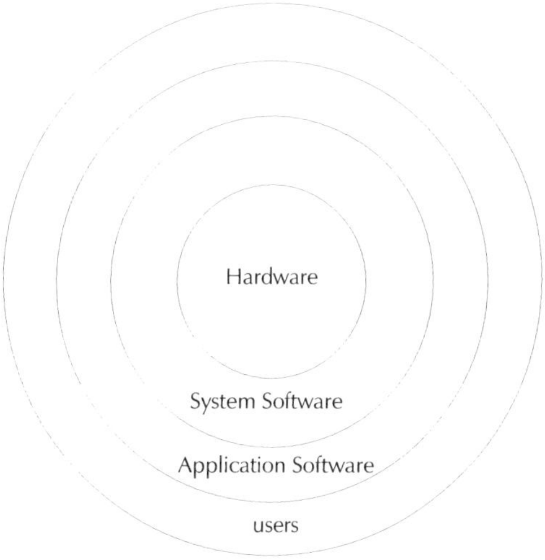

Figure 5.1 : Hardware, System Software, Application Software and Users

Categories of Software

Software can be classified as system software and application software. System software control and coordinate the hardware components and manage their performances, whereas application software enable the users to accomplish their required tasks.

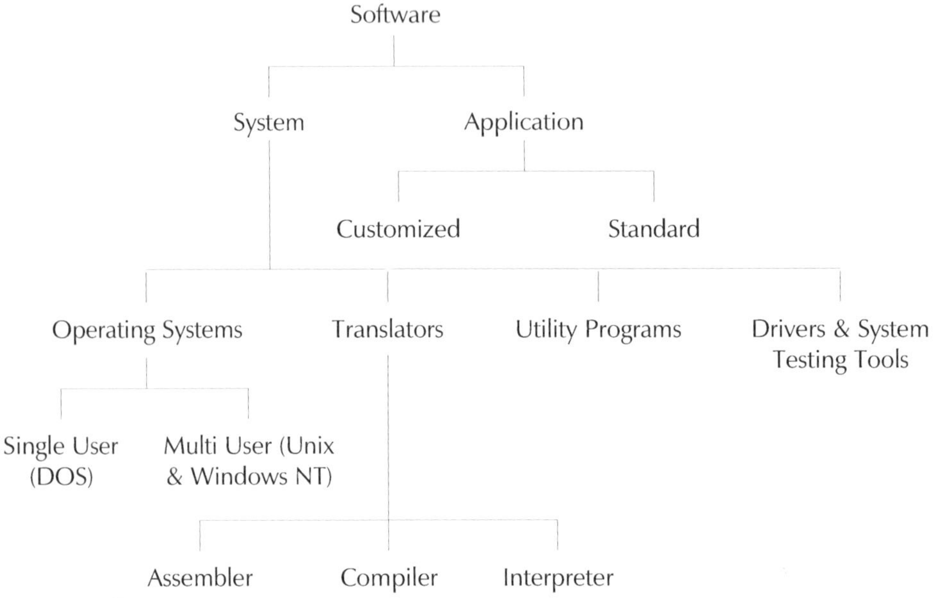

Figure 5.2 : Software Categories

System Software

System softwares are programs used to control the operation of the computer system and assist the programmer in doing his/her work efficiently. Some of them are stored permanently in the computer memory and relieve the programmer from some mundane tasks; in turn improve his/her productivity. In general, a computer's system software performs one or more of the following functions:

1. Supports the development of other application software.
2. Supports the execution of other application software.
3. Monitors the effective use of various hardware resources such as CPU, memory, peripherals etc.
4. Communicates with and controls the operations of peripheral devices such as printer, disk, tape, etc.

The programs included in a system software package are called **system programs** and the programmers who prepare system software are referred to as **system programmers**.

They make very efficient use of hardware resources. System softwares can be further categorized as operating system, language translators, system utility and device drivers.

Operating System

An operating system is an essential component of a computer system, which manages the resources of the system. It is a set of large and complex programs that act as an interface between computer hardware and its users. It not only serves the purpose of interpreting the user program instructions to the hardware, but also provides coordination services necessary to enable a group of users to share computer system resources efficiently.

The operating system complements the hardware by providing a layer of services which manage the resources of the hardware and allow the users to drive the system. It keeps track of the status of each resource such as, memory, processor, and I/O devices and decides which job will have control over computer resources for how long and when.

The position of operating system in the overall computer system has been depicted in figure 5.3. It clearly explains how the OS ensures communication between the user and the hardware devices via a set of application programs and system programs (e.g. translators).

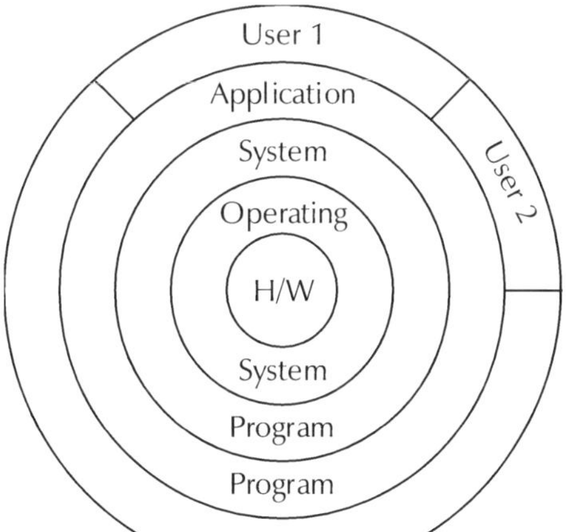

Figure 5.3 : Place of OS in the computer system

Operating System — Need and Usage

In earlier days, the user had to design the applications according to the internal structure of the hardware. There was a need to enable the user to design the application without getting into the intricacies of computer's internal structure. This need led to the evolution of the operating system.

It is the OS through which the user interacts with the machine, to accomplish any task. Thus, the OS is the primary interface for the user to interact with the machine. It helps the user to interact with the machine very closely and most of the concepts and techniques found in an OS have general applicability in other applications.

The operating system is used for:

- Easy interaction between humans and computers.
- Starting computer operation automatically when power is turned on.
- Loading and scheduling user's programs.
- Controlling input and output.
- Controlling program execution.
- Managing use of the main memory.
- Providing security to users' jobs and files.
- Account resource usage.

Functions of Operating System

The functions of an operating system can be outlined as follows:

1. Process Management
    - i) Schedules the user processes.
    - ii) Controls the execution of user processes.
    - iii) Maintains status of the individual process.
    - iv) Coordinates with other components of the OS.
2. Device Management/ Input/Output Management
    - i) Controls functioning of I/O devices.
    - ii) Controls allocation, access and deallocation of devices.
3. Memory Management
    - i) Decides which process must reside in main memory.
    - ii) Monitors the amount of primary memory available.
    - iii) Allocates memory to each process.
    - iv) Ensures that memory space of one process is protected from the other processes.
    - v) Frees the memory when process execution is complete.

4. Information/File Management

   i) Controls the reading and writing of information on the physical media.

   ii) Usually implemented through an elaborate file system.

5. Job Control / Security

   i) When the user wants to run an application program, he must communicate with the OS, telling it what to do.

   ii) He does this using OS's job control language or JCL. JCL consists of a number of OS commands, called system commands that control the functioning of the operating system.

6. House Keeping / Command Interpretation

   i) Includes all the support services necessary to ensure smooth operation of the computer system, namely, security, protection, and resource accounting backup and restoration.

Language Translators

Computer only understand a language consisting of 0's and 1's called machine language. Programs written in this language are difficult to write and understand. Therefore special programming language called high-level language were developed that reassembled natural languages like English. Therefore, a tool was required which could translate a program written in a programming language to machine language. So whenever a new programming language developed, a language translator was also developed. Language translators help in converting programming instructions into the 0s and 1s that the computer is able to process. Depending on the programming language used, language translators are divided into three major categories : Compilers, Interpreter and Assembler.

Assemblers

Compared to all the types of programming languages assembly language is closest to the machine code. An assembly language program cannot be directly executed by a computer. It has to be converted into machine language before the computer can interpret and execute it. An assembler is a program that translates a program written in assembly language into a machine executable code.

Compilers

Compilers are the translators that translate high level language programs (source code) into machine code at once and this machine code is executed afterwards. The translated machine code is known as an **object code**.

Interpreters

An interpreter is the language translator for the third-generation programming languages. Rather than generating object code for the entire source code, this class of translators examines and executes source code on a line by line basis. Each line of source code is scanned, parsed, translated, and executed before moving on to the next line.

Interpreter takes one statement of a high-level language program, translates it into machine language instructions, and then immediately executes the resulting machine language instructions. That is, the translation and execution processes alternate for each statement encountered in the high-level language program.

The input to an interpreter is the source program, but unlike a compiler, its output is the result of program execution instead of an object program. Since no object program is saved for future use, repeated interpretation (translation plus execution) of a program is necessary for its repeated execution. Note that since an interpreter translates and executes a high-level language program statement-by-statement, not only the entire program must be reinterpreted for its repeated execution, but even a program statement must be reinterpreted every time it is encountered during program execution.

The difference between interpreter and compiler:-

INTERPRETER	COMPILER
It takes one statement of a high-level language program and translates it into a machine instruction which is immediately executed.	It is called so because it translates each high-level language instruction into a set of machine language instructions rather than a single machine language instruction.
Translation and execution are alternate for each statement encountered in the high-level language program.	This merely translates the entire source program into an object program and is not involved in its execution.
The object code is not saved for future use because the translation and the execution processes alternate.	The whole source program is translated into its equivalent machine language program. The object code obtained is permanently saved for future use and is used every time the program is to be executed.
An instruction is interpreted and translated into machine language every time changes are incorporated in the program.	Repeated compilation is not necessary for repeated execution of a program.
Interpreters are slower than compilers.	A compiled program runs much faster than an interpreted program.

Table 5.1 : Difference between Interpreter and Compiler

System Utility

Utility programs are a collection of programs that assist the users in performing routine tasks and in system maintenance tasks. These programs or system utilities greatly speed up and simplify the user of a computer and improve program efficiency. The tasks that are commonly performed by utility programs are as follows:

- Finding a specific file from a repository of files.
- Checking the amount of available memory and storage space on hard disk.
- Formatting hard disks or floppy disks.
- Taking file backups on a tape or floppy disk.
- Scanning the system for computer viruses.

In addition to the major tasks mentioned above, the utility programs also help in conserving storage space by reorganizing files. Disk Defragmenter and virus scanners, backup, data recovery, firewall are few commonly used utility programs.

Device Drivers

Device drivers are special software programs created by peripheral device manufacturers to facilitate the computer in communicating with the peripheral devices, like printer and mouse. Drivers, according to the device setting, have the ability to convert the data supplied by the computer and then transfer it to the device to work on it. In other words, a device driver instructs a hardware device the way it should accept the input from the operating system and the way in which it should communicate with the other units of the computer system.

Application Software

Application software is a collection of programs developed to solve a specific problem or do a specific task rather than just managing a computer system. For instance, an application software for order processing produces invoices as the major output and an application software for processing examination results produces marksheets as the major output. Application softwares are dependent on system softwares. They can be broadly classified into two groups.

- Customized application software
- Standard application software

Customized Application Software

Customized application software are programs written by the user or programmer in order to perform specific jobs for the user. They are written in a variety of programming languages depending on the task at hand. Normally these are sets of programs used in conjunction with one another, such as a payroll system or customized accounting packages for a company.

Standard Application Software

These are generalized set of programs used to deal with a particular application. These softwares are normally developed by specialist software developers to solve common problems faced by many users. Some of the most commonly known application softwares are briefly described below:

- **Word Processor** — Word processors a software that is generally use to create, edit, view, format, store, retrieve, and print documents. The word processor application software also allows us to perform different operations, such as cut-paste for moving the text within the document, copy-paste for copying the text. It also check the spelling and grammar of text and arrange it correctly on the page. Microsoft Word and WordPerfect are the most common examples of a word processor.
- **Spreadsheet** — Spreadsheets are used for tasks that require number crunching, such as financial analysis, budget preparation, and grade calculation. Spreadsheets can sort and analyze data, create charts, graphs and figures, and perform "what-if" analysis to assess the impacts of changes to input variables. Microsoft Excel is a popular spreadsheet software.
- **Database Management System** — A database management software is a set of one or more programs that enable users to create a database, maintain it, organize its data in desired fashion, and to selectively retrieve useful information from it. Database software is widely used today by both large and small organizations to maintain employee data, customer data, assets data, accounting data, etc. Some of the examples of the database management programs are MS-Access, Oracle, and FoxPro.
- **Image Editors** — Image Editor software enables us to use a computer system for creating, editing, viewing, storing, retrieving and printing designs, drawings, pictures, graphs, etc. These computer programs enables the user to adjust an image to improve its appearance. Examples of these programs are Adobe Photoshop, CorelDraw, and Adobe Illustrator.
- **Multimedia Software** — Multimedia software packages are the latest craze in the users. A user can very easily create animations and modify them using such programs. Using these programs, one can create 3D objects, move objects on a definite or a random path, and can animate objects in a number of ways. Some of the examples of the multimedia programs are Flash, Director, Maya and Sound Forge.

Public Domain Software

A public domain software is a software that is available for free on the Internet. Users can find it either on bulletin boards or user-group libraries on the Internet. The developers of these software distribute their products just in order to popularize them. The fact that there is no price tag attached to these software and their easy accessibility has made them very popular amongst the users. Public domain software is also referred to as **shareware** or **free domain software**.

Some of the apprehensions that strike the users who go in for downloading these software are:

- These software may not be properly tested before release.
- They may not come with requisite support like the one that users of commercial software get.
- They may fail during operation and may adversely affect the project due to the non-availability of technical support.

Software Licensing

The illegal and unauthorized duplication of software is called **software piracy**. The most frequently used deterrents to software piracy are warning and license labels found on most software packages. Software piracy is an offence. The warnings clearly state that the user has only purchased a license to use the software on a single machine and that any copy must be made for backup purposes only. Authorized users of licensed software enjoy the following benefits:

- They receive complete documentation along with the software.
- They receive all the change/modification notices about the software from the supplier.
- Upgrades to higher versions of the software are available for nominal prices, to licensed users.
- Users can get benefit by sharing experiences with other licensed users through user groups.

Computer Languages

A computer, being an electronic device, cannot understand instructions if provided in a general language. Therefore, a special language is used to instruct a computer system. This language is known as computer programming language. It consists of a set of symbols and characters, words and grammar rules that allow the user to frame instructions in the format that can be understood and acted upon by the computer system. Computer scientists are striving to develop computer systems which can accept instructions in normal human language known as **natural language processors**.

Generations of Programming Languages

The term "generation" of computer languages is used to categorize the generic enhancements in various computer languages. It shows the step-by-step evolution of programming languages. Each generation indicates significant progress towards making computers easier to use. Table below summarises the generations and history of development of programming languages.

Generation	Period	Programming Language	Features
First	1940s	Machine Language	• Machine dependent • Better utilization of machine • difficult to learn and use • Error Prone • Difficult to modify
Second	1950s	Assembly Language	• Machine dependent • Faster execution • Relatively easier to modify • Relatively simple to use • Knowledge of hardware required
Third	1950 -1970	High Level Language	• Machine independent • Easier to learn and use • Fewer errors • Lower program preparation cost • Easier to maintain
Fourth	1970 -1990	Very High Level Language	• Highly portable • Easier to learn • Example C, C++, Perl, SQL
Fifth	1990s	Internet based Languages	• Object oriented • More efficient • Reliable and fast • Employed Artificial Intelligence

Table 5.2 : Generations and History to Development of Programming Languages

Types of Programming Languages

Computers understand only one language and that is machine language which consist of 0s and 1s. The development of programs in machine languages was not an easy task for the programmers. During the 1950s assembly language was evolved. The programmers enjoyed working with this programming language because it was easy to develop a program in the assembly language as compared to machine language. During the period of 1950 and 1960 many high-level programming languages were developed. Programming languages can be divided into three major categories:

1. Machine Language
2. Assembly Language
3. High-Level Language

Machine Language

In machine-language programs, the computation is based on binary numbers. All the instructions including operations, registers, data and memory locations are given in their binary equivalent.

The machine directly understands this language by virtue of its circuitry design so these programs are directly executable on the computer without any translations. This makes the program execution very fast. Machine-languages are also known as first-generation languages.

Assembly Language

Assembly languages are also known as second-generation languages. These languages substitute alphabetic or numeric symbols for the binary codes of machine language. That is, we can use mnemonics for all opcodes, registers, and for the memory locations which provide us the more readable form of the program.

These languages require a translator known as "**Assembler**" to translate the program code written in assembly language to machine language. Because computer can interpret only the machine code instructions, once the translation is completed, the program can be executed.

High-Level Language

All high-level languages (HLL) are procedure-oriented languages and are intended to be machine independent. Programs are written in statements akin to English language. That is, the high-level languages use natural language like structures. These languages require translators (compilers and interpreters) to translate high-level language programs into machine-language programs for execution. The programs written in a high-level language can be ported on any computer, that is why they are known as machine-independent. The early high-level languages come in third generation of languages, for example COBOL, FORTRAN, PASCAL, BASIC, and APL.

Introduction to Some High-Level Languages

Today, a large number of high-level programming languages are available for developing different types of software applications. However, only few of these programming languages are popular among programmers. The following are some of the popular high-level programming language.

FORTRAN

FORTRAN (FORmula TRANslator) was developed by IBM in 1957. It is extremely suitable for expressing formulae, solving equations, and performing iterative calculations. FORTRAN is oriented towards solving problems of a mathematical nature and has been designed as an algebra-based programming language. It is one of the oldest and most widely used high-level languages.

COBOL

COBOL (COmmon Business Oriented Language) was designed specifically for business data processing so that the processed output could have the appearance and structure of a business report written in English. Thus, it is constructed from sentences, paragraphs, sections, and divisions.

BASIC

BASIC (Beginner's All-Purpose Symbolic Instruction Code) was developed by John Kemeny and Thomas Kurtz at Dartmouth College, USA. Interpreter is used to translate BASIC language instructions into machine-language code. It is a very simple and versatile language and can be used for different types of tasks like data file handling, graphics, and games. The various versions of BASIC language are — MS-BASIC, QBASIC, BASICA, and GW BASIC.

PASCAL

PASCAL was developed in 1968 by Professor Nicklaus Wirth of Switzerland and named after the French mathematician, Blaise Pascal. Pascal was the first structured programming language which was designed to force us to look at a problem in a logical way. It was used for both scientific and file processing applications and was standardized by ANSI in 1983.

LISP

LISP (LISt Processing) was developed in 1960 by Professor John Mc. Karthy. It is suitable for non-numeric applications and widely used in artificial intelligence projects. It is a functional language, that is, each instruction is defined in LISP as a function.

C

The C language, developed at Bell laboratories in early 1970s, was used to write an early version of the UNIX operating system. It is a mid level scientific language better than BASIC or FORTRAN. It is a compiler based, structured, language. Commonly used in many workplaces because its programs are easy to transfer between different types of computers.

C++

Created in 1983-1985 by Bjarne Sroustrup at Bell Labs it is object-oriented types language and is advanced version of C. It expands C by providing support for data abstraction and object-oriented design. It provides various enhancements over C and has became more popular among developers. C++ is used in numerous fields, such as accounting and finance systems, and computer-aided design.

Java

Java is an object-oriented programming language developed by Sun Microsystems to write programs to run on the Internet. The programs written using Java can be distributed on World Wide Web (WWW) and executed on a variety of computers. Programs written in Java are translated by the Java compiler in a format called **bytecodes** which can be executed on any computer. Programs can be developed in Java and the executable code can be distributed on the Internet. Anyone with a program to interpret the code can download and use the program.

C#

C# (pronounced as 'C sharp') is a new computer programming language developed by Microsoft Corporation USA. C# is a fully object-oriented language like Java and is the first component-oriented language. It has been designed to support the key features of .Net Framework, the new development platform of Microsoft for building component-based software solutions. It is simple, efficient, productive and type-safe language derived from the popular C and C++ languages. Although it belongs to the family of C/C++, it is a purely object oriented modern language suitable for developing web-based applications.

Summary

- Software is a set of programs which provide the facility to manage and use the data and other computer resources.
- Software can be one of the following two types: system software, and application software.
- System software comprises the programs that provide the interaction between user and computer.
- Application softwares are made by the user or programmer utilizing programming languages, DBMS software or any other system software.
- Customized softwares are softwares designed specially for a particular user or an organization.
- Utility software enables the computer to improve its performance.

- There are two types of programming languages available known as low-level languages and high-level languages. Low-level languages are of two types — machine languages and assembly languages.
- Assembly languages use mnemonics for the opcode, memory locations, and registers for calculations.
- High-level languages provide us with the English like structure to develop our programs.
- The compiler translates complete code simultaneously and generates the machine-level object codes which are non-executable until loaded into the memory.

Review Exercise

Multiple choice questions

1. Compiler translates
   a) line by line
   b) whole program
   c) using interpreters
   d) none of the above
2. Utility software enables users to
   a) manage CPU resource
   b) improve system performance
   c) create different documents
   d) create their own programs
3. DBMS software comes under
   a) Operating systems
   b) Translators
   c) System softwares
   d) Standard packages
4. Software that is available for free on the Internet
   a) Customized Software
   b) Public domain software

c) Operating system

d) None of the above

5. High level language is

a) easy to understand

b) uses simple english-like words

c) generally uses compiler to translate the program

d) All of the above

State whether true or false

1. System software consists of all the operating systems, translators and languages to ensure smooth efficient functioning of the computer.
2. Compiler is a program that translates a program written in assembly language into a machine executable code.
3. Compilers are slow as compared to interpreters because of line by line translation and execution.
4. All high-level languages are procedure-oriented.
5. C++ language is used to create web-based applications.

Fill in the blanks

1. Interpreters interpret programs ___________ .
2. Software enables user to ________ his/her own tasks.
3. Humanware is the person who ________ , ________ or ________ the computer to perform the particular task.
4. _________ are the special softwares that provide a helping hand to other types of softwares.
5. _________ language programs are translated by an assembler.

Descriptive questions

1. Write drawbacks of machine language.
2. What do you understand by system software? Draw the software classification diagram.
3. How can you say that a software is an application software?

4. Differentiate between
   a) Machine language and High level language
   b) Customized and Standard application software
   c) Interpreter and Compiler
5. Write short notes on:
   a) Translators
   b) Operating system

CHAPTER

6 MULTIMEDIA

FEATURING

- Multimedia : Definition
- Categorization of Multimedia
- Major Characteristics of Multimedia
- Why is Multimedia Important?
- Multimedia Development System
- Multimedia Building Blocks
- Multimedia Applications
- Common Multimedia File Formats

The multimedia revolution has redefined the communication system that forms a significant part of the infrastructure of our society. New developments in computing and communications technologies are at the forefront of the multimedia revolution. The word multimedia refers to the integration of multiple media — such as visual imagery, text, video, sound, and animation — which together multiply the impact of the message. It provides the presenter with a powerful tool that can greatly enhance communication by delivering a multi-sensory experience.

In this chapter, you will get to know the standard definition of multimedia, its various applications, and the reasons for its popularity.

Multimedia : Definition

Multimedia is media and content that uses a combination of different content forms. The term can be used as a noun (a medium with multiple content forms) or as an adjective describing a medium as having multiple content forms. The term is used in contrast to media which only use traditional forms of printed or hand-produced material. Multimedia includes a combination of text, audio, still images, animation, video, and interactivity content forms.

Multimedia is usually recorded and played, displayed or accessed by information content processing devices, such as computerized and electronic devices, but can also be part of a live performance. Multimedia (as an adjective) also describes electronic media devices used to store and experience multimedia content.

Figure 6.1 : Multimedia System

Categorization of Multimedia

Multimedia may be broadly divided into linear and non-linear categories. Linear active content progresses without any navigational control for the viewer such as a cinema presentation. Non-linear content offers user interactivity to control progress as used with a computer game or used in self-paced computer based training. Hypermedia is an example of non-linear content.

Multimedia presentations can be live or recorded. A recorded presentation may allow interactivity via a navigation system. A live multimedia presentation may allow interactivity via an interaction with the presenter or performer.

Major Characteristics of Multimedia

Multimedia presentations may be viewed in person on stage, projected, transmitted, or played locally with a media player. A broadcast may be a live or recorded multimedia presentation. A laser show is a live multimedia performance. Multimedia games and simulations may be used in a physical environment with special effects, with multiple users in an online network, or locally with an offline computer, game system, or simulator.

Why is Multimedia Important?

Multimedia is highly effective as Computer Technology Research (CTR) reports that people retain only 20 percent of what they see and 30 percent of what they hear. But they remember 50 percent of what they see and hear, and as much as 80 percent of what they see, hear, and do simultaneously. That is why multimedia becomes such a powerful tool for teaching and learning.

Multimedia has brought about an astounding change in the very nature of reading itself. Instead of confining the readers to the traditional linear presentation of text as printed in books, multimedia makes reading dynamic by giving words an important new dimension. Words in multimedia serve as triggers that readers can use to expand the text in order to learn more about a topic. In addition to providing more text, it also enlivens the text with sound, pictures, music, and video.

A multimedia document can be searched automatically to find any topic, while a printed book makes it almost impossible. Multimedia uses links to let you navigate the universe of connected information at an incredible speed. Multimedia has the potential to spread the information to millions of people who have not yet used a computer. A survey sponsored by IBM found that more than half of the survey's respondents did not want a computer that required a manual to use it. Multimedia provides the computer industry with an effective tool to reach to these clients.

Multimedia has entered into public domains and is easily accessible. An example is the way how the world shopping scenario is changing. Electronic home shopping is becoming increasingly popular. Multimedia has changed the face of the newspapers as well. Daily news has been brought to life with graphics and audio and video clips. Succinctly in the 21st century knowledge about multimedia is essential to function productively.

Multimedia Development System

Multimedia applications usually require more computer memory and processing power than the same information represented by text alone. For instance, a computer running multimedia applications must have a fast central processing unit (CPU), which is the electronic circuitry that provides the computational ability and control of the computer. A multimedia computer also requires extra electronic memory to help the CPU in making calculations and to enable the video screen to draw complex images. The computer also needs a high capacity hard disk to store and retrieve multimedia information, and a compact disc drive to play CD-ROM applications. Finally, a multimedia computer must have a keyboard and a pointing device, such as a mouse or a trackball, so that the user can direct the associations between multimedia elements.

Multimedia computers should support the capture, editing and viewing of video and audio data and provide facilities for the transfer of these data types between computers either through modems or through local and wide area networks.

To develop the system of multimedia we use the various hardware/ software components are:

- **The CPU** The CPU, which is recommended for a multimedia computer should be Pentium IV or other advanced chips.
- **The Monitor** The multimedia PC should be equipped with a monitor having Super Video Graphics Arrays (SVGA) card. The basic advantage of having SVGA is that it has a better resolution, thus display will be of better quality for the graphics and pictures.
- **Input** Output Devices: Keyboard and mouse are two important components for any multimedia PC.
- **CD- ROM** Multimedia uses digitized audio and video, which not only take huge amount of storage space but also require high-speed storage media, which can send large amount of data back and forth quickly to keep audio and video playing and recording smoothly.
- **DVD** Digital Video Disk technology improves the storage capacity to 4.7 to 17 Gbytes.
- **Sound Card** Sound output from a computer has been a feature of machines usually used for sending warning error message or games. If better quality and capabilities for sound output or inputs are required, then there must be a device, which can be added to the basic machine. This device is known as sound Card, which is added to the basic machine.
- **PhotoCD** It is used to save photos in the compressed form. The compression allows for 100 photos to be recorded in one CD.

Software for Multimedia

We can classify multimedia software as system software and authoring tools used to develop multimedia applications. The former sets up the communications between the system resources and the application programs. Examples are:

- Video for Windows
- Quicktime

- Indeo and Digital Video Interactive
- Microsoft Multimedia Technologies

Some of the recent software used in multimedia industry are:

- **Photoshop** Industry standard digital imaging software.
- **Director** Authoring multimedia for CD-ROM and the web.
- **Premiere** Digital video and postproduction tool.
- **Sound Edit** Sound capture and editing for multimedia.
- **Flash** Vector capture and editing for multimedia.
- **Front-page** Authoring tool for Internets and the www.
- **Alias/Wave front** 3d tools for games, films.

Multimedia Building Blocks

Multimedia is a combination of various elements, such as text, images, video, sound, and animation. Interactive multimedia allows the user to control what and when the elements are delivered. With the rapid changes in the field of technology, the interactive multimedia has become increasingly popular in education, business, entertainment, and public places. Now multimedia, which has the capability of incorporating various media from text to graphics and from video to sound, is a new way to present information.

- **Using text in Multimedia** With the recent explosion of and increasing demand for the Internet and the World Wide Web, text is an essential aspect of presenting the information. Like each element of the multimedia design, effective use of text can either direct users/readers attention or divert it.
- **Using Sound in Multimedia** Sound is one of the most powerful elements of interactive multimedia presentation. How you use the power of sound, either linking text or image with sound, can enhance the multimedia presentation. For any computer application, such as Web pages, audio resources need to be digitized. There are some important considerations in order to do that : quality, file formats, and file size considerations; digitizing process; and understanding constraints and limitations.
- **Using Images in Multimedia** Graphics are the visual elements that make up a multimedia screen. The images, such as pictures, clip art, 3-D graphics, animations, are widely used in designing for both multimedia and the Web. Hence, understanding of various graphic formats, that is how the particular image formats work, and where to use each type of image in your web pages. There is a great number of resources about graphic formats on the web. The following tutorials discuss different aspects of multimedia graphics:

- **Using Animations in Multimedia** There is no doubt that animation adds visual impact to interactive multimedia and web pages. Besides traditional animation methods made famous by Walt Disney, there are computer-generated animation programs which typically follows the same logic and procedures using layer, keyframe, and tweening. Available multimedia authoring tools, which usually have the capability of creating animations, make it easier to create computer animations for the web.
- **Using Video in Multimedia** Carefully planned and high-quality video in which one can perceive text (title), image, animation, and sound all together can make an amazing difference in an interactive multimedia product. With the digital video technology we can use the power of video for multimedia and Web delivery. In order to make the best use of this technology in multimedia design, we need to understand basic concepts, such as streaming video and video compression. Therefore, I think the following resources will be helpful for beginner multimedia designers.

Multimedia Applications

Multimedia is appropriate whenever a human interface connects a user to electronic information of any kind. Multimedia enhances traditional text-only computer interfaces and yields measurable benefit by gaining and holding attention and interest; it improves information retention. It can provide entertainment as well.

Multimedia is now being used in training and education systems for large corporations, government departments, and military installations. Such computer-based training systems were typically large customized projects, designed and built by professional courseware developers, often in specialist consultancies. Here are some of the possible areas where the use of multimedia applications has replaced the conventional system with new technology.

Education

Multimedia gives teachers instant access to thousands of slides, videos, sound tracks, and lesson plans. These materials can be called up instantly, either as material for a lecture, or as a resource for cooperative learning, critical thinking, discussions, question-and-answer sessions, reviews, problem solving, or self study.

Networks add an important dimension to educational computing. The information superhighway is linking universities, colleges, schools, and homes. Through cooperative learning on networks, students can collaborate on worldwide project, share data and contribute findings to reach more immediate results.

Multimedia is a natural medium to display art because it is visual and has 16 million colours to work with. Multimedia computers offer art educators all the advantages of hypermedia. Biology teachers are taking advantage of multimedia's ability to bring classrooms to life with animations, full-motion video clips, and stereo sound. For example, *Mammals:*

A Multimedia Encyclopedia, a multimedia CD from the National Geographic Society, covers more than 200 mammals. Several chemistry teachers are using multimedia tools to make presentations in classrooms, publish electronic journals, illustrate the periodic table, develop animations of ions and molecules, and make multimedia chemistry instruction available on the information superhighway.

Multimedia computers are a natural medium to teach language. Digital audio gives them pronunciation capabilities, and full motion video can put students in real-life situations. The highly visual nature of geography makes it a natural medium for multimedia. **Picture Atlas of the World** is a CD-ROM from the National Geographic Society covering both physical and cultural geography, it includes world, continental, and regional maps, in addition to high-resolution interactive political and topographical maps. Animations, illustrations, and diagrams enliven map projections and show the earth's rotation.

CD-ROMs that present stories for children in a hypermedia format are gaining popularity. They display full-colour illustrations and let the child interact by clicking items on the screen to have words spoken, defined, or used in sentences, to trigger sound effects and animations, and to link to related materials.

Entertainment

Much of the innovation in multimedia sound and graphics has happened because of the demand of the entertainment industry. There is intense competition among cinematographers and video game producers to deliver the most dazzling special effects. Research and development in virtual reality has broken new grounds in visual effects and mobility.

Moviemakers are investing heavily in the development of multimedia software to make movies more engaging. Producers use multimedia computers to create realistic special effects through digital imaging, rendering, animation, morphing, superimposition, replacement, and surround sound.

Digital audio has made video games more realistic by providing instant access to recordings of the actual sounds made by characters and objects in the game. Advances in computer graphics have replaced stick figures and cartoon-like drawings with actual photographs of scenes and characters digitized on multimedia computers. Interactive movies played on multimedia computers let the viewer influence how the story unfolds.

Virtual Reality (VR) gives the user a simulated experience which seems real. VR systems often use special hardware to enhance the experience, including visual displays (monitors, head-mounted viewing goggles, and direct eye scanning), tracking devices (data gloves, joysticks, body suits), and mobility devices (motion platforms, treadmills, stationary bicycles, and trackballs that let you move in a 3-D space).

The entertainment industry is using VR to create virtual actors, known as **VActors**. Virtual actors appear on-screen as animated characters whose actions are controlled by humans wearing VR sensors. Special input devices track the actor's face, body, and hand movements.

Marketing

Multimedia provides businesses with powerful new ways to reach and service customers. Multimedia computers are being used in businesses to solve the problem of time and effort required to locate a product you want in the style, colour, and size you need. These businesses provide interactive merchandising systems that can help you find the product you want in the size you need. You can also do comparison shopping without having to spend all day visiting different stores. Kiosks, in public places, can make everyday life simpler. For example, the Florsheim's merchandising kiosk lets you shop for shoes by style, size and colour, by touching the screen and following voice instructions. The kiosk includes a keyboard that lets you enter your name, address and credit card number, and the system then arranges to ship the shoes by UPS overnight.

Figure 6.2 : Kiosk

The information superhighway provides consumers with convenient shopping in any store connected to an online service. This benefits not only the shopper, but also the manufacturer. Online shopping bypasses the traditional distributor to put information-rich virtual storefront right where the customer is waiting.

Anyone who invests in the stock market knows what a dramatic effect current events have, on the day-to-day value of volatile stocks. This is why the financial services industry is using multimedia to provide on-screen windows that display broadcast videos including the **Financial News Network (FNN), Cable News Network (CNN)** and other related services. Brokers can buy or sell quickly when news breaks.

Another natural avenue for multimedia is the real estate industry. Visiting properties for sale is time consuming for brokers and buyers alike. Multimedia computers enable buyers to visit hundreds of properties virtually, view on-screen photos of homes, inspect floor plans, see street maps, and study neighbourhood demographics to minimize the number of actual visits required.

Multimedia is wide open for entrepreneurs who can make a lot of money dreaming up ways to use it in mass market applications. For example, New Image Industries has made clever use of multimedia to help people decide which hairstyle suits them best. They use a multimedia computer with a video capture board and a camera to digitize a person's head onto the computer screen. Then the operator uses the digitizing tablet and stylus pen to remove the person's hair and put other hairstyles to show how a person looks in different styles and colours.

Common Multimedia File Formats

The most commonly used audio formats on the Web are the AU(Audio format), WAV (Waveform Audio), AIFF (Audio Interchange File Format), and MIDI (Musical Instrument Digital Interface) file types.

The most commonly used video formats on the web are Quicktime (MOV), MPEG (Moving Picture Expert Group), and AVI (Audio Video Interleave).

Summary

- Multimedia is a woven combination of text, graphic art, sound, animation, and video elements.
- In 1991, the Multimedia PC Marketing Council announced for Multimedia PC (MPC) standard that defines the minimum hardware requirements for multimedia.
- There are different kinds of linked objects in a multimedia application: text, graphics, sound, video and animation.
- Animation adds visual impact to your multimedia project. Computer animation programs employ the layer, keyframe, and tweening techniques to create animated sequences.
- Cel Animation computer Animation, Kinematics and morphing are some of the animation techniques.
- Multimedia is being used extensively in the areas of business, education, marketing, engineering, entertainment, Communication and Medicine.

Review Exercise

Multiple choice questions

1. MIDI stands for

   a) Multimedia Instruction on Digital Interface

   b) Music Interpreter and Digitizer Interface

   c) Musical Instrument Digital Interface

   d) None of the above

2. Which of the following is a type of sound object that can be used in multimedia productions?

   a) Digital Video

   b) Waveform Audio

   c) Videodisc

   d) Videotape

3. Which of the following is not an animation file format?

   a) 3D Studio Max (max)

   b) Windows Audio Video Interleaved Format (avi)

   c) CompuServe (gif)

   d) None of the above

4. Which one of these is a collection that may contain a random assortment of images or a series of graphics, photographs, sound and video related to a single topic?

   a) E-books

   b) Animation

   c) Bitmap

   d) None of these

5. Which of the following is a popular effect that transforms one image to another?

   a) Kinematics

   b) Morphing

   c) Splicing

   d) Kerning

State whether true or false

1. Cel animation is a technique made famous by Disney and it uses a series of progressively different graphics on each frame of movie film.
2. When parts of pictures are used to trigger multimedia events, they are called hyperpictures.
3. JPEG file format is used for creative video.
4. Multimedia computer system requires small main memory.

5. Text, graphics, audio and video are multimedia objects.

Fill in the blanks

1. _________deals with the generation, representation manipulation and display of pictures with the aid of a computer.
2. __________ is the study of the movement and motion of structures that have joints.
3. _________ add the power of multimedia to web browsers by allowing users to view and interact with new types of documents and images.
4. In Windows, digitized sounds are most commonly stored as ________ files.
5. ____________ refers to the study of movement and motion of structures that have joints.

Descriptive questions

1. Define Multimedia and list five reasons, why multimedia is important?
2. What is multimedia system? Explain all desirable features of a good multimedia system.
3. What is a text? What are different kinds of text?
4. List the various applications of Multimedia. Also describe how multimedia technology has made its effect in the area of education.
5. Explain the importance and role of animation in making a multimedia application.

CHAPTER 7

AN INTRODUCTION TO MICROSOFT WINDOWS

FEATURING

- **An Overview of Different Versions of Windows**
- **Introduction to Windows XP**
- **Getting Started with Windows**

Every computer requires an operating system, which is a set of instruction to organize a file system and to launch programs. Initially DOS (Disk Operating System) was the dominant operating system for PCs but it could run only one program/process at a time. It used a character-user interface. Soon the need to run more than one program at a time and clearly understandable interface was felt. So a new working environment Windows was discovered which supported graphical-user interface. In this chapter, you will study some basic facts about Windows.

An Overview of Different Versions of Windows

The operating system in early 1980's was DOS. DOS is a single-user, character-based operating system. Microsoft came up with various versions of Windows, during 1985-1988. However, the software was not very powerful and user-friendly.

Windows 3 was introduced in 1990. In 1992 Windows 3.1, which was an enhanced version of Windows 3, was introduced, but it was also not a full-fledged operating system. Windows NT, on the contrary, includes the networking software. The GUI used in Windows NT is similar to Windows 3.1, but is more reliable. However, Windows NT did not become popular as it needed a lot of hardware resources which were not easily available in 1990's.

In 1993, Microsoft introduced Windows for Workgroup. It was same as Windows 3.1, except that it contained the networking software.

In 1995, Microsoft introduced Windows 95. The user interface of Windows 95 was redesigned, and it was a great success. It did not need DOS to run it.

Microsoft introduced Windows 98 which was an enhanced version of Windows 95, and it was also very successful.

Towards the end of 1999, Microsoft combined Windows NT technology and Windows 98 graphical user interface and released Windows 2000.

At the end of year 2000, another version of windows called Windows ME introduced.

In 2001, Microsoft released Windows XP which was an updated version of Windows 2000.

In year 2003, enhanced version of Windows, called Windows Server 2003 was introduced, which has in-built Internet Information Services (IIS). In the year 2006, Window Vista version was introduced which was multilingual user interface.

In this book we shall discuss the features of Windows XP. Windows 7, is the latest version of windows released in year 2010.

Introduction to Windows XP

Microsoft Windows XP is an operating system which controls the overall activity of the system. The main tasks of an operating system program are:

- To ensure that all parts of the computer work together smoothly and efficiently.
- To provide an interface to the computer, for the user to work on.

Windows XP provides a Graphical User Interface (GUI), which is more discoverable and easier to use. It can be used as an operating system for a stand-alone machine, a small network, or a large corporate network i.e., Windows XP can also act as a full-fledged Network Operating System. Windows XP is the successor of Windows NT Workstation.

NOTE In a network, a workstation is a personal computer that is attached to a network, and a server is a computer that makes access to files, printing, communications, and other services available to the user's workstations via the network.

Features of Windows XP

There are number of features and enhancements that are incorporated in Windows XP since Microsoft Windows 2000 was released. Some of them are:

- **Automatic Updates (AU)** This feature allows users with administrative rights to download and install OS updates like security fixes and patches.
- **Copying Files and Folders to a CD** Users of Win XP information like photos and software, to a compact disc (CD) without the support of third party software.
- **The File System** The file system is the set of principles by which files are stored on the hard drive. Windows XP supports two file systems. They are — FAT (File Allocation Table) and NTFS (New Technology File System).
- **Compressed Folders** Users can create ZIP folders and view their contents with this feature.
- **Fast User Switching for Multiple Users of a Computer** This feature is useful when multiple users want to share a computer simultaneously without closing all of their applications first.
- **Instant Messaging** This feature allows users to quickly communicate with one another over the Internet. Internet Explorer 6.0 shows MSN Messenger, Outlook Express, and Outlook contacts in a side panel.
- **Internet Connection Firewall (ICF)** A protection is provided on computers that are directly connected to the Internet. It is available for LAN or dial-up networking, Virtual Private Networking (VPN), and Point-to-Point protocol over Ethernet (PPoE) connections. Scanning of ports and resources (file and printer shared) from external resources are also prevented by this feature.

Getting Started with Windows

After you switch on the computer or the PC and load Windows XP into the RAM, it first contacts the hard drive and then loads a software to allow communication between itself and its hardware. Windows XP tests all the hardware components and loads graphic files, font files, etc. which are needed for displaying the desktop. Finally after the checking Windows XP displays its desktop.

Desktop

Desktop is what you see when Windows XP starts. It is the background area of the screen. It resembles a physical desktop on which you keep the most recently used papers, files, telephone numbers, etc. The Desktop is actually an invisible folder called Desktop folder (you can access this folder by using Windows Explorer). You can move files and folders to the Desktop for easy access. Desktop, by default, contains a number of icons (e.g. My Documents, My Computer, Recycle Bin) and the Start button and Taskbar at the bottom of screen.

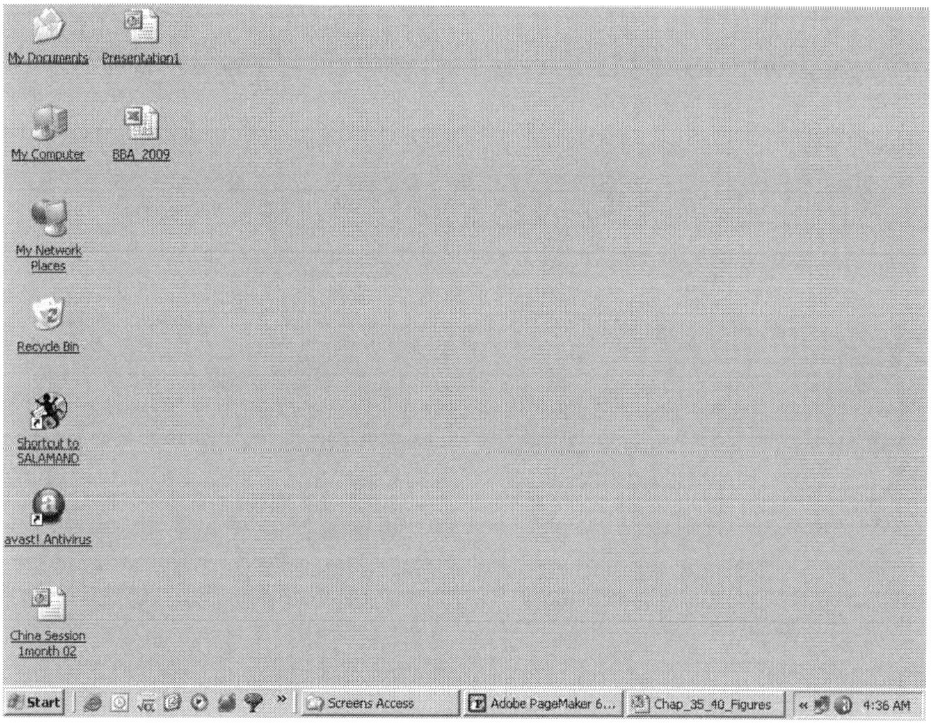

Figure 7.1 : Windows XP Desktop

My Computer Icon

The My Computer icon is usually displayed near the upper left corner of the Windows desktop. It is the easiest tool for browsing the contents of the PC. Single clicking this icon displays the icons for all the drives, plus a folder for the Control Panel and a Printers Folder.

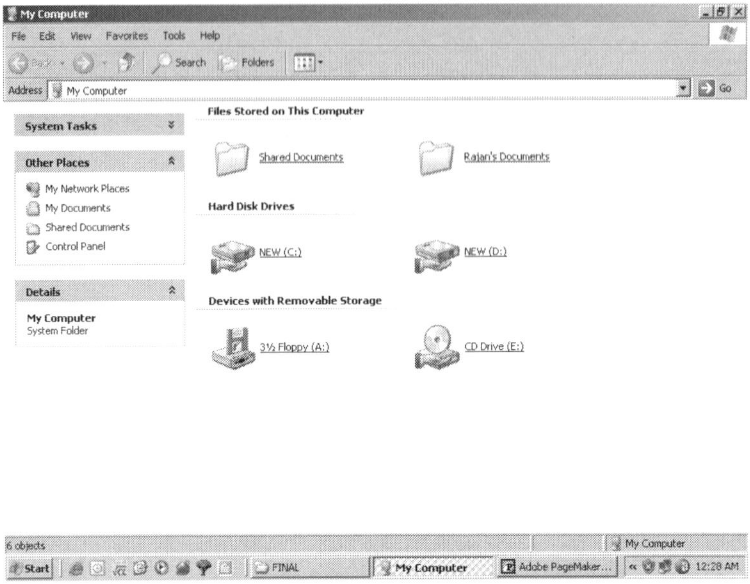

Figure 7.2 : Browsing with My Computer

The Start Button

It is used to gain access to system shutdown options, help, configuration options, recently used documents/files, applications etc. It is by default located in bottom left corner of the Desktop. Clicking on this button activates the Start Menu, displaying the menu of choices:

1. **Windows Update** — Brings up the Update wizard, which connects to the Microsoft's web site for updation (www.windowsupdate.microsoft.com) and updates your computer automatically.

2. **Programs** — Displays a cascading submenu which includes all the programs currently installed on your computer including the Windows 2000 Accessories, DOS prompt, Windows Explorer, Internet Explorer, etc.

3. **Documents** — Displays a submenu displaying a list of shortcuts to recently used files (maximum 15).

4. **Settings** — It displays a submenu having options such as Control Panel, Printers etc., which can customize the way Windows 2000 looks and works.

5. **Search** — Brings up a submenu for searching for files or folders on the network, for printers on network, etc.

6. **Help & Support** — Here you can find answers to all of your Windows 2000 related questions. It also contains a Favorites tab which can store and quickly access Help topics that are frequently looked up.

7. **Run** — Displays the Run dialog box, which lets you run various applications and open folders, documents, etc.

8. **Turn Off Computer** — Brings up the Turn off Computer dialog box, having options to Turn off, Restart or Hibernate the computer.

Taskbar

It appears at the bottom of the screen by default, containing the Start button, and the Quick Launch toolbar. It also displays a button for each open program window, which can be used to switch between the open application windows. The status area which displays the system date and time is on the right side.

To change the location of taskbar, click-and-drag it to the desired side of screen. To increase its size, position the mouse pointer at the upper edge of the taskbar and click-and-drag the border. The taskbar and Start properties can be set by Clicking Start> >Settings> >Taskbar & Start Menu. The Properties dialog box that appears, as shown in Figure 7.3, has two tabs: Taskbar and Start Menu.

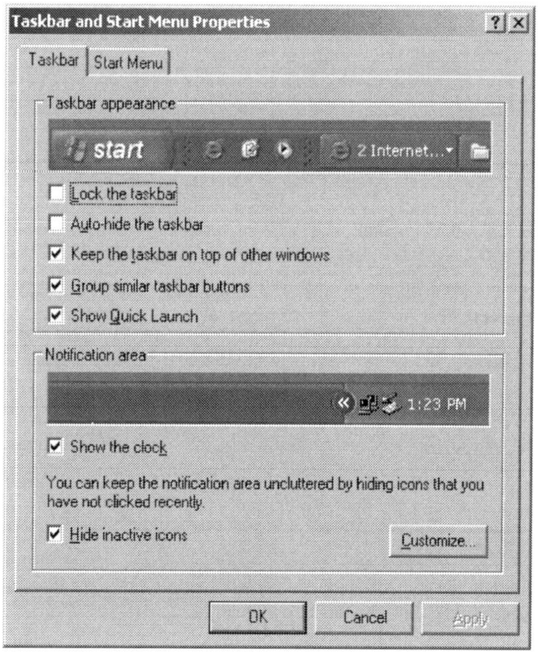

Figure 7.3 : Task bar and Start Menu Properties dialog box

The options available on **Taskbar** tab are as follows:

1. **Lock the taskbar** — When checked, it cannot be moved to a new location on the desktop.

2. **Auto-hide the taskbar** — Selecting this option makes taskbar visible as a thin line, and is displayed only when mouse is moved over it.

3. **Keep the taskbar on top of the other windows** — Check if you want to see taskbar on top of all the windows so that it is always visible.

4. **Group similar taskbar buttons** — When checked, all the buttons for the same program are grouped together on the taskbar.

5. **Show Quick Launch** — When checked, this bar displays icons you can click to quickly open programs.

6. **Taskbar Notification** — It is the area of the taskbar where you usually see the current time displayed. This area can become crowded with notification icons that appears when certain events occur such as when you receive e-mail.

The options on **Start Menu** tab are:

1. **Start Menu** — Specifies that your default start menu is the one that gives you quickest access to e-mail and the Internet, your documents, pictures, and music and the programs you have used recently.

2. **Classic Start Menu** — Specifies that your default start menu has the same look and behaviour as earlier versions of windows.

Recycle Bin

The Recycle Bin icon on the Desktop is a reserved space on the hard disk drive, which can be used to dispose off the files and folders which are no longer required. When a file or folder is deleted, it is moved to this reserved space. You can recover a file or folder deleted previously from the Recycle Bin (if available in it) by selecting the object in the Recycle Bin folder and choosing File >> Restore.

To delete a file or folder permanently, you have to delete it from the Recycle Bin by selecting the object and pressing Delete Key. To remove all the files or folders from the Recycle Bin, select File >> Empty Recycle Bin.

Control Panel

Windows XP comes with many options or tools which help in customizing the Windows session and make the operating system more usable. These tools are available in the Control Panel. To start Control Panel : Click Start>>Settings>>Control Panel. A window as shown in Figure 7.4 appears.

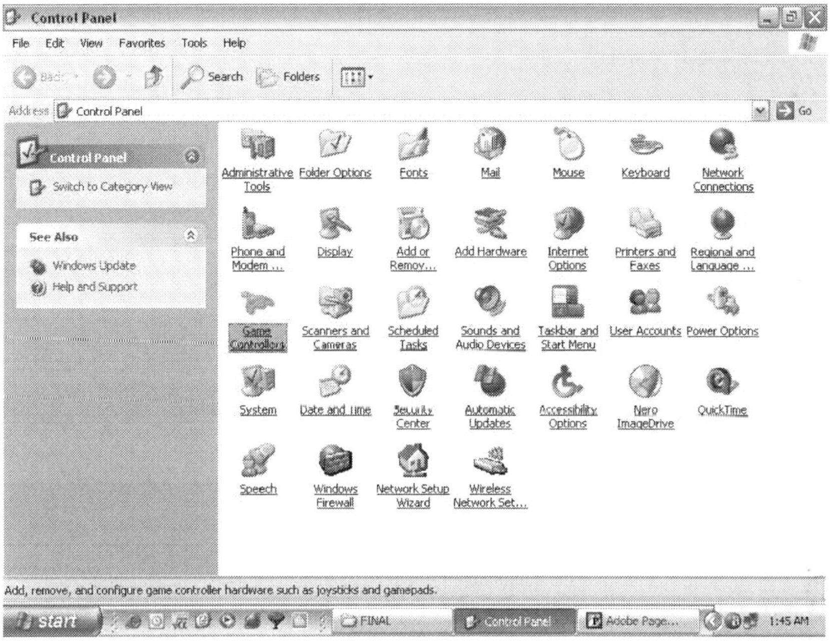

Figure 7.4 : Control Panel

Accessibility Options

The Accessibility Option in Control Panel provides functionality so as to make Windows XP more accessible to users with special needs, such as some physical impairments. To open Accessibility Options dialog box, click its icon in the Control Panel.

Add Hardware

Hardware components which support PnP (Plug and Play) specifications, are detected and setup by Windows XP automatically as soon as they are installed on the system. Other devices which are not PnP compatible such as network cards, modems, etc., must be explicitly specified by the user, before the user can use them. This can be done using Add Hardware Wizard. To start the wizard, click Start>>Settings>>Control Panel >>Add Hardware.

Add/Remove Programs

The programs and Windows XP components installed on the computer have an entry in the Windows Registry. So, before deleting a program or Windows component its entry must also be removed from Registry. The Add/Remove Programs option in Control Panel displays the Change or Remove Programs screen, as shown in Figure 7.5 which contains buttons for changing, removing or adding programs and for adding or removing Windows components.

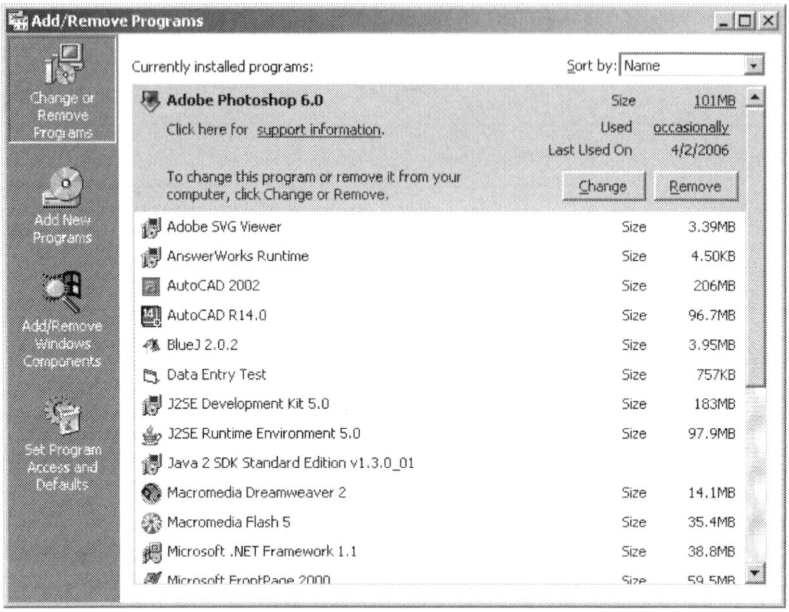

Figure 7.5 : Add/Remove Programs dialog box

Date and Time

It can be used to reset the date and time settings of the computer. It also allows you to change the time zone e.g., Indian time zone is +5:30 GMT.

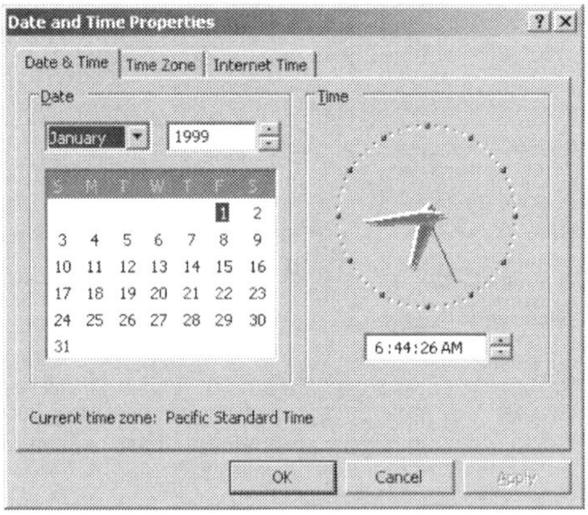

Figure 7.6 : Date/Time Properties dialog box

Display

It opens the Display Properties dialog box as shown in Figure 7.7, which allows to set a background for the Desktop, specify a screen saver, change the appearance of Windows by changing the color scheme, and change and specify the monitor resolution and color depth.

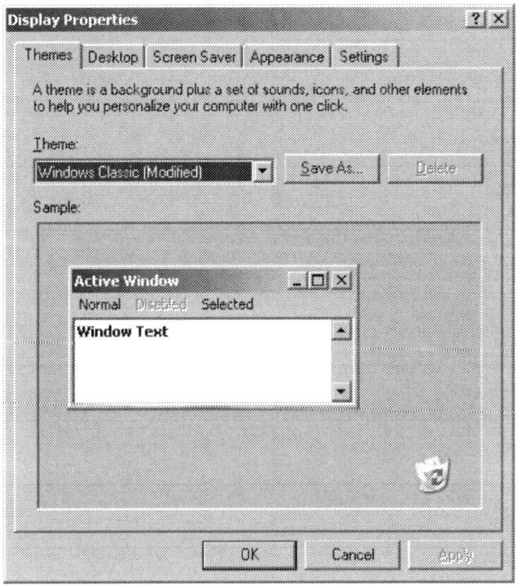

Figure 7.7 : Display Properties dialog box with Themes tab activated

The various tabs of the Display Properties dialog box are discussed below:

1. **Themes** — List the available desktop themes. A desktop theme determines the overall appearance of your desktop by providing a predefined set of icons, fonts, colors, mouse pointers, sounds, background pictures, screen saver, and other window elements.

2. **Desktop** — The wallpaper and background pattern is what appears as the Desktop. On the Desktop tab, you can select a background from the list box or can click on Browse button to locate the file that you want to use as picture.

3. **Screen Saver** — A screen saver is a picture or pattern that appears on the screen when you do not use your computer for a specified period of time. You can choose a screen saver and also set a password for the screen saver, and the idle time before the screen saver is displayed.

4. **Appearance** — It allows the user to change the color scheme of the different Desktop elements such as title bars, menus, border size, etc. To change the settings of any element click the element in the preview window and change the size, color or font of that element. Click on Apply to apply the selected settings.

5. **Settings** — It lets you specify the screen resolution and color quality for your display.

Mouse

To change how your mouse operates, settings are available in the Mouse icon in the Control Panel. Various tabs of Mouse properties dialog box are as follows:

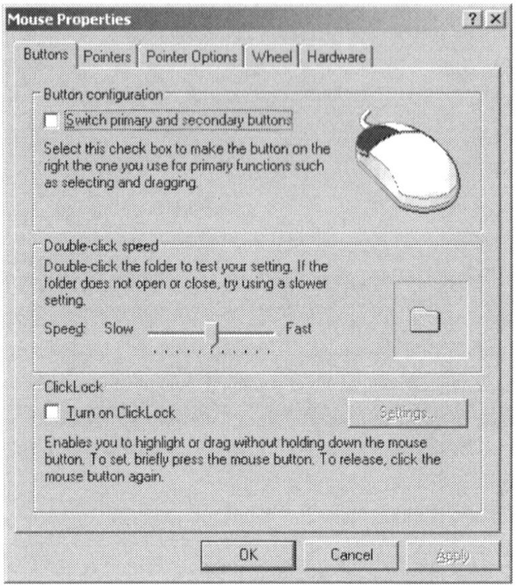

Figure 7.8 : Mouse Properties dialog box with Buttons tab activated

1. **Buttons** — You can configure the mouse for the right or left hand use and the internal setting of the left and right click will change accordingly. You can also specify whether to open files and folders with a single or double click. The double-click speed of mouse, i.e., the duration between two simultaneous clicks can also be adjusted. There is a test area which can be clicked to check the double click speed settings.

2. **Pointers** — It lets you choose a design scheme for the pointers. To change the mouse pointers, click the down arrow in the Scheme box to display a list of available design schemes and choose the scheme that you want. Click OK.

3. **Pointer Options** — It lets you adjust the speed of pointer movement. When check to Snap To box, it will automatically move pointer to the default button in a dialog box.

My Network Places

It lets you view and navigate the resources, such as printers, folders, on the network. Only those resources can be accessed which are made shareable over the network. By default, a shortcut to My Network Places is placed on the desktop, which can be double-clicked to open it. You can also open My Network Places, by clicking on it in the left pane of Windows

Explorer. The My Network Places folder, includes the Entire Network icon, which can be double clicked to browse the complete network hierarchy, such as other computers connected to the network.

Basic Windows Elements

- **Control-Menu Box** If you click on the upper left corner of the window (or press Alt and Spacebar keys together) the control menu appears. The control menu can be used to restore, more, size, minimize, maximize and close a window. You can press Esc to close the window.
- **Title Bar** All Windows have a title bar. It's the long narrow box across the very top of a window. The title bar shows the system menu icon, the title of the window or name of the program being run in the window, and the buttons for resizing and closing the window.
- **Menu Bar** All Windows have a Menu Bar. It's the long narrow box below the Title bar of a Window. However it can be dragged and moved according to the user's choice to any part of the window. The Menu bar shows File, Edit, View, Help options generally on all the Windows.
- **Tool Bar** All Windows have a Toolbar. It's the long narrow box below the Menu Bar of a Window. However it can be dragged and moved according to the user's choice to any part of the window. The Toolbar shows various icons which help in the working of that particular application.
- **Scroll Bars** There are vertical and horizontal scrollbars which are used to move through the window when the entire content does not fit in the window.
- **Maximize Button** On clicking this button using the mouse, the active window is enlarged so that it covers the entire desktop.
- **Minimize Button** On clicking this button using the mouse, the active window is reduced to an icon which can be re-arranged on the desktop.
- **Restore Button** On clicking this button, the window returns to its previous size if at all it was maximized or minimized.
- **Window Border** The outer edge of the active window is called the window border. The window can be resized by increasing or decreasing the border with the help of mouse.
- **Insertion Point** The linking vertical bar or the cursor indicates the insertion point where the matter has to be inserted on typing or drawing.
- **Mouse Pointer** It is an arrow that points items and appears on the active window only if the mouse is installed on the system.

- **Client Area** The area inside the window where the actual operation (insertion, deletion etc.) has to be performed.

Shortcuts

Shortcuts let you access various Windows objects by acting as a pointer to them. They are a means of convenience in the Windows environment. A shortcut, identified by a small arrow in its icon, can be created to folders, programs and other files. It can be created on the desktop or in other folders such as Start menu. The steps for creating a shortcut on the Desktop are:

1. Right click in a blank area on the Desktop and Choose New >> Shortcut to open the Create Shortcut dialog box (refer Figure 7.9).

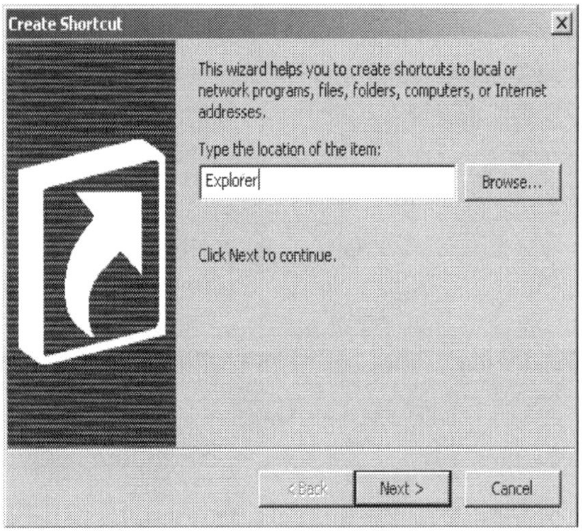

Figure 7.9 : Create Shortcut dialog box

2. Enter the name (along with the path) of the file or folder, or click on Browse to locate it.
3. Click Next> to open the dialog box, where you can select a title for the program.
4. Type a name for the shortcut.
5. Click Finish.

The shortcut will appear on your Desktop.

Each shortcut has a Properties sheet associated with it that can be seen by right-clicking on the shortcut icon and selecting Properties from the pop-up menu (refer Figure 7.10).

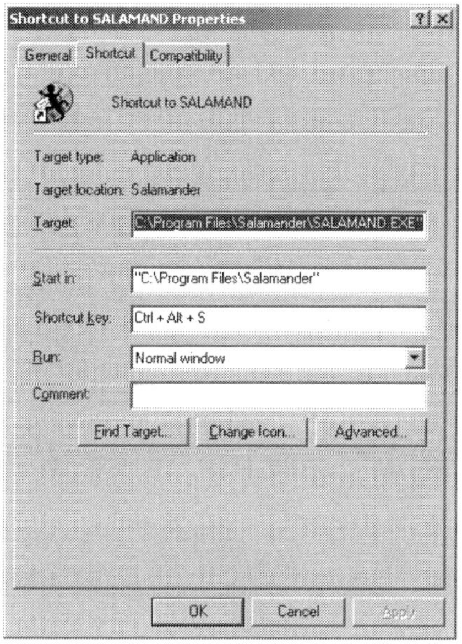

Figure 7.10 : Properties Sheet

The Target text box on the Shortcut tab of the Properties sheet displays the path of the destination object for shortcut. To change the icon of the shortcut:

1. Select Shortcut tab from the Properties sheet of the shortcut.
2. Click the Change Icon button. A dialog box appears.
3. Use the Browse button to look in other files. Select the icon you want to use.
4. Click OK twice.

Search Feature

The search command is an invaluable tool in helping you locate a document, file or folder. You can choose to search by various criteria including file name, a specific word present in the file or the last modified date. Windows XP allows you to search for media files, such as pictures, music and video; documents, such as those created with word processing and spreadsheet programs; or all files and folders. To perform search, follow the steps given below:

1. Click Start >> Search, this displays Search Results Window.
2. A search companion appears on the left side of the window, which ask you what type of item you want to search for.
3. Click on the desired option.
4. Click search button to start the search.

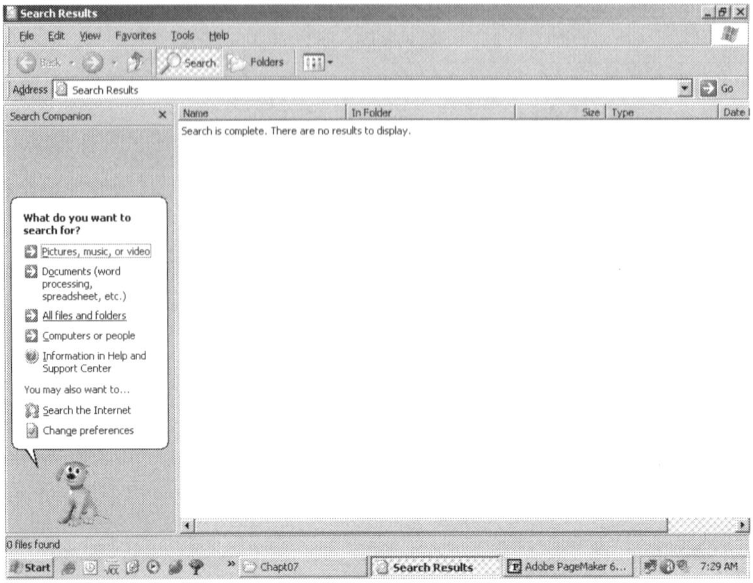

Figure 7.11 : Search dialog box

Properties

Sometimes, it is important to have information about files folders and programs. This information about any object can be found in the property sheet of that object. To invoke the property sheet of any item, right click it's icon & choose properties from the menu that appears. The property sheet of that item will appear containing the characteristics of that item like color, size, shape etc.

Right clicking (Context Menu)

Every thing on the desktop including the desktop can be right clicked. It displays a short-cut menu of commands appropriate for the item on which the mouse is right clicked. Example:

- Right clicking a file icon displays a menu of multiple options, including opening the file with its associated program.
- Right clicking a folder opens a menu which is similar to the one for a file.
- Right clicking the start button brings up three choices :
  - **Open** — It opens the start menu folder that contains the files and folders which are dropped on the start menu as well as another folder called programs that contains all the shortcuts that make up the programs menu.
  - **Explorer** — Opens the start menu folder in the Explorer view.
  - **Search** — A shortcut for finding a file in the start menu folder.

Turning OFF the Machine

Before you turn OFF your machine, you should shut down Windows XP properly. If you don't, the next time you will startup, you'll have to wait while Windows XP does some file checking and maintenance and you could even loose some data and settings.

1. Click Start >> Turn off Computer.

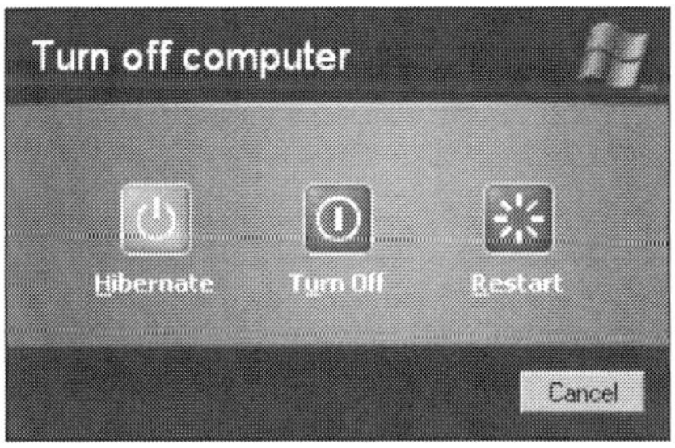

Figure 7.12 : Turn off Windows dialog box

2. Select Turn off.

Summary

- On starting Windows, you see the desktop that provides an interface between Windows and the user.
- Start button appears in the lower left corner of the screen, clicking which Start menu appears.
- The taskbar is a bar containing a button for each open window on the desktop.
- Shortcuts enable users to access various Windows objects by acting as a pointer to them.
- The Control Panel is used to control the properties of the computer system.
- The Accessibility option provides functionality to users with special needs.
- On-screen keyboards are used by users with physical disability to type.
- To change how your mouse operates, settings are available in the mouse icon in the control panel.
- Background, Appearance, and Screen saver can be changed with the help of Display Properties.
- You can install/uninstall fonts and printers.
- Before you turn OFF your machine, you should shut down Windows XP properly.

Review Exercise

Multiple choice questions

1. Which of the following features make(s) Windows desirable?
   a) It is easy to learn and use.
   b) It works with virtually every kind of program.
   c) It brings all the exciting new electronic communication and entertainment technologies to your PC desktop.
   d) All of the above.
2. Identify the incorrect statement
   a) by default taskbar appears at the bottom of the screen.
   b) taskbar contains a button for each open window on the desktop.
   c) it is not possible to move the taskbar from its position.
   d) none of the above.
3. In order to add new fonts, which path is valid?
   a) Start>>Settings>>Control Panel>>Fonts>>File>>Install New Font
   b) Start>>Settings>>Control Panel>>Fonts>>Install New Font
   c) Both (a) & (b)
   d) None of the above
4. Small interactive programs that guide us through multistep procedures are called
   a) templates
   b) wizards
   c) dialog boxes
   d) none of the above
5. Collections of sounds, icons, fonts, colors, and screen saver are known as:
   a) Appearance
   b) Themes
   c) Colors
   d) Settings

State whether true or false

1. Control Panel can be used to control the available hardware and software settings.
2. Each little picture on the desktop represents an application.
3. Clicking the Start button actually initiates the working of Windows.
4. Only one window can be opened at a time on the desktop.
5. The Accessibility Options of Control Panel are meant for people who are physically challenged.

Fill in the blanks

1. The ______________ enables the desktop and other Windows applications to look and act as a web page.
2. The __________ button appears in the lower left corner of the WINDOWS screen.
3. In Control Panel, there is _____________ option and tools to help people with disabilities.
4. To add, remove and change mouse settings, there is an icon called __________ in Control Panel.
5. Right clicking the start button brings up three choices : ______ , ________ and _______ .

Descriptive questions

1. Describe any five major features of Microsoft Windows.
2. What is the Start button used for?
3. Define the role of Taskbar.
4. What are main features of the Display option on the Control Panel?
5. What are Desktop Icons? Describe some of the desktop icons.

CHAPTER 8

WINDOWS ACCESSORIES & FILE MANAGEMENT

FEATURING

- Windows Accessories
- Windows Explorer
- Command Prompt
- Files, Directories and Drives
- Installing Applications
- Uninstalling Applications

Windows XP comes with a set of small programs (applications). These applications usually have a limited capability, so are known as applets or accessories. In this chapter you will study a wide range of items categorized under Accessories, such as, Notepad, WordPad, Paint, etc. You will also go through a set of disk tools used for system maintenance.

Windows XP offers a new version of Windows Explorer, which has more functionality and ease of use as compared to its predecessors. This chapter gives an insight into the Windows Accessories and file management tools.

Windows Accessories

Windows XP comes with a set of small programs (applications). These applications usually have a limited capability, and are more aptly known as Applets or Accessories. To access these Applets click Start >> Programs >> Accessories menu. The Accessories menu includes a wide range of items such as Games, Notepad, Paint, etc.

System Tools/Disk Tools

Windows XP provides a set of disk tools for the system maintenance. You can access the list of tools by clicking the Start >> Programs >> Accessories >> System Tools menu. Under this menu we can select from various options. Some of them are:

Disk Cleanup

It can find files on your hard disk that can be deleted to free up hard disk space. These files may be temporary internet files, unnecessary program files, Windows XP components which are not required (specified by user), cache files, and files in recycle bin.

To start Disk Cleanup (refer Figure 8.1) select it from System Tools submenu of Accessories option, in Programs menu, and follow the following steps :

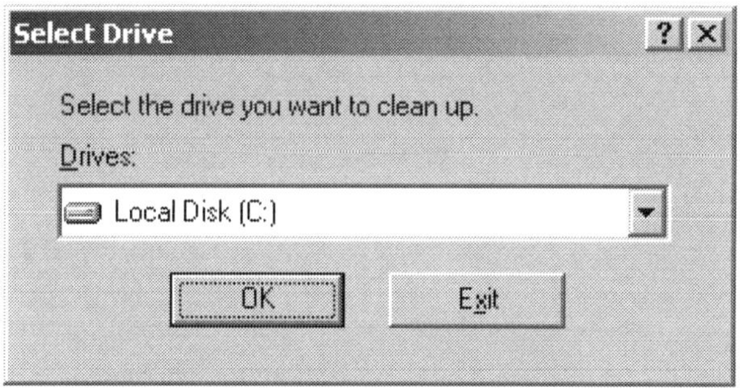

Figure 8.1 : Disk Cleanup dialog box

1. Select the drive you want to clean. Click OK.
2. On the Disk Cleanup tab, place a check mark next to the type of files you want to delete and click View Files to see which files will be affected. Click OK after finishing the selection of files.
3. Confirm the deletion process by clicking Yes.
4. Windows will return to desktop after finishing the task assigned to Disk Cleanup.

Disk Defragmenter

When an operating system stores/writes a file to a disk, it puts the file blocks anywhere it finds room which may make a file fragmented. When a file is spread over multiple places the system takes more time in accessing it (which may be a program or data file), thereby slowing down the system. Disk Defragmenter is a tool that lets you arrange these fragments (parts) of a file, so as to improve the access speed. To start Disk Defragmenter select it from System Tools menu and a dialog box as shown in Figure 8.2 appears.

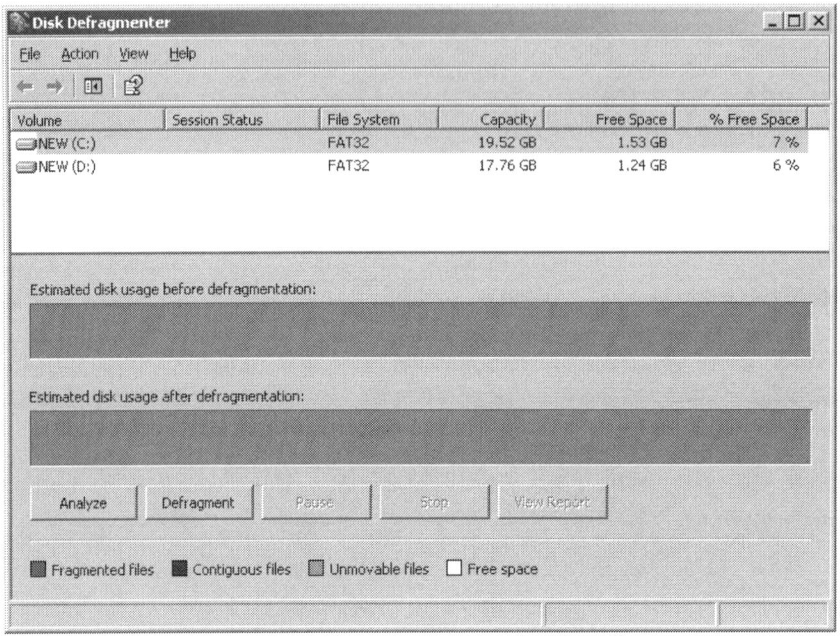

Figure 8.2 : Disk Defragmenter dialog box

To defragment a disk :

1. Select a disk/volume from the list in upper pane of Disk Defragmenter.
2. Click the Defragment button to start the process.
3. When the process is complete Windows XP displays you a message that defragmentation is complete.

System Restore

System Restore is a component of Windows XP that you can use to restore your computer to previous state, if a problem occurs, without losing your personal data files : System Restore monitors changes to the system and some application files, and it automatically creates easily identified restore points. These restore points allow you to revert the system to a previous time. They are created daily and at the time of significant system events.

Using the System Restore Wizard:

- Click Start >> Programs >> Accessories >> System Tools >> System Restore. A System Restore wizard guides you through the steps of each task in system restore.

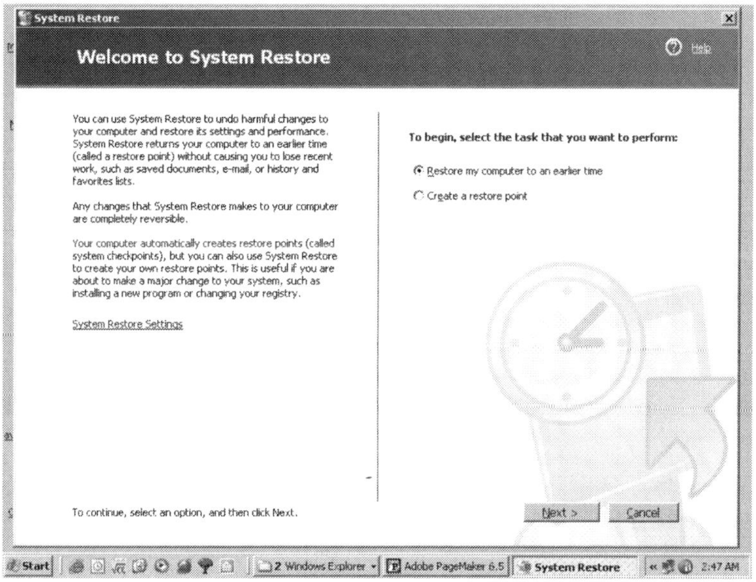

Figure 8.3 : System Restore Wizard

Calculator

It is just similar to the hand-held Calculator device. It has two versions — Standard and Scientific.

To open Calculator : Click Start >> Programs >> Accessories >> Calculator. When the Calculator is started, it displays the version last used, standard or scientific. To change the view (version), click View menu and select the desired version. On selecting scientific version, the calculator as shown in Figure 8.4 appears.

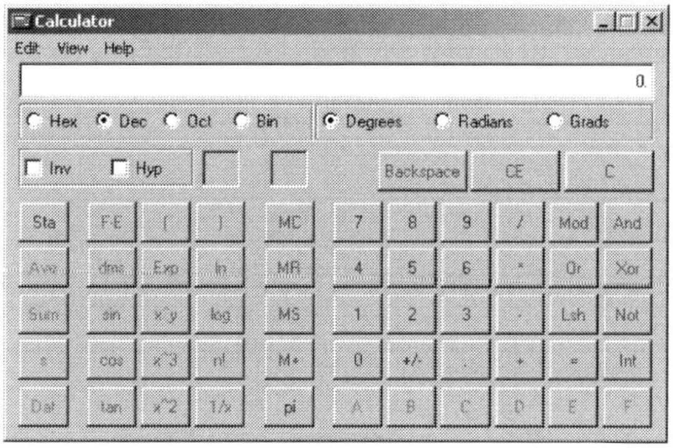

Figure 8.4 : Scientific Calculator

Notepad

Notepad is a miniature text-only word processing program. It is very limited in comparison to other word processors. Notepad cannot centre text, nor does it support multiple fonts in a document. It also does not have provision to add graphics to a Notepad document. Notepad has the bare minimum of facilities on its menus. Using Notepad, it is possible to:

- Search for characters or words.
- Use Page Setup to set margins, paper orientation, customize the header and footer, and select a printer.
- Copy, cut and paste text.
- Insert the time and date into a document.

Figure 8.5 shows a new document opened in the Notepad editor.

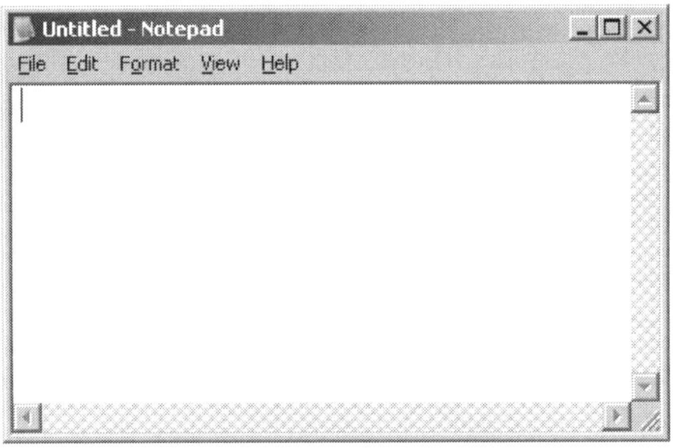

Figure 8.5 : Notepad Editor

To start Notepad, click on Start button and choose Programs >> Accessories >> Notepad. The Notepad program launches and begins with a clean editing screen.

Notepad does not have any toolbars and offers only four menu choices to select from. The word-wrap facility is available in Notepad but the first time you use the program, you must turn on the feature. If word-wrap is turned on, the text you type wraps to the next line. Notepad ignores your margin settings when word-wrap is activated. To turn this feature on, choose Format >> Word Wrap. To change the font, choose Format >> Font.

To save a file in Notepad, choose File >> Save. The Save As dialog box, prompts you to enter a file name. Enter a file name and then click OK.

To open a file in Notepad, choose File >> Open. The Open dialog box appears on the screen. Double click on the desired file to open it. If a Notepad document is to be printed, the word-wrap feature must be turned off prior to printing. Then choose File >> Print.

Paint

Every drawing is made up of a series of small objects — usually one or more shapes such as circles or rectangles, combined with other objects such as lines or text. The Paint program helps in making drawings. To start Paint, click on the Start button and choose Programs >> Accessories >> Paint.

Identifying the Tool Box

A feature called the Tool Box appears on the left of the Paint window as shown in figure 8.6. If the toolbox is not displayed, click on the View menu and choose Tool Box. The tool button appears to be pressed in when a tool is active. Also, some tools display additional options at the bottom of the Tool Box when they are selected.

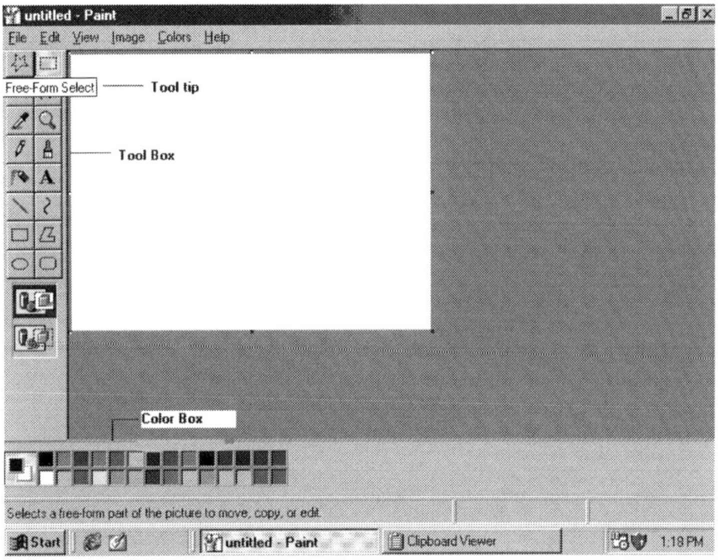

Figure 8.6 : Paintbrush Program identifying the toolbox

Editing the Color Box

The color box, appears at the bottom of the screen with a palette of 28 colors that can be used while making a drawing. Clicking on a color with the left mouse button selects a color for the foreground or frame of the object. Clicking on a color with the right mouse button selects a color for the background or interior of an object.

Resizing the Drawing Screen

The size of the Paint working area can be changed. Click on Image>>Attributes. A dialog box, as shown in Figure 8.7, appears.

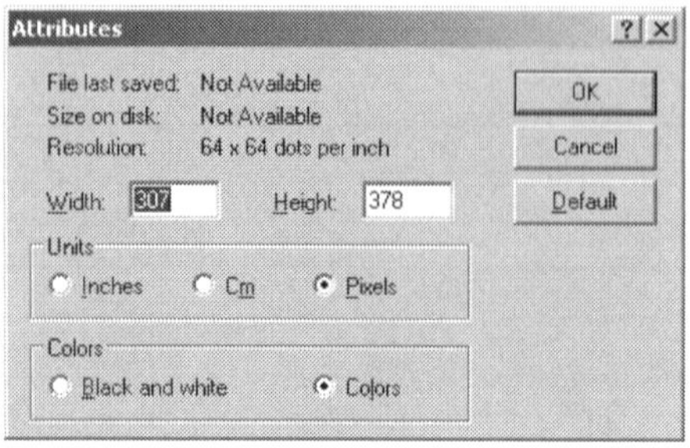

Figure 8.7 : Attributes dialog box

From the Units area, choose Inches. Enter the desired page Width and Height (measured in inches); then click on OK. The new page size remains in effect for all new drawings. The default size can be restored by clicking on the Default button from the Attributes dialog box at the top of the drawing window.

Saving a Drawing

Paint Program saves the files in bitmap format, that is, files have .BMP extension. Choose File >> Save. Type a descriptive name for the drawing in the File Name box and then click on Save. It is also possible to save a drawing as your wallpaper for the Windows desktop by choosing File >> Set as Wallpaper (Tiled) or Set as Wallpaper (Centred).

Flipping and Rotating an Object

In Paint you can flip an area upside down or reverse its direction. You can also rotate an area by a specified number of degrees. Use the selection tool to select the object to be flipped. Choose Image >> Flip/Rotate. Make the desired selection in the dialog box that appears, and then click on OK.

Wordpad

WordPad is another handy applet for working with text. But unlike Notepad, which creates plain, simple text files, WordPad can help in creating true word processing documents with fonts, boldface, and other print features. To start WordPad, click the Start button and choose Programs >> Accessories >> WordPad, and a screen as shown in Figure 8.8 appears.

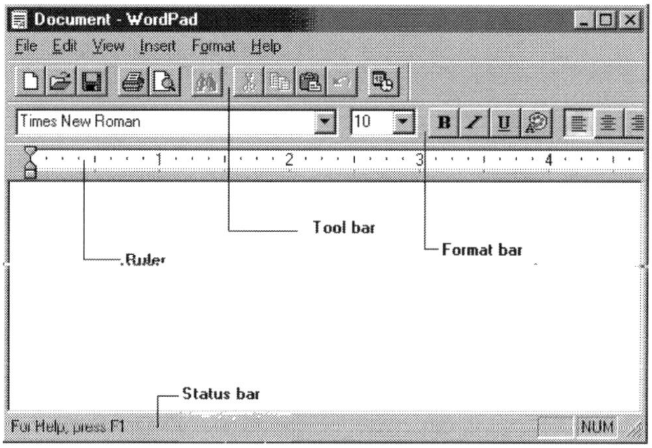

Figure 8.8 : Wordpad Document

- **Editing a WordPad Document** After typing, anything is changeable in a word processing document. Just move the insertion pointer to the location where the changes are to be made and then make the changes.
- **Selecting Text in a WordPad Document** To make changes in the text of two or more characters, that text must be selected. WordPad includes several special techniques to select a block of text. Block can be anywhere from two characters to the entire document in length. Table 8.1 lists some block selection techniques:

Do This	To Select
Double click on a word	A word
Triple click on a word	A paragraph
Click and drag across characters	Any amount of text you drag the mouse across
Ctrl + A	The entire document
Shift + (Arrow key)	One character at a time from the insertion point in the direction of the arrow key.

Table 8.1 : Block Selection Techniques

- **Moving a Block of Text** For moving a block of text, select the text and then choose Edit >> Cut. Place the insertion point where the text is to be moved and choose Edit >> Paste.
- **Copying a Block of Text** For copying a block of text, select the text and then choose Edit >> Copy. Then place the cursor where the text is to be copied and then choose Edit >> Paste.

- **Adding Bullets** A bullet is a small black circle or other character that precedes each item in a list. Choose Format >> Bullet Style. A bullet is added in front of each item, and the text is indented 1/2 inch to the right.
- **Changing Page Attributes** Page attributes are settings that affect the layout of the text on the page. Choose File >> Page Setup. The Page Setup dialog box, displays selections for the paper size, source, orientation and margins available.
- **Saving a WorPad Document** Choose File >> Save. Type a descriptive filename in the File Name text box. Click on OK to save the document with the specified name.

Entertainment

Under this option there are facilities which support multimedia capabilities to play sound effects and MIDI (Musical Instrument Digital Interface) music and to display digital video and 3D. It provides following facilities:

Windows Media Player

Windows Media Player is a universal media player you can use to receive audio, video and mixed media files in most popular formats. Windows Media Player has several features that make it the most comprehensive, simple and efficient multimedia player. These features are:

- A wide range of files are played in a simplified way.
- It is made easier according to the users preferences.
- High Quality multimedia experience.
- Quick access to media content.

Select Start >> Program >> Accessories >> Entertainment >> Windows Media Player.

Sound Recorder

If there is an audio input device on the computer (either a microphone or a CD-ROM player) Sound Recorder can be used to make a .wav file which can be used to associate with a windows event or send a message.

Select Start >> Program >> Accessories >> Entertainment >> Sound Recorder.

Volume Control

The volume control panel helps in adjusting sound level. It also individually tunes different types of files. Select Start >> Program >> Accessories >> Entertainment >> Volume

Control. A window will appear. Select Advanced Controls from the options menu for controlling tones. Use slider controls to increase or decrease the various tones. These settings will affect at the sound files.

Games

This icon can be used to add, remove or change settings for game controllers. Windows XP even offers a package of four exciting games for your relaxation from the braintaxing work on the computer.

To reach the Games section of Windows XP, select

Start >> Programs >> Accessories >> Games

The four games you can play are : Free Cell, Minesweeper, Pinball, Solitaire. To know how to play each of these games, just open the game and go to Help Menu

Imaging

All the faxed, scanned and other image documents can be viewed using imaging. The captured image's are sent directly to the imaging application, where they can be re-sized, or their colors can be changed etc. There is a special toolbar for imaging which contains several tools for editing the images. You can access the imaging by clicking the Start >> Program >> Accessories >>Imaging.

Windows Explorer

Windows Explorer is a powerful tool which provides the utilities you need to work with files and folders, and associate files with applications. It can be used for :

- Viewing files and folders on the hard drives, floppy disks or other storage media, such as CD-ROM.
- Creating shortcuts to and locating the executable files for applications that are not automatically installed on the Desktop or the Start Menu.
- Copying, Moving, Renaming or Removing files or folders.

To start Explorer :

Click Start >> Programs >> Accessories >> Windows Explorer. A window, as shown in Figure 8.9, appears.

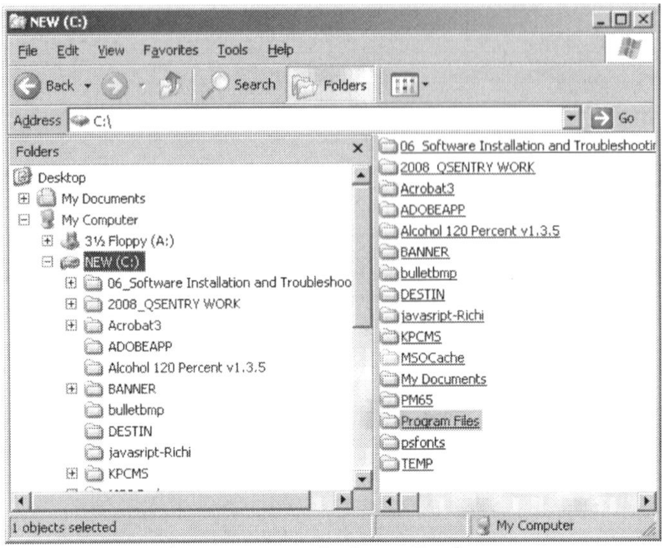

Figure 8.9 : Windows Explorer

Working with Files and Folders

A **file** is a collection of your data or information, stored on the secondary storage. It can be used to access the data or information later on.

Folders are part of the Windows XP file system structure. Folders can be used to organize files on your computer. A folder can contain files or subfolders. Folders are equivalent to DOS directories.

Selecting Files and Folders

Before performing any action on a file or folder, it must first be selected. To select a file or folder, just click on it in any Explorer window. To select continuous group of Files or Folders, click on the first file or folder you want to select and holding down the Shift key click on the last file or folder of the group. To select noncontinuous files or folders, click on a file or folder you want to select and holding down the Ctrl key, click on other files or folders you want.

Creating a New Folder

A folder can be created by any of the following tools:

- My Computer
- Windows Explorer

With My Computer

To create a folder with My Computer, follow these steps:

- Open the My Computer icon.
- Open the icon of the drive / existing folder on / inside which you have to put the new folder.
- Choose File >> New >> Folder from the menu bar or right click some empty space between existing icons and choose New >> Folder. A new folder is created.
- A folder titled New Folder appears. The folder name is highlighted and it is ready to accept the new name. Type a new name for the folder.
- To save the new folder, click on the empty place inside the folder window or press Enter.

With Windows Explorer

To create a new folder with Windows Explorer, follow the steps given below:

- Click the Start button and choose Programs >> Accessories >> Windows Explorer.
- In the left column, select the drive or folder one level above when the new folder is to be created.
- Choose File >> New >> Folder. A new folder titled New Folder appears at the bottom of the list in the right hand pane and the folder name is highlighted.
- Type a new name and to save the folder press Enter or click on the empty area in the right pane of the Explorer window.

Managing Folders

Following things can be done while working with folders.

- To open a folder, double click (in Classic style) or click (in Web style) it. If folder is open but covered by other windows on the desktop, click the hidden folder's taskbar button to bring it to the forefront.
- To close a folder, click the Close button in its window.
- To rename a folder, right click it and choose Rename or select it and press F2. Give a new name and press Enter.
- To move or copy items into a folder, right drag the selected objects to the folder's icon or the folder's open window, release the mouse button and then choose Move Here or Copy Here. To move or copy items out of a folder, open the folder, select the item and follow the same method.

- To delete a folder, select the folder's icon and then press Delete or right click the folder's icon and then choose Delete. Choose Yes when asked for confirmation.

Creating a File

A file can be created in one of the following three ways :

1. **From the Desktop**
   - Right click on the empty space on Desktop and choose New.
   - From the submenu, select the type of file you want to create.
   - Type a name for the file and click outside it.
   - This file is stored in the Desktop folder in your username folder.
2. **From Explorer**
   - Start the Explorer window and select the folder that will contain the new file.
   - Right-click in a blank space in the right pane of Explorer.
   - Select New, and the file type from menu that appears.
   - Type a name for the file and click outside it.
3. **From within an Application**
   - Generally files are created from within an application.
   - In the application window (e.g., Notepad, Paint), choose File >> Save As.
   - Select the folder in which you want to save the file, so that the folder name appears in the Save in list box.
   - Enter a name in the File name text box. Click Save.

Renaming Files and Folders

To rename a file or folder:

1. Select the file or folder and select File >> Rename.

   OR

   Select the file or folder and press F2 key.

   OR

   Right click on the file or folder and select Rename.
2. Type the new name and click outside it or press Enter.

Moving and Copying Files and Folders

When a file or folder is moved, it is no longer in its original place. Creating a copy means the copy is created in some folder, but the original still remains. A file or folder can be copied or moved in the following three ways:

1. Moving or Copying using Right mouse button:
   - Locate the file or folder in Explorer.
   - Right-click it, and drag it to its destination.
   - Release the mouse button and then choose Copy Here or Move Here from the pop-up menu.
2. Moving or Copying using Left Mouse button:
   - When you use the left mouse button to drag-and-drop, if the source and destination are on same drive then the file is moved, otherwise it is copied.
   - To move a file or folder when the source and destination are on different drives, click the file and hold down the Shift key while you drag the file.
   - Similarly, to copy a file or folder when the source and destination are on same drive, click the file and hold down the Shift key while you drag and drop the selection to destination or same file.
   - In an Explorer window, select the file or folder and click the Move To, or Copy To tool button. In the dialog box, select the destination for the file or folder and click OK.

Sharing Folders

As discussed earlier, My Network Places icon can be used to access a network share that can be a printer, folder, etc. To share a folder, follow these steps :

1. Open the Explorer window, and browse to the object you want to share.
2. Right-click to display the shortcut menu, and choose Sharing and Security to open the Properties dialog box, as shown in figure 8.10, for the selected object.
3. Select the Sharing tab and checked Share this folder on the network checkbox. Enter a share name.
4. Check the Allow network users to change my files checkbox if you want to specify the permission for the share.
5. Click OK.

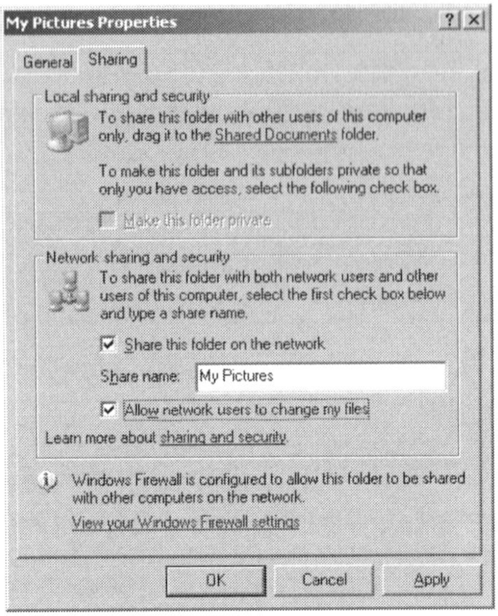

Figure 8.10 : Folder Sharing Properties dialog box

The shared folder can now be accessed over network by the Share Name in My Network Places folder.

Command Prompt

If DOS or MS-DOS alone is installed on your computer, starting of computer means starting of DOS. However, if you have MS-Windows installed as an operating system and you want to switch over to DOS mode following step have to be performed:

Start >> Programs >> Accessories >> Command Prompt

Or

Start >> Run, then type **cmd** in the Run dialog box and press Enter or OK button.

Command Prompt Window

On switching to DOS Prompt window, another small window is displayed on the monitor. Details of the DOS version being used is indicated in the first two lines. The next line before the blinking cursor is called the prompt or the system prompt. The following are the two purposes of this prompt:

- Indication that DOS can now accept the command from keyboard.
- Display of the default drive and directory (folder) name.
- For example, C:\Documents and Settings\Administrator directory (folder) is selected in drive C.

If the user does not specify any drive name and/or folder, DOS uses the default drive and folder.

Files, Directories and Drives

Files are logical containers of data that are always present at the leaf level of a directory tree, i.e., they are the last element of any tree. A file cannot be a collection of other files or directories and can only contain data or instructions. Each file has a set of properties associated with it.

1. **File name** Each file is recognized by its filename. Filename has two parts; name and extension. File naming conventions must be followed while naming a file. A filename can have a maximum of 8 characters.

   Extension identifies the type of the file or the application to which a particular file belongs. It can be 3 characters long.

2. **Size** determines how much space the file is occupying on the disk.
3. **Date created** corresponds to the date when file was created.
4. **Date accessed** corresponds to the date when file was last accessed.
5. **Date modified** corresponds to the date when file was last modified.
6. **Path** specifies the location of file on the disk. It comprises of a series of predecessor (parent) directories and moves up to the root.

Directories are a collection of files or other directories. Directory at the highest level is called the root directory. There can be only one root in a directory structure. Directories at lower levels are called child and those who share the same parents are called siblings. A directory structure can be viewed as a way to organise files on the hard disk. Figure 8.11 depicts a typical directory structure.

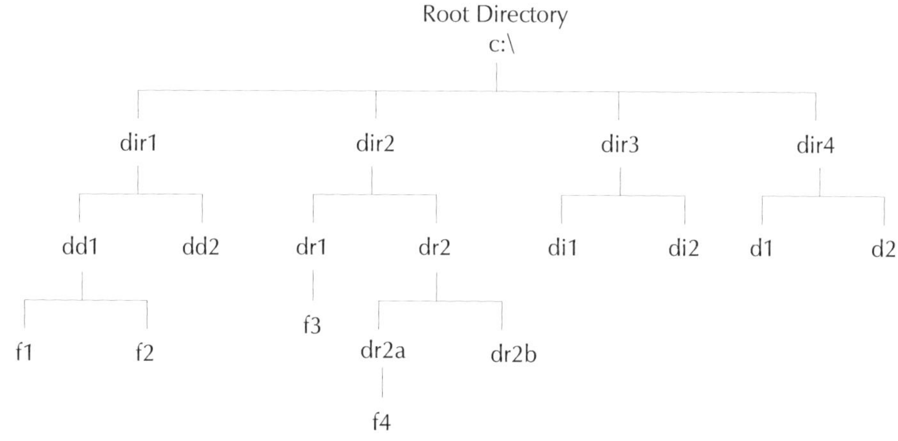

Figure 8.11 : Directory Structure

Path specifies the location (exact or relative) of a particular file or directory. Path generally starts with the root directory name (i.e., the drive letter), all predecessors of the concerned sub-directory or file and finally the filename or the directory name. For example, path of dr2a in figure 8.11 will be C:\dir2\dr2\dr2a

Moving along the Directory Tree

1. **cd..** moves you one level up the directory tree. i.e., it takes you to the parent directory.
2. **cd <dirname>** moves you one level down i.e., takes you to one of the children of the current directory.
3. **cd** moves you directly to the root directory, irrespective of your location on the directory tree.

Using Relative and Absolute Pathnames

Absolute pathname is the complete path of a file/directory starting from the root. For example, the absolute path of dr2a in figure 8.11 is:

C:\dir2\dr2\dr2a

Relative pathname is the path of a specified file or directory, relative to another file or directory. For example, the (relative) path of dr2b relative to dr2a will be

..\dr2b

Here .. takes you to the parent directory, i.e., dr2 and dr2b brings you to dr2b.

Drives are logical partitions of the hard disk or may be extension to the hard disk. A convention is followed while giving names to these partitions. For example, A:, B: represents Floppy disk. C:, D:, E: represents Hard Disk, and F:, G: represents the Compact Disk.

To switch from one drive to another, only the drive letter followed by a colon needs to be specified. For example, at C:\> type A: and press <Enter>. This will take you to A:

While doing any directory or file manipulation you must take note of your location. Location of a file or directory always starts with the drive letter (which is the root) followed by the name of its parent in one order and finally its own name.

For example, C:\Program Files\Microsoft Office\Office\MS Word

Implies that the root is C:\, one of the folders in C:\ is Program Files, Program Files contains Microsoft Office folder, which in turn contains office folder, which in turn contains MS Word.

DOS Commands

DOS Commands are predefined instructions which when issued at MS-DOS command prompt direct the operating system to perform a particular task using hardware resources. Below are some of the DOS commands.

DIR

DIR is used to display the contents of a drive or directory.

Syntax : DIR [drive:] [path] [filename] [/P] [/W]

Parameters

[drive:] [Path]	:	Specifies the drive and directory for which you want to see the listing.
[filename]	:	Specifies a particular file or group of files for which you want to see the listing.

Switches

/P	:	Displays one screen of listing at a time. To see the next screen, press any key.
/W	:	Displays the listing in wide format, with as many as five filenames or directory names on each line.

Examples:

DIR/P	:	Gives page wise listing of directories.
DIR/A	:	Displays only attributes.
DIR/D	:	Displays only directories.
DIR/H	:	Displays only the hidden files.
DIR/O-D	:	Displays the directory sorted according to date and time, latest first (descending order).
DIR A:	:	Displays the directories of A drive.
DIR *.COM	:	Displays all those files that have COM as extension name.
DIR D???.*	:	Displays all files starting with D and having less than or equal to four characters in the file name and any extension.

NOTE Here ? and * characters are called **"Wild Card Characters"**. * stands for any number of characters and ? stands for any one character. Wildcard characters are used to match the occurrence of one or more than one character.

MD (Make Directory)

The MD command is used to create a new directory.

Syntax: MD [drive :] [Path] dirname

Parameters:

drive	:	Specifies the drive on which you want to create the new directory.
Path	:	Specifies the name and location of the new directory.
dirname	:	Name of directory to be created.

Examples:

C:\> MD INDIA

C:\> MD INDIA\UP

C:\> MD A:\MICROSOFT

RD (Remove Directory)

The RD command is used to remove or delete a directory. Before deleting a directory, all the files and sub-directories must be removed. The DELTREE command can be used to recursively remove the contents of a directory and the directory itself.

Syntax: RD [drive:] Path

Examples:

C:\> RD INDIA\UP	Removes the subdirectory UP from the parent directory INDIA.
C:\> RD A:\MICROSOFT	Removes MICROSOFT directory from floppy disk.

CD (Change Directory)

The CD command is used to change the current directory or to make any subdirectory as current directory.

Syntax: CD [Drive:] Path

Examples:

C:\> CD INDIA	Changes the current working directory to INDIA which is present in root.
C:\> CD INDIA \UP	Changes the current working directory to UP which is in turn present in INDIA.

C:\> CD A:\MICROSOFT	Changes the current working directory to MICROSOFT which is present in the floppy disk.
C:\INDIA\UP>CD..	Moves you to the parent directory i.e., INDIA.
C:\INDIA\UP>CD\	Moves you to the root directory i.e., C:.
C:\> CD	Displays the name of current directory.

PATH

The PATH command is used to define the route of all the directories in which executable files are stored. Once the path is defined, the file can be directly executed from any other directory.

Syntax: PATH [drive :] [path] [; [drive :] [path]......]

Parameters:

None	:	Displays the current search path.
drive	:	The disk drive that DOS is to include in the command file search path.
Path	:	A DOS subdirectory to be included in the command file search path.

Examples:

C:\>PATH=\abc1\abc5 abc5 contains the executable files.

C:\>PATH=C:\abc1\abc5; C:\abc1\abc6; C:\abc\abc2

Path containing different executable files can be set using the same command delimiting each path with a semicolon.

Type **PATH**; to clear all search-path settings and direct Windows to search only in the current directory.

Type **PATH** without parameters to display the current path.

COPY CON

The COPY CON command is used to create a new file. F6 or Ctrl-Z can be used as end-of-file markers. When the COPY CON command is given, the system waits for you to enter the contents into the file. After the contents are typed into the file, F6 or Ctrl+Z can be pressed to exit from the edit mode.

Syntax: COPY CON [Drive :] [PATH] Filename

Example:

C:\>COPY CON FILE1

This is file number one.

^Z

TYPE

The TYPE command is used to display the contents of a file.

Syntax: TYPE filename

Parameter:

filename : Name of the file to be typed.

Example: TYPE ABC.TXT

Batch Files

Some times, you may find yourself typing a series of commands over and over again to perform some repetitive task. Suppose, at the end of each day you have to take up the back up of all the data from hard disk (C:) to thumb drive (F:). For doing this following command to be issued.

```
C:\> Copy C:\*.txt  F:
     Copy C:\*.bak  F:
     Copy C:\*.dbf  F:
     Copy C:\*.doc  F:
```

In such a case, you have to type those commands daily at the end of day. In this situation you can create a batch file to simplify your operations. A batch file contains commands for a sequence of operations. Batch files, have one advantage that single command can replace a series of commands. Extension of these files must be .BAT.

Batch File Commands

There are certain DOS commands for batch files. These commands are known as batch file commands. Some special batch file commands available are:

- **Echo** In general, every command is displayed on screen when they are being executed. You can turn off these commands by giving the Echo off. Echo on turns on the display of commands.
- **Pause** When pause command is encountered, the execution of the batch file stops and the following message is displayed on screen:

  Press any key to continue ....

  At this point, you complete your tasks and then key can be pressed to execute subsequent commands of the batch file.

- **REM** This command allows you to include comments in batch files. REM stands for Remark.

  Example of Batch file :

```
REM this batch file is for creating backup
ECHO OFF
DATE
TIME
COPY C:\ABC.TXT C:\BACKUP
TYPE ABC.TXT>PRN
```

Installing Applications

Installation (or setup) of a **program** (including **drivers**, **plugins**, etc.) is the act of putting the program onto a computer system so that it can be **executed**.

Some software can be executed by simply copying it to a computer and executing it with no further ado; no installation procedure as such is required. Other programs are supplied in a form not suitable for immediate execution, and require an installation procedure. Installation may include unpacking of files supplied in a compressed form, copying them to suitable locations, tailoring the software to suit the hardware and the user's preferences, providing information about the program to the **operating system**, and so on. The installer may test for system suitability and available **mass storage** space.

Because the requisite process varies for each program and each computer, many programs (including **operating systems**) come with a general-purpose or dedicated **installer**- a specialized program which automates most of the work required for their installation.

Some software is designed to be installed simply by copying their files to the desired location, and there is no formal installation process. This was once usual for many programs running under **MS-DOS**, **Mac OS**, **Atari TOS**, **AmigaOS** since early versions of these operating systems and actually it is very common and "de facto" standards in **Mac OS X applications** and is also used for many **Windows applications**.

Installation usually implies that once installed, the program can be executed again and again, without the need to reinstall before each execution, until the program is uninstalled or the program prevents further execution, for example by coming to the end of its demonstration period.

An installation program or **installer** is a computer program that installs files, such as applications, drivers, or other software, onto a computer. Some installers are specifically made to install the files they contain; other installers are general-purpose and work by reading the contents of the **software package** to be installed.

Uninstalling Applications

Uninstall, when referring to software, is the act of removing program files and folders from your hard disk and removing related data from your registry so that software is no longer available. When referring to a device, it is the act of removing the corresponding device drivers from your hard disk and physically removing the device from your computer.

An uninstaller, also called a deinstaller, is a application software which is designed to remove all or parts of a specific other application software. It works opposite as an installer.

Summary

- Notepad is a miniature text-only word processing program.
- Notepad cannot centre text, nor does it support multiple fonts in a document.
- WordPad is another handy applet for working with text.
- The Windows Clipboard is a temporary holding place for data. It can hold only one thing at a time i.e., the most recently cut or copied data.
- The Paint program helps in making drawings.
- The Character Map lets you access all kinds of symbols, including Greek letters and special signs.
- Hyperterminal is used to connect to other computers, bulletin board systems and on-line services via modem.
- Disk Cleanup can find files on your hard disk that can be deleted to free up hard disk space.
- Disk Defragmenter is a tool that lets you arrange these fragments of a file, so as to improve the access speed.
- Task Scheduler schedules tasks to be executed by the computer.
- Windows Explorer is a powerful tool which provides the utilities you need to work with files and folders.
- My Computer is the easiest tool for browsing the contents of the PC.
- My Network Places icon lets you view and navigate the resources.
- Files and folders can be created, copied, moved, renamed, deleted, shared, etc.
- Recycle bin is similar to a dustbin and can be used to dispose off files and folders.

Review Exercise

Multiple choice questions

1. In which of the following views can you display the calculator?
   a) General
   b) Fixed
   c) Scientific
   d) Statistical
2. System restore utility helps to restore files and folders from:
   a) unreliable and unstable system
   b) Disk drives
   c) My network places
   d) CD-ROM
3. To access system information utility which of the following paths should be followed?
   a) Start>>Programs>>Accessories>>System Tools>>System Information
   b) Start>>Programs>>Accessories>>Tools>>System Information
   c) Start>>Programs>>Accessories>>Information
   d) None of the above
4. The maximum angle by which an image can be skewed is
   a) 45^0
   b) 89^0
   c) 90^0
   d) 87^0
5. Which of the following features is not supported by Notepad?
   a) Word-wrapping
   b) Test-center
   c) Both (a) and (b)
   d) None of the above

State whether true or false

1. Using Maintenance Wizard, we can schedule only Scandisk and Disk Cleanup.
2. Notepad ignores the margin settings when word wrap is activated.
3. In Paint, the color box contains a palette of 28 colors.
4. To move the insertion point to the end of current line, Alt+End keys are pressed.
5. Folders cannot be shared.

Fill in the blanks

1. __________enables you to see what is currently inside windows clipboard.
2. __________ utility deletes files which are no more required and makes the disk space available for useful programs.
3. ___________collects all the pieces of a file and places them together on the disk.
4. ___________ does not support multiple fonts in a document.
5. If toolbox is not displayed in the Paint application click on _________ menu and choose Toolbox.

Descriptive questions

1. What are desktop icons? Describe some of the Desktop icons.
2. What is Disk Defragmenter and what is its use?
3. What is the difference between viewing the data through Windows Explorer and My Computer?
4. What is a folder? How can you create a new folder?
5. What are the advantages of on-screen keyboard over physical keyboard?

CHAPTER 9

THE LINUX OS

FEATURING

- An Overview of Linux
- Features of Linux
- Structure of Linux Operating System
- Installation of Linux
- Linux File System
- Starting Linux Session (Logging in)

Linux is the kernel or core operating system. Linux has become widely popular around the world in the last few years since its initial release in 1991 by author, Linus Torvalds, then a graduate student at the University of Helsinki, Finland. Linux follows the open source development model. Source code will be available with the software, so that you can customize the software as per your requirement. Torvalds has made the source code of the Linux Kernel available for study and change over the Internet. ***Torvalds*** *also accepts modifications to the kernel code.*

Linux has an ***official mascot*** *— the Linux penguin, called Tux, which was selected by Torvalds to represent the image he associates with the operating system he created. This chapter gives an insight into this popular operating system.*

An Overview of Linux

Linus Torvalds, a student at the University of Helsinki, Finland, introduced Linux in 1991. Torvalds worked on the Linux project and wrote the source code for the Linux Kernel (that is the core program of the Linux OS). He has made Linux available on the Internet. Many programmers added to the code, changed it, and built in support for all kinds of hardware. In fact now, there are several versions of Linux **available for different hardware platforms**. Linux version 0.02 was introduced in 1991. Torvalds and hundreds of developers from across the world worked on it, and in March 1994, version 1.0 of the Linux Kernel was released. Red Hat Linux 6.0 uses version 2.25 of the Linux Kernel.

Linux is a Unix operating system clone which runs on a variety of platforms, especially personal computers with Intel 80386 or better processors. Linux follows the open source development model. This means that the source code of Linux is always open to everybody. This has been a major factor for the success of Linux.

Linux is written and distributed under the GNU, GPL (General Public Licensing) which means that it is a software which can be copied and distributed to any number of users, it is not required to purchase this software as you can easily download and use it free of cost.

The first Linux Kernel is the core of operating system and Linux strictly is an operating system kernel. It was first released to the public in the year 1991. It had no networking support. It ran only on 80386 compatible Intel processors and PC hardware. It had very little device driver support. Later Linux version 1.0 was released as a production software in March 1994. Linux was integrated with other GNU softwares to produce a fully functional operating system.

Advantages of Linux

- **Reliability** Linux is a stable operating system. Linux servers are not required to shut down for years together. This means that users on the Linux operating system work consistently with the Linux server, without reporting any operating system failures.
- **Backward Compatibility** Linux is said to be backward compatible. This means that Linux has excellent support for older hardware as well as old features of Linux are supported by newer versions.
- **Simple Upgrade and Installation Process** The installation procedure of most Linux versions is menu-driven and easy. It includes the ability to upgrade from prior versions.
- **Low Total Cost of Ownership** Linux and most of the packages that come with it are free, therefore, the total cost of ownership in procuring a Linux server software is low. The system configuration requirements to install a Linux machine is less, hence the hardware cost goes down. Linux is itself an OpenSource software that comes with General Public Licensing (GPL).

- **GUI Interface** Linux has GUI environment and the graphical interface for Linux is the **Xwindow system**. Linux has a number of graphical-user interfaces called Desktop Environments, such as K Desktop Environment (KDE) and GNU Object Model Environment (GNOME), both of which are versions of the X window system. GNOME and KDE are discussed in detail, later in the chapter.
- **Text and Word Processing Applications** In addition to commercial word processing softwares such as WordPerfect, StarOffice and Applixware, Linux offers powerful tools for editing text files and processing text in an automated fashion. Some of the popular GUI applications are GIMP, gEdit and GNOME Calculator.
  - **GIMP** — General Image Manipulation Program (GIMP) is an attempt to offer the Linux users, a full featured image-editing package like Adobe Photoshop or CorelDraw. GIMP is included on the CD-ROM as a part of the Standard Red Hat Linux 6.0 distribution. GIMP can be invoked from Graphics submenu of the main GNOME system menu. GIMP can also be run from an xterm window with the command:

    $ /usr/bin/gimp&
  - **gEDIT** — gEdit is a GNOME application that provides functionality similar to the Windows Notepad text editor. gEdit can be used to open and change the contents of a plain text file, search and replace text, and create new files. It can be invoked using the Applications submenu of the main GNOME system menu. It can also be run against the $ prompt as - $ gedit &.
  - **GNOME Calculator** — It can be run by selecting simple calculator from the Utilities submenu of the main GNOME SYSTEM menu. It can also be run by the command - $/usr/bin/gcalc&.
- **Security Features** Linux offers high security. This is the reason why many Internet Service Providers (ISPs) are replacing their current OSs with Linux systems.
- **Development Libraries** Linux offers an excellent platform for many development languages like C++ and Perl.

Limitations of Linux

- Linux does not have a considerable commercial support and service which is the biggest obstacle of implementing it.
- A limited support for databases containing more than a terabyte of data is offered by Linux.
- A relatively few commercial Linux-based applications are available because of the existence of so many Linux distribution versions. There is a lack of standard among various Linux distribution versions such as what are the file formats to be

used, how and where to keep the system files, how and where to add new programs to menus, etc. This is the reason why commercial software developed for Linux must be tested on every version of Linux it runs and on every version of the libraries and services it requires.

Distributors of Linux

There are many distributors who provide Linux. All the distributors use the Linux kernel, which is controlled by Linus Torvalds. These distributors add their own utilities and applications and sell these as a customized package.

Some of the distributors and their site addresses are given below:

Red Hat	http://www.redhat.com is the most popular commercial distribution of Linux.
Caldera	http://www.calderasystems.com
Linux Mandrake	http://www.linux-mandrake.com
Debian	http://www.debian.org
Suse	http://www.suse.com
Slackware	http://www.slackware.com

Features of Linux

Linux is undoubtedly a highly successful operating system. It owes its success partly to its technical properties and partly, as a consequence to its early history when it was distributed widely among universities and companies. The Linux operating system offers many salient features, the important ones are:

Multi-user Operations

Linux is a multi-user operating system designed to support a group of users simultaneously. The system allows for the sharing of processors and peripheral resources, while at the same time providing excellent security features.

Multi-Tasking

A program in Linux is broken down into tasks, where each task can be something like reading from or writing to the disk, or waiting for input from the user, and so on. When a program is waiting for completion of a task, the CPU, rather than wasting time, starts executing the next task. Therefore, while a program is waiting for input from the user, another program could be reading from the hard disk.

Time-Sharing

Multiprogramming is made possible on the Linux system by the concept of time-sharing. Since there is only a single CPU to take care of various programs to be executed, the active programs are queued and the CPU time is shared among them. Each program gets CPU time for a specific period and is then put back in the queue to wait for its turn again as it attends other programs in the queue.

Virtual Memory

The amount of physical memory may not always be sufficient to execute large applications or have multiple applications active at a point in time. In such situations, a partition (that is a logical portion of the hard disk) can be utilized as the artificial or virtual memory. The system places the programs and data that are not frequently required or currently active, in this portion of the hard disk and loads them in the memory, whenever required. Thus, it uses the resources of the computer to the fullest.

Shared Libraries

There are sets of functions or sub-routines maintained as a set of files. All the applications that use these functions access them from the shared library files instead of individually maintaining code for them, thus saving hard disk space and memory.

Network Information Service (NIS)

NIS is an authentication service run by NIS server for providing a Centralized Authentication System for all the host available on network. It is possible to share passwords and group files across a network in Linux using the Network Information Service (NIS). NIS is a client and server database system.

DOS Emulator

Linux has a program called DOSEMU. It creates DOS emulator that can execute many DOS applications. DOSEMU uses an image file of a hard disk to **emulate** a DOS hard drive so that you need not have a DOS partition. Linux can also use a DOS partition, if you have one on your system.

CRON Schedular

Linux has a scheduler program called **cron**. It is used to run commands, scripts, or programs at scheduled times. For example, scheduled tasks in windows on the basis of date, time, min, hours, days, weeks, months, etc. Linux accepts all command in lower case and is strictly case sensitive.

Office Suites

Linux supports many office suites like **Applixware, Open Office** and **StarOffice**. They can be used for reading and writing Microsoft Word and Excel files. Applix Spreadsheet and Applix Presentation Graphic are similar to Microsoft Excel and Microsoft PowerPoint.

Data Archiving Utilities

Linux provides utilities for basic data backup (archiving), such as **tar**, **cpio**, and **dd**. **Read flat Linux version 5.0** onwards also provides a Backup and Restore system Unit (BRU), which can be purchased. BRU offers automated back-up and scheduling.

Licensing

Linux is copyrighted under the General Public License, GNU. The licensing for Read flat Linux states that a person can make any number of copies of the software and distribute it freely or charge a price for it. One can freely download Linux from the Internet for use.

Web Server

Server software provides you the facility of executing server side scripts & generating web pages to be accessed by web clients. Linux comes with the **Apache Web Server**, which is the most popular web server in use today.

GUI Environments for Linux (GNOME, KDE)

The graphical user interface for Linux is the **X Window system**. Xwindows is highly flexible and configurable GUI environment that runs on Linux as well as on most Linux Systems. It is divided into two sub-systems consisting of a server and a client. As it has been mentioned earlier, Linux has a number of graphical-user interfaces called Desktop Environments, such as K Desktop Environment (KDE) and GNU Object Model Environment (GNOME), both of which are versions of the X Window system. They run on the X server.

Structure of Linux Operating System

The Linux system's parts may be functionally categorised as having three levels : The Kernel, The Shell and the Tools and applications.

- The Kernel schedules tasks and manages data storage.
- The Shell is a program that connects and interprets the commands typed by a user. It interprets user requests, calls programs from the memory and executes. Them one at a time or in a series called a "pipe".
- The supplies tools and applications add special capabilities to the operating system.

The parts of the linux system are illustrated in the following figure:

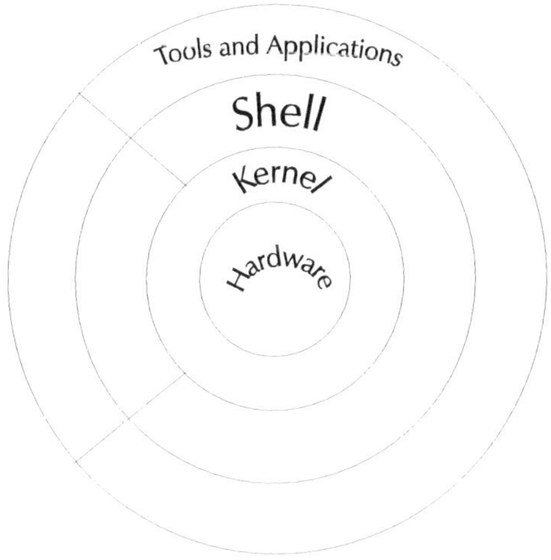

Figure 9.1 : System Architecture

Kernel

The kernel is the heart of the operating system. It performs the following jobs:

- It performs all the low-level jobs necessary to control all the tasks and hardware devices.
- Schedules all the processes.
- Carries out all the crucial functions of the operating systems.
- Kernel contains routines to carry many tasks that the operating system has to handle.

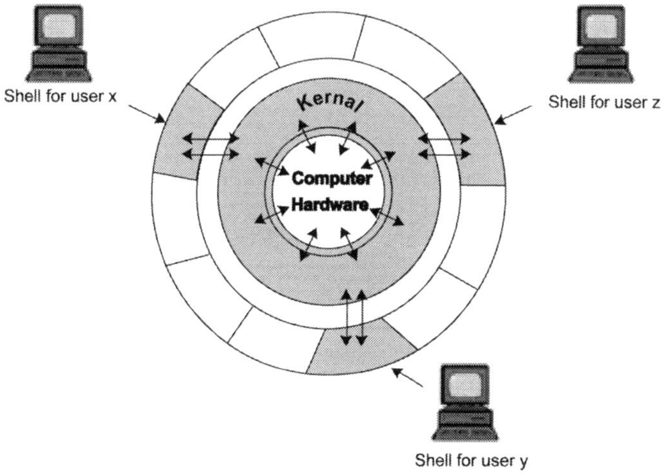

Figure 9.2 : The Kernel and the Shell

Shell

Shell is an interface between the user and the kernel. It is termed as the command line interpreter. The shell thus, is a blanket around the kernel and eliminates the need for the programmer to communicate directly with the kernel. The mechanics of command interpretation by the shell can be explained as follows:-

- On logging in, shell displays a $ sign indicating that it is ready to receive commands from the user.
- The user now issues a command, for example: ls <directory name>
- The shell reads the commands, searches for and locates the file with that name in the directory which contain the command, loads, it into memory, and execute it.
- After the execution is completed, the shell once again displays the $ prompt, conveying that it is ready for the next command.

Linux consists of the following popular types of shells:

- **Bourne Shell** This is the original command processor and named after its developer, Stephen R. Bourne. This is the standard shell that is distributed with LINUX system. The Bourne shell is the fastest LINUX command processor available and can be used on all Linux systems, it is also one of the most widely used shell, at present. The executable filename is sh. The prompt issued by this shell, on the terminal is usually a Dollar sign ($).
- **C Shell** This is another command processor developed by William Joy and others at the University of California at Berkeley, and gets its name from its programming language, which resembles the C programming language in syntax. The executable filename is **csh** and the prompt used by this shell is the percent sign (%).
- **Korn Shell** This combines the best features of both the above shells. The executable file name is **ksh**.

Bourne Again shell is the default shell installed with Linux distributions. Each shell allows you to write your own shell scripts which are small set of programs similar to batch files but more powerful than that.

Linux Utilities and Application Programs

The Linux utilities or commands are a collection of programs that service day-to-day processing requirements. These programs are invoked through the shell, which is itself another utility. Apart from the utilities provided as part of the Linux operating system, more than a thousand Linux-based application programs like database management systems, word processors, and various other programs are available from independent software vendors.

Installation of Linux

In the past, the long and involved installation process was a barrier that kept many people from installing and experimenting with Linux. Installation of Linux has been somewhat automated, which takes a lot of the difficulty out of the task. This section will show you how to perform the easiest Linux installation — running Linux as the sole operating system on your computer.

Installation Options

Linux is a very flexible operating system that can be easily modelled to meet your specific needs. You have three choices for the type of installation you can perform:

1. **Workstation** This option is for those who are new to Linux and want an easy and automated installation. You will also want to use this option if you are planning to use your Linux computer as a stand-alone workspace or as a workstation connected to a network.
2. **Server** You should use this option if you intend to use your computer as a server. Here too, like the workstation class, the settings such as partitions, their size and data to be stored in these partitions is standardized. Do not use this method if you have window or some other OS installed on the same hard disk (on another partition), as all partitions existing on your hard disk are removed and replaced with a new one to suit Linux. All previous data is irreversibly lost.
3. **Custom** If your requirements for the operation of your Linux computer do not really fit either of these two options, you may elect to install Linux by using the custom option. Do not go for custom installation unless you have installed Linux before and completely understood its installation process.

If Workstation or Server installation was selected, the rest of the installation will proceed easily. If custom installation was chosen the disk partitioning procedure will follow. The window that comes up gives you an option to either use fdisk or Disk Druid. If you have never used fdisk then it is better to go in for Disk Druid, which is more comfortable and interactive.

Preliminary Steps Before Installation

Before you begin, take time to plan and organize your Linux installation. To help Linux configure itself properly, you need to collect some basic information about the hardware installed on your computer. The main reason for this is that unlike Microsoft Windows, Linux is not widely supported by the manufacturers of hardware. The following steps must be taken before installation:

Hardware Checklist for Linux Installation

- **Keyboard** Though fairly standardized, check for any language specific features. In India, most of us would be using the US keyboard.
- **Mouse** The brand, number of buttons and port type Serial, PS/2, is essential.
- **Monitor** Look up the manual for details like brand, size and horizontal and vertical refresh rate parameters.
- **CD-ROM Drive** Check the interface type (IDE, SCSI), make and model number.
- **SCSI Adapter** You need to find the make/model.
- **Floppy Drive** No specific make, but essential for making the boot-disk during installation.
- **Hard Drive** Specifically, the number, size, and type — IDE or SCSI.
- **Sound Card** Though not required for installation, knowing the I/O address, IRQ and DMA values will be useful later.
- **Video Card** Card's Chipset and onboard RAM is to be noted.
- **Network Card** The card's make and model number. It you are connected to a network, make sure you know the Network Interface Card and your IP address, netmask, gateway IP address of your machine.

You will need at least 150 MB of free space for a really useful Linux installation. You will need upwards of 450 MB if you intend to load most of the software — such as the compiler and programming tools, kernel source, and have a comfortable margin for additional programs later. Also, note that for a "complete" installation of everything, you will need at least 4.5 GB just for the OS and applications.

Record Your Hardware Configuration

After you have all the Hardware information, you need to check your computer hardware with the Red Hat Linux Hardware Compatibility List. You must record the configuration of your hardware for later use at the time of configuring your Linux system.

Partitions Required by Linux During Installation

Ideally, you would install Linux on its own hard disk. Some of us will have to create a partition on the hard disk we are using for DOS/Windows. Since the operating systems are contained on separate partitions, they can co-exist in the same computer. In fact, Linux can access all the files on a DOS/Windows partition, and through an emulation program WINE, run Windows programs.

You will need a swap partition to act as virtual RAM. If you have more than 32 MB RAM you may not need a large swap partition. When data is placed on a drive, it is written into the structure, called a file system in the Linux community. A file system is the format in which data is stored.

There are six major types of file systems used on Intel-compatible PCs today, as given below:

File System	Used By
FAT	Windows 95, Windows 98, Windows NT
FAT32	Windows 98, Windows NT, Windows 2000, Windows XP
NTFS	Windows NT, Windows 2000, Windows XP
ext2	Linux
os2	OS/2
Swap	All operating systems

Table 9.1: File System Types (Intel PCs)

Thus, in order to install Linux on your PC, you will need to create an ext2 partition on your hard drive.

Rather then using drive letters to denote partitions, Linux uses a different naming convention:

/dev/[Drive Type] [Device where Partition Resides] [Partition Number]

The following table explains the variable used in this naming convention:

Variable	Definition
/dev/	All devices in Linux are managed in the /dev/ directory, including hard drives and their partitions.
Drive Type	This is a two-letter indicator of the hard drive type. Possible values are hd (IDE disk) and sd (SCSI disk).
Device where partition resides	This is the device the partition is on. Possible values are /dev/sda (first SCSI disk) and /dev/hdc (third IDE disk).
Partition Number	This denotes the partition. Possible values are 1-4 (primary or extended partitions) and 5 + (logical partitions). For example, /dev/hda1 here hd represent hard disk, a is used for primary master and 1 is used for first partition on this hard disk.

Table 9.2 : Partition naming convention

Red Hat Linux recommends that you have three partitions for optimal performance. The following table lists the desired partitions, their space, and their mount points:

Partition	Mount Point	Memory Allotment
Boot partition	/boot	No more than 16 MB
Root partition	/	A minimum of 600 MB for minimal install, 1.5 GB to install all packages
Swap partition	None	Equal to your PC's RAM, a minimum of 32 MB

Table 9.3 : Recommended Linux partitions for Intel PC

Steps of Linux Installation

1. Enable your CD-ROM as the first boot device.
2 Boot your system with Linux CD-ROM.
3. Language Selection.
4. Keyboard Configuration.
5. Mouse Settings.
6. Choosing the Installation Class
7. Selecting Partition Options.
8. Setting the Time Zone.
9. Configuring Accounts.
10. Selecting Package Group

Language Selection

The very first screen of the installation path requires you to select the language you will use. From the list of languages, select you preferred language and then click the Next button.

The Language Selection Screen is shown in Figure 9.3.

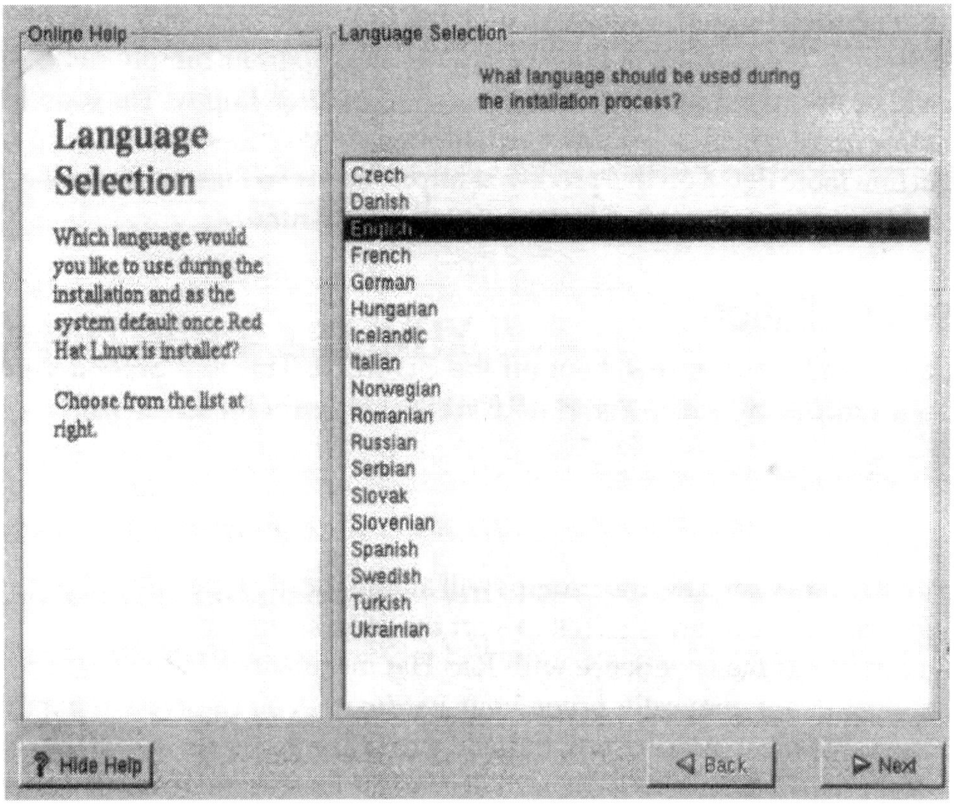

Figure 9.3 : Selecting a Language during installation

Keyboard Configuration

From the dialog box choose the model of the keyboard that best fits your system. If no match is found then choose the Generic match. If you do not see your specific keyboard model, select Generic 101-key PC.

The Keyboard Configuartion Screen is shown in Figure 9.4.

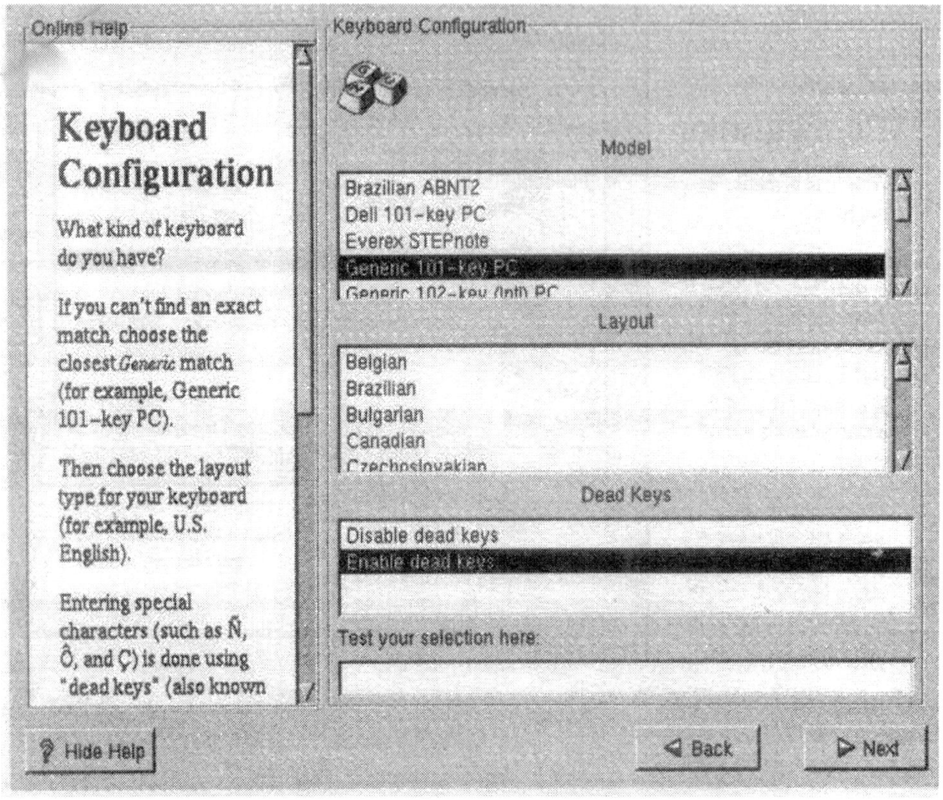

Figure 9.4 : Keyboard Configuration Screen

Mouse Settings

Select the mouse type you have. Select Generic if no match is found.

The Mouse Configuration Screen is shown in Figure 9.5.

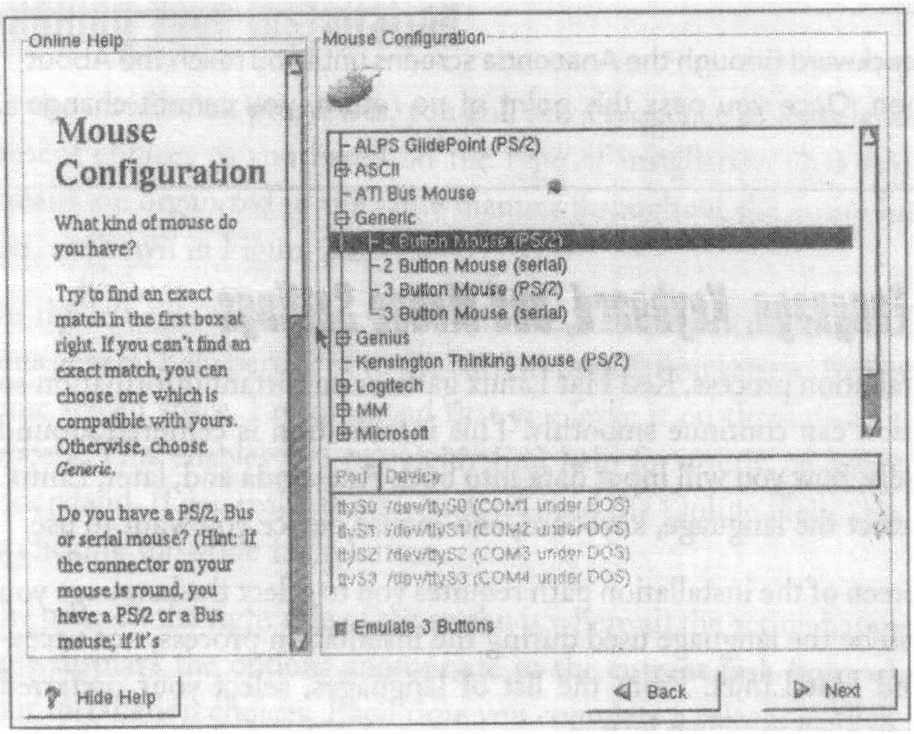

Figure 9.5 : The Mouse Configuration screen

Choosing the Installation Class

There are three primary installation options that can be selected.

- **Workstation** — A standard PC Workstation.
- **Server System** — A server with server packages and can be used as Application server.
- **Custom System** — Customize the installable packages selection.

When you finish selecting all installation options, click Next to continue.

The Install Options Screen is shown in Figure 9.6.

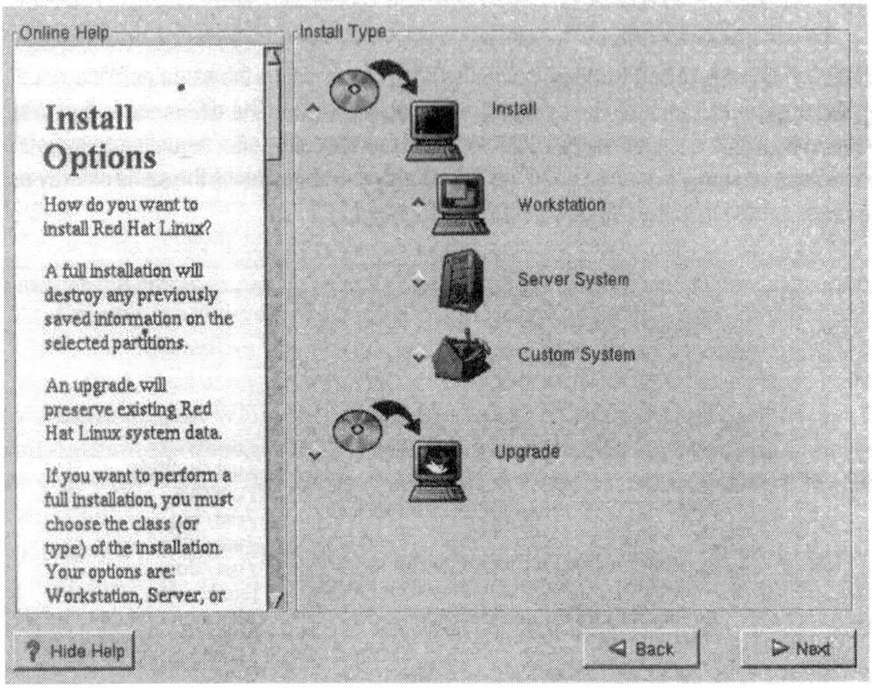

Figure 9.6 : Install Options dialog box

Selecting Partition Options

The Automatic Partitioning screen is the next to appear in the installation process. Here, you decide whether to partition your hard drive yourself or to have Linux do it. If you have not partitioned your hard disk then you can choose from the options:

- **Automatic Partition** — If no other operating system and data exists on Hard disk.
- **Manual Partition** — If you want to manually partition the Linux portion of the hard drive yourself. Manual Partition can be done either with Disk Druid or with fdisk.

You can use one of the two tools: Disk Druid and Linux fdisk. Click the Next button to advance to the next screen.

The Partitions Screen is shown in Figure 9.7.

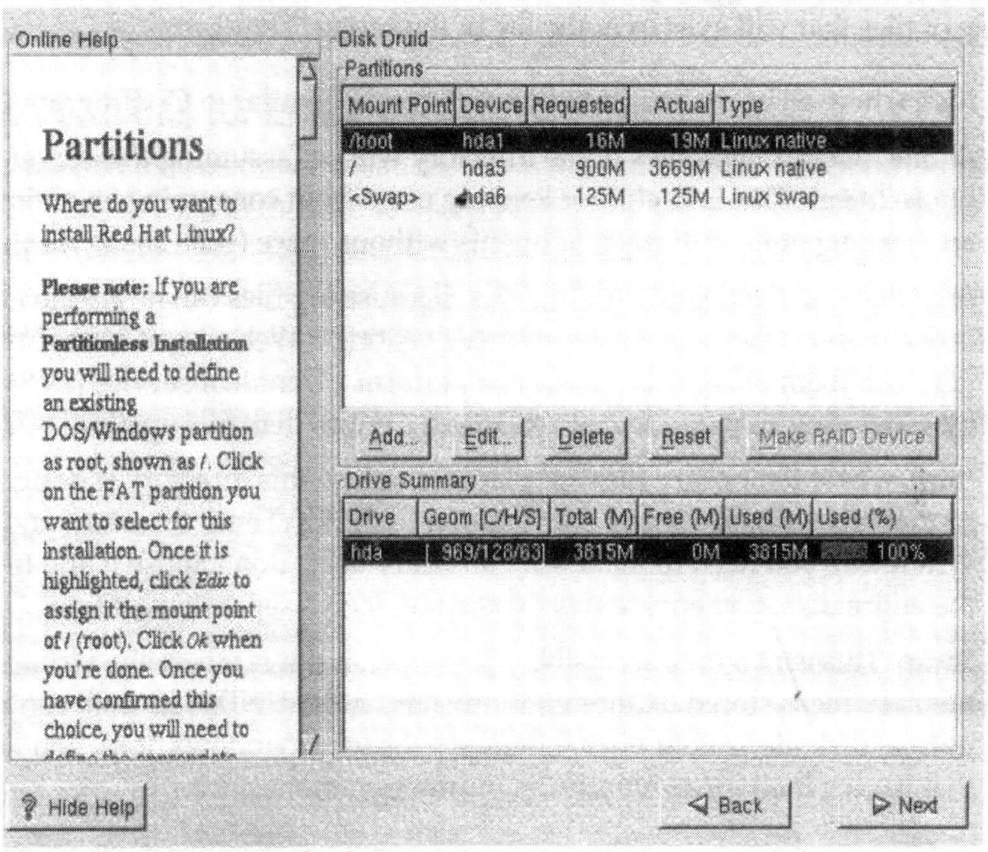

Figure 9.7 : Partitioning dialog box

Setting the Time Zone

To set your time zone, simply click the city/region closest to you on the map. Alternately, you can select your city/region from the list that appears below the map. Your choice then appears in the field immediately below the map. When complete, click the Next button.

The Time Zone Selection Screen is shown in Figure 9.8.

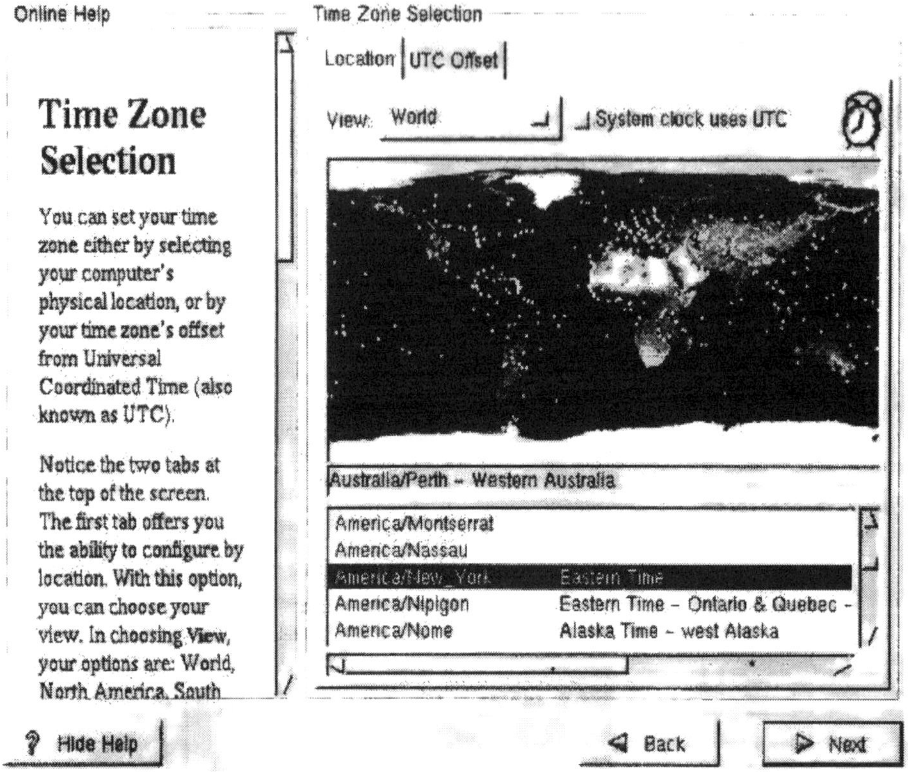

Figure 9.8 : Time Zone Selection dialog box

Configuring Accounts

Whenever a Linux system is created, the root account must be created as well. The root account is the administrator account for the Linux PC. All you need to do to set up the root account is to enter the same password in both the Root Password and Confirm fields. You can create additional user accounts on the system. User accounts are analogous to user profiles found in Windows. After you have added users to the system, click the Next button to continue.

The Account Configuration Screen is shown in Figure 9.9.

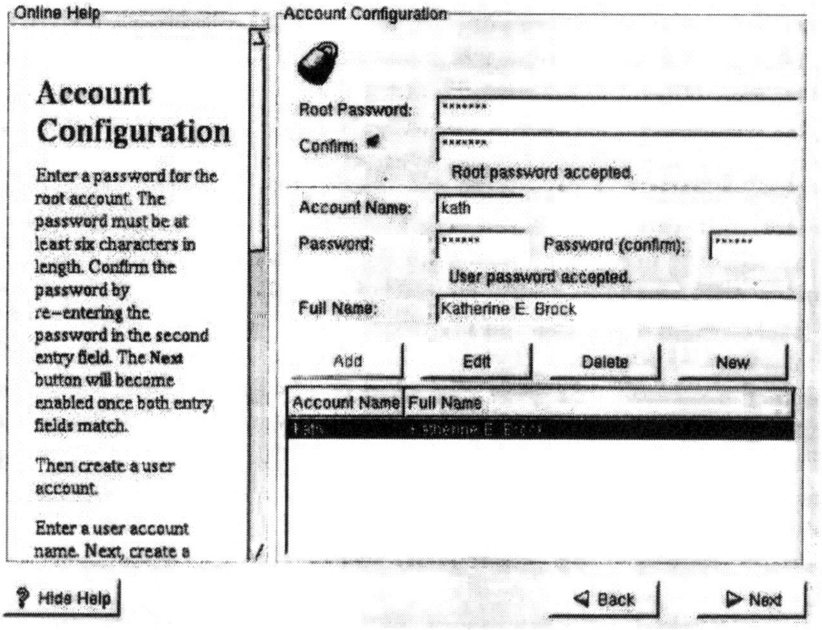

Figure 9.9 : Account Configuration dialog box

Selecting Package Group

Packages in Red Hat Linux are synonymous with application installation programs. The first package selection screen, gives you three choices: GNOME, KDE, and Games. To select a package for installation steps are:

- Step1 : Double-click the package name. A red check mark appears on the package icon, indicating its readiness for installation.
- Step2 : Click Next to continue to the Unresolved Dependencies screen. This screen addresses packages that may need additional files within other packages in order to work.
- Step3 : Click the Install packages to satisfy dependencies option.
- Step4 : Click Next. All the needed files will be added to the installation set automatically.

Immediately after installation finishes, you will arrive at the login prompt. Type the account login name and password you created during the installation process. After successful login, you will get a shell prompt to type in your commands for execution. The shell prompt appears as given below:

username @ localhost current workdir:

The Selecting Package Groups Screen is shown in Figure 9.10.

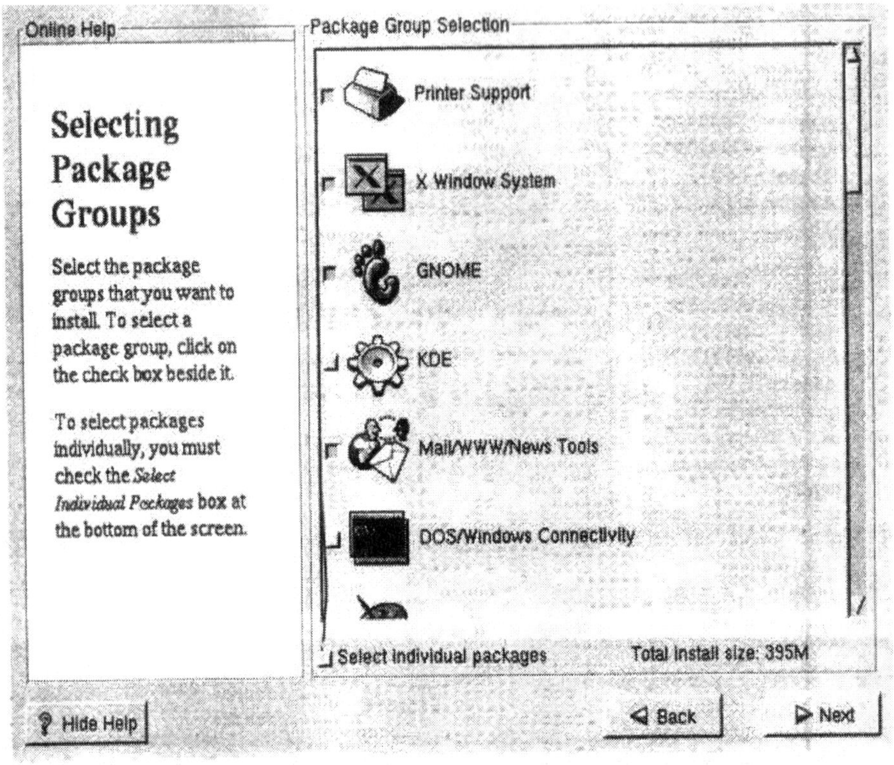

Figure 9.10 : Selecting Package Groups dialog box

Linux File System

In Linux File System there is a top level directory called the "root". The root directly is denoted by a slash(/). From the root, originate several directories namely "bin", "etc", "usr", "dev", "tmp" and an ordinary file named "LINUX" which is the kernel program itself. This is the file which is loaded into the memory during system startup.

The directories are called subdirectories of the root and conversely the root directory is called the "parent" directory of these directories. Each subdirectory in turn can contain other directories and files which give rise to the branching, upside down tree structure. The following diagram shows hierarchical file system:

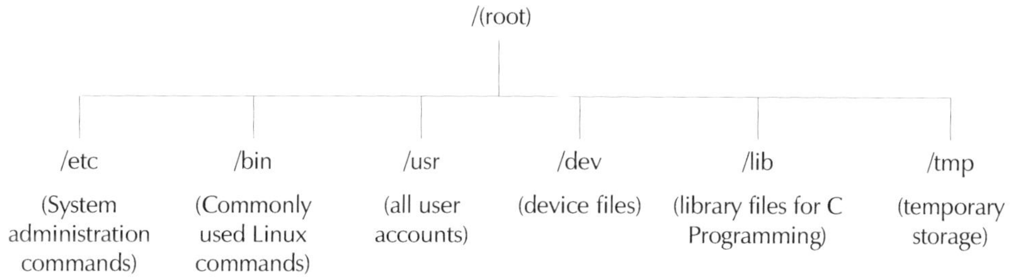

Figure 9.11 : Linux File Structure

A single fixed disk can store thousands of files. To organize data by grouping files on the disk, the operating system provides a file system. Linux follows the Unix file system convention i.e., the hierarchical system.

The following are some of the directories under the /directory. Each of these directories has been organized to store a specific type of file.

- The /**bin** directory stores many utilities of Linux. These utilities are the commands available under the Linux system. These are in the binary format, hence the name "bin".
- The /**dev** directory stores all the device-related files for the system.
- The /**etc** directory stores the system-related data which users and the system need to refer to, such as the passwd file. These are generally the essential miscellaneous system programs and configuration files, and are usually used by the system administration.
- The /**lib** directory contains libraries of data for the compilers installed in the system, for example, the C language routines.
- The /**usr** directory stores the operating systems files, which are not involved in the boot process. Many utilities are available in the bin directory under the usr directory.
- The /**tmp** directory contains temporary files. Whenever the user writes his own tools, he must use /tmp directory for temporary files, built while the tool runs, and not needed afterwards.

Types of Files in Linux

In Linux, all information is treated as a file. There are three categories of files in Linux:

1. **Ordinary Files** All the files created by a user come under this category of files. These include all the data files, program files, object files, and executable files. A user can make changes to such files.

2. **Directory Files** Linux automatically creates a directory file when a directory is created. This file has the same name as the directory, and contains information about the files under the directory. A directory file cannot be modified by a user but is, instead, modified automatically by the system when a new file or a sub-directory is added to the directory.

3. **Special files** These files are typically associated with input/output devices and are found in the standard Linux directories, such as /dev and /etc. Users cannot alter special files. Special files are not really files, but they are pointers to device drivers located in the kernel that handles the data flow.

Linux supports the following types of special files:

- Character device files (read and write data one character at a time)
- Block device files (can access a block of data at a time)
- Hard links (allow a single file to have multiple names)
- Symbolic links (similar to hard links except that they can work across different file systems)

Starting Linux Session (Logging in)

To gain access to a Linux system you must go through a process usually known as "logging in" or sometimes "logging on". When you approach a terminal connected to linux, it should be displaying, among other things.

- **Login** Against the "login" string type the user name is lowercase, followed by pressing the Enter key. If you type in the correct username you get the Linux prompt which is either a $, # or % sign.

- **Password** To protect your files from other users Linux provides the facility of defining password, which when set once remains applicable till it is removed or changed. System asks for the password at the time of login and validates it. If found correct the user is placed in home directory else the user's attempt to log on to the system is rejected.

- **Logging out** When you have finished working with the Linux system, you can "log out" or "log off". At the $ prompt press Ctrl+d key combination to come out from Linux session.

Directory Manipulation Commands

Some of the directory manipulation commands are:

- **Pwd** Pwd stands for Print Working Directory, which displays the full path of the current working directory. At the command prompt ($) issuing the pwd command lists the current location of the user who is logged in.

- **cd** cd stands for Change Directory. It performs the same function as in DOS for example, moves you one level up or one level down within the directory tree.

  - **cd .. (cd space dot dot)** this command moves you one level up the directory tree. For example, if your current location is dir1 and you say cd.. at $ prompt you will be moved up to dirroot. Issuing the pwd command shows you the new location.

  - **cd <dirname> (cd and the name/path of another directory)** This command will take you to the location specified by dir name. For example, cd usr1/bca19/diroot will take you to dirroot from your current location.

  - **cd / (cd forward slash)** This command will take you to the root directory.

  - **cd \ (cd backward slash)** The command will take the user to his home directory.

- **mkdir** stands for Make Directory. This command is used to create a new directory in the current location.

  $ mkdir dirroot

  The above command creates a new directory called **dirroot** in the user's current working directory.

- **ls** stands for list. The ls command is used to display the contents of the current working directory.

The ls command does the same work as the dir command of DOS. It can also be used with various options as given in Table 9.4.

Option	Function
-a	Lists all the files, including hidden files
-F	Shows the file type along with the name ('/' for a directory, '*' for an executable)
-R	Does a recursive listing, that is, displays the contents of the specified directory and all the sub-directories
-r	Displays files and sub-directories in the reverse order
-S	Sorts by file size
-l	List in long format, given mode, number of links, owner, group size in bytes, the time of last modification for each file.

Table 9.4 : Options with ls command

Figure 9.12 shows the result of ls command when used with the -a and -l options — (-l) shows long listing. (-a) shows hidden files as well.

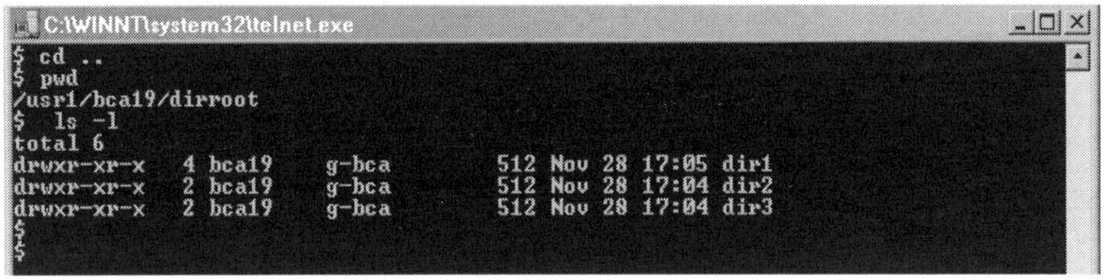

Figure 9.12 : Result of ls-l

File Manipulation Commands

Some of the File Manipulation Commands are described in Table 9.5:

Command	Used To
cat	display the contents of the specified file. create a new file. concatenates 2 or more files.
cp	duplicate the contents of the source file into a target file Syntax : cp [options] <source file/s> <destination directory/file>
rm	delete files or directories Syntax : rm[options] file/s
mv	move a file or directory from one location to another or to change the name of a file or directory Syntax : mv[option] source destination

Table 9.5 : File Manipulation Commands

- **cat** is used to perform the following three functions:
  1) Display contents of an existing file. e.g : $ cat file1
  2) Create a new file. e.g: $ cat > new file
  3) Concatenate (join) two files. e.g : $ cat file 1 file 2 new file
- **cp** is the copy command of UNIX. The cp command is used to create a copy of a file. For example,

  cp pledge pledgecopy

  will create a copy of pledge file and name the copy as pledgecopy.

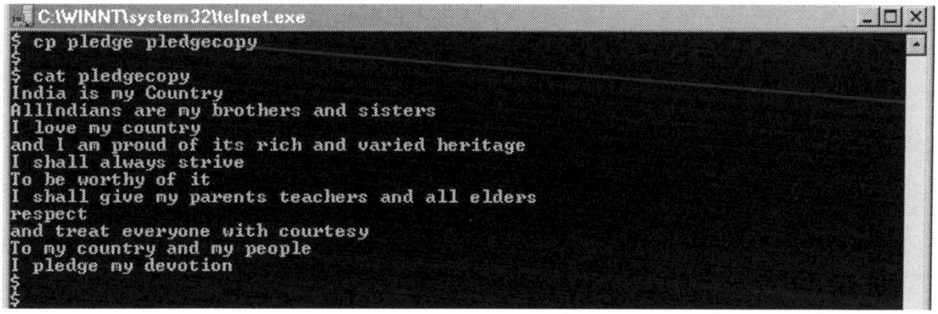

Figure 9.13 : cp command

Options available with the cp command are shown in Table 9.6.

Option	Function
-f	Overwrites the existing destination by force
-i	Interactive, prompts before overwriting at the destination location
-v	Verbose – explains what is being done, in detail

Table 9.6 : Options with cp command

- **rm** stands for remove/delete files or directories.

  $ rm pledgecopy

Options available with the rm command are shown in Table 9.7.

Option	Function
-i	Prompts before removing (Interactive mode)
-f	Removes a file by force. It ignores the non-existence of a file, that is, if the file does not exist, the command will not flag an error
-r or –R	Deletes recursively, that is, deletes a directory along with its sub-directories
-v	Verbose – explains what is being done, in detail

Table 9.7 : Options with rm command

Working with File Permissions

Any user who wishes to access a file belongs to one of the following user classes:

- **Owner** Each directory and file has an associated user, called owner, who created the directory or file.
- **Group** Each user belongs to one or more sets of user known as groups. Each directory and file has an associated group, which is assigned when the directory or file is created.
- **Others** Any user who is neither the owner nor a member of the owner's group.

When working with commands that involve ownership (e.g. : **chmod**) following abbreviations are used:

u — owner (user)

g — group

o — others

Take a look at the following entry, which is the output from an ls-l command applied to a hypothetical file named file1.

-rwxrw-r-- 1 root root 1213 Aug 28 12:30 file1

Permissions are based on the character on the far-left end of the output. The 10 characters determine what different users can do with this file.

If the first character is not a dash (-), it's not a regular file. It could be directory (d) or a file that is linked (1) to another.

The remaining characters can be grouped in threes as shown below with explanation.

- **rwx** The owner of the file named file1 can read (r), write(w) and execute(x) this file.
- **rw-** users in the same group as the file owner can read this file (r) or edit and write to this file (w). These users cannot execute the file.
- **r--** users that don't belong to the same group as the file owner can read this file. They can't write to it, nor can they execute it.

You can setup these permissions on any file using the **chmod** command.

- **chmod** command is used to set the access modes of a directory or file. Access permissions determine what operations a user can perform on a directory or file. There are two modes for setting file permissions.

Using Symbolic mode

Permission	Meaning for directory	Meaning for file
r	Lists the directory	Read contents
w	Create or remove files	Write contents
x	Access files and subdirectories	Execute

Examples:

$chmod u + wx file1	(add write and execute permission to owner of file1)
$chmod g - x file1	(remove execute permission from group members of file1)
$chmod o = rx file1	(set the read and execute permission to other members of file1, erasing all existing permissions).

Using Numeric mode

Table 9.8 depicts the numeric codes for setting the file permissions.

Example :

$chmod 751 file1

This command gives the following access permission of file1:

- First number (7) sets read, write, execute permissions for the owner.
- Second number (5) sets read, execute permissions for the other users in the owners group.
- Third number (1) sets execute permission for every one else.

Value	Meaning
0	- - - -
1	--x
2	-w-
3	-wx
4	r--
5	r-x
6	rw-
7	rwx

Table 9.8 : Numeric codes for file permissions

Other Important Linux Commands

The other important commands in Linux are date, clear, who and man that have been explained in Table 9.9:

Command	Used To	Example
date	display the current date and time and also for changing the system date and time	$ date
clear	clear the terminal screen	$ clear
who	display the names of all users who are currently logged in	$ who
man	displays pages from the Linux reference manual that is installed along with the Linux OS	$ man ls

Table 9.9 : Other Linux Commands

Summary

- The number of Linux installations is growing rapidly and it has become an ever growing competition for windows.
- Linux is the kernel or core operating system. It follows the open development model.
- Linux Torvalds, a student at the University of Helsinki, Finland, introduced Linux in 1991.
- Features of the Linux operating system include: Multiprogramming, Time-Sharing, Multitasking, Virtual Memory, Shared Libraries, POSIX compliance, DOS Emulator, NIS, CRON Scheduler, Office Suites, Data Archiving Utilities, Licensing and Web Server.
- The graphical interface for Linux is the X window system.
- Linux has a number of graphical user interfaces called Desktop environments, such as K Desktop Environment (KDE) and GNU
- All the files are stored on the disk under one main directory called the root directory.
- The root directory is further subdivided into directories-bin, boot, home, usr, etc, and dev.

Review Exercise

Multiple choice questions

1. Which of the following options can be used with the cp command to prompt the user if there is an existing file of the same name in the destination directory?

   a) -p

   b) -i

   c) -r

   d) -f

2. Which of the following options can be used with the mv command to create a backup file of any file that would be overwritten by moving a file?

   a) -b

   b) -i

   c) -f

   d) -r

3. Which option can be used with the mkdir command to create a directory with specified permission?
    a) -p
    b) -r
    c) -o
    d) -m
4. Which of the following characters is a shortcut that refers to your home directory?
    a) ^
    b) ~
    c) -
    d) +
5. Which of the following commands can be used to print the name of the present working directory?
    a) pwd
    b) cd
    c) cd/
    d) /

State whether true or false

1. Format>>Frames is primarily useful for creating Web pages that contain multiple panes.
2. Every document on a Web site has the same file.
3. In the context of Web documents, bookmarks serve as the destination of hyperlinks.
4. Marquee is a scrolling piece of text on a Web page.
5. Web toolbar and Web Tools toolbar are the same.

Fill in the blanks

1. Linux follows the ___________ model.
2. Linux has an official mascot — the Linux penguin, called ___________ .
3. The ability of any OS to handle the execution of multiple tasks is known as ________ .

4. It is possible to share passwords and group files across a network in Linux using the ________ .
5. __________ is a Linux scheduler program.

Descriptive questions

1. Give at least five features of the Linux Operating System.
2. Give an overview of the Linux Architecture.
3. How many types of installation choices you have for Linux?
4. How many types of files are there in Linux?
5. Explain any three directory and file commands.
6. What do you understand by file permissions? Explain.
7. Which command is used to set the file permissions? Explain it using suitable example.

CHAPTER 10

MICROSOFT WORD BASICS

FEATURING

- ❐ **Introduction to Word Processing**
- ❐ **Introduction to Microsoft Word 2003**
- ❐ **The Word 2003 Environment**
- ❐ **Creating a Document**
- ❐ **Word's Document Views**
- ❐ **Opening a Document**
- ❐ **Saving a Document**
- ❐ **Printing Documents**
- ❐ **Exiting Word**
- ❐ **Typing in a Document**
- ❐ **Selecting Text**
- ❐ **Editing Text**
- ❐ **The Clipboard**
- ❐ **Moving and Copying Text**

A word processor is a computer program which we use to type documents such as letters, office memos, magazine articles and even complete books. Any program which allows us to use the computer in similar manner is called a "word processor". Some popular word processors are Word Star, MS-Word, and Word Perfect. All these are basically computer programs. They have been developed by different companies and offer various features useful in preparing a document. This chapter gives you an overview of Microsoft Word and explains how to perform some basic tasks in it.

Introduction to Word Processing

More than 85 percent of the personal computers in existence today are equipped with word processing programs. Word processing programs allow the user to write, edit, format, save, and print a document with ease. Using word processing software, the user can produce a high-quality document in much less time than a typewriter. The reason is that word processing software separates document creation from document printing.

With a word processing program, the user can enter his work without being concerned about how the document will appear. Editing the document is much easier and more efficient with a word processing program. The user's creativity comes handy in formatting the documents. Formatting is the process of adjusting the appearance of the document.

A few special features most word processing programs include are: spell-checker, thesaurus, style and grammar checker, mail-merge, and macros.

Word Star, Word Perfect and MS Word are few popular word processing programs.

Introduction to Microsoft Word 2003

Microsoft Word is a word processor, created by Microsoft Corporation, US. It is one of the most advanced and powerful word processing software packages in the market. It replaces your pen, paper, dictionary, thesaurus, and typewriter, and helps the user to create professional documents in record time.

With the help of Word, users can write letters, memos, faxes, brochures, newsletters, and even books. Word and other applications of Microsoft Office suite are integrated to give greater flexibility and also provide a document-centric approach rather than an application-centric approach.

Microsoft Word strives to provide more interconnectivity between the user and the world by linking Word documents to the Word Wide Web and between the user and other office-mates by allowing many people to edit the same document without confusion.

Microsoft Word 2003 is a word processing program designed for windows XP or later versions. Word can integrate information with other Microsoft Office products such as Excel and PowerPoint.

Starting Word

Use one of the following three methods to activate Word:

- Click the Start menu button and choose Microsoft Word from the Programs menu.

- Click the Start menu button, choose Microsoft Office from the Programs menu and then select MS-Word.
- Choose Start>>Run, enter the path and program name in the Open text box and then click the OK button to start Word.

Word can be started automatically, whenever Windows starts, if Word is placed (WinWord.exe file) into Startup folder in the Start menu.

The Word 2003 Environment

Initially, Word displays a new document that is based on a Normal template (NORMAL.DOT) in full-screen size. Word's Normal template determines the initial settings. The following elements of the Word environment are shown in Figure 10.1:

- **The Title Bar** The title bar at the top of the screen displays the program name (Microsoft Word), document filename (Document1), Word control menu, and three buttons on the upper-right corner of the screen to either minimize, restore, or exit document, respectively.
- **The Menu Bar** Just below the title bar is the menu bar. It contains drop-down menus like File, Edit, View and so on.
- **Toolbars** By default, the *Standard* and *Formatting* toolbars are displayed just below the menu bar. Additional toolbars are available for different features. Choose *View >> Toolbars* to show or hide any of Word's toolbars.
- **The Ruler** The horizontal ruler is displayed across the top of the document window and enables to change paragraph indents, adjust margins, change the width of newspaper style columns, change the width of table columns and set tab stops. To display or hide the ruler, choose the *View >>Ruler* command.
- **The Status Bar** The first section of the status bar shows the current page number, the section number and the total number of pages in the document. The next portion shows the distance (in inches) from the top edge of the page to the insertion point, followed by the insertion point's line and column numbers. The last section displays the current time and modes. To turn it off choose the **Tools>>Options** command. Select the *View* tab and click the Status bar check box.
- **Task Pane** In Word 2003 whenever you open a new document a task pane appears at right side from which you can select the task you want to perform.

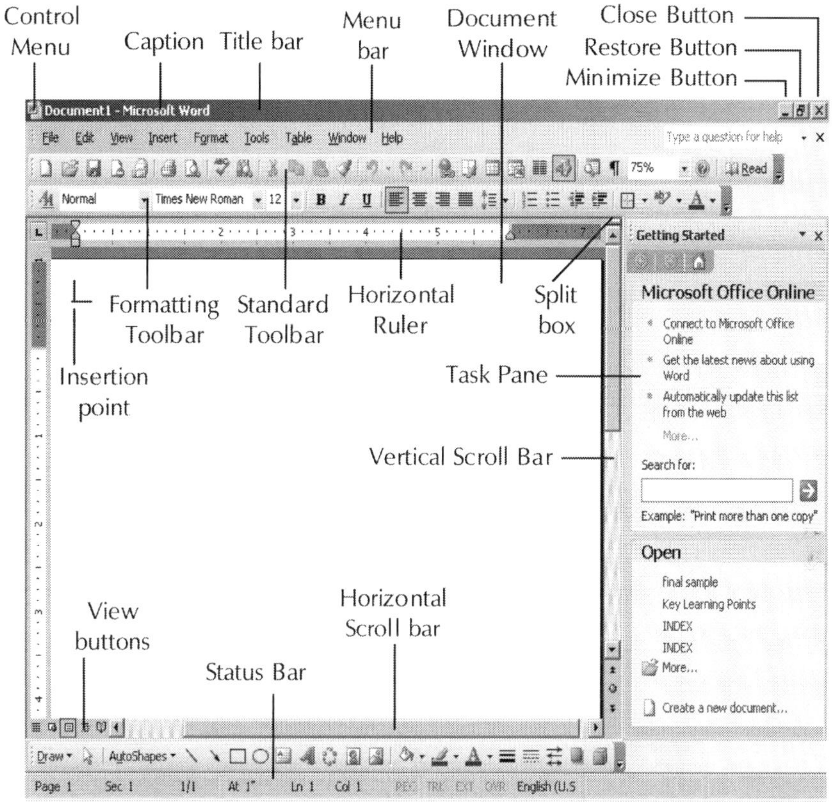

Figure 10.1 : Main elements of a Word Window

- **The Style Area** The vertical pane along the left edge of the document window displays the style name for each paragraph visible in the window. To display or hide the style area, follow these steps:
  - Choose **View>>Normal** (only available in Normal and Outline views).
  - Choose **Tools>>Options**.
  - Choose View tab, specify width in the **Style area width** box. For example, enter 0.5".
  - Click OK button.
  - To hide the style area, drag the style area boundary to the left until the style names disappear.
- **The Document Window** One can create, edit, format, and view the document files in the document window. The blinking vertical bar is called the **insertion point**. It indicates where text is to be entered into a document.
- **The Scroll Bars** The vertical and horizontal scroll bars, which are a part of the document window, are used to scroll the document either from top to bottom

or bottom to top and from left to right or right to left respectively. The horizontal scroll bar also contains buttons that allow to switch quickly between the four most common document views (explained later).

- **The Office Assistant** When Word starts, a little paper clip icon appears on the lower right corner of the screen. This icon is called the Office Assistant. Office Assistant is the best bet to get help with Word. To close it, click on Help>>Hide the Office Assistant.

Creating a Document

When Word opens, a new blank document called *Document 1.doc* appears on the screen, based on the Normal template. Template is a blueprint or pattern for all documents of a certain type, such as a letter, memo, or report. To begin working, just start typing. To create a new document with Normal template:

- Choose the **File >> New** command or click the New button on the Standard toolbar.
- On choosing **File >>New** a task pane appears on right side as in Figure 10.2. Choose blank document hyperlink to create blank document.

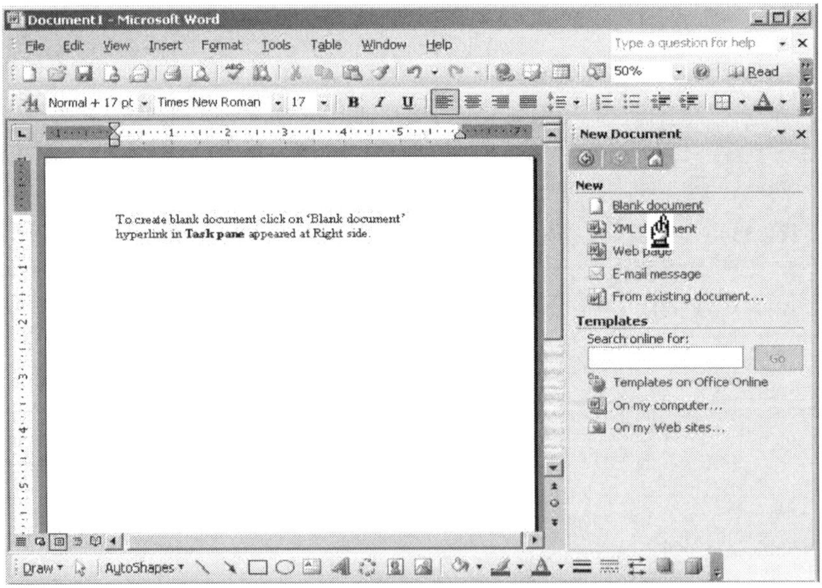

Figure 10.2 : Window with Task Pane

Word's Normal Template (Normal.dot) Default Settings are shown in Table 10.1.

Option	Default Setting
Paper size	Letter ($8\frac{1}{2}$ inches × 11 inches)
Left and right margins	1.25 inches
Top and bottom document margins	1 inch
Line spacing	Single
Justification	Align Left
Tabs	0.5 inch
Font	Times New Roman
Point size	10 points
View	Normal

Table 10.1 : Word's Normal Template default settings

Word's Document Views

Word lets the user view documents from a number of different perspectives to make them easier to visualize and quicker to work with. These display options are called *views*. Word provides the following views *Normal, Outline, Print Layout, Web Layout,* and *Print preview*. To change the view either use *View* menu or *View* buttons on the horizontal scroll bar.

Normal View

Normal view is the default view. It is not a true WYSIWYG view (WYSIWYG stands for What You See Is What You Get) because one cannot see headers and footers, footnotes and annotations but the **formatting** and **layout** elements of the document can be *seen*. Working with this view is relatively *speedy*. You should work in Normal view to type, edit, and format text.

Print Layout View

Print Layout view should be used to see how text, graphics, and other **elements will be positioned on the printed page**. This view is useful for editing headers and footers, for adjusting margins, and for working with columns and drawing objects.

Outline View

Outline view is a specialized view that one can use to organize a document. In Outline view, the users can expand or collapse portions of the document to see only the headings of their choice. Users can quickly and easily move and copy large portions of the document in Outline view.

Web Layout View

Web Layout view should be used while creating a Web page or a document that is viewed on the screen. In Web Layout view, backgrounds can be seen, text is wrapped to fit the window, and graphics are positioned just as they are in a Web browser.

Reading Layout View

The goal of reading layout view is to increase legibility. The text is automatically displayed using microsoft clear type technology. You can easily increase or decrease the size in which

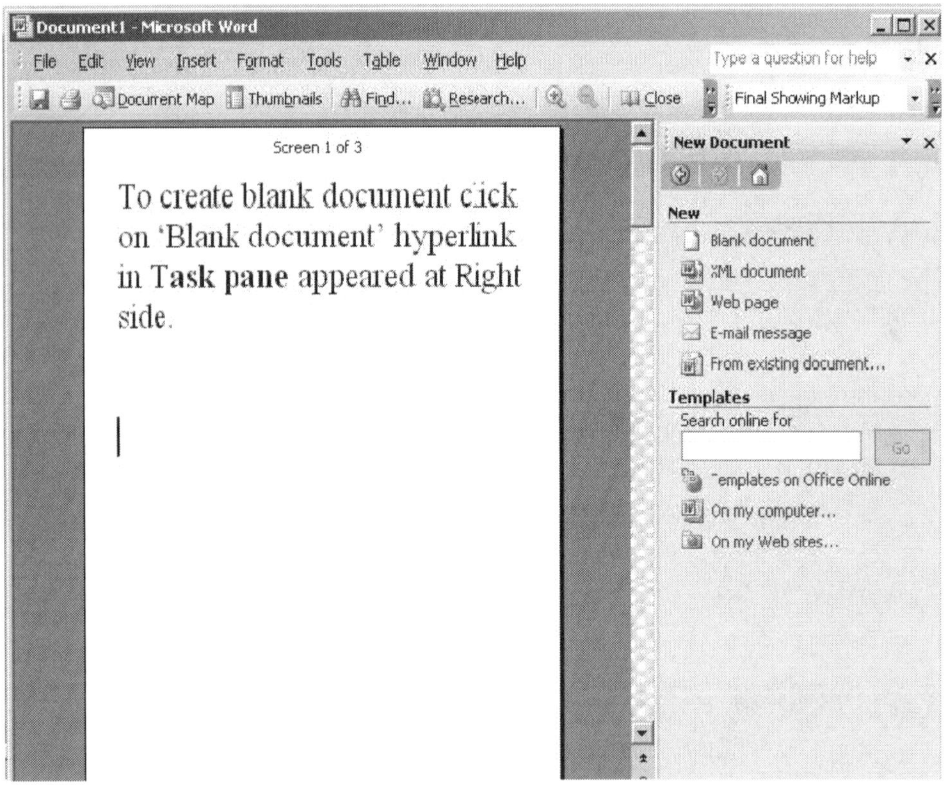

Full Screen View

Use the **Full Screen** view to hide all of Word's menus, toolbars, and rulers and have the whole screen to write. On selecting **View >> Full Screen**, nothing is displayed on the screen except the document and the one-button toolbar. To return to the previous view, click once on the button or press Esc.

Web Page Preview

In Web page preview, users can see how their document will look in a Web browser. Microsoft Word saves a copy of the document and then opens it in the default browser. If the Web browser is not already running, Word starts it automatically. The users can return to their document in Word any time.

Print Preview

Print preview, display multiple pages of a document in reduced size. In this view, the user can see page breaks, hidden text, and watermarks, and can make editing or formatting changes before printing the document.

Zoom

Zooming changes the magnification of the document. The default is 100 percent. User can zoom up to 500 percent. Higher zooms are good for overall design checking and lower zooms are good for detail checking.

NOTE Each view can have a different zoom level.

Opening a Document

- Choose File >> Open to display Open dialog box.
- Select the appropriate drive and folder, using Look In combo box.
- Select the file on which you want to work.
- Click on Open button or press Enter.

Saving a Document

Click the Save button, or choose **File >>Save**. The **Save As** dialog box appears as shown in Figure 10.5. By default, the **File name** text box lists the first sentence of the document.

Enter a name of up to 255 characters for the file. Word automatically adds the filename extension *.doc* to the filename. Choose **OK**, or press **Enter** to save the document.

The Save Options: Fast Save Or Full Save

The **Save As** dialog box includes a **Tools** button. Click it and then choose **Save Options**, a **Save Options** dialog box appears as shown in Figure 10.4.

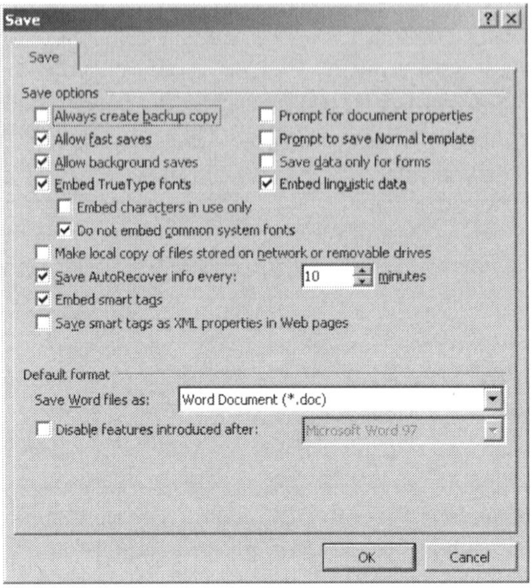

Figure 10.4 : Save Options dialog box

The **Allow fast saves** check box instructs Word to save only the changes to a document. This is faster than a full save, in which Word saves the complete, revised document.

Saving a File with a New Name

Various reasons to save a file with a different name are listed below:

- To track modification made by others.
- To save a copy in a different folder than the original.
- To make changes to the original document but also keep the original intact in order to compare the different versions.
- To save the file in a different format so another application can use it.

Steps to save a document with a new name are as follows:

- Choose *File >> Save As*. The *Save As* dialog box appears.
- Type the new name in the *File name* box.
- Select the appropriate drive, if the file is to be saved on a different location.
- Select the desired format by clicking the *Save as type* box.
- Click *Save* or press *Enter*.

Printing Documents

Click the *Print* button in the Standard toolbar, the document goes directly to the printer. To specify what exactly has to be printed use the *File>>Print* command to display *Print* dialog box.

Print Preview command is used to view document in a number of ways. To preview a document in Print Preview:

- Choose *File >> Print Preview* or click the *Print Preview* button on the Standard toolbar.

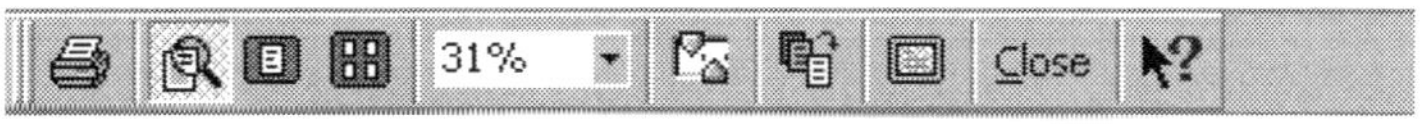

Figure 10.5 : The Print Preview Toolbar

- To close Print Preview, choose the Close button.

The various options available on the Print Preview toolbar are detailed in Table 10.2.

Button Name	Action
Print	Prints the document by using default print options.
Magnifier	Enlarges or reduces the document view.
One Page	Displays the document in single-page view.
Multiple Page	Views one or more pages of a document.
Zoom Control	Select different magnifications, from 10 to 500 percent and other options.
View Ruler	Displays or hides the horizontal and vertical rulers.
Shrink to Fit	Shrinks document to fit on one page or less if the last page of document contains only a few lines of text.
Full Screen	Removes title bar and toolbars to show a full screen display of the document in Print Preview.
Close Preview	Closes Print Preview and returns to your document.
Context Sensitive	Provides Context-Sensitive Help for Print Preview Help options.

Table 10.2 : Print Preview Options

Exiting Word

Any of the following five methods may be used to correctly exit Word.

- Choose the *File >> Exit* command.
- Press Alt+F4.
- Click the *Close* button in the right corner of the Word program title bar.
- Double-click the control menu icon in the left corner of the Word program title bar.
- Right-click in the Microsoft Word button in the taskbar, and choose *Close* from the pop-up menu.

Typing in a Document

When a document is first created by using the Normal.dot template, the insertion point rests at the top of the document, ready for the user to begin typing. To add text to a document, just start typing. By default, Word will automatically wrap the text to the next line when the text reaches the right margin. The Enter key is pressed when the user wants to create a new paragraph in Word. Show/Hide button, on the Standard toolbar, displays nonprinting characters. These are the characters that can be displayed on-screen but do not print. Common nonprinting characters and their names are: Line break or new line (↵), Paragraph mark (¶), Space (.), Tab (→).

Selecting Text

Before moving, copying, deleting, or making changes in the text, the first step is to select the item. The general rule is to select first and then perform any action. This rule applies to nearly every action performed in Word.

Using the Mouse

The shortcuts to selecting different text items using a mouse are listed in Table 10.3.

To Select	Do This
A word	Double-click the word.
A graphics	Click the graphic.
A line of text	Click in the selection bar to the left of the line.
Multiple lines of text	Click in the selection bar in the direction of the lines you want to select.
A sentence	Hold on Ctrl, and click in the sentence you want to select.
A paragraph	Double-click in the selection bar to the left of the paragraph.
Multiple paragraphs	Drag in the selection bar in the direction of the paragraphs you want to select.
Any item or amount of text	Click where you want the selection to begin. Then hold down Shift, and click where you want the selection to end.
An entire document	Triple-click in the selection bar.
A vertical block of text	Hold down Alt, click the mouse button, and drag.

Table 10.3 : Methods to select the text using the mouse

With the Keyboard

The keyboard shortcuts for selecting text are listed in Table 10.4.

To Select	Press
One character to the right	Shift + right-arrow key
One character to the left	Shift + left-arrow key
To the end of a word	Ctrl + Shift + right-arrow key
To the beginning of a word	Ctrl + Shift + left-arrow key
To the end of a line	Shift + End
To the beginning of a line	Shift + Home
Insertion point to the end of the paragraph	Ctrl+Shift+Down arrow
Insertion point to the start of the paragraph	Ctrl+Shift+Up arrow
To the end of the document	Ctrl + Shift + End
The whole document	Ctrl + A

Table 10.4 : Keyboard shortcuts for selecting the text

Editing Text

When the text is typed in, the user is quite likely to make mistakes. Correction of these mistakes is called ***editing***. Editing the text is an essential feature of a word processing package. Word makes it easy to add a new thought, change a word, or replace one phrase with another.

Finding and Replacing Text

The *Find and Replace* option of Word is a convenient way of searching for a particular word in a document and replacing it with another. The *Find* command moves to a specific point in the document quickly and the *Replace* command searches for and replaces the text.

Find Command

- Choose *Edit >> Find* or click the *Select Browse Object* button in the vertical scroll bar and click the *Find* icon.
- Enter the text to be searched in the *Find What* text box in the dialog box.
- Specify *Search Options* and other check options if required.
- Choose *Find Next*. Word begins the search and highlights the first occurrence of the text it was searching.

Replace Command

To search and replace text in a document:

- Choose *Edit >> Replace*.
- Enter the text to search for in the *Find What* text box.
- Choose *All, Up* or *Down Search Options*.
- In the *Replace With* text box, enter the replacement text.
- Do one of the following:
  - To confirm each replacement, choose *Find Next*. Then choose *Replace* to replace the text or *Find Next* to skip to the next occurrence.
  - To change all occurrences of the search text without confirmation, choose *Replace All*.
- Choose *Close* to end the replace session.

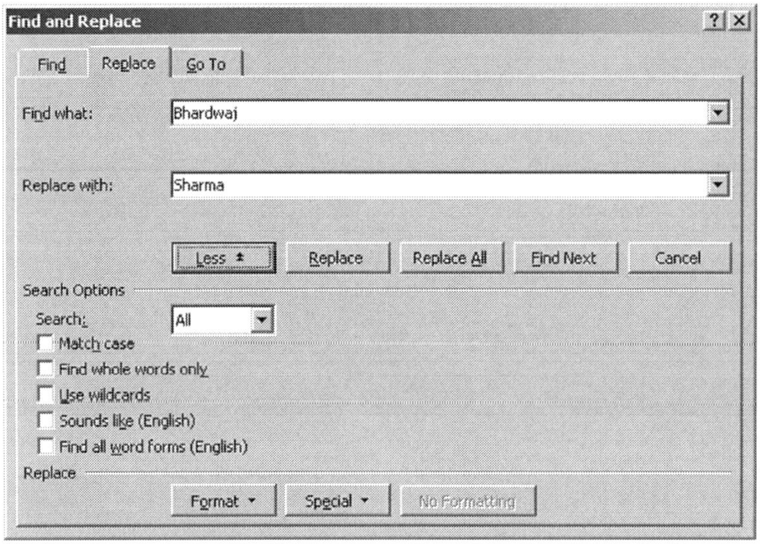

Figure 10.6 : Replace tab active in Find and Replace Dialog Box

Options for search Criteria

Select one or more options of *Find and Replace* dialog box (explained here) as search criteria.

- **Match case** Find only the text that matches the uppercase and lowercase letters of search text.
- **Find whole words only** Restrict the search to entire words that match the specified search text.
- **Use wildcards** Allows to specify wild card symbols in search text.
- **Sounds like** Used to find different spelling of words that sound similar.
- **Find all word forms** Finds different grammatical versions of a specified word.
- **Search** Controls the direction of the search beginning at the insertion point. The default direction is All. It also includes two other search options: Up and Down.
- **Special** Specify this option to search for and replace Word's special characters, such as paragraph and tab marks.
- **Format** Word can find and replace any kind of formatting including character and paragraph formatting style. Formatting can be specified in the *Find and Replace* dialog box in three ways: using formatting dialog boxes, using buttons on the Formatting toolbar, or using shortcut key combinations.

Deleting Text

There are several ways to remove unwanted text from the document. Table 10.5 lists the Word's keyboard deletion options. Selected text can also be deleted using *Edit >> Clear* command.

To Delete	Press
Selected text	Backspace or Delete
Character before the insertion point	Backspace
Character after the insertion point	Delete
A word before the insertion point	Ctrl + Backspace
A word after the insertion point	Ctrl + Delete

Table 10.5 : Keyboard Options for Deletion

Undoing Actions

The *Undo* command is used to reverse actions. The user can Undo an Undo with the help of *Redo* command. Word provides *three methods* to undo or redo the most recent action:

- Clicking the *Undo* button or *Redo* button on the Standard toolbar.
- Choosing *Undo* or *Redo* from the Edit menu.
- Pressing the shortcut keys Ctrl + Z (Undo) or Ctrl + Y (Redo)

The Clipboard

The clipboard is a temporary storage area maintained by Windows. Applications can put data into the clipboard and recall it later. In fact, one application may put its data into the clipboard and another application may read this data. Clipboard is a convenient interface to transfer data from one application to another. For example, we may copy data from DOC 1 into the clipboard, then switch to Word and paste the data from the clipboard into the document DOC 2.

The Office Clipboard is a new feature allowing you to copy up to 12 items at a time and paste them in any Office 2003 product. The text can be pasted in the same order in which they were copied or in any order or combination.

Moving and Copying Text

Word supports all the usual Windows techniques for copying and moving information. It provides a feature called drag-and-drop, a handy one step, mouse-assisted move to take information from one place to another on the same page. Cutting removes the original selection from the document. Copying makes a copy of the selected text and leaves the original selection unchanged.

Smart Cutting and Pasting

When cut or paste operations are carried out, Word adjusts the remaining spaces in the sentence. To deactivate the *Smart Cut and Paste* feature, Choose *Tools* >> *Options*, select *Edit tab*, and clear the *Use Smart Cut and Paste* check box.

Drag-and-Drop Editing

This feature is especially convenient for copying and moving text, where the source and destination are visible in the same screen.

To move or copy text by using drag-and-drop editing between Windows:

- Select the desired text.
- Do one of the following:
  - To **move** a selection, point to the selection, and hold down the mouse button until it changes to a drag-and-drop pointer.
  - To **copy** a selection, hold down the Ctrl key, point to the selection, and hold down the mouse pointer until it becomes a drag-and-drop pointer.
- Drag the pointer to the new location.
- Release the mouse button to drop the text into place.

Using the Cut, Copy, and Paste Buttons

Use the *Cut*, *Copy*, and *Paste* buttons on the Standard toolbar to move or copy text or graphics within a document, among different documents, or among other applications. To move or copy text and graphics with Standard toolbar

- Select the text to move or copy.
- Do one of the following:
  - To **move** the selection, click the *Cut* button on the Standard toolbar.
  - To **copy** the selection, click the *Copy* button on the Standard toolbar.
- Position the insertion pointer at the new location.
- Click the *Paste* button.

Using Commands and Keyboard Shortcuts

To copy a selection, choose Edit >> Copy, move the insertion pointer at the new location, and choose Edit >> Paste. To move a selection, choose Edit >> Cut and after specifying the location choose Edit >> Paste.

Keyboard Shortcuts for Copying and Moving are given in Table 10.6.

Operations	Standard Windows Shortcut	Other Shortcut
Cut	Ctrl + X	Shift+Del
Copy	Ctrl + C	Ctrl+Ins
Paste	Ctrl + V	Shift+Ins

Table 10.6 : Keyboard Shortcuts for Copying and Moving

Summary

- Word is a word processor, created by Microsoft Corporation, US.
- The available views are Normal view, Print Layout view, Outline view, Web Layout view, reading layout view, Full Screen view, Web Page Preview and Print Preview.
- Print Preview option can be used to view the document before printing.
- To display nonprinting characters, Show/Hide button on the Standard toolbar can be used.
- To perform any operation on any piece of text, first of all it must be selected.
- It is possible to undo or redo any action by using Undo or Redo buttons available on the Standard toolbar.
- Text can be moved from one location to another using Cut and Paste options.
- The Find command searches for a specified text and moves the cursor to that location where that text appears.

Review Exercise

Multiple choice questions

1. In Word's Normal template, default value of point size is
   a) 10
   b) 15
   c) 20
   d) 25
2. Which of the following options is available under Print Preview toolbar?
   a) Zoom Control
   b) Magnifier

c) Shrink to fit

d) All of the above

3. Which of the following views is useful for editing headers and footers and for adjusting margins?

a) Normal view

b) Print layout view

c) Outline view

d) Web layout view

4. Keyboard shortcut for Redo is

a) Ctrl+A

b) Ctrl+Y

c) Ctrl+E

d) Ctrl+R

5. Which of the following options is not valid for search criteria (in 'Find and Replace' dialog box)?

a) Match case

b) Use Wildcards

c) Format

d) None of the above

State whether true or false

1. It is possible to save an existing file with a different name.
2. Using Word you can search a file by specifying the text it contains.
3. More than one document window can be made active at one time.
4. Default magnification is 75 percent.
5. Show/hide button on the Standard toolbar can be used to show and hide the selected parts of a document.

Fill In The blanks

1. Word can be started automatically, whenever Windows is started, if Word is placed into ________ folder in the Start menu.

2. A ________ ________ ________ option instructs Word to save only the changes to a document.

3. The magnification range available is from 0 percent to ________.

4. To delete a word before the insertion point, press CTRL + ___________ key.

5. To display nonprinting characters ___________ button is used.

Descriptive questions

1. What are the advantages of using a word processor?

2. What are the various views available to see a document in Word?

3. Briefly explain how will you search for a particular word in the document and replace it with another.

4. What is the difference between cutting and copying a text?

5. How will you perform drag-and-drop editing?

CHAPTER 11

PROOFING DOCUMENTS

FEATURING

- Proofing Documents
- Correcting Spelling Errors
- Quick Spelling Checking
- Using Automatic Spell-Check
- Using the Grammar Command
- Using the Thesaurus
- Using AutoCorrect and AutoText
- Using the AutoComplete
- Hyphenating Documents

People generally make errors in spelling or grammatical syntax when writing either because they focus on the ideas and concepts they are writing about or because of simple typographical errors. With careful reading of finished documents you can catch most such errors, but that takes time. Word provides some document proofing tools such as spell-checker and grammar-checker. These automatic checking features catch the misspelt words and other errors immediately so that you can correct them as you come across the same. Word offers convenient ways to store, retrieve, and insert frequently used text, graphics, and other document elements. The techniques employ Word's AutoText, AutoCorrect, and AutoComplete commands. Each has strengths and weaknesses. In this chapter, we will learn about document proofing tools provided by Microsoft Word.

Proofing Documents

One of the many useful features of Word is that it can automatically check the documents for spelling mistakes. It has a built in English language dictionary. This dictionary is stored in the hard disk of the computer and it contains commonly used words in the English language.

Word has a **Spelling-Checker** and **Grammar-Checker** programs to check documents for misspelled words, duplicate words, grammar, style, punctuation, and word usage. These programs also offer advice to fix potential problems. The automatic checking features catch the misspelled words and other errors immediately.

Correcting Spelling Errors

The user can check the spelling of an entire document, a selection of text, or a single word. To run the spell-checker from the menu:

- Select the word or text to be checked. To check the entire document, make sure that nothing is selected.
- Choose **Tools** >> **Spelling and Grammar**.

Word stops automatically each time it finds what it considers an error and then the **Spelling and Grammar** dialog box opens showing the error highlighted in red (refer to Figure 11.1). The spelling error options are detailed in Table 11.1.

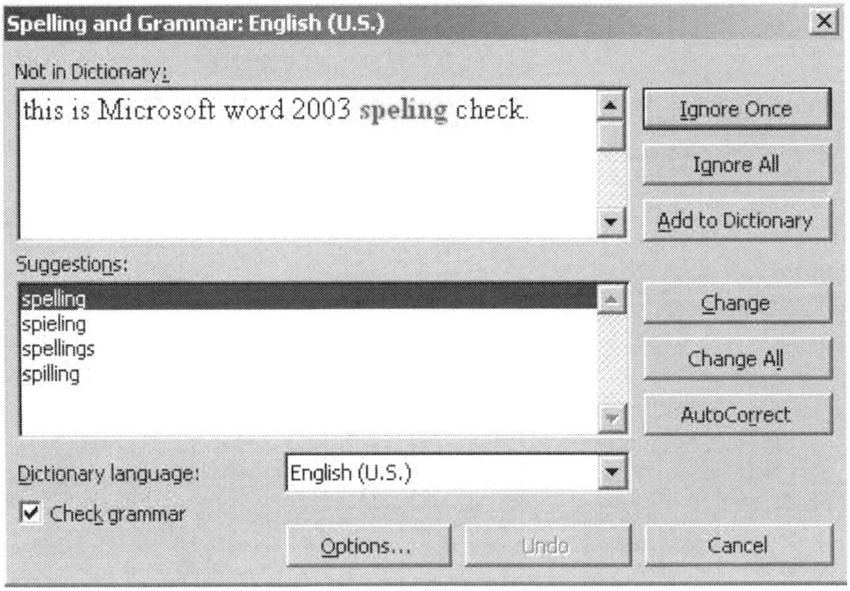

Figure 11.1 : Spelling and Grammar dialog box

Spelling Error Options

Not in Dictionary	The text is not a misspelled word but is being flagged because it is not in the dictionary.
Suggestions	Displays a list of suggested corrections and puts the most likely one at the top.
Ignore	To keep the word as it is. However, the checker will query the word if it reappears.
Ignore All	If the user wants the checker to accept the word for the entire document, click this option.
Add to Dictionary	Adds the selected word to the active dictionary.
Change / Delete	Accepts the suggestion in the **Suggestion** box. If the error is a repeated word, this button changes to **Delete** which removes the repeated word.
Change All / Delete	Changes all instances of the selection in the current document. If the error is a repeated word, this button changes to **Delete All**.
AutoCorrect	Adds the error and its correction to the **AutoCorrect** list.
Options	Opens **Options** dialog box.
Undo	Undoes the last correction made during the current spell-check session.
Cancel / Close	Closes the dialog box. The **Cancel** button becomes the **Close** button after at least one change takes place.

Table 11.1 : Spelling error options

Quick Spelling Checking

The **Spelling and Grammar** button on the Standard toolbar is a quick way to check the spelling of a single word, a paragraph or any other selection of text.

Another way to check spelling quickly is by pressing F7.

Word can automatically check spelling as the user types the text in. To correct the error immediately, right-click the offending word to open a **context-sensitive shortcut menu**. The status bar also displays three icons indicating the current spelling grammar status of document.

Using Automatic Spell-Check

Word automatically underlines misspelt words with a red wavy line. Spell-checking and underlining occurs as the user types. The steps to run an automatic spell-check are:

- Select **Tools** >> **Options** menu. The **Options** dialog box is displayed as in Figure 11.2.
- Select the **Spelling & Grammar** tab.
- Select the **Check spelling as you type** check box.

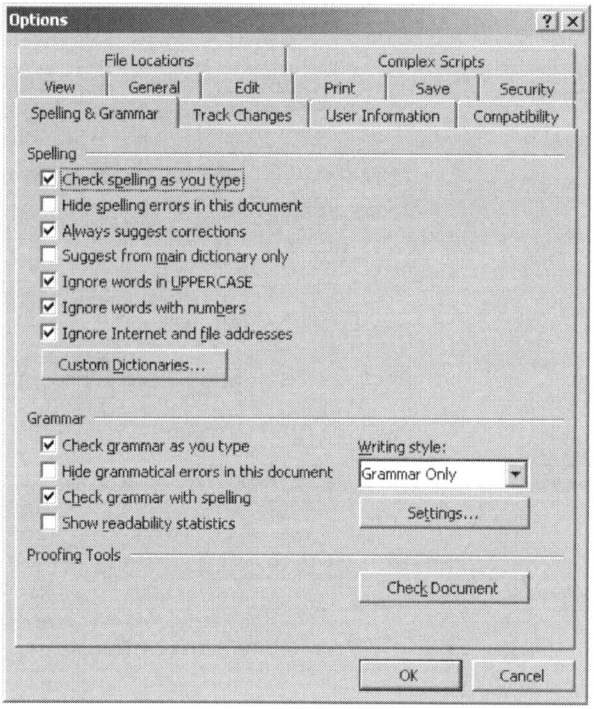

Figure 11.2 : Options dialog box with spelling and grammar tab active.

Using the Grammar Command

Word's grammar-checker uses rules to identify problems in the user's writing such as passive verbs, pronoun errors, possessive noun errors, homonym problems (like "'*there*" and "*their*"), and even political incorrectness. To deactivate spell-checker while checking grammar, choose **Tools** >> **Options**, click the **Spelling & Grammar** tab, and uncheck the **Check spelling** option and other rules.

To run the grammar-checker from menu:

- Select the sentence to be checked. For entire document, do not select anything.

- Choose **Tools** >> **Spelling and Grammar**, to begin the grammar check.
- The **Spelling and Grammar** dialog box appears each time, when possible error is caught (refer Figure 11.3).

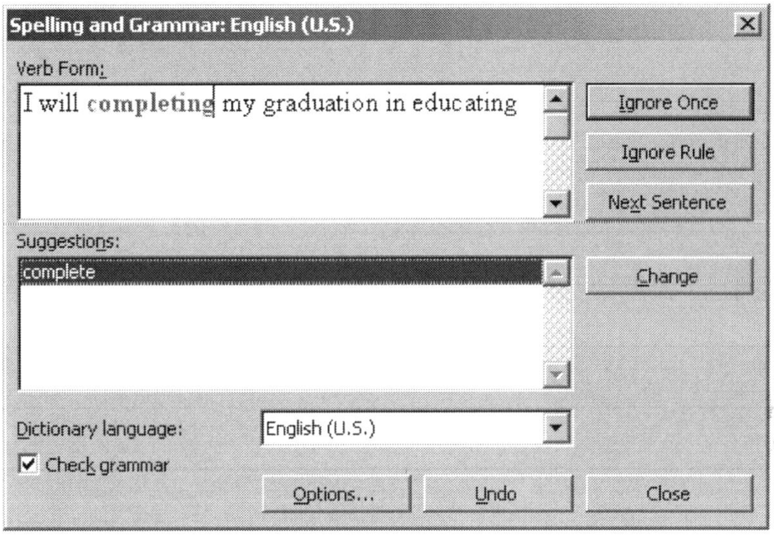

Figure 11.3 : Grammar suggestions in Spelling and Grammar dialog box

Using the Thesaurus

A Thesaurus is a tool used to find a **synonym** (a word that means essentially the same as the word it replaces). Word's Thesaurus also displays antonyms for some words. An **antonym** is a word that means the opposite of the selected word. To use the Thesaurus to find synonyms:

- Select the word whose synonym has to be found.
- Choose '**Tools**' menu click '**Research**'.
- In the 'Search for list', select thesaurus.
- Press Alt and click the word you want to lookup. Results appear in the Research task pane. Instead of using above 3 steps you can take an alternative approach.
- Select the word then choose Tools >> Language >> Thesaurus. A dialog box appears as in Figure 11.4.
- After you select an synonym for the looked up word, you can either insert, copy, that word or you can lookup for more synonyms by selecting one of the options showing in Figure 11.4.

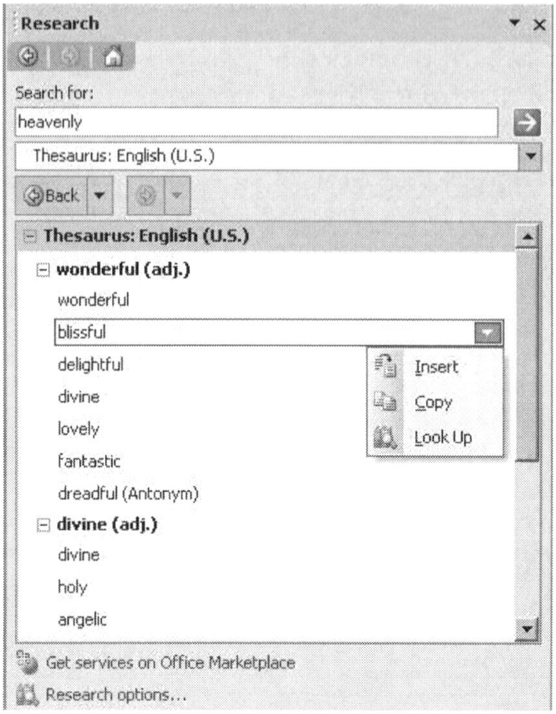

Figure 11.4 : Thesaurus dialog box showing insert, copy, lookup option

- After you choose an antonym for the looked up word, you can either replace your word with the chosen antonym or you can also look up synonyms for the antonym.

Using AutoCorrect and AutoText

Both the **AutoCorrect** and **AutoText** commands quickly insert frequently used boilerplate text and graphics.

With **AutoCorrect**, Word inserts previously created entries (by user) automatically as the user types. Because AutoCorrect inserts text automatically as the user types, the user can use it to automatically correct the most common typing and spelling errors.

AutoText offers a powerful way to substitute one item for another, yet it keeps its hands off the document until you explicitly command Word to make the substitution. **AutoText** entries are inserted after the user chooses the AutoText command or types the entry name and uses a shortcut key.

Creating AutoCorrect Entries

Word comes with a set of predefined **AutoCorrect** entries, for example, to correct two initial capitals and to capitalize first letter of each sentence. There are two ways to create an **AutoCorrect** entry:

- Add entries to **AutoCorrect** during a spell-check.
- Add entries to **AutoCorrect** directly.

To add entries to AutoCorrect directly:

- Choose **Tools** >> **AutoCorrect Options**.

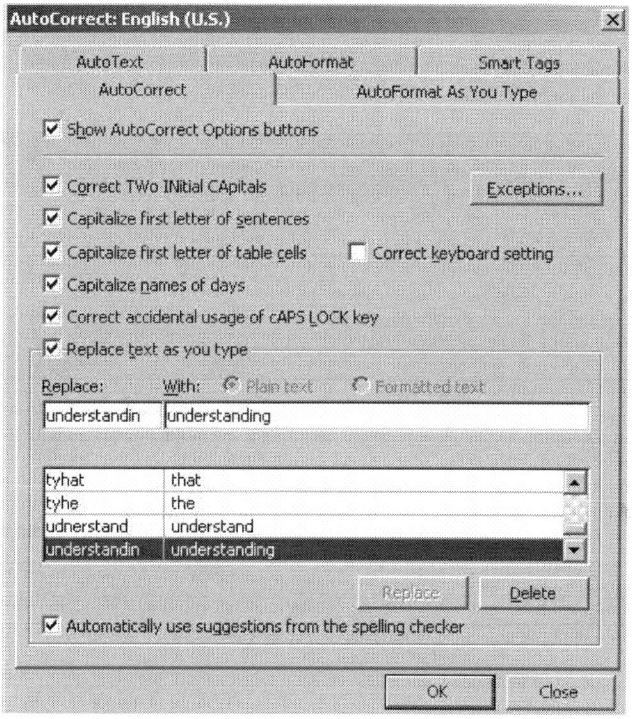

Figure 11.5 : AutoCorrect dialog box

- In the **Replace** text box, type the desired word that is often misspelt and need to be corrected automatically.
- In the **With** text box, type the correct spelling of that word.
- Click on the **Add** button.
- Click the **Exceptions** button to enter exceptions to **First Letter** tab or the **INitial CAps** tab (optional step).
- Click **OK** twice to return to the document.

Creating AutoText Entries

To create an AutoText entry :

- Select the text to store as an Autotext entry, then choose Insert >> AutoText >> AutoText. Your selected text is appeared in the "Enter Autotext entries here" box, click on add button, and your Autotext entry is added.

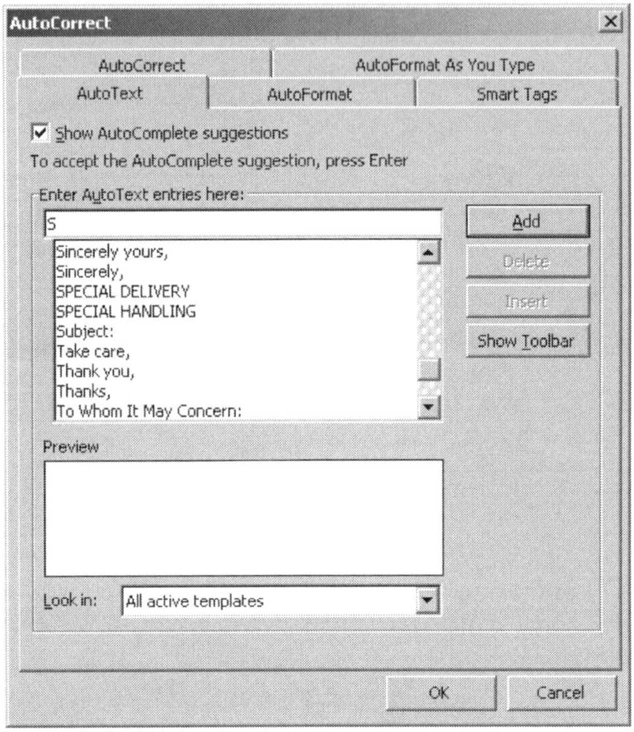

Figure 11.6 : Autocorrect dialog box with Autotext tab active

Inserting AutoText Entries

There are three ways to insert an AutoText entry.

- Using Keyboard Shortcut
  - The insertion point is positioned where the AutoText entry will be inserted.
  - Type the name of the entry or just enough letters to uniquely identify the name of an **AutoText** entry.
  - Press F3 function key.
- Using the AutoText toolbar
  - The insertion point is positioned where the AutoText entry will be inserted.
  - Click the scroll down menu in the middle of the AutoText toolbar.

- Select the desired entry to insert, and press Enter.

♦ Using the AutoText dialog box

  - The insertion point is positioned where the AutoText entry will be inserted.
  - Choose **Insert** >> **AutoText** or click the "**AutoText**" menu on the AutoText toolbar.
  - In the **Enter AutoText entries here** box, type or select an AutoText name.

Using the AutoComplete

Word automatically finishes the word "Thursday" if user types thur and presses Enter. Similarly, typing the first couple of letters in user's name prompts Word to finish it. This feature extends to months, current date, and the user's own AutoText entries.

On the **Tools** menu, click **AutoCorrect Options** and then click the **AutoText** tab.

Select or clear the **Show AutoComplete Suggestions** check box.

Hyphenating Documents

Hyphenating allows more text to be fitted on a page. It tightens justified paragraphs and reduces the ragged appearance of unjustified text. Word offers four methods of hyphenating text:

♦ Automatically hyphenate

♦ Manually hyphenate

♦ Insert optional hyphens

♦ Insert non-breaking hyphens

The hyphenation options are available through the **Language** option on the **Tools** menu.

Summary

♦ Word has a Spelling-checker and Grammar-checker programs to check documents for misspelt words, duplications, grammar, style, punctuation, and word usage.

♦ To check spelling and grammar, choose **Spelling and Grammar** command from the Tools menu.

♦ A **Thesaurus** is the tool used to find a synonym or antonym for a particular word.

♦ **AutoCorrect** feature can be used to correct typing mistakes for those words already created as AutoCorrect entry.

- **AutoText** feature is used to insert words automatically at any location.
- Word has **AutoComplete** feature, that is, it automatically finishes the words incompletely typed by the user.

Review Exercise

Multiple choice questions

1. Identify the invalid statement.
   a) Word can automatically check documents for spellings mistakes.
   b) Word has a built-in English Language dictionary.
   c) Word has a spell check facility.
   d) Word does not provide any grammar checking facility.
2. Keyboard shortcut for spell check is
   a) F5
   b) F6
   c) F7
   d) F8
3. Under which menu item is the option for enabling the AutoComplete tip for AutoText and dates is available?
   a) Tools
   b) Insert
   c) View
   d) Edit
4. Hyphenation option of Word is present in
   a) Tools >> Language
   b) Format >> Language
   c) Insert
   d) Edit
5. Which of the following is not displayed in Readability Statistics?
   a) Number of characters in the document.
   b) Number of lines in the document.
   c) Number of sentences in the document.

d) Number of words in the document.

State whether true or false

1. A Thesaurus looks up for synonyms and antonyms.
2. All the words highlighted during a spell-check are spelled incorrectly and must be changed.
3. Spelling-checker checks only for spelling not usage.
4. AutoText feature is used to convert numeric entries into character entries.
5. AutoComplete feature can be used to complete the documents automatically by inserting specified text at specified location in the document.

Fill in the blanks

1. In spell-checking process, __________ option is used to keep the word as it is.
2. A __________ is a tool used to find a synonym or antonym.
3. __________ feature is used to automatically insert previously created entries while typing.
4. AutoCorrect option can be found under __________ menu.
5. __________ feature automatically finishes the word if user types that word partially.

Descriptive questions

1. List some of the word proofing tools. What is the AutoText feature used for?
2. How can you automate the word correction process? How will you create an AutoCorrect entry?
3. What are the various spelling error options available in Word?
4. What is the use of Grammar command?
5. In your document, you have typed the word file as "'*file*" but you want to find and replace all the occurrences of this word to "'*File*". How would you do this?

C H A P T E R

12 DOCUMENT ENHANCEMENT

FEATURING

- **Formatting Text**
- **Character Formatting**
- **Paragraph Formatting**
- **Section Formatting**
- **Page Formatting**

Enhancing a document's appearance is Word's speciality. In seconds, the user can create professional-looking documents. Text and document enhancements are called formats. Formatting a document includes assigning text into columns, adjusting the line and paragraph spacing, and setting margins. Paragraphs are the basic building blocks of any document and it is also possible to apply formatting to paragraphs. Paragraph marks store the formatting applied to each paragraph. The next level applies to formatting individual sections of a document. Working with sections is essential if you want to create a page with multiple columns, the format used for most newsletters. In this chapter, you will learn the fundamentals of character and paragraph formatting. This chapter also explains how to change the formatting of a page such as margins, headers, footers, and page numbers.

Formatting Text

Formatting text means making the content readable and presentable. Word allows you to format the text by applying various text styles. Word divides formatting into following categories:

- Character Formatting
- Paragraph Formatting
- Page Formatting
- Section Formatting

Character Formatting

Word can embellish the appearance of a single font to create bold, italic, shadow and other effects. The techniques that accomplish this are referred to as character formatting.

Word offers the following ways to change character formats

- From the Formatting toolbar (Figure 12.1), you can select a font, change to a different point size, toggle bold, italic and underline, and much more. The buttons generally toggle between applying and removing their effects on the currently selected text; otherwise the effect is applied to whatever is typed at the insertion point.

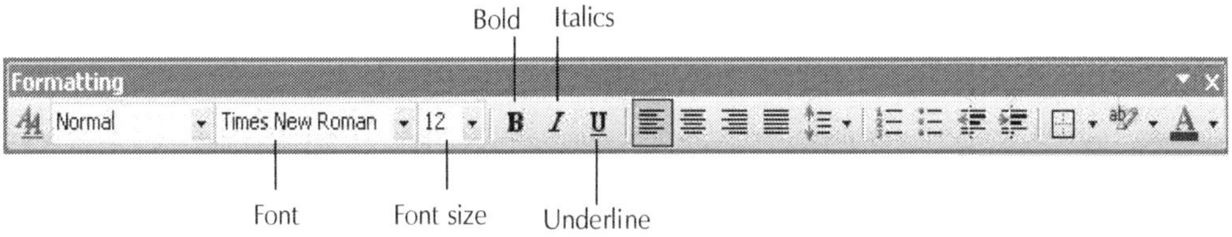

Figure 12.1 : Formatting Toolbar

- The **Font** dialog box which enables the user to apply one or multiple character formats at one time (refer Figure 12.2).

The Font dialog box can be accessed by choosing **Format** >> **Font** or by displaying the shortcut menu (click the right mouse button in the document window or press Shift+F10).

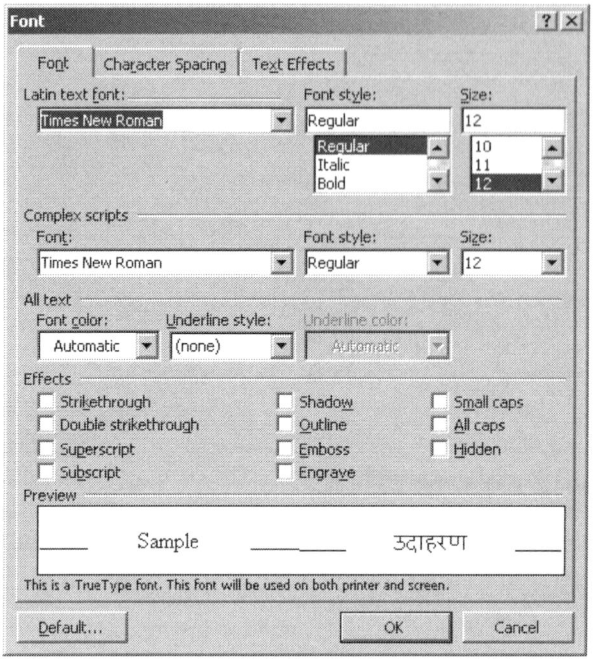

Figure 12.2 : Font dialog box

- Shortcut keys can be used to apply a format as the text is inserted. Word provides an extensive collection of shortcut keys for applying most of Word's character formats.

Boldfacing Text

Boldfacing makes characters heavier in their stroke weight, so that it will appear darker and attract the reader's attention. To format text in boldface:

- Select the text to boldface, or, for new text, position the insertion point where the boldfacing has to begin.
- Click the **Bold** button on the Formatting toolbar, or press Ctrl+B or choose **Format** >> **Font >> FontStyle >> Bold**.

Italicizing Text

An italic format is a script version of a font style that slants the characters to the right. To italicize text:

- Select the text to italicize, or, for new type, position the insertion point where the italicized text has to begin.
- Click the Italic button on the Formatting toolbar, or press Ctrl+I or choose **Format >> Font >> FontStyle >> Italic**.

Underlining Text

You can emphasize text by placing a line underneath it. Word lets the user format text with four types of underlines : single, words only, double, and dotted. To underline text:

- Select the text to **underline**, or, for new type, position the insertion point where the underline text has to begin.
- Click the Underline button on the Formatting toolbar or press Ctrl+U or choose **Format >> Font >> Underline Style**.

Using Superscripts and Subscripts

The **superscript** format places text slightly above a line of normal printed text, and the **subscript** format places the text slightly below a line of normal printed text.

For example, $E = MC^2$ (Superscript)
H_2O (Subscript)

To format text as superscript or subscript

- Select the text to be formatted.
- Select the **Superscript** or **Subscript** check box in the **Effects** section of the **Font** dialog box, and choose OK.

All Caps and Small Caps

Word's **All Caps** format changes selected lowercase characters to uppercase characters. The **Small Caps** format changes lowercase characters to uppercase characters and reduces their size. To format text as Small Caps or All Caps

- Select the text to be formatted.
- Select the **Small Caps** check box in the **Effects** group of the **Font** dialog box, and choose OK.

Some other formats that can be applied on the selected text by using the **Font dialog** box are — coluring the text with Font color option, creating shadow, outline, and embossed or engraved text using options available in **Effects** group (refer Figure 12.3).

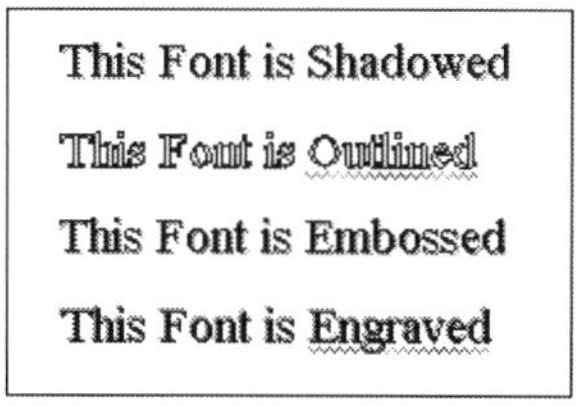

Figure 12.3 : Formatted Effects on text

Changing Character Spacing

Character spacing increases or decreases the amount of space between characters in the selected text by the amount specified. **Kerning** reduces or expands the spacing between certain letter pairs to improve the appearance of these character pairs. To make changes to either kind of spacing, display the **Font** dialog box and then choose the **Character Spacing** tab (refer Figure 12.4).

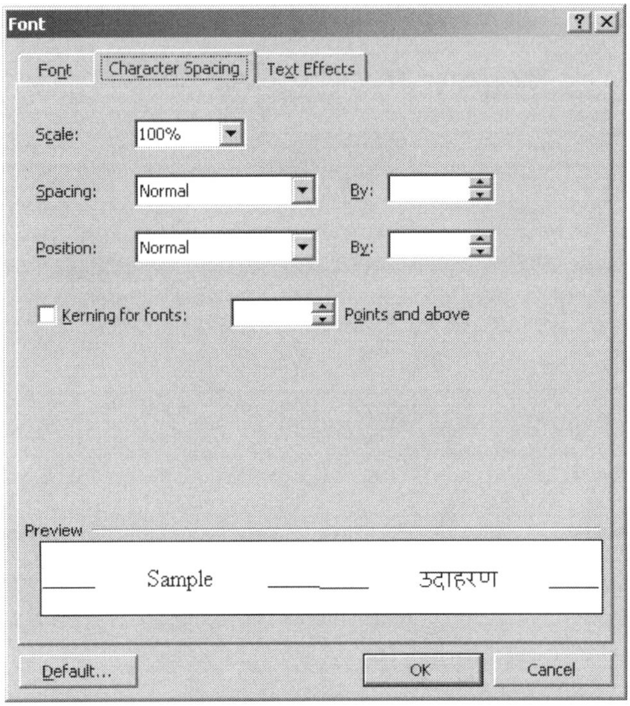

Figure 12.4 : Character Spacing tab of Font dialog box

Using Text Effects

Word offers a creative feature in the **Font** dialog box's **Text Effects** tab (refer Figure 12.5). It can be used to give a blinking background to the text, making the text sparkle, or creating a "light show" around the parameter. These special effects are not printable. To apply text effects to the text:

- Select the text.
- Choose **Format >> Font**, click the Text Effects tab.
- Select any of the animations and click the OK button.

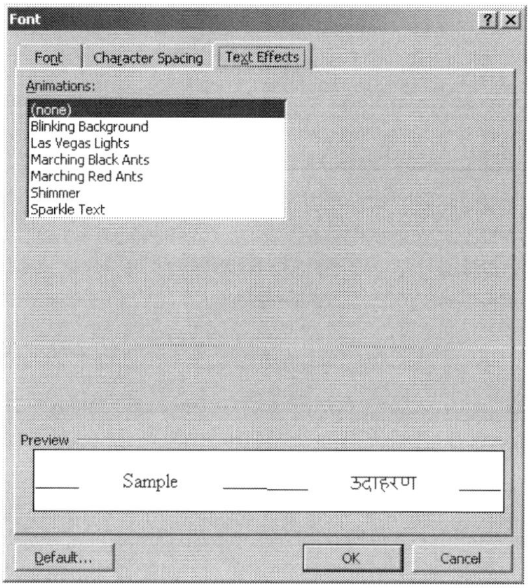

Figure 12.5 : Text Effects tab of Font dialog box

Displaying Character Formatting

- To see which formats are applied to a given section of text, choose **Help >> What's this**.
- When the pointer changes to an arrow with a question mark, click the text to check the formatting.

Repeating Character Formatting

- The **Edit >> Repeat** command allows the user to copy formatting immediately after the user has formatted characters.
- This method repeats only the most recent format.

Copying Character Formatting

- Use the **Format Painter** tool button to copy character formatting from place to place.
- To copy character formatting using Format Painter tool:-
  - Select the text containing the formatting that the user wants to copy.
  - To copy the formatting to one location, click once on the **Format Painter** button on the Standard toolbar. (To copy to several locations, double-click.) The mouse pointer will change to a paintbrush.

- Select the text to be formatted.
- If the user has double-clicked in Step 2, press ESC after using the **Format Painter**.

Highlighting Text

- Word's **Highlight** button on the Formatting toolbar is used to highlight any text in a document with a range of colors.

Changing the Case of Character

- The **Change Case** command automatically changes selected characters from uppercase to lowercase, or vice versa.
- **Format >> Change Case** displays the **Change Case** dialog box as in Figure 12.6. Choose one of the options and choose OK.

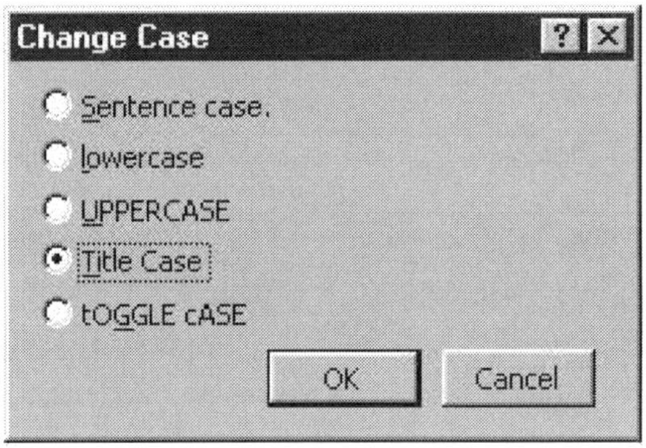

Figure 12.6 : Change Case dialog box

Paragraph Formatting

Each time the ENTER key is pressed, a new paragraph is created. Word paragraphs can be simple blank "lines" or complex collections of indentation, tab, line spacing, and other settings. The attributes of a paragraph are stored with its paragraph mark. Deleting the mark removes a paragraph's formatting.

Using Paragraph dialog box you can align paragraph, adjust paragraph spacing, and even adjust line spacing of paragraph. To activate Paragraph dialog box, first position the insertion point in a paragraph, or select the paragraphs, that are to be formatted. Choose **Format >> Paragraph**, select **Indents and Spacing** tab (Figure 12.7).

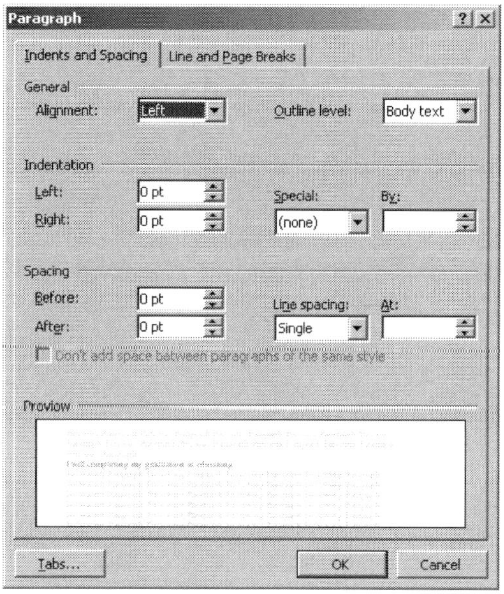

Figure 12.7 : Paragraph dialog box with Indents and Spacing tab active

- **Alignment** means to organize the position of the text relative to the margins. Choose following alignment option from the Alignment list.

Left aligned (default)	:	Text is said to be left-aligned if it is aligned with the left margin of the page.
Centre aligned	:	This option is normally used to centre the heading and text.
Right aligned	:	Text is said to be right aligned if it is aligned with the right margin of the page.
Justified	:	This feature aligns a paragraph with both the left and right margins. Inter-word spacing is adjusted such that each line of text begins at the left margin and ends at the right margin.

- **Adjust paragraph spacing** by adding a line space before or after a selected text type a number in the **Before** or **After** box in Spacing section (refer Figure 12.7).
- **Adjust line spacing** of selected text or paragraph(s) by choosing **Line spacing** options (Single, 1.5 lines, Double, At least, Exactly, Multiple) (refer Figure 12.7).

Setting Tabs

Tabs are great to create quick, relatively simple lists. The default tab is a left-aligned tab that occurs after every 1/2 inch. Word offers five specialized types of tab stops

Left	L
Centre	⊥
Right	┘
Decimal, and	⊥.
Bar	¦

Tabs can be set by either using the **Ruler** or the **Tabs** dialog box.

The steps to set tab stops using **ruler** are:

- Position the insertion point in a paragraph.
- Click the **Tabs Alignment** button, select the desired tab style.
- Position the pointer just below the mark on the ruler where the user wants the tab stop to appear. Click to place the tab stop on the ruler.

To clear the Tab setting, just click the tab stops on the ruler, drag it downwards and release the mouse pointer.

The steps to set tab stops using the **Tabs** dialog box are:

- Position the insertion point in a paragraph.
- Choose **Format >> Tabs**, the Tabs dialog box appears as in Figure 12.8.

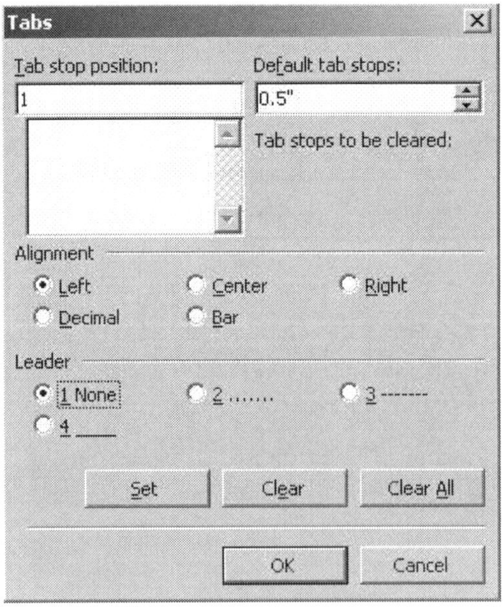

Figure 12.8 : Tabs dialog box

- Type the position of the tab stop in the **Tab stop position** box.
- From the Alignment group, choose tab style.

- Select the tab leader style from the **Leader** section.
- Choose the **Set** button to set the tab stop.
- Choose OK.

Setting Indents

Indenting lets the user set off a paragraph from other text. It makes the text more eye-catching. Indents are added to margins, thereby increasing the white space and decreasing the text area for specific paragraphs. The users text can be indented by using ruler, paragraph dialog box, and formatting toolbar.

Using the Ruler

The ruler contains triangular markers, called **indent markers**, at the left and right margins (refer Table 12.1).

Drag	To Set
	First-line indent
	Left indent
	First-line and left indent
	right indent

Table 12.1 : Indent Markers of Ruler

Using the Paragraph Dialog Box

Any type of indent can be set by using the paragraph dialog box (refer Figure 12.7). The advantage is that the user can enter precise measurements instead of experimenting with text alignments with ruler measurements.

Using the Formatting Toolbar

The "Decrease Indent" and the "Increase Indent" buttons on the Formatting toolbar can be used to create left indents only.

Adding Borders and Shading

Border and shading are generally used in conjunction with either paragraphs or tables. Other objects in Word, such as frames and pictures, can also have formatted borders. Word includes a **Tables and Borders** toolbar for applying borders and shading. To add boxes or lines to paragraphs by using the Tables and Borders toolbar the steps are:

- Select the paragraph(s) to enclose.

- Click the Tables and Borders icon on the Formatting toolbar. A Tables & Borders toolbar appears as shown in Figure 12.9.

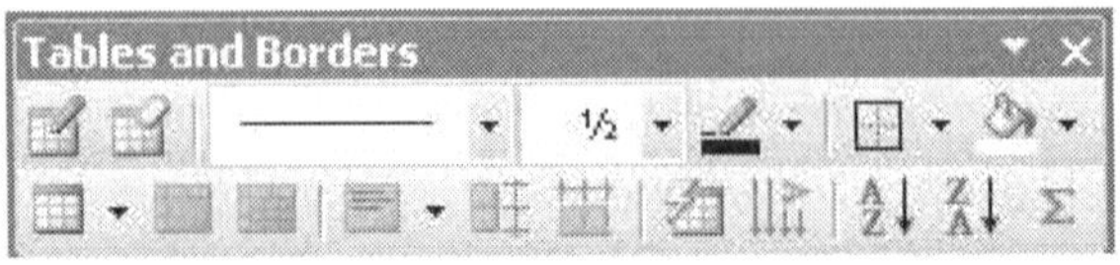

Figure 12.9 : Tables and Border toolbar

- Choose line style by clicking Line Style box.
- Choose width of line by clicking on Line Weight box.
- Choose color of the border by clicking on Border color box.
- Choose type of border by clicking on outside Border box.

Borders and shading can also be added by using **Format >> Borders and Shading** dialog box as shown in Figure 12.10.

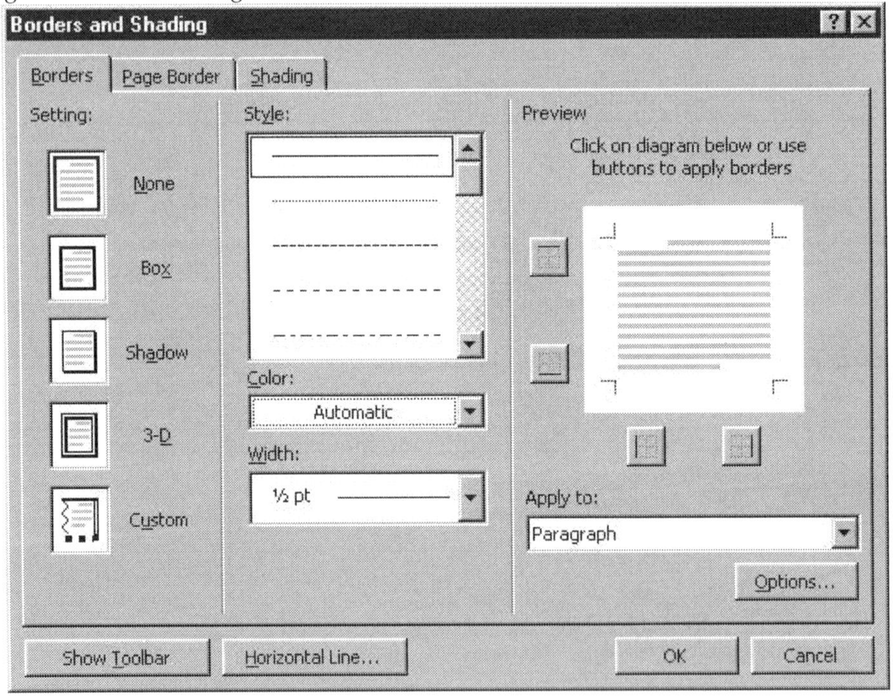

Figure 12.10 : Borders and Shading dialog box

Many options are self explanatory, such as the type of border (plain box, 3D, and so forth), the style of line for the border (solid, dotted, and so forth), and the color and width of border's lines. As you make your selections, the results appear in the preview region of the dialog box.

Bordering Pages

Click on the Page Border tab of the Borders and Shading dialog box, and a dialog box as shown in Figure 12.11 appears.

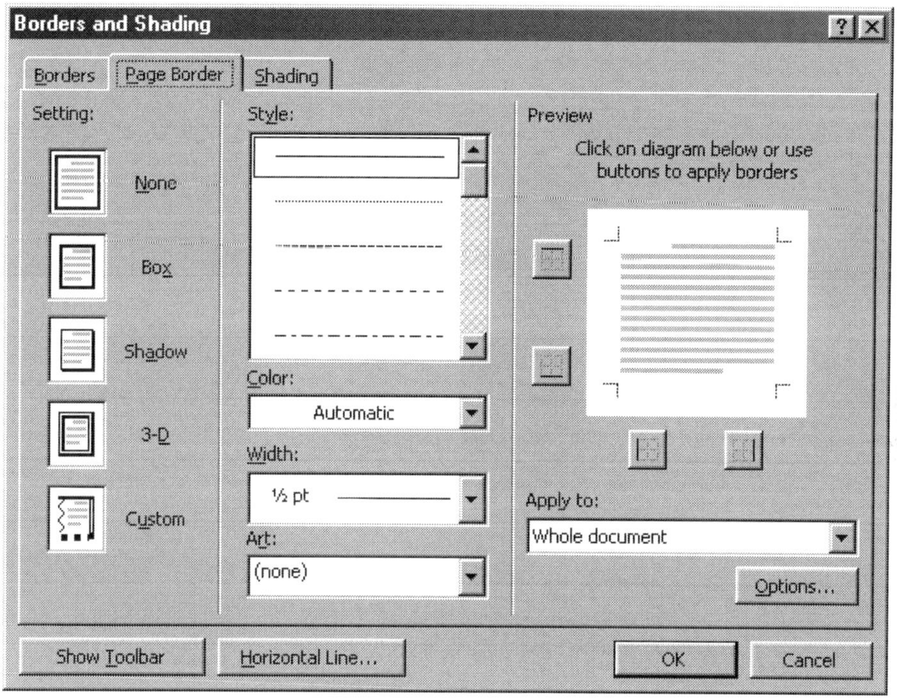

Figure 12.11 : Borders and Shading dialog box with Page Border tab active

The Page Border dialog box has three basic differences from the Borders page:

- The effects that you choose will be applied to entire pages rather than to individual elements on a page.
- You have options to apply your choices to all pages, to only the first page, to all pages except the first page, and to sections of a document by choosing the **Apply to** list box.
- The Page Border dialog box contains an **Art** drop-down pick list. Instead of consisting of pedestrian lines, your borders can depict a string of repeated, tiny images of objects.

Creating Bulleted Lists

Bulleted and Numbered lists help in distinguishing a series of important items or points from the rest of the text in a document. To create a bulleted or numbered list:

- Type the list at the left margin and select it.

- Choose **Format >> Bullets and Numbering** (refer Figure 12.12).
- Choose the Bulleted tab. Select the bulleted list format from the predefined choices.
- Choose the Numbered tab. Select the numbering style from the predefined choices.

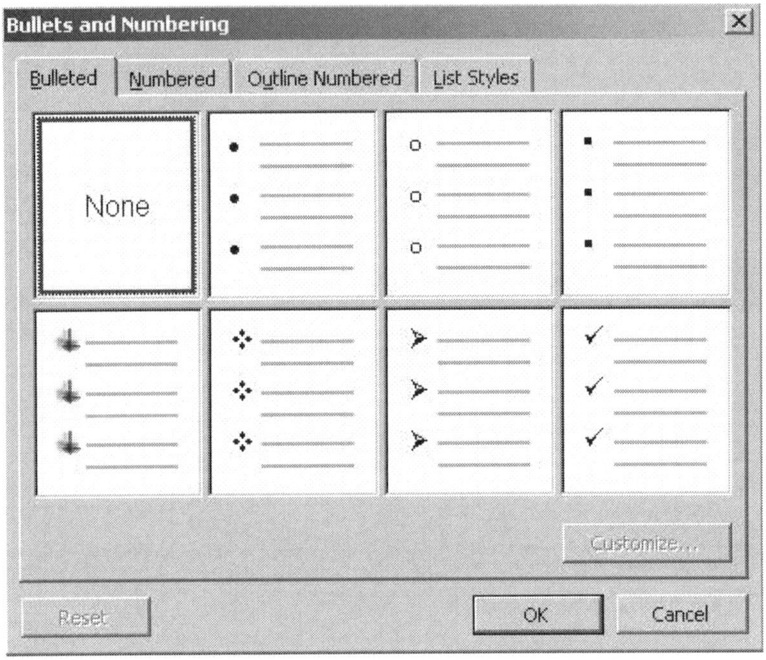

Figure 12.12 : Bullets and Numbering dialog box with Bulletted tab active

Inserting Large Initial Caps and Drop Caps

Large initial caps are big letters at the beginning of paragraphs and are used for decorative effect. Drop caps are large initial caps that are dropped below the baseline of its paragraph or into the margin next to the paragraph. The general steps to achieve the drop cap effect are:

- Select the character or characters you want to drop.
- Select Format >> Drop Cap. The dialog box as shown in Figure 12.13.

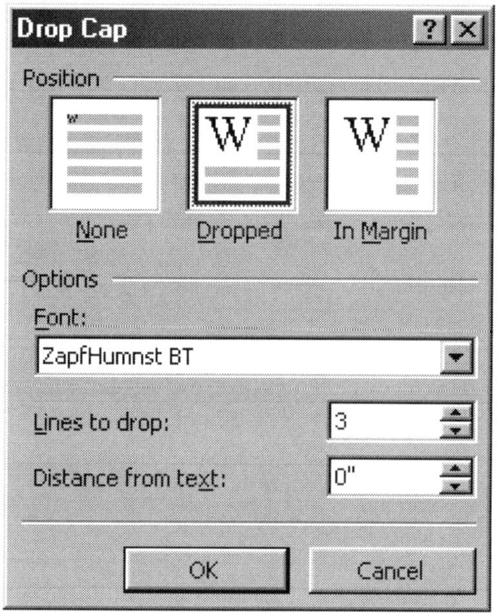

Figure 12.13 : Drop Cap dialog box

- Click one of the three drop-cap styles, and adjust the options.
- Click OK.

Note that Drop Cap is designed to work with single-spaced text. It will not work in tables, headers, or footers. It is not possible to see the position of drop caps or create them in Outline view. Drop Caps can't be placed in the margins of multicolumn documents, though they can be placed in text in such documents.

Section Formatting

Working with sections is essential to create a page with multiple columns. Section breaks divide a document into sections. By default, Normal template creates and entire document as a single section. Sections are used for any of the following types of formatting.

Inserting Section Breaks

Section breaks are always visible in Normal view. They appear as double-dotted lines containing the words "End of Section". A section break marks the point in a document where new formatting begins. To insert a section break:

- Position the cursor from where a new section starts.
- Choose **Insert >> Break**.

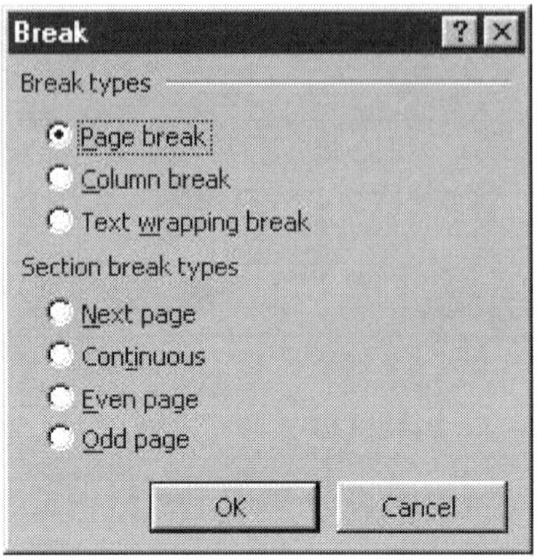

Figure 12.14 : Break dialog box

- Choose one of the following options in the Section breaks types (refer to Figure 12.14).
  - **Next page** radio button to insert a section break and begin the new section at the top of the next page.
  - **Continuous** radio button to insert a section break and begin the new section on the same page, below the previous section.
  - **Even page** radio button to insert a section break and begin a new section on an even-numbered page.
  - **Odd page** radio button to insert a section break and begin a new section on an odd-numbered page.
- Choose OK.

To delete a section break, select the section break and press the Del key.

Working with Columns

Word enables the user to create newspaper-style columns to make text more appealing and readable. Two methods of creating columns are:

- Choose the **Format >> Columns** command.
- Choose the **Columns** button on the Standard toolbar.

The first method opens a dialog box as shown in Figure 12.15, from which the desired formatting can be selected.

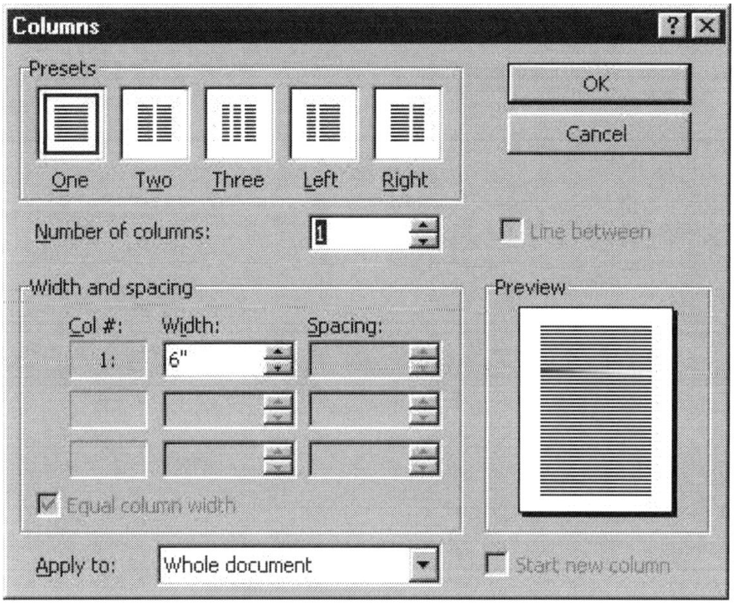

Figure 12.15 : Columns dialog box

The second method can be used to select the number of evenly sized and spaced columns (upto six). Both methods automatically switch to Print Layout view.

Page Formatting

Formatting pages can mean changing the margins, paper size, orientation or headers and footers. Word enables the user to apply page setup formatting options to a selection, a section, multiple sections, or the entire document.

Setting Margins

Margins are the borders on all four sides of a page within which the text of the document is confined. Word sets default margins with a 1 inch top and bottom margins and 1.25 inch left and right margins.

Setting margins by using the **Page Setup** dialog box:

- Position the cursor in the section for which you want to set the margins, or select the text or sections you want formatted.
- Choose **File >> Page Setup**. The Page Setup dialog box appears as in Figure 12.16.

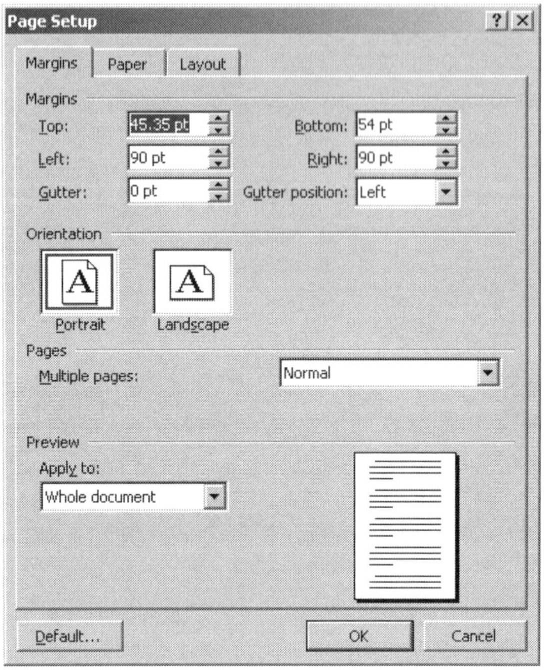

Figure 12.16 : Page Setup dialog box with Margins tab active

- Select the **Margins** tab.
- Choose the Top, Bottom, Left, or Right margin settings.
- Choose OK after you are satisfied with the new margins.

A convenient way to set margins for the document or for a section is to use the ruler and mouse. The document must be displayed in **Print Layout** or **Print Preview** view to change the margins on all four sides of the document. To change margins with a ruler:

- Position the cursor in the section where the margins are to be set.
- Choose **View >> Print Layout**. If the ruler does not appear, choose **View >> Ruler** to display it.
- Position the pointer over the margin boundary that is to be changed.
- Drag the margin boundary towards the edge of the page to make the margin smaller or towards the centre of the page to make the margin wider. A dotted line appears showing where the new margin will be. Holding down the **Alt** key while dragging enables the user to see margin measurements in the ruler.

Changing Paper Size and Orientation

Changing the paper size enables you to create documents other than the standard 595.35 x 841.95 points. To set paper size and orientation:

- Position the cursor in the section for which the paper size and orientation has to be set, or select the text or sections.
- Choose **File >> Page Setup**.

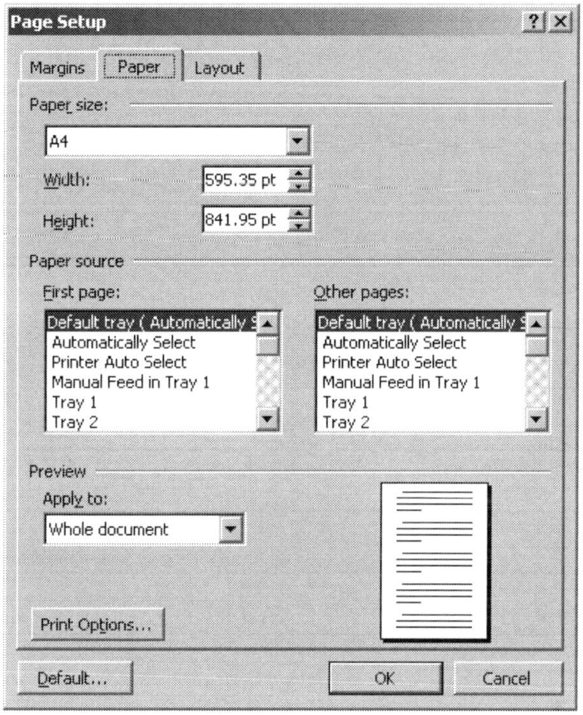

Figure 12.17 : Page Setup dialog box with Paper tab active

- Select the **Paper** tab, choose a predefined paper size from the Paper size list, or type the width and height of customized paper size to set paper size. (See Figure 12.17)
- Select **Margins** tab, choose Landscape (horizontal, sideways page) or Portrait (default vertical, upright page) from Orientation group to set page orientation. (See Figure 12.16)
- Choose OK.

Aligning Text Vertically on a Page

Word provides three options for vertical alignment of text on a page: Top, Center, and Justified. These options determine how Word aligns a partial page of text between the top and bottom margins. To vertically align text on the page

- Position the cursor inside the section containing the text for alignment.
- Choose **File >> Page Setup**.
- Select the **Layout** tab.
- Choose one of the options in the **Vertical alignment** list.
- Choose OK.

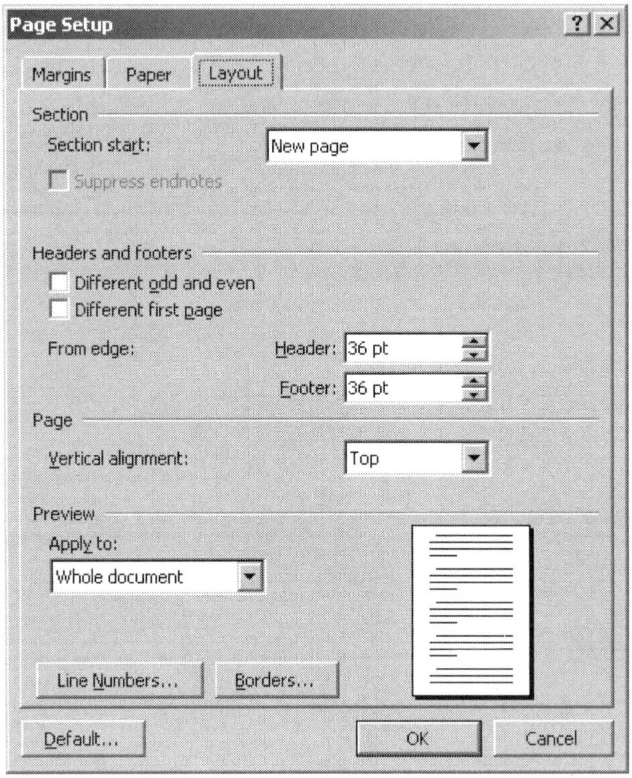

Figure 12.18 : Page Setup dialog box with Layout tab active

Creating Headers and Footers

Headers and footers are word processing holding areas for repetitive information that must appear either in the top margin (header) or in the bottom margin (footer) of every page of the document. The user can create different headers and footers for different sections of document. They can also be different for odd and even pages. Table 12.2 explains the function of the buttons on the **Header and Footer** toolbar.

Button Name	Description
Insert AutoText	Displays drop-down list of AutoText entries.
Insert Page Number	Inserts a page number field.
Insert Number of Pages	Inserts total number of pages in document.
Format Page Number	Opens Page Number Format dialog box.
Insert Date	Inserts a date field. Uses whichever date format you last chose in using the Insert >> Date and Time command.
Insert Time	Inserts a time field.
Page Setup	Opens Page Setup dialog box.
Show/Hide Document Text	Toggles between displaying dimmed body text and graphics in the background or showing no text in background.
Same as Previous	Links or unlinks a header from preceding section.
Switch Between Header and Footer	Toggles between displaying header and footer.
Show Previous	Shows header or footer for preceding section.
Show Next	Shows header or footer for next section.
Close	Closes the Header and Footer toolbar.

Table 12.2 : Options available on Header Footer toolbar

To add header or footer to the entire document:

- Choose **View >> Header and Footer**. Word displays the Header and Footer toolbar (refer Figure 12.19).
- To switch between header and footer click the Switch Between Header and Footer button.
- Type the text for header or footer within the dashed line that surrounds the header or footer area.
- Use the Header and Footer toolbar buttons to insert the fields in the header or footer.
- Choose Close or double-click the document to close Header and Footer toolbar and return to document.

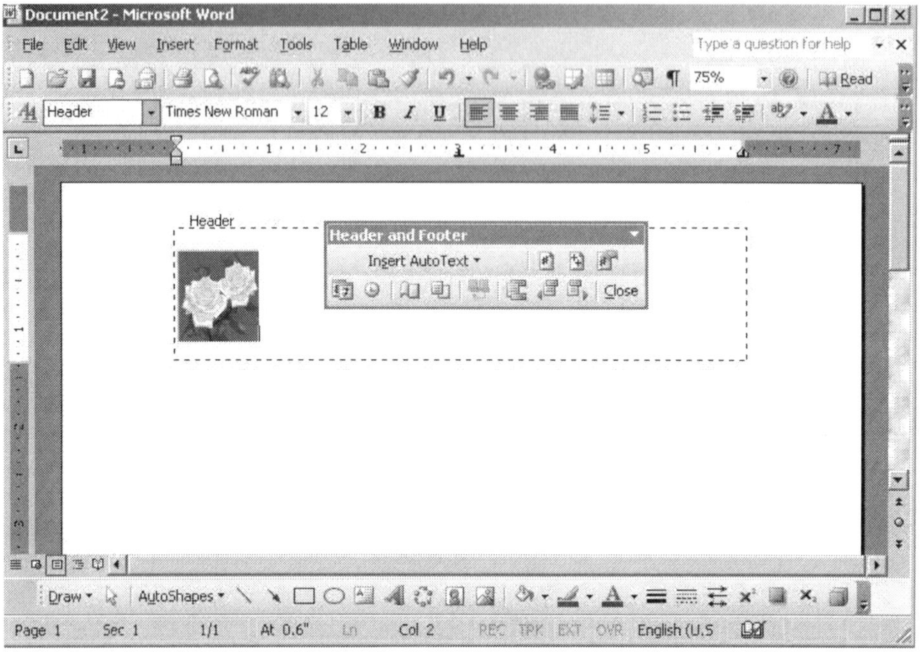

Figure 12.19 : A floating Header Footer toolbar

NOTE

- You can use most of the commands in the Insert, Format, Tools, and Table menus to format headers, and footers.
- To edit a header and footer, use the same command you used to create it, or in the Print Layout view, double-click the header or footer.

Summary

- It is possible to give your documents a professional look using formatting options available in Word 2003.
- Using character spacing feature of Word it is possible to increase or decrease the amount of space between characters.
- Text effects facility can be used to give a blinking background to the text, making the text sparkle or creating a light show around the parameter.
- Using the various buttons available on the Formatting toolbar, the font, font style, and font size can be changed.
- Like character formatting, paragraph formatting can also be applied.
- Paragraphs can be aligned in four ways: left-aligned, right-aligned, centre-aligned and justified.

- Word offers five specialized type of tab stops: Left, Centre, Right, Decimal and Bar. Tabs can be set by either using Ruler or the Tabs dialog box.
- Indenting lets the user to set off a paragraph from other text.
- Borders and Shading can be applied to paragraphs using Tables and Borders toolbar.
- Bulleted, Numbered or Outline Numbered lists can be created by using Bullets and Numbering option from Format menu.
- Drop caps can be used in a document to drop the selected character below the baseline of its paragraph or into the margin next to the paragraph.
- To create multiple column documents, it is essential to create multiple sections.
- Formatting pages provides changing the margins, paper size, orientation or header and footers.

Review Exercise

Multiple choice questions

1. Shortcut key combination for superscript is
   a) Ctrl + Shift + =
   b) Ctrl + =
   c) Ctrl + Shift
   d) None of the above
2. Which of the following options will let you select a raised character effect?
   a) Tools >> Customize
   b) Tools >> Languages
   c) Format >> Font
   d) Format >> Paragraph
3. Besides left, center and right, the other types of tab stops are
   a) Bar
   b) Decimal
   c) Both of the above
   d) None of the above

4. Shortcut key combination for center aligning the text is
   a) Ctrl + L
   b) Ctrl + E
   c) Ctrl + C
   d) None of the above
5. To convert first character of each word of selected text to uppercase, select
   a) Format >> Change Case >> Upper Case
   b) Format >> Change Case >> Title Case
   c) Format >> Change Case >> Sentence Case
   d) Format >> Change Case >> Lower Case

State whether true or false

1. The current date cannot be inserted in the header.
2. Even and odd pages can have different footers.
3. Bold, italics and bold italics are available for all fonts.
4. All sections in a document necessarily use the same margin.
5. In case of multiple columns, a vertical line can be drawn between columns.

Fill in the blanks

1. In ____________ type of alignment, text gets aligned along both left and right margins.
2. ____________ is the left limit of the page and marks the beginning of the line.
3. Margins, indents and tabs are shown on the ____________ ruler.
4. The default spacing in Word is ____________.
5. The default tab-stop position is ____________ inch.

Descriptive questions

1. Name the different types of tab stops that you can set in Word.
2. How can you modify an assigned bullet or a number?
3. How will you type the following symbols in your document?
   a) O_2
   b) a^2+b^2
4. How will you create a new line without creating a new paragraph?
5. What is the use of inserting section breaks?

CHAPTER

13 MAIL MERGE

FEATURING

- ❑ **Mail Merge — An Introduction**
- ❑ **Introducing Main Documents and Data Sources**
- ❑ **Writing Form Letters**
- ❑ **Creating the Data Source Document**
- ❑ **Merging Specific Records**
- ❑ **Setting the Record Order**
- ❑ **Creating Envelopes and Mailing Labels**

Word's mail merge feature helps in quickly creating documents by combining information from two different files. In mail-merge, you write a letter in one document, enter all your recipients names and addresses in another, and then merge the two to produce as many copies as needed. Mail merge enables you to personalize form letters for mass mailing, product announcements, customer letters, reports, and invitations. With mail-merge, it is also possible to combine a list of names and addresses to create invoices and mailing labels. So, instead of typing many individual letters and changing the variable information in each letter, you can tell Word to merge the letter and the variable information, which saves you effort required to type and time. So, if you have a dozen identical letters to write, then you can use mail-merge feature of Word to get the desired results in no time. In this chapter you will learn how to use the mail-merge feature to create form letters, envelopes, and mailing labels.

Mail Merge – An Introduction

Mail Merge helps in generating multiple copies of a base document (the content of a letter) incorporating some variable information (the name and address of a person) such that each copy appears to the recipient as an original document. Mail Merge saves the user from the effort of typing in each copy separately. The process is called "merging", and does the following operations:

- Print personalized letters addressed to any number of recipients.
- Print envelopes for the letters.
- Print mailing labels.
- Print lists and catalogs.

The Mail Merge process involves:

- Creating a main document that contains text with some placemarkers embedded within the text.
- Creating a data source document that lists sets of text that will replace the placemarkers in the main document.
- Finally, when Word merges the two files, the result is a set of documents, one document for each set of text in the data source document.

Introducing Main Documents and Data Sources

The two main documents used by Word in the mail merge process are:

- a main document
- a data source document.

NOTE Presently, think only about Mail Merge to create personalized form letters.

The Main Document

The *main document* for a form letter contains the unchanging text, and perhaps graphics, that should be in every letter. The words enclosed in chevrons (<< and >>) in the main document are the *field codes* that identify data to be inserted from the data source document. Other text in the main document (text not enclosed in chevrons) will appear in every letter. A sample example of such main document is shown in Figure 13.1.

NOTE When you open a main document in Word, it is associated with the data source with which it was last saved. If you use a previously created main document, attach it to any new data source that you want to use.

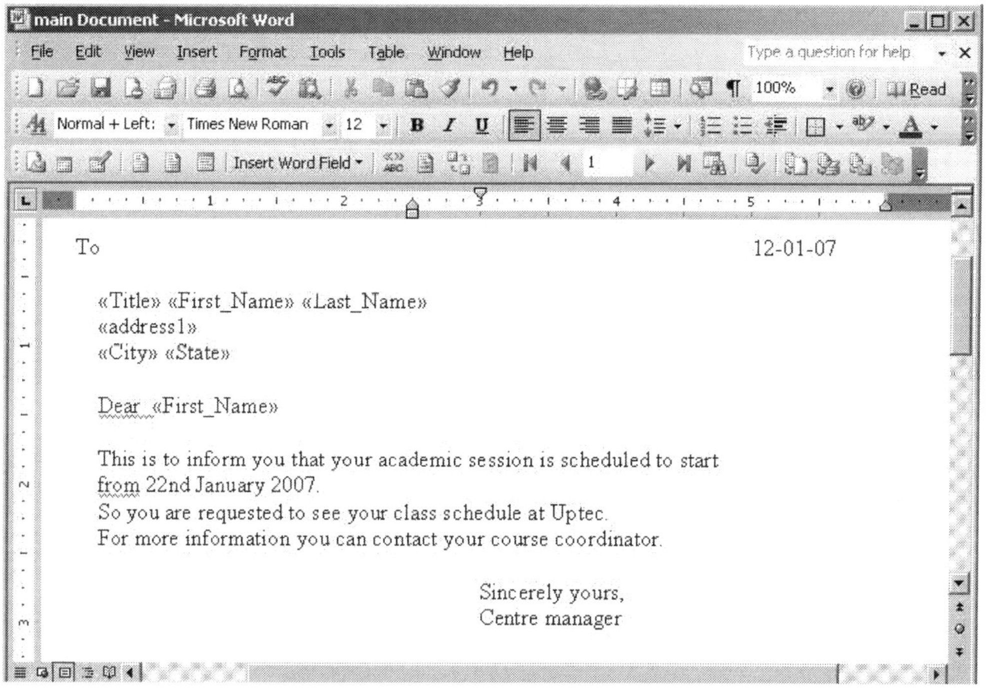

Figure 13.1 : Main Document

The Data Source Document

Data sources are organized collections of information — databases — that you can create easily as a Word table. Word can also use data from other applications, such as Microsoft Excel or Microsoft Access. All data sources, no matter where they come from, contain *records* and *fields*. A record is a complete set of related information, and a field is each separate element in a record. Data contains the information that replaces field codes in the main document. It is actually just a table as shown in Table 13.1.

Title	First Name	Last Name	Address 1	City	State
Ms.	Neetika	Saxena	A-22, Indira Nagar	Jaipur	Rajasthan
Mr.	Rajan	Awasthi	84/278 KMG	Lucknow	UP
Mr.	Vikas	Bajpayee	Asharfabad	Lucknow	UP
Ms.	Leenu	Jain	16, RP Marg	Lucknow	UP
Mr.	Surya Prakash	Sharma	Thakurganj	Lucknow	UP

Table 13.1 : Data Source

Putting the Two Together

After creating a main document and a data source document, the only thing left is to tell Word to merge them. The result is a set of customized letters.

Writing Form Letters

Word guides you smoothly through the process of creating a form letter. You simply follow the instructions in a sequence of dialog boxes.

Building a New Merge Structure

To begin creating a set of form letters proceed in the following steps:

- Open an empty document, choose Tools >> Letters and Mailing >> Mail Merge. Mail Merge Task Pane appears as shown in Figure 13.2

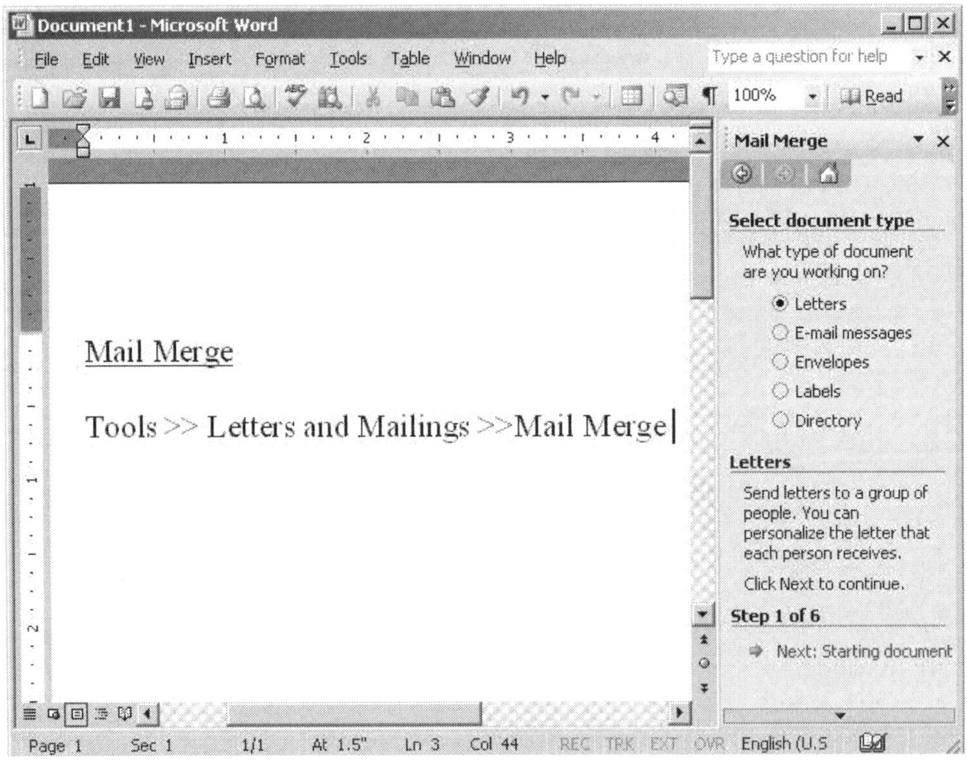

Figure 13.2 : Mail Merge Task Pane

NOTE In Microsoft Word 2000, Mail Merge is available in Tools >> Mail Merge.

In 'Select document type' click on **Letters** Radio button, and in next wizard step (Step 1 of 6) click on **Next : Starting document**, next task pane appears which asks for '**Select starting document**'. In which you can select to 'Use current document' Radio button or you can 'Start from a template or Start from existing document as in Figure 13.3.

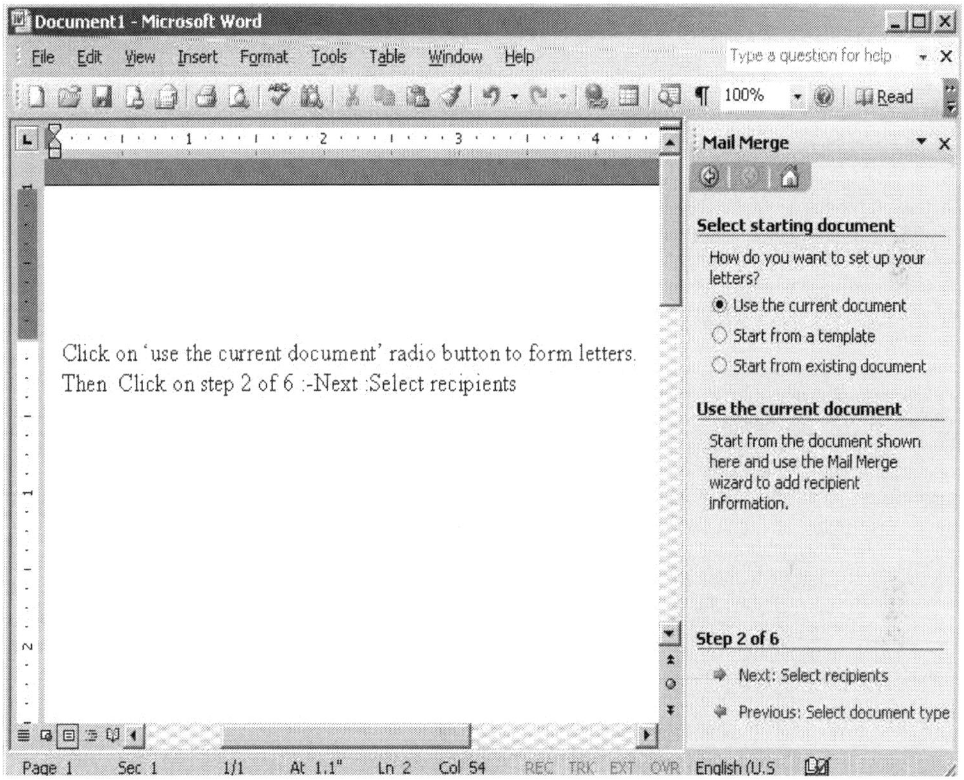

Figure 13.3 : Mail Merge task pane _step 2

Now click on step 2 of 6 Next select recipients . Next task pane appears asking '**Select recipients**' click on **type a new list** radio button. Then to type the names and address of recipients click on '**Create..** hyperlink (refer Figure 13.4) a New Address List dialog box appears, as shown in Figure 13.5.

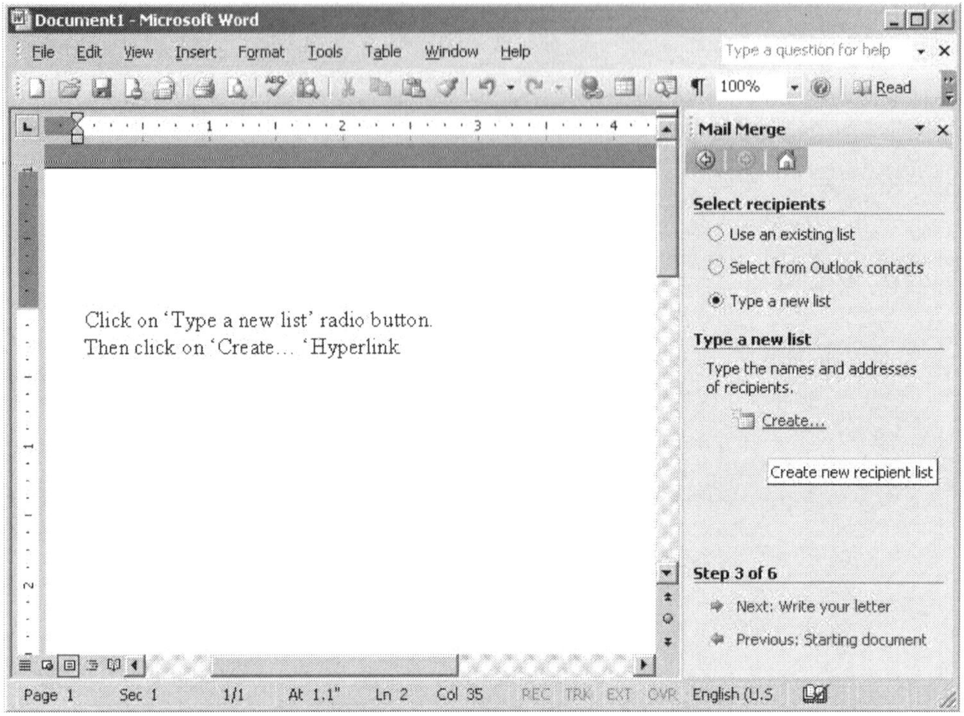

Figure 13.4 : Mail Merge task pane _Step3

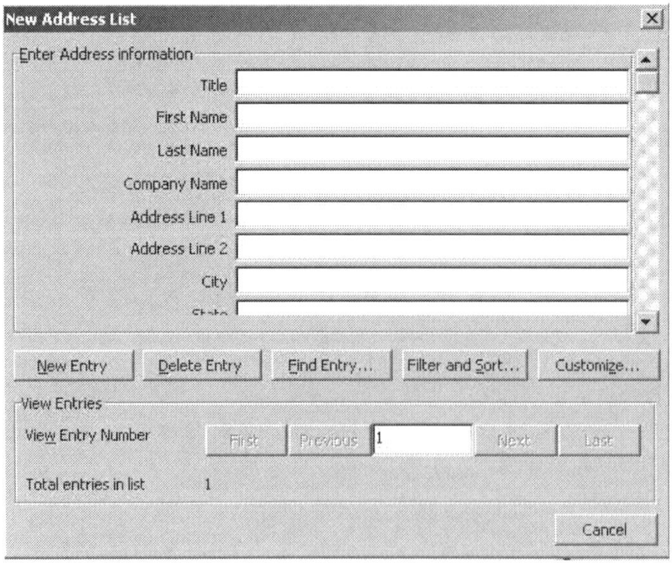

Figure 13.5 : New Address List dialog box

Creating the Data Source Document

Now you have to Enter address information, To enter new address headings and to delete the one you don't want in your address information you can customize your address information to do this in Figure 13.5 click on '**Customize**' button, 'Customize Address List' dialog box appears as shown in Figure 13.6.

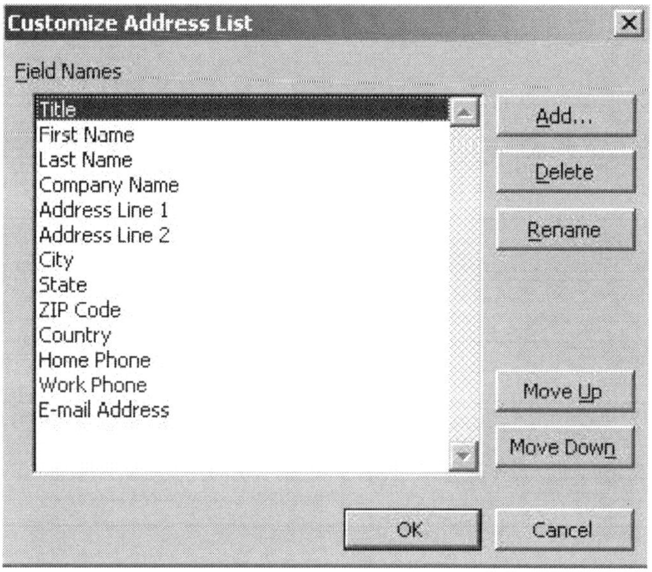

Figure 13.6 : Customize Address List

Now delete the address headings which you don't want and add new address entries you want to add, you can also rename already existing entries by clicking 'Rename' button, and using 'Move up' & 'Move down' button you can arrange field names in the order you prefer at the time of entering address information.

Now click OK button to close Customize Address List dialog box, and you will be back at 'New Address List' dialog box, fill the entries you want and at last click Close button. Now Save address list dialog box appears. Type the File name here, it will be saved as type 'Microsoft Office Address Lists' (which is basically 'Ms-Access database' here).

- Click on **Save** button.
- Next '**Mail Merge Recipients**' dialog box appears which facilitates sorting, editing, deleting, & also adding more records to database (refer Figure 13.7).

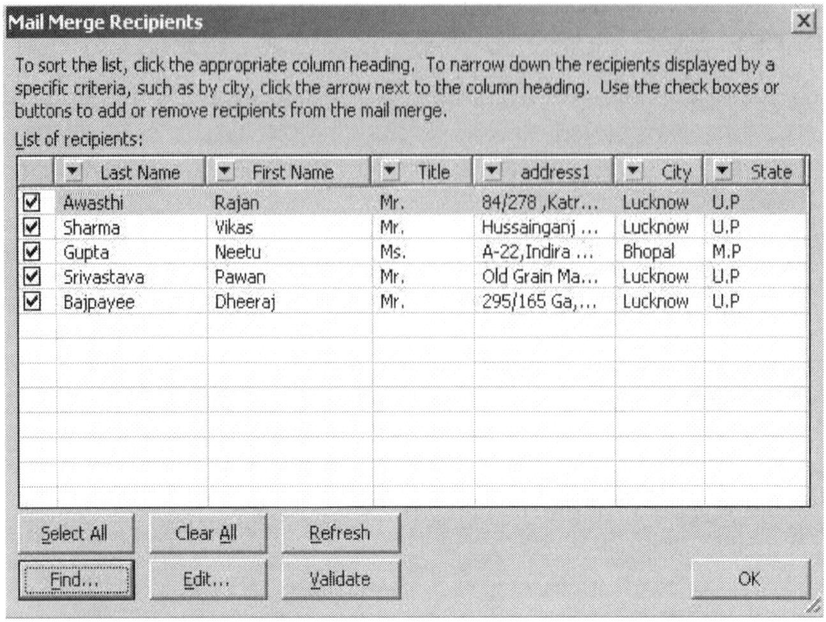

Figure 13.7 : Dialog box giving options for editing data source or main document

- Click **OK** button. Now 'Mail Merge' toolbar appears.

Figure 13.8 : Mail Merge toolbar

Functions of the Mail Merge Toolbar Buttons

Name	**Function**
Main document setup	To select document type to create.
Open data source	To open datasource already created.
Mail Merge Recipients	To show the Mail Merge recipient dialog box.
Insert Address block	To specify address elements
Insert Greeting line	To specify greeting line.
Insert Merge Field	To insert merge field while making main document.
Insert Word Field	To insert a word field into the main document.

View Merged Field	To complete & view merge document.
Highlight Merge Field	To highlight merge fields.
Match fields	To activate match fields dialog box.
Propagate labels	To propagate among the labels.
First record	To directly skip to first merged document.
Previous record	To move record pointer one record back.
Go to record	To type record no. move directly on desired record.
Next record	To move record pointer one record ahead.
Last record	To move pointer at last record
Find Entry	To activate find entry dialog box.
Check for errors	To check errors in merged document.
Merge to new document	To merge records in a new main document.
Merge to printer	To send merged document directly to printer to get printout.
Merge to EMail	To send merged email message using outlook express.
Merge to Fax	To send merged document on Fax.

Table 13.2 : Listing of functions of Mail Merge toolbar buttons

Creating the Form Letter

In the empty main document, place two types of data: text that appears in every letter, and field codes to mark the positions where text from the data source document will be inserted.

Inserting Merge Field

- Place the insertion point where you want to insert field name. Choose the Insert Merge Field button of the Mail Merge toolbar to display a list of fields in the data source document (refer Figure 13.9).

Figure 13.9 : Insert Merge Field dialog box

- Select the desired field name to insert into the document & click insert button.
- The field name is enclosed in chevrons automatically.
- Click the Insert Merge Field button again to insert each field in the document.
- Type the body of the letter, i.e., the text that is common.
- After completing the main document, save it.

Merging the Main and Data Source Document

Choose '**Merge to New Document**' button from mail merge toolbar to create a new document that contains all your merged documents as a single document as shown in Figure 13.10 or you can take the help of task pane wizard to complete the remaining merge steps.

NOTE In this step, you can choose Merge To New Document button of the Mail Merge toolbar for the same.

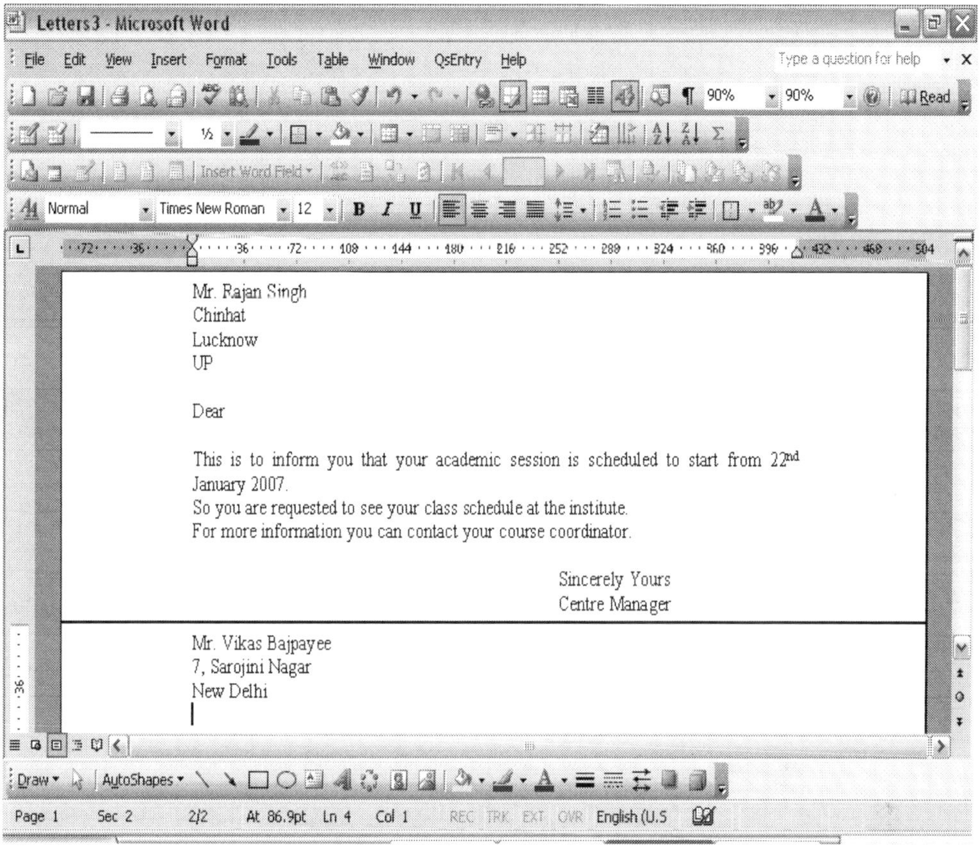

Figure 13.10 : Merged document

Merging Specific Records

A query enables the user to specify conditions under which a record in the data source document is included when merged. A query can be quite simple, such as asking for records for people in one state, or more complex, such as asking for all the records that have surname "Singh" living in "New Delhi" city. To create a query:

- In new address list dialog box (refer Figure 13.5) click on 'Filter and Sort' button, a dialog box appears as shown in Figure 13.11.

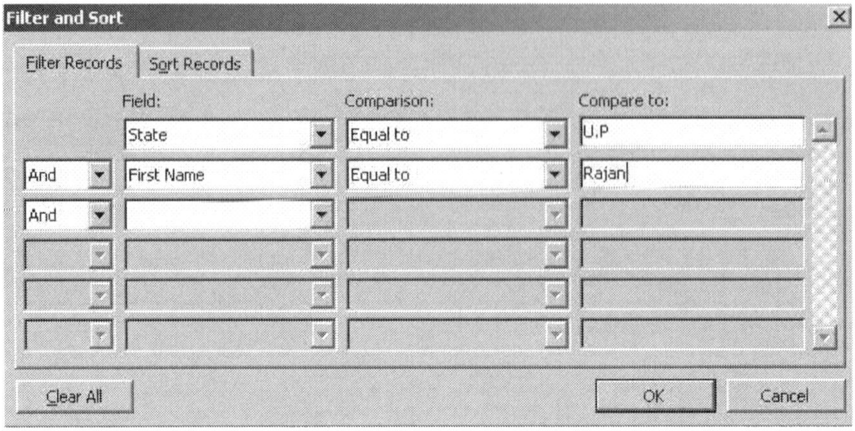

Figure 13.11 : Filter and Sort dialog box with filter records tab activated

- Select the **Filter Records** tab.
- In the **Field** column choose the field you want to use as a filter, for example, City.
- In the **Comparison** drop-down list, choose the appropriate comparison operator (Equals to, less than, etc.).
- In the **Compare to** box, type the required filtering criteria, for example, Lucknow.
- Word automatically prepares for an additional query condition by adding And/ Or to the second line for more complex queries.
- Choose OK to return to New Address list dialog box.

Setting the Record Order

By default, Word prints merge documents in the same order as records occur in the data source document. By using the Sort option, you can change this order. To sort records:

- Display the **Filter and Sort** dialog box (described above). Then display the Sort Records tab as shown in Figure 13.11.
- In the **Sort By** list box, select the field by which records will be sorted.
- Choose the Ascending or Descending option according to the preference.
- Choose OK.

Creating Envelopes and Mailing Labels

You can also use Word's Mail Merge Helper to merge labels and envelopes of various kinds. The procedures to merge labels and envelopes are similar to that of form letters, we will discuss them briefly here.

Using Mail Merge to Print Envelopes

The steps you follow to print envelopes, using an existing data source document, are similar to those you use to create form letters except that the envelope is the main document.

Getting Ready to Print Envelope

Preparing to print envelopes is a matter of identifying the data source document, or creating one if it does not already exist, and selecting the envelope size and layout. To identify the data source document:

- Choose Tools >> Letters and Mailings >> Mail Merge.
- In the Mail Merge Task pane in 'Select document type' click 'Envelopes radio button, and in step 1 of 6 click Next : Starting document.
- Now in step 2 select your starting document.
- In change document layout click on 'Envelope options' hyperlink to choose envelope size as shown in Figure 13.12, also you can set printing options (refer Figure 13.13).
- Click OK.

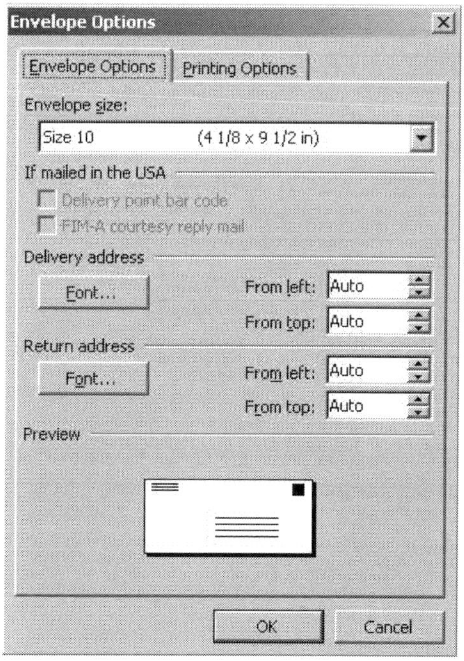

Figure 13.12 : Envelope Options dialog box

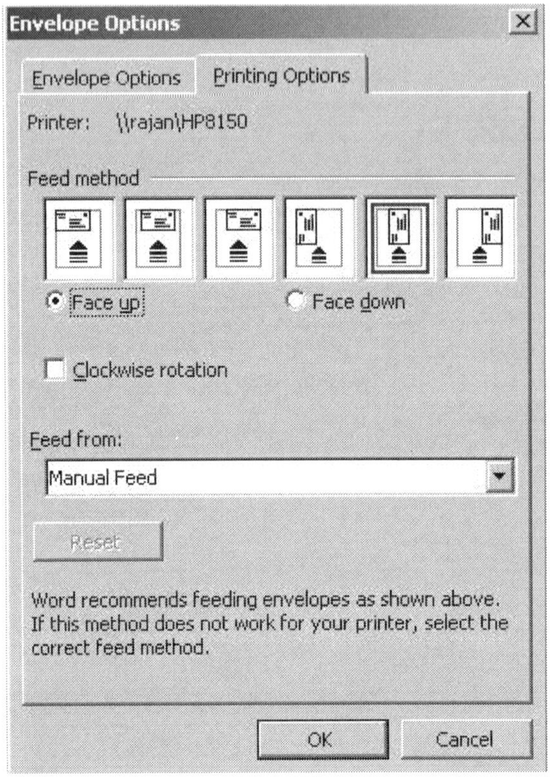

Figure 13.13 : Envelope Options with Printing Options Tab activated

- Now click Step 2 of 6; Next Select recipients.
- Now you can use and browse existing list (Data Source) or you can create new list.
- Next Mail Merge toolbar appears, select 'insert merge field button' & insert required merge fields at the recipient address area on an envelope as shown in Figure 13.14.

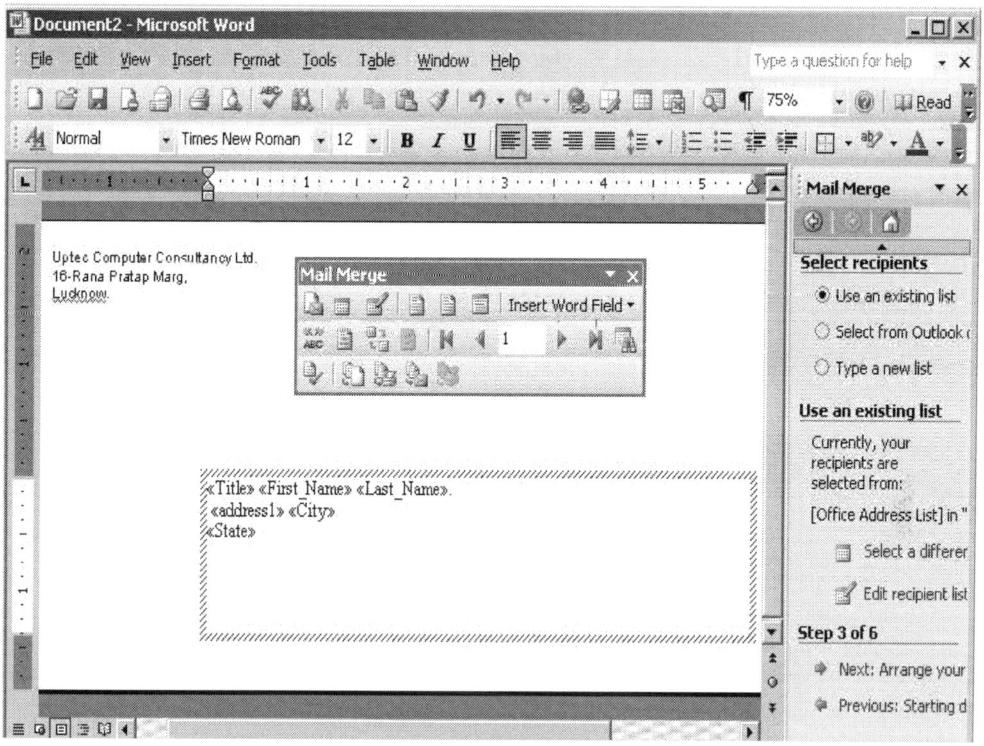

Figure 13.14 : Main document having label Fields

Printing the Envelopes

To print one or two sample envelopes:

- Choose 'Complete the Merge' (step 5 of 6) from Mail Merge task pane.
- Select 'Print' in Mail Merge task pane.

Mailing Labels

The process of preparing and printing mailing labels is same as that of envelopes.

- Choose Tools >> Letters and Mailings >> Mail Merge.
- Choose Labels radio button in Mail Merge task pane.
- Click Label options... (refer Figure 13.15).

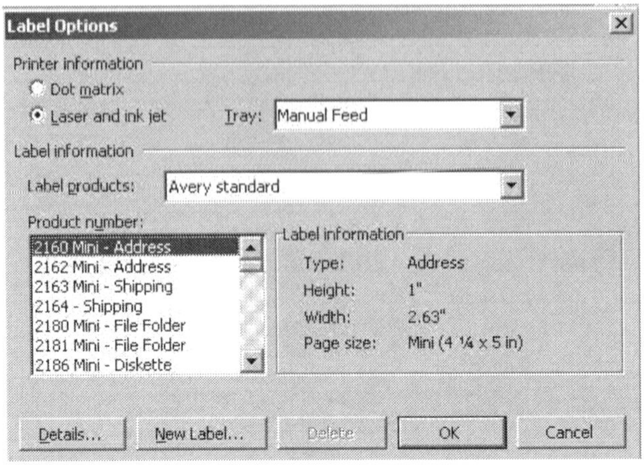

Figure 13.15 : Label Options dialog box

- When you have chosen the labels to use, choose OK to close the dialog box.
- Next select recipients and click browse and select a datastore (it already created) Next click step 3 of 6 : Arrange your labels.
- Next click on 'More items' hyperlink to insert merge fields in labels (as shown in Figure 13.16).

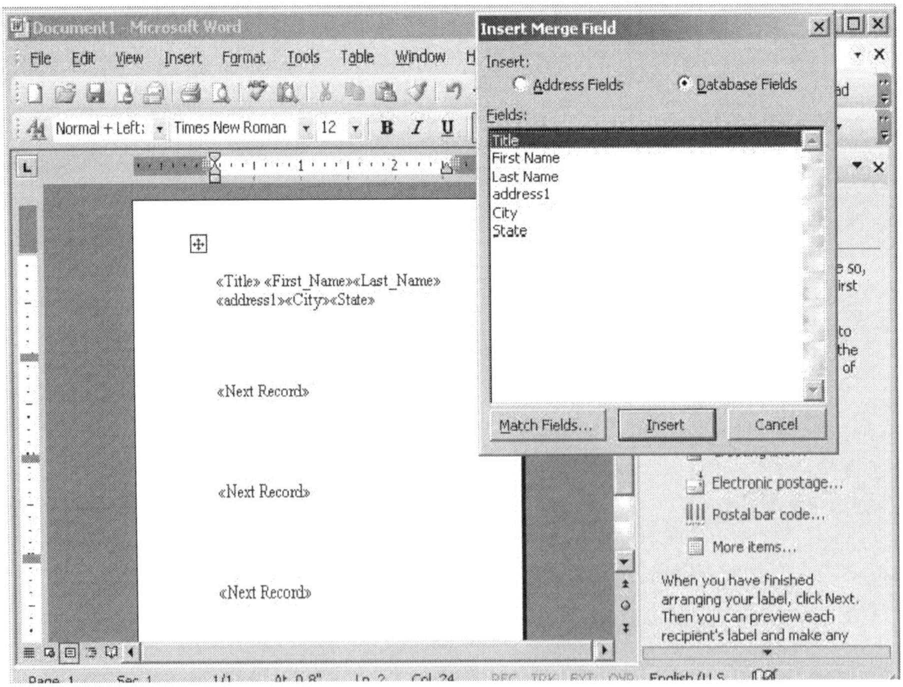

Figure 13.16 : Create Labels dialog box

- Choose Next : Preview your labels.
- Click Next : Complete the merge. To print labels click on 'Print..' hyperlink.

Summary

- Mail merge allows you to generate multiple copies of a base document incorporating some variable information such that each copy appears to the recipient as an original document.
- In the mail-merge process, two main documents are used by Word: a main document and a data source document.
- The main document contains the text and graphics that should be in every copy.
- The variable information in each copy is stored in the data source document.
- Some specific records can be merged as per the requirement.
- Records can be sorted based on some criterion, before printing the merged document.
- Using mail-merge, it is also possible to create and print envelops and mailing labels.

Review Exercise

Multiple choice questions

1. Which of the following options is not available in Mail Merge toolbar?

    a) Check for Errors

    b) Merge to Printer

    c) Edit Data Source

    d) Edit Main Document

2. Select the most appropriate method used to merge selected records.

    a) Tools >> Mail Merge >> Query

    b) Tools >> Merge Query

    c) Tools >> Mail Merge >> Filter

    d) None of the above

3. Identify the incorrect statement.
   a) Using Mail Merge, it is possible to create and print envelopes and mailing labels.
   b) Word uses three main documents in the Mail Merge process.
   c) Catalogs and lists can also be created using Mail Merge.
   d) None of the above
4. The Restore button on the Data Form dialog box
   a) Deletes a record.
   b) Brings the entries to their previous state.
   c) Saves a record.
   d) None of the above.
5. 'Check For Errors' option is available under
   a) Mail Merge
   b) Database
   c) Both of the above
   d) None of the above

State whether true or false

1. Merge printing is used to generate multiple copies of the same document with personalized information on each copy.
2. Mail merge feature of Word can be used to create greeting cards containing text and pictures.
3. Data source contains the information that is to be sent to all the recipients.
4. If errors occur during the mail-merge process, there is no way to correct those errors.
5. Specific records of data source can be combined during the merge process.

Fill in the blanks

1. Merge printing takes the data from a ___________ and inserts it into a ___________ where specified by ___________.
2. The words enclosed in << and >> in the main document are called ___________.

3. ____________ button in mail-merge toolbar is used to insert a merge field into the main document.
4. ____________ button of mail-merge toolbar is used to print merged documents.
5. ____________ tab of Query Options dialog box allows to print merged document in sorted order of records.

Descriptive questions

1. What do you understand by mail merge?
2. What are the various buttons available on the mail-merge toolbar?
3. Is it possible to check errors that may have occurred during the mail-merge process. If yes, how?
4. How will you merge specific records of data source?
5. Briefly explain the process of preparing and printing mailing labels.

C H A P T E R

14 WORKING WITH WIZARDS AND TEMPLATES

FEATURING

- **Word's Wizards**
- **Introducing Templates**
- **Handling Graphics**

Word cannot create documents by doing your writing for you but it does give you a variety of tools that can save you the trouble of formatting generic documents such as letters, memos, reports and other similar documents. There is no use worrying about setting margins, where to put the text, or what typeface to use. Users just need to click and type — Word does the real work. Word has a helpful feature called Wizard which can be used to quickly create almost any kind of document such as a letter, memo, report, and fax-cover sheet. Wizards are computerized assistants that help in creating the required document after asking some questions and making a few design decisions on their own. Word has another helpful feature called Template. Templates are read only documents containing styles and other design elements that you can use to create or restyle your own documents. A template provides a pattern for shaping a document. It contains boilerplate text, styles, and glossary items. It enables you to create a new document based on the special text and formatting elements that the template provides. In this chapter you will learn how to work with wizards and templates.

Word's Wizards

Wizards are easy-to-use programs that the Word supplies to enable the user to create documents by answering a series of questions. The extension of Wizard file is .WIZ. To choose Wizards for different types of documents, choose File >> New, in new document task pane in template heading click on "On my computer" hyperlink, Word displays a template dialog box as shown in Figure 14.1.

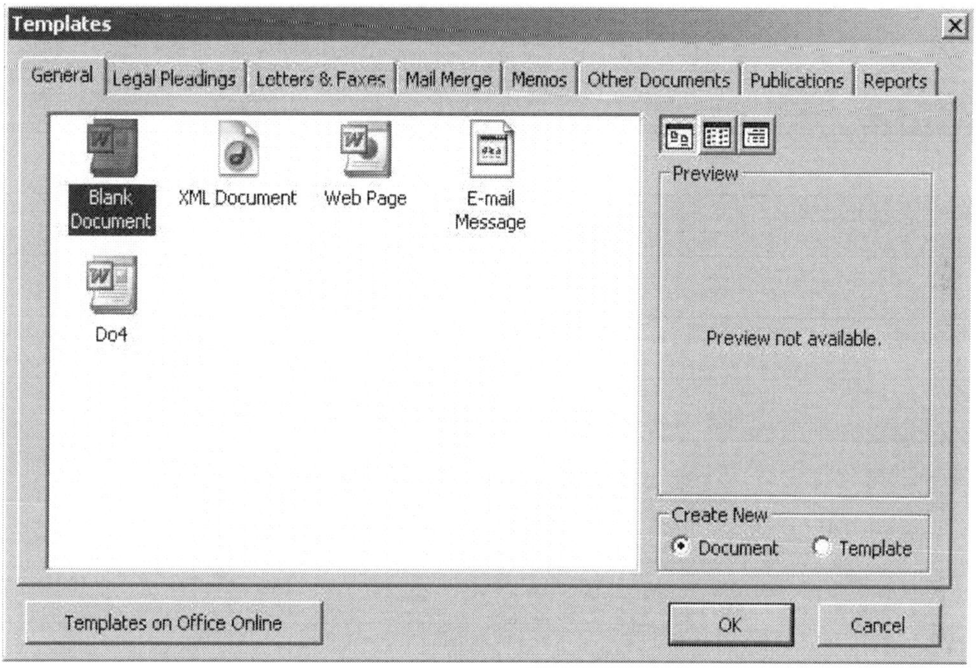

Figure 14.1 : Template dialog box

Using a Letter Wizard

All Word's wizards are used in much the same way. This section explains how to use the **Letter Wizard** to create a letter based on various page designs and styles.

To create the letter using wizard:

- Choose **Letters and Faxes** tab of Templates dialog box.
- Choose **Letter wizard.** Letter wizard dialog box appears as shown in Figure 14.2.

Figure 14.2 : Letter Wizard dialog box

- Choose Send one letter option. Click OK. Step 1 of Letter wizard open as shown in Figure 14.3.

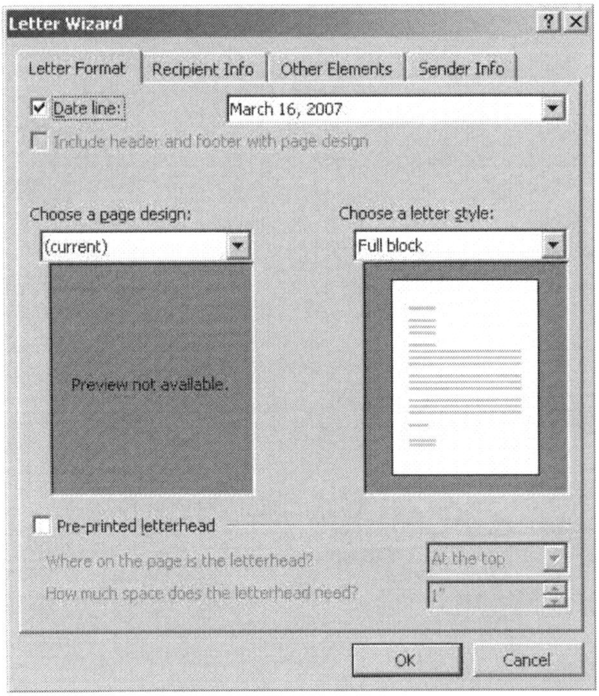

Figure 14.3 : Letter Wizard dialog box with Letter Format tab active

- The tabs that appear in Step 1 of Letter Wizard are: **Letter Format**, **Recipient Info**, **Other Elements**, and **Sender Info**.
- Choose the **Recipient Info** tab and specify the required details about the recipient.

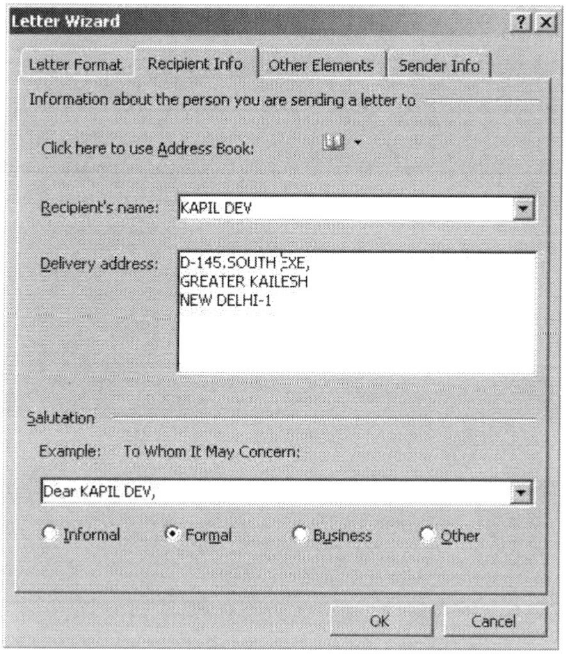

Figure 14.4 : Recipient Info Tab

- The **Sender Info** tab contains Sender's name, return address and other options.
- Click on **Finish** button, the word displays your letter as shown in Figure 14.5.

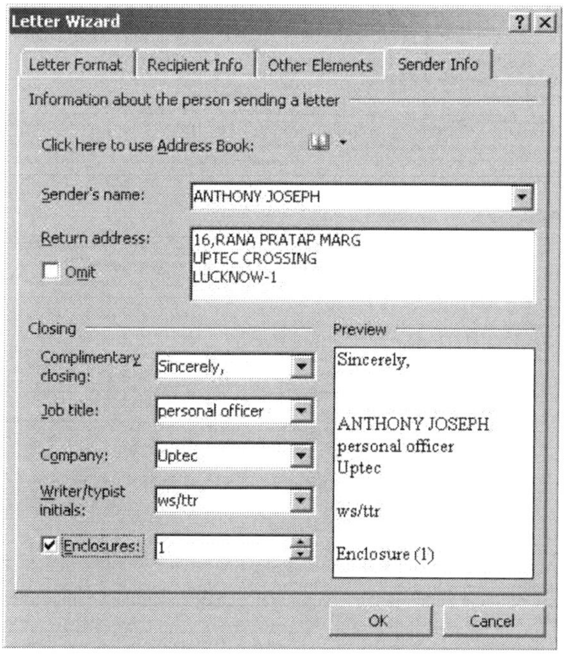

Figure 14.5 : Sender Info Tab

At any point, choose **Finish**, and Word displays the letter as shown in Figure 14.6.

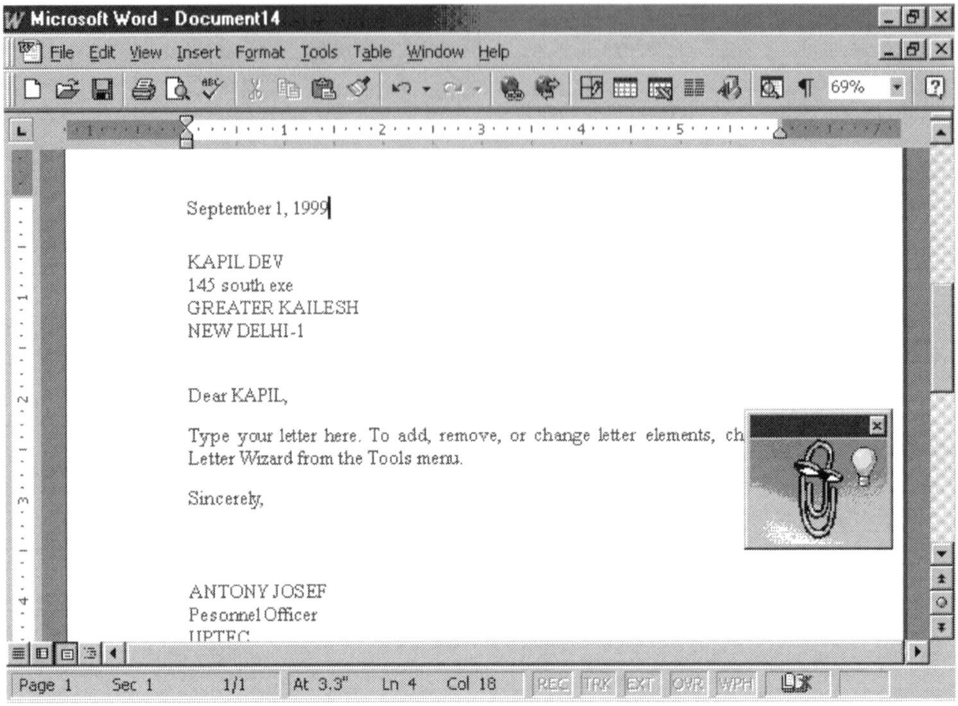

Figure 14.6 : A document letter created using the Letter Wizard

Introducing Templates

Every Word document is based on a **template**. Template is like a framework boilerplate or master pattern that defines a document's appearance and may define some of its contents. Word has numerous templates, each suitable for a specific type of document. The users can modify any of the supplied templates, including the Normal template, and can create their own templates.

What a Template Contains

A template can contain many components. The following explains each possible component of a template.

- **Layout information** includes character formatting, paragraph formatting, and section and page formatting. It also includes styles.
- **Boilerplate text** in a template appears in every document based on that template. A template used for letters, for example, may include the return address as boilertext. It can also include boilerplate graphics, such as a company's logo.

- **Field codes** represents certain kinds of data. For example, the current date.
- **AutoText** entries while typing or editing a document can be accessed in the template on which that document is based.
- A template can contain **macros** that are available to all documents based on that template.
- Custom command setting simplifies working with Word. User can place the custom features in specific templates.

Using a Sample Document to Preview a Template

Suppose the user is about to write a letter and is thinking of using one of the letter templates supplied by Word. To see how the letter will look, access the Style Gallery dialog box, as described in the following steps:

- Choose **Format >> Theme >> Style Gallery** to display the Style Gallery dialog box as shown in Figure 14.7.
- In the **Template** list box, choose the template to view.
- Choose Example, in the **Preview** section at the bottom left, corner of the dialog box.
- Choose OK.

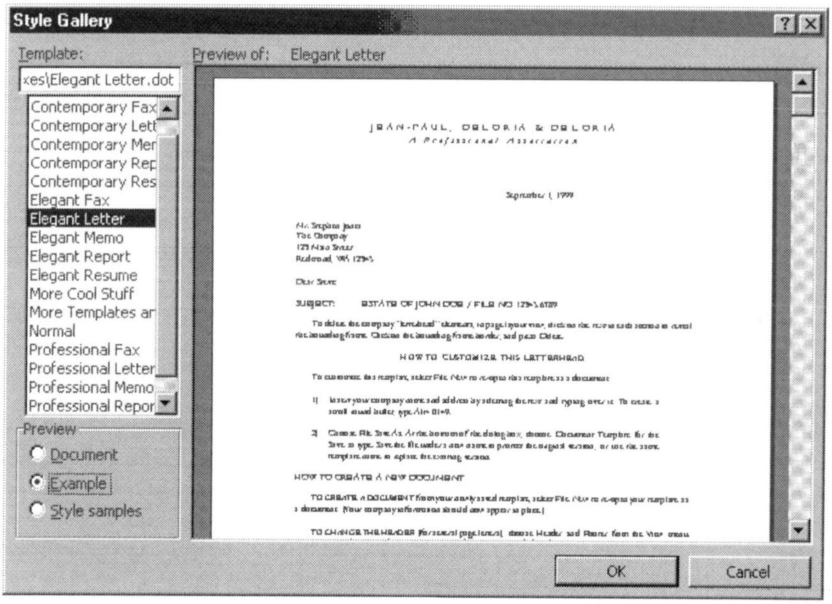

Figure 14.7 : Style Gallery dialog box

Creating a New Document Based on a Template

As mentioned earlier, all Word documents are based on a template. By default, each document is based on the Normal template. To create a document based on any template (other than Normal):

- Choose **File >> New** to open New document task pane
- Choose to search for a template on your computer, on Microsoft's website or some other site.
- Choose a template of your choice from the templates dialog box. A sample appears in preview to help you choose. (refer Figure 14.8).
- Click OK.

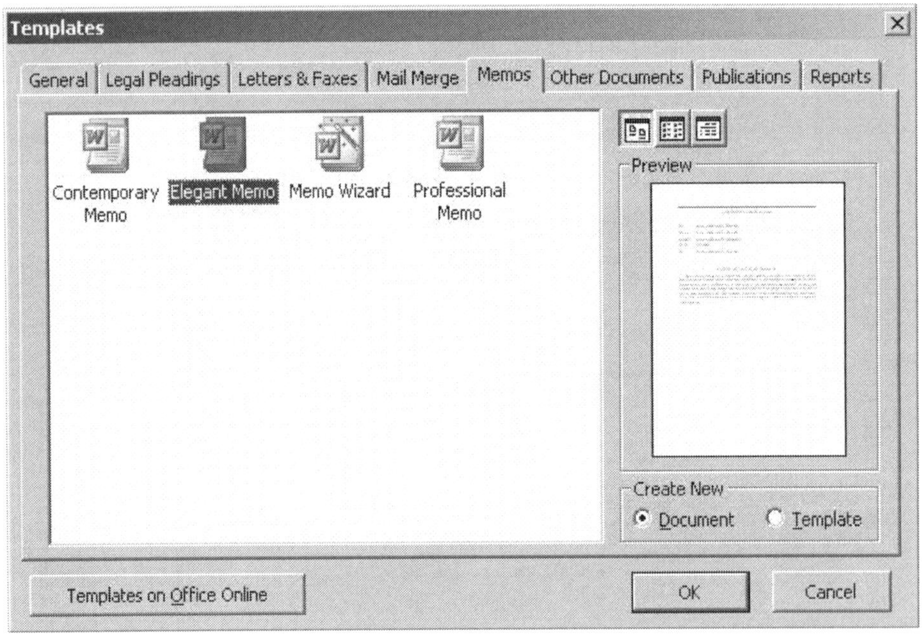

Figure 14.8 : New dialog box

Figure 14.9 shows an example of a new document based on the **Elegant Letter** template under memo tab.

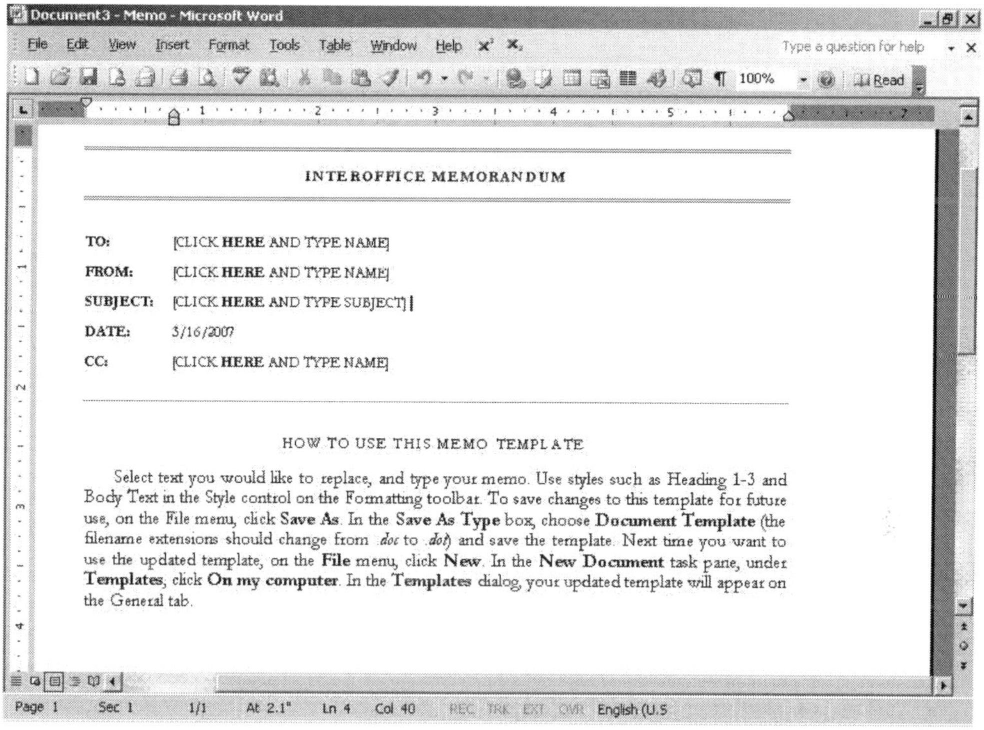

Figure 14.9 : An example of a New Document based on the Elegant Letter Template

Creating a Template

User-defined templates can be created by modifying an existing template or by converting document to a template.

Suppose the user likes the general style of the **Contemporary Letter** template but would prefer to have Word graphic appear at the top of the page. The user can easily modify the supplied template, and save the modified version for future use. To create a template by using an existing template, begin by opening the existing template as explained in the following steps:

- Choose **File >> Open** to display Open dialog box.
- In the **Files of type** list box, choose Document Templates.
- In the **Look in** list box, choose the folder that contains the template files. Figure 14.10 shows the 1033 folder.

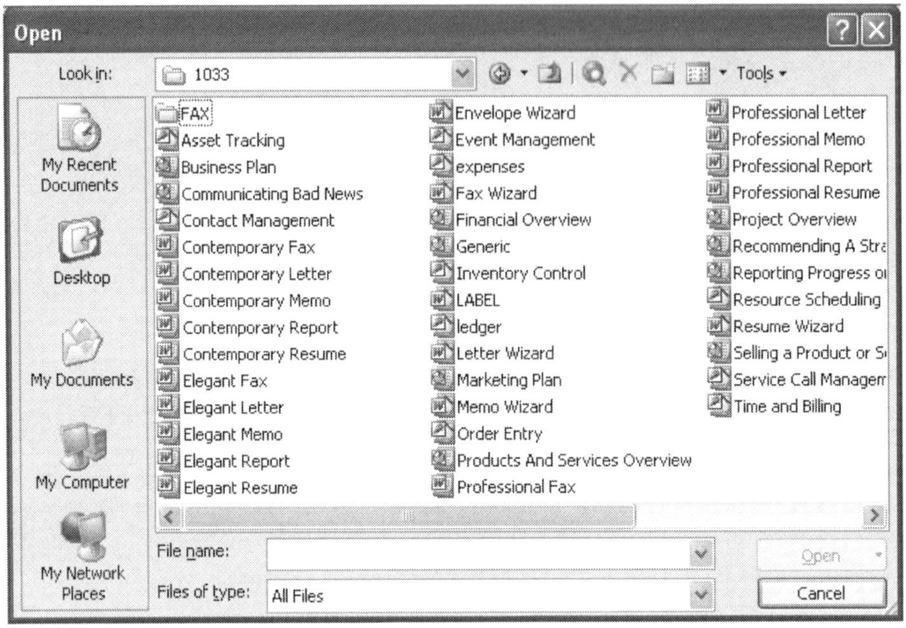

Figure 14.10 : 1033 folder in the Open dialog box

- Double-click the icon for the template to modify. For example, open the **Contemporary Fax**.
- Choose OK.

Saving a Modified Template

To save a modified template with a new name:

- Choose **File >> Save As**.
- Change the folder where the user wants to save the template. Type a name for the new template.
- Choose OK.
- Choose **File >> Close** to close the template.

Using a Document to Create a Template

Instead of creating a new template by modifying an existing one, you can create a template from a document. To create a template based on a document:

- Choose **File >> New.**

- Choose on my computer in the **Templates Option**. The templates dialog box will open.
- Choose General Tab >> Blank document.
- Check the template button on the lower right hand corner as shown in Figure 14.11.

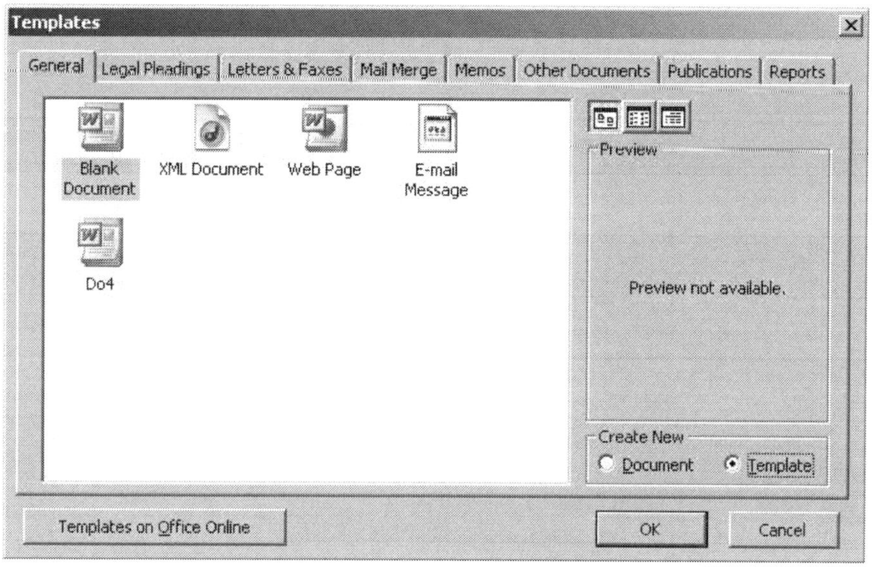

Figure 14.11 : Save As dialog box

- Click OK.
- Add styles, text, graphics, toolbars etc. to include in new template.
- Choose **File >> Save**.

Attaching a Different Template to a Document

After a document has been created, it remains attached to its original template until a different one is attached. The user may want to change the template attached to a document to modify the document's appearance. To attach a template to a document based on a different template:

- Open the document to which the user wants to attach a different template.
- Choose **Tools >> Templates and Add-ins** to display the Templates and Add-ins dialog box as shown in Figure 14.12.

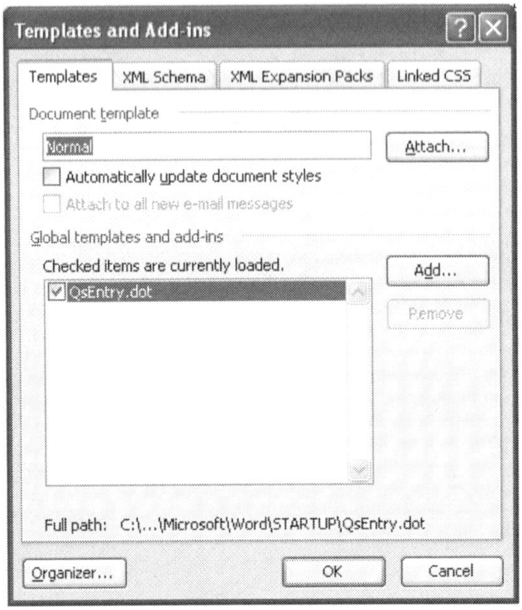

Figure 14.12 : Templates and Add-ins dialog box

- Enable the **Automatically update document styles** check box.
- Choose the **Attach** button to display the Attach Template dialog box, which lists the available templates.
- Choose the name of the template that the user wants to attach to the document.
- Choose OK.

Handling Graphics

Adding graphics or pictures to illustrate the documents and make them more appealing. Graphics format are available under two categories: **bitmap** and **vector**. Bitmap graphics are composed of small dots, called **pixels**. Each pixel is represented by one or more bits in the computer's memory that define color and intensity. Vector graphics, in contrast, comprise of a set of drawing instructions that describe the dimension and shape of every line, circle, arc, or rectangle.

Inserting Pictures in Documents

A picture can be inserted in a Word document in one of the following three ways:

- Use the **Insert >> Picture** command and choose either the **Clip Art** or **From File** submenu.
- Use the **Insert** >> **Object** command to insert a picture that the user plans to link to a graphics program.

- Open the program used to create picture, and copy (or cut) a picture to the Windows clipboard. Then use the **Edit >> Paste** command to paste it into a Word document.

Inserting Clip Art and Pictures

Choose **Insert >> Picture >> Clip Art**, Microsoft Clip taskpane appears with search options as shown in Figure 14.13.

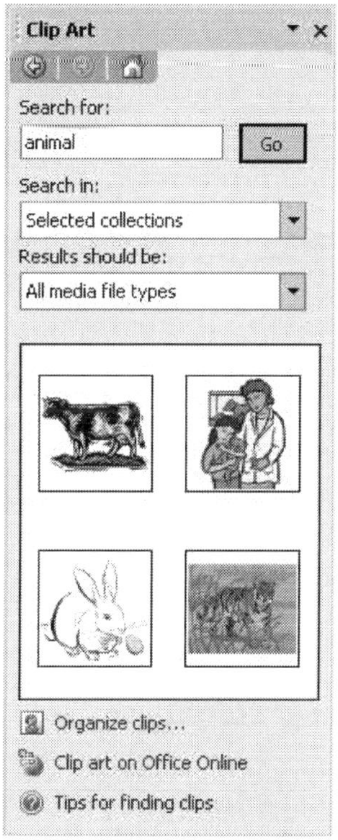

Figure 14.13 : Microsoft Clip Gallery 3.0 with ClipArt tab active

- In the search box enter key words to search.
- Specify the search location in the **Search in** dropdown box.
- In the **Result should be** drop down box specify clipart.
- Left click on the picture to insert it.
- To insert a picture from a file into document:
    - Position the insertion point where the picture will be inserted.
    - Choose **Insert >> Picture >> From File**.
    - From the File Name list, select the picture file that is to be inserted.
    - Choose **Insert**.

Linking Graphics

If the user is using a graphic created in another Word-compatible program, then the **Link to file** option can be chosen in the Insert Picture dialog box or in the **Create from File** tab in the Object dialog box. To link picture file to a Word document:

- Position the insertion point where the picture will appear.
- Choose **Insert >> Picture >> From File** and select the picture file to insert.
- Choose the picture.
- Click on the **Insert** button.

If the user moves or edit the original picture file, the link can be updated by positioning the insertion point on the picture placeholder & pressing F9.

Drawing in Word

Word's drawing features are built directly into Word. Using Word, the user can create vector images, called "objects". A Word drawing can comprise many objects, such as lines and circles. These objects drawn by the user, appear directly on the page. These can then be moved anywhere on the page.

Using the Drawing Toolbar

- In Word, a drawing can be created using the **Drawing** toolbar.
- Click the Drawing button on the Standard toolbar.
- Figure 14.14 shows a floating drawing toolbar.

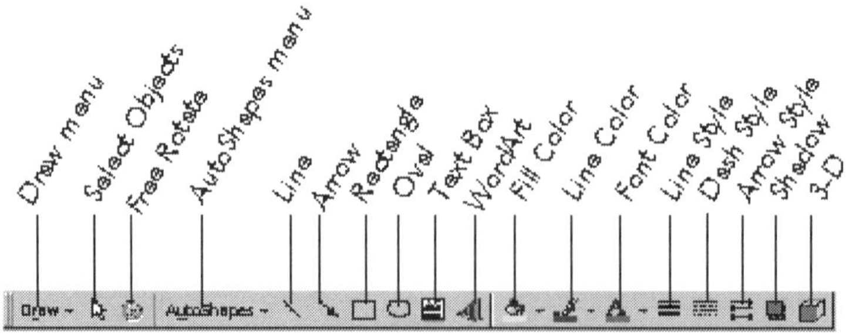

Figure 14.14 : Floating Drawing Toolbar

Summary

- Wizards are easy to use programs supplied with Word that enable the user to create documents by answering a series of questions.
- A wizard creates a formatted document for the user and prompts to include items the user may otherwise forget.

- Using a Letter wizard, it is possible to create a letter by providing the recipient's name, delivery address, sender's name, and return address.
- Template is like a framework boilerplate or master pattern that defines a document's appearance and may define some of its contents.
- Components of a local template affect only those documents which are based on that template while components of global template affect other documents also.
- Word permits to add graphics or pictures to illustrate your documents.
- It is possible to insert pictures in your document and also resize and crop them.
- Users can create their own drawing by using various drawing buttons on the Drawing toolbar.

Review Exercise

Multiple choice questions

1. Choose the most appropriate method for creating a letter using a wizard
   a) Tools >> Letters and Mailing >> Letter wizard
   b) Tools >> Letters and Faxes >> Letter wizard
   c) Tools >> Faxes >> Letter wizard
   d) None of the above
2. Which one of the following is not a category of the standard template?
   a) Contemporary
   b) Elegant
   c) Professional
   d) None of the above
3. The Normal template is
   a) Local
   b) Global
   c) Both of the above
   d) None of the above
4. Templates can store
   a) AutoText entries
   b) Toolbars

c) Macros

d) All of the above

5. The extension of a wizard file is

a) .wiz

b) .wizard

c) .wizards

d) None of the above

State whether true or false

1. Templates are used to create different types of document formats.
2. A template can save macros.
3. Wizards guide you through detailed procedures in a step by step manner.
4. The components of global template affect only those documents which are based on that template.
5. Pictures can be inserted in your document but you cannot change their size and location.

Fill in the blanks

1. The extension of wizard files is ___________.
2. While using a letter wizard, to check your address ___________ tab is to be selected in Options dialog box.
3. The text in a template that appears in every document based on that template is called ___________ text.
4. In a template, a certain kind of data, for example, current date is represented by ___________.
5. A ___________ template always has priority over a ___________ template.

Descriptive questions

1. What is the use of letter wizard? How do you use it?
2. What is a template? What does it contain?
3. What is the difference between Local and Global templates?
4. How will you create a template using another template?
5. How will you create a template using a document?

CHAPTER

15 CREATING TABLES AND HTML DOCUMENTS

FEATURING

- **Word Tables**
- **Creating Tables**
- **Modifying the Table Layout**
- **Sorting Table Data**
- **Calculating in a Table**
- **Creating a Web Page**
- **Converting an Existing Document to HTML**
- **Inserting Hyperlinks**
- **Previewing Web Page**

A table is a collection of rows and columns. By using tables, it is possible to arrange columns of figures, lists of information, and even paragraphs of different sizes placed side by side. Graphics can also be placed together with text in tables. Tables in Word are easy to create and modify, and it is possible to insert them anywhere in a Word document. The web authoring tools in Word allow you to create multimedia web pages. Word's web authoring tools are based on many of the same commands you use to create Word documents which makes it easy to create a web document. In this chapter you will learn how to create tables, and perform various operations on it. You will also learn how to create web pages in MS-Word.

Word Tables

A table gives the user an efficient, concise method to present a lot of related data in a document. Tables are grid-like structures, similar to spreadsheets, and consist of cells arranged in rows and columns. A **cell** is a box where a row and a column meet. A cell can contain text, numbers, or even an image. A user can create a new table structure and enter text, or can convert existing text to a table grid layout.

Creating Tables

If table is relatively simple, with evenly spaced rows and columns, it is easy to use the **Insert Table** button on the Standard toolbar.

- Position the insertion point where the table is to be inserted.
- Choose the **Insert Table** button on the Standard toolbar (refer Figure 15.1).

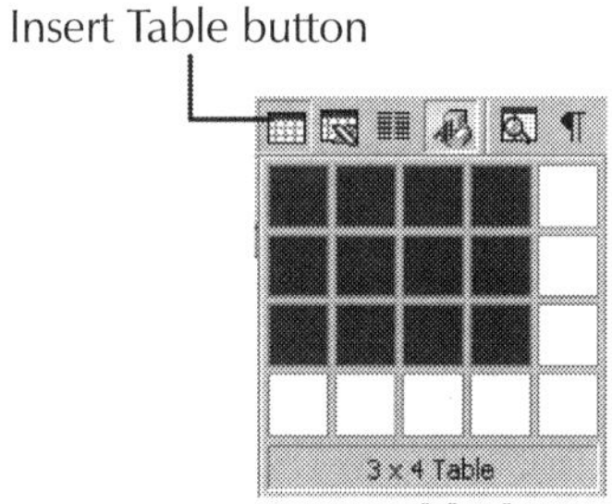

Figure 15.1 : Insert Table button

- Drag over to the number of columns and rows, release the mouse button to have Word insert the table.
- Alternatively, choose **Table >> Insert >> Table** to display the Insert Table dialog box as shown as in Figure 15.2.

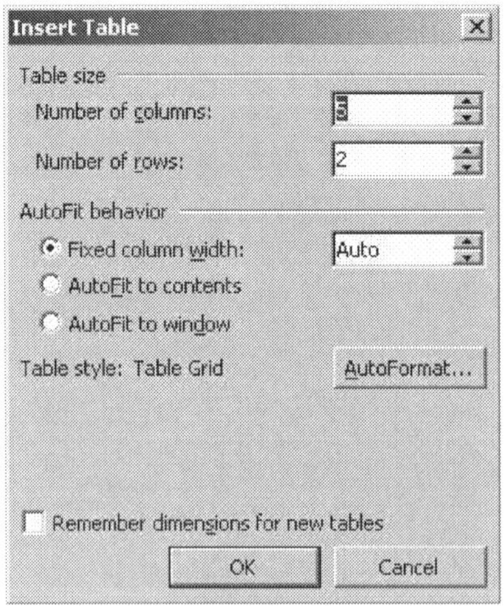

Figure 15.2 : Insert Table dialog box

- Enter the number of rows and columns in the Insert Table dialog box (Figure 15.2), you can also select the autofit behaviors.
- Click **OK**.

To create a non-uniform table, use the new **Draw Table** feature of the Table menu.

- Choose **Table >> Draw Table** or click the **Tables and Borders** button on the Standard toolbar. The new Tables and Border floating toolbar appears (refer Figure 15.3). The mouse pointer also changes to a pencil icon.

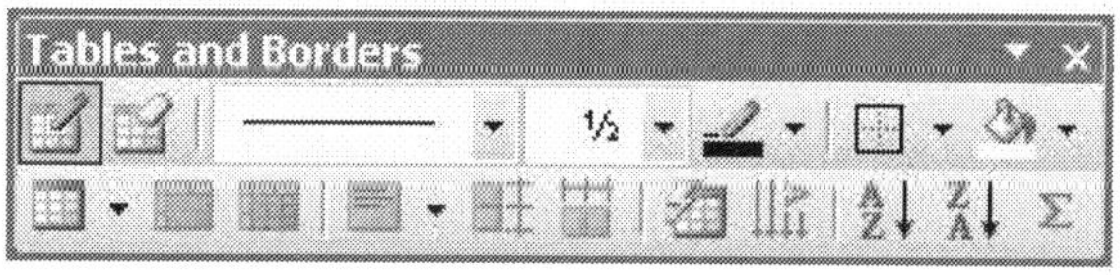

Figure 15.3 : Tables and Border floating toolbar

- Click in the document where the upper left corner of the table will appear, drag to the opposite corner and release the mouse button.
- Use the pencil to draw row and column gridlines in the table.
- Use the **Eraser** button on the Tables and Borders toolbar to remove a line.

NOTE When you are drawing a table you are automatically shifted to print layout or web layout view.

If you have text which are separated by comma or tab space you can convert it into a table like this:

- Type the text separated by paragraphs, commas, tabs or any other delimiter.
- Select the text you wish to appear in the table.
- Select Table >> Convert >> Text to Table.
- In the dialog box specify the delimiter you used in the text.
- Specify the number of columns in the table. Word will automatically determine the number of rows.
- Click OK.

Modifying the Table Layout

Modifying a table layout means altering the structure of the table including copying, moving, inserting, and deleting rows, columns, and cells.

Inserting Cells, Rows and Columns

To add cells to a table:

- Select a cell or cells adjacent to where the new cell or cells are required .
- Choose **Table >> Insert >> Cells**. This displays the Figure 15.4.

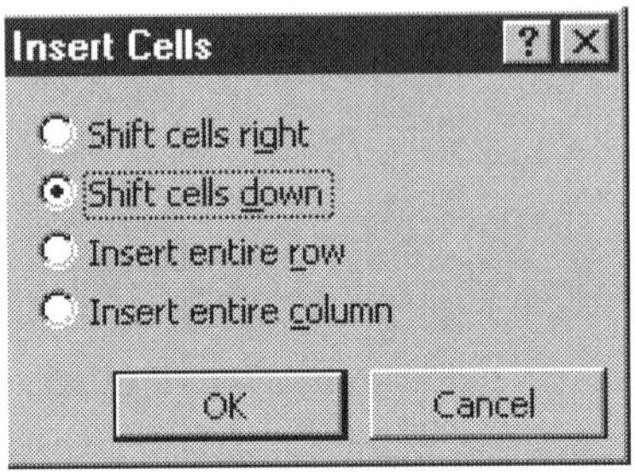

Figure 15.4 : Insert Cells dialog box

- Make the appropriate choice. Choose OK.

To insert rows and columns:

- Select the row or rows below where the user want the new row or rows to be inserted.
- Choose the **Insert Rows** button or choose **Table >> Insert Rows**.

Word inserts the new column to the left of the selected column. To insert columns in a table:

- Select the column or columns to the right of where you want the new column or columns are to be inserted.
- Choose the **Insert Column** button, or choose **Table >> Insert >> Column to the left** or **Column to the Right**.

Deleting Cells, Rows, and Columns

- To delete the contents of a cell, select the contents that the user wants to delete and press the Del key.
- To delete a cell, select the cell to be deleted and choose **Table >> Delete >> Cells** to display the **Delete Cells** dialog box (refer Figure 15.5).

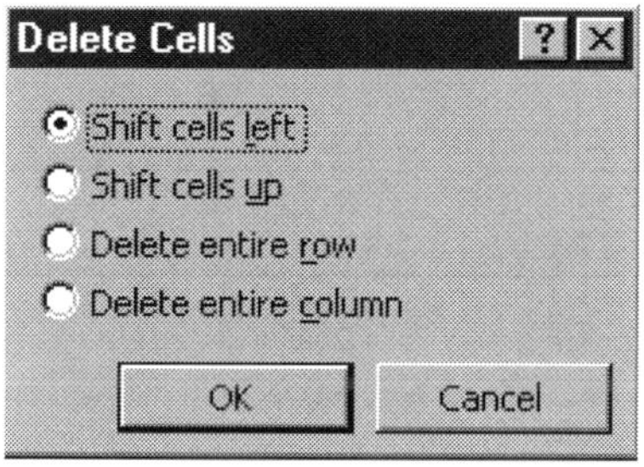

Figure 15.5 : Delete Cells dialog box

- To delete row(s) and column(s), select the row(s) or column(s) the user want to delete and then, use any of the following options:
  - Choose **Table >> Delete >> Rows** (or **Columns**).
  - Choose **Edit >> Cut**.
- To delete an entire table, select all rows and columns, and then choose **Table >> Delete Rows** (or **Delete Columns**).

Merging and Splitting Cells

Headings can be created using columns by merging several cells into one wide cell. Merging cells refers to merging adjacent cells in a row or rows. Splitting cells refers to dividing the selected cells horizontally. To split and merge cells:

- Select the cells you want to split or merge.
- To merge the selected cells, choose **Table >> Merge Cells** or click the **Merge Cells** button on the Tables and Borders toolbar.

To split the selected cells, choose **Table >> Split Cells** or click the **Split Cells** button, a Split Cells dialog box appears (refer Figure 15.6).

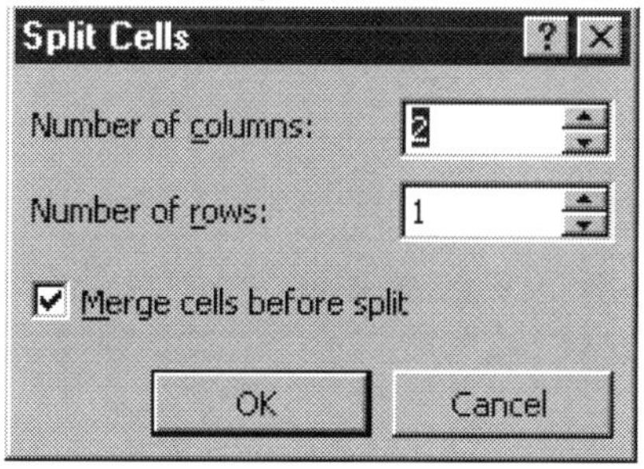

Figure 15.6 : Split Cells dialog box

Specify the number of columns or number of rows that need to be split in the document and choose OK.

Borders and Shading

The gridlines that appear on the screen while creating a table are used only to design and cannot be printed. However, the user can print borders for the whole table or for selected cells in a table. The user can also shade selected cells in a table. To quickly apply preset border and shading formats to a table, use the AutoFormat feature.

To apply custom border and shading formatting, choose **Format >> Borders and Shading**. (for more details refer chapter 17).

When **AutoFormat** is used, the selection applies to the entire table. To use the AutoFormat feature:

- Position the insertion pointer inside the table.
- Choose **Table >> Table AutoFormat** to display the **Table AutoFormat** dialog box (refer Figure 15.7).
- After specifying all options, choose OK.

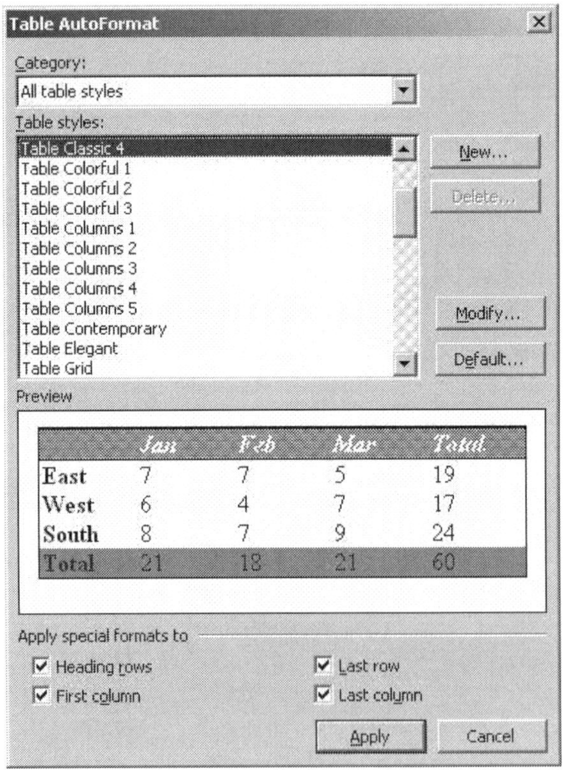

Figure 15.7 : Table AutoFormat dialog box

Sorting Table Data

Word enables the user to sort up to three columns at a time. When the user sorts the information in a table, Word arranges the rows according to the criteria set by the user. To sort rows:

- Select the rows for sorting, if the user is sorting only part of the table.
- Choose **Table >> Sort** to open the Sort dialog box (refer Figure 15.8).

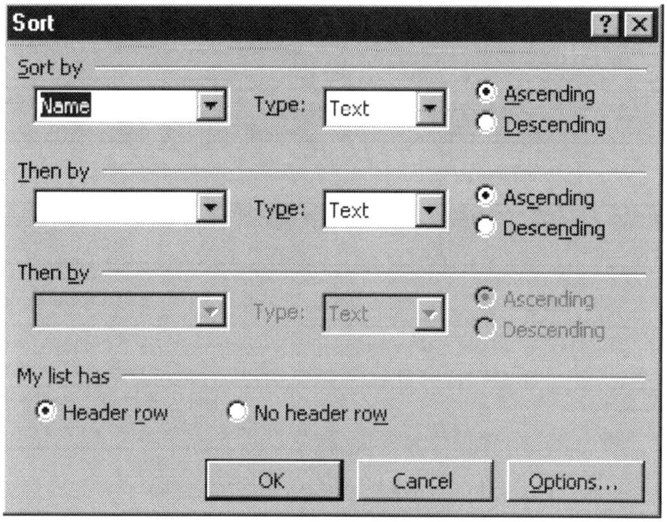

Figure 15.8 : Sort dialog box

- Select the first column from the drop-down list, in the first **Sort by** box.
- Check header row option to display the column header.
- Under **Type** drop-down list select Number, Text, or Date.
- Select Ascending or Descending order option for the sort.
- For more complex sort, repeat the previous three steps, by using the **Then by** boxes.
- Choose OK.

Calculating in a Table

Word's **Table >> Formula** command will add, multiply, and divide numbers that are typed in the document. It is perfect for creating simple financial reports or for proofreading columns of numbers.

To calculate in a table:

- Position the insertion pointer in the cell where the user want the answer to appear.

- Choose **Table >> Formula** to open the Formula dialog box as shown in Figure 15.9.

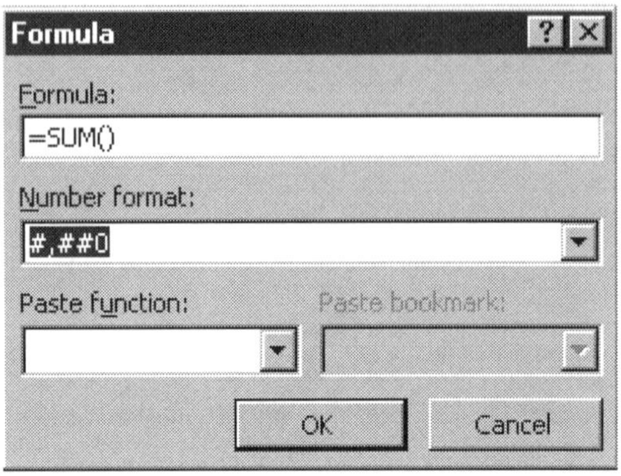

Figure 15.9 : Formula dialog box

- Select formula from the **Paste function** box, or enter custom formula in **Formula** box.
- Select a number format if required, from the **Number format** list box.
- Choose OK.

Figure 15.10 is an example of Word table with possible table options like formatting, splitting cells, calculating in a table and borders and shading.

THE TIME - SHARE OPTIONS							
	Destinations						
Name	Operational	Proposed	Locations	Seasons	Period	Size	Membership
Resort Club	1	None	Gurgoan	3	33	Studio 1Room 2Room	5000.50 6000.00 8000.00
Mahindra Holidays	6	2	Mussouri Goa, Ooty Shimla	3	33	Studio 1Room 2Room	53000.00 600.00 250000.00
Sterling	15	6	Chail, Goa, Lucknow, Panchgani	3	99	Studio 1Room 2Room	10000.00 5000.00 400000.00
Royal Goan	1	1	Goa	3	Forever	Studio 1Room 2Room	100000.00 300000.00 600000.00
TOTALS							1737600.5

Figure 15.10 : Example of a Word Table

Creating a Web Page

Word allows user to create web pages with the help of the web page template.

To create a web page:

- Choose File >> New.
- In the New Document task pane, click on My computer under templates (refer Figure 15.11).
- On the general tab, double-click the web page template.
- The user can then build the web page using word's tools.
- Choose File >> Save to save the document. The document is saved as an html document with .html extension.

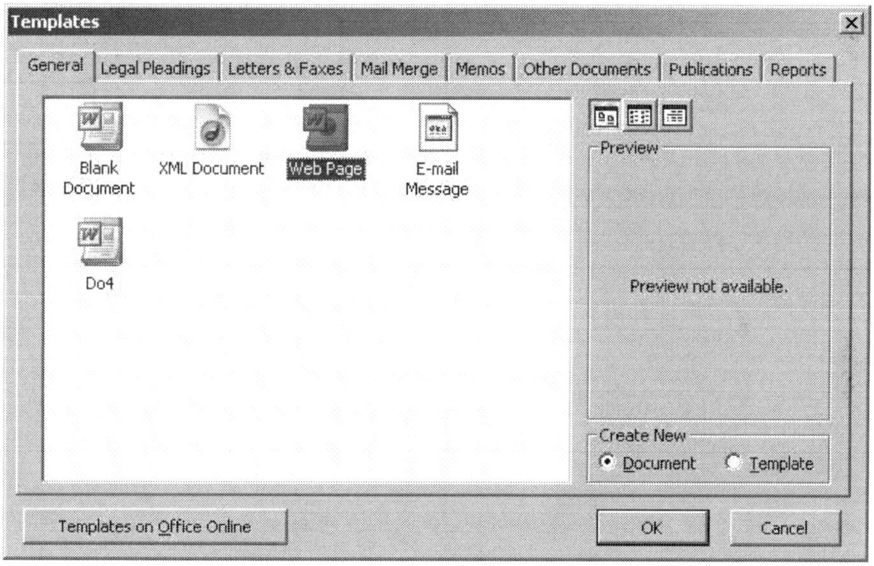

Figure 15.11 : New dialog box

Converting an Existing Document to HTML

Word's conversion filters make the work of turning other document formats to web pages easier. The user can create a web page by saving an existing Word document in HTML format. However, some aspects of the document may not be available in HTML and, therefore, may not appear correctly. Formatting and other items that are not supported by HTML are removed from the file. Word's HTML conversion filter takes care of the following tasks:

- It changes the filename extension to .html (so, for example, if you convert a file called report.doc into a web page, Word names the resulting file report.html).
- It converts the document into a web page, applying the HTML formatting effects that most closely resemble the styles used in the document.
- It converts embedded graphics and objects into GIF images and saves copies of the graphic files in the same folder as the new web page.
- It makes web page authoring toolbars, styles and menu commands available.
- It saves the new page in the same directory as the original file.

To convert a document into a web page, follow these steps :

- Open the document.
- Choose File >> Save As Web Page.
- In the Save As dialog box, click OK.
- A Microsoft Word dialog box appears with a warning about information and formatting loss when the user converts a Word document to HTML. To proceed with the conversion process, click on Yes.

Inserting Hyperlinks

Hyperlinks are the bits of text or images within each web page that, when clicked on, jump to another location. It is also used to jump to multimedia files, such as sound files or video clips. To insert a hyperlink, do the following:

- In a previously saved web page, position the insertion pointer where the user wants the hyperlink or select the text or object you want as a hyperlink.
- Press **Ctrl + K**, or click the **Insert Hyperlink** button and the Insert Hyperlink dialog box will appear (refer Figure 15.12).
- Under the Link to, click existing file or web page.
- In the Address box, type the address to which you want to link or, click the down arrow in the look in box and navigate to and select the file.
- In case you are working with frame pages specify the Target Frame.

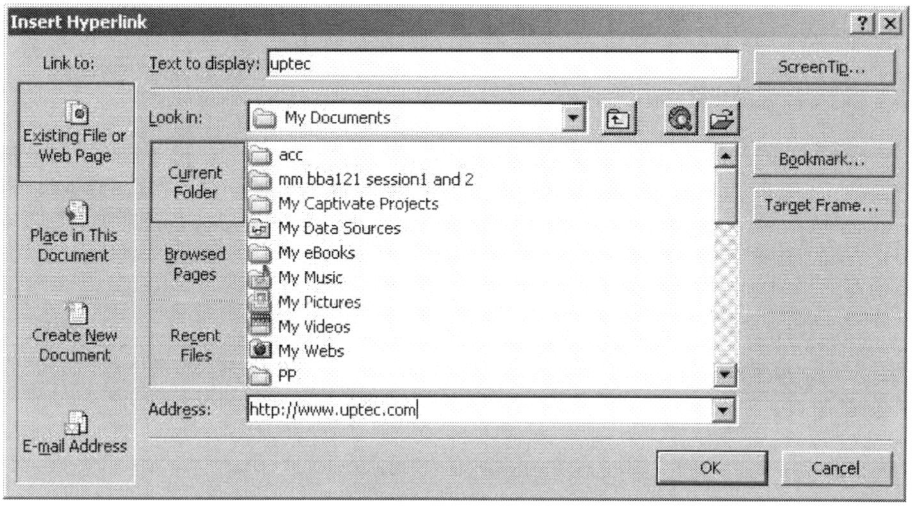

Figure 15.12 : Insert Hyperlink dialog box

Previewing Web Page

While the Web page in Word's authoring environment looks a lot like the finished Web page as a user would view it, but it is not. Choose **File >> Web Page Preview** or click the **Web Page Preview** button on the Standard toolbar to display the web document in the Internet Explorer web browser.

Summary

- Tables are grid-like structures and consist of cells arranged in rows and columns.
- A table gives the user an efficient, concise way to present related data in a document.
- It is possible to insert, delete, move and copy cells, rows and columns.
- There is a provision to create table headings and apply borders and shading to the tables.
- Tables can be sorted based on the contents of their columns. It is also possible to number the cells of a table.
- Hyperlink is a piece of text or images within each web page which moves you to another location whenever they are clicked.

Review Exercise

Multiple choice questions

1. Which of the following keys should be pressed to select multiple cells in a table?

   a) Shift
   b) Ctrl
   c) Alt
   d) None of the above

2. Which of the following ways can be used to create a new table?

   a) The Insert Table button on the Standard toolbar
   b) The Insert Table dialog box
   c) The Table and Borders toolbar
   d) All of the above

3. Which of the following keys should be held down while dragging the column, to see the exact column measurements in inches displayed on the ruler?

   a) Shift
   b) Ctrl
   c) Alt
   d) F7

4. Which of the following option is not available under the Table menu?

   a) Draw Table
   b) Rows
   c) Hide Gridlines
   d) Autofit

5. Shortcut key combination to insert a hyperlink is

   a) Ctrl + K
   b) Ctrl + H
   c) Ctrl + I
   d) None of the above

State whether true or false

1. Using Insert Table button on the Standard toolbar, 8 columns and 15 rows can be inserted.
2. It is possible to remove row and column gridlines in the table.
3. Deleting a cell will result in deleting the entire row and column containing that cell.
4. The extension of a web page is .doc.

Fill in the blanks

1. A ____________ is a box where a row and a column meet.
2. A Word table may have up to ____________ columns.
3. To split a table the shortcut key combination is ____________.
4. The extension of an HTML document is ____________.
5. Hypertext is text that is specially coded using a standard system called ____________.

Descriptive questions

1. What do you mean by splitting cells and merging cells?
2. How will you sort a table using three columns at a time?
3. How can you convert text to a table? Write steps.
4. What are the tasks performed by HTML conversion filter while converting an existing document to HTML document?
5. How will you insert hyperlinks into a document?

CHAPTER 16

MICROSOFT EXCEL BASICS

FEATURING

- Introduction to Excel 2003
- Starting Excel
- Excel's Parts
- Navigating through Cells
- Essential Workbook File Operations
- Workspace Files
- Types of Worksheet Data
- Entering Data into a Cell
- Editing a Worksheet
- Selecting Cells, Rows and Columns
- Copying and Moving Cells
- Deleting Cells, Rows and Columns
- Inserting Cells, Rows and Columns
- Changing Column Widths
- Changing Row Heights
- The Formatting Toolbar
- Number Formats
- Using AutoFormats
- Essential Spradsheet Operations
- Printing Your work

"Spreadsheet" *allows you to perform detailed analysis on numeric data. Spreadsheets, also known as* "worksheets", *display data in the form of rows and columns. With the help of spreadsheets, you can analyze data which involves performing statistical and mathematical calculations, presenting the data in the form of graphs, and relating tables of data from more than one source to generate a consolidated data set. Excel is a software product that falls into the spreadsheet category. Lotus 1-2-3, Quattro Pro, and Visicalc are other examples of spreadsheets. This chapter gives you an overview of Excel.*

Introduction to Excel 2003

'Excel' is a Window-based **'spreadsheet'**, created by **Microsoft Corporation**, US. It includes all the standard features of a **spreadsheet package** like automatic recalculation, graphs, and functions. It also includes several advanced utilities like the facility to include other objects within a spreadsheet and pivot tables and form designing.

Excel can be used for a variety of applications. It is mostly used to automate financial statements, business forecasts, inventory control, and accounting. The package spreadsheet provides statistical, financial and scientific functions. Therefore, Excel can be used in many scientific and engineering applications to analyze numeric data. Excel is currently the most popular Windows spreadsheet. This part of Microsoft Excel explains 2003 version.

Features

Excel is a feature-rich product that can be used at many different levels.

- **Multisheet files** Excel's files (called workbooks) can consist of any number of sheets. The sheets can be worksheets, chart sheets, macro sheets, or custom dialog boxes. The user's work becomes more organized with this feature.
- **Multiple document interface** This capability of Excel makes it easy to transfer information between worksheets in different workbooks.
- **File compatibility** Excel can read files created by other spreadsheet programs. It can also read and accept text files, dBASE files, and HTML documents.
- **Interactive help** While working in Excel, the user can get help on-screen. The help feature is available in the main menu of Excel. Excel's on-line help is excellent and extremely detailed.
- **List management** It is easier to sort, filter, summarize, and manipulate the data stored in the worksheet by using the list management feature.
- **Built-in functions** Excel includes an enormous collection of built-in mathematical and scientific functions.
- **Charts** The data written in figures can be displayed graphically using charts. Excel's charting features enable the user to modify and augment a wide assortment of graph types.
- **Integrated mapping** This feature allows the user to display the data in terms of a geographic map.
- **Pivot tables** Pivot tables help the user view the data in summarized table form.
- **Advanced analytical tools** Goal seeking, a powerful Solver feature, and the analysis ToolPak add-in features are the advanced analytical tools that provides extensive statistical, financial, engineering, and scientific functions and procedures.
- **Scenario management** Excel is often used for **what-if analysis**, that is, you can change one or more assumptions for calculations and observe the effects on dependent formulas.

- **Templates** Excel has a template wizard that walks the user through the steps required to create a custom template.
- **Internet support** Excel includes a variety of new features that make it easy to access, save document as HTML files and even create hyperlinks directly in spreadsheet documents.

Starting Excel

To invoke Excel choose any of the following three methods:

- Click the **Start** menu button and choose **Microsoft Excel 2003** from the **Programs** menu.
- Click the **Start** menu button, select the **Program** menu, Now choose **Microsoft Office** and then select **Microsoft Excel 2003**.
- Choose **Start >> Run**, enter the path and program name in the **Open** text box and then click the OK button to start Excel.

Excel can be started automatically whenever Windows starts, if Excel is placed (**Excel.exe** file) into **Startup** folder in the **Start** menu.

Excel's Parts

Various parts of Excel can be seen in Figure 16.1.

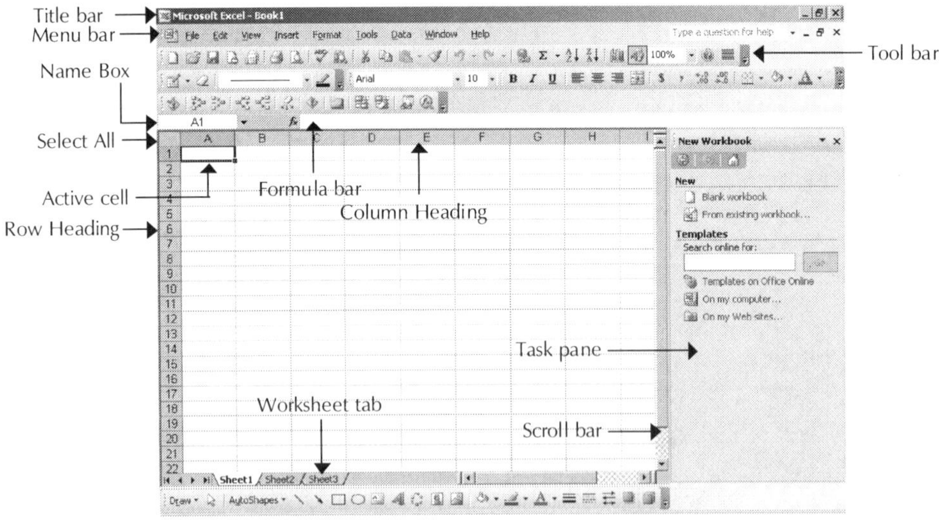

Figure 16.1 : Excel Screen Elements

- **The Title Bar** This identifies the name of the program (on the upper left corner of the window) and also holds some control buttons (on the upper right of the window) which can be used to modify the window.
- **Windows control menu buttons** There are three buttons which control the Excel's application window: minimize, restore, and close. The restore button itself may become the maximize button in case the application window is not on full screen.
- **Menu bar** One way of issuing Excel commands is through the Menu bar.
- **Toolbars** It holds buttons to issue commands when clicked. These buttons are shortcuts to the command present inside the menu items on the menu bar.
- **Formula bar** Information and formulas when entered into Excel, appear in this text area.
- **Name box** Displays the name of the active cell in the current workbook. It is also used to quickly assign a name to the selected range or cell.
- **Status bar** It is present at the bottom of the Excel window. It usually contains mode indicator button and keyboard mode buttons.

Parts of a Workbook Window

The user's work is stored in **workbooks**. Each workbook appears in a separate window within Excel's **workspace**. The major parts of a workbook window that can be seen in Figure 16.1 are:

- **Select All button** Clicking on the intersection of the row and column 'headers' selects all cells on the active **worksheet** of the active window.
- **Active Cell Indicator** The dark outline around a cell indicates the currently active cell.
- **Row Headings** Numbers ranging from **1 to 65,536** — one for each row in the worksheet are the row headings. 65,536 is the maximum number of rows possible in a worksheet.
- **Column Headings** Letters ranging from A to IV — one for each of the 256 possible columns in the worksheet.
- **Sheet Tabs** A workbook can have any number of sheets, and each sheet has its name displayed in a sheet tab.
- **Tab Scroll Buttons** These buttons help to scroll the sheet tabs to display tabs that are not visible.
- **Scroll Bars** The horizontal and vertical scroll bars help to scroll the **workarea**, i.e., the columns and rows respectively.

Navigating through Cells

Table 16.1 summarizes all the worksheet movement keys available in Excel.

Key	Action
Up arrow	Moves the active cell up one row.
Down arrow	Moves the active cell down one row.
Left arrow	Moves the active cell one column to the left.
Right arrow	Moves the active cell one column to the right.
PgUp	Moves the active cell up one screen.
PgDn	Moves the active cell down one screen.
Home	Moves the active cell to the beginning of row.
Ctrl + Home	Moves the active cell to cell A1.
End	Moves the active cell to the last cell in the current row.
Ctrl + End	Moves the active cell to lower-right corner of the worksheet.
End (with Scroll Lock on)	Moves active cell to the lower-right corner of the window.
Home (with Scroll Lock on)	Moves active cell to the upper-right corner of the window.

Table 16.1 : List of Movement Keys

Essential Workbook File Operations

Operations that can be performed with workbook files are: creating, opening, saving, closing and deleting.

Creating a New Workbook

When you start Excel, it automatically creates a new (empty) workbook called **Book1**. By default, this workbook consists of three worksheets — **Sheet1, Sheet2** and **Sheet3**. To create another new workbook can be used one of the following methods:

- Use the File >> New command.
- Press the Ctrl + N shortcut key combination.

If the first method is chosen, **New workbook task pane** appears as shown in Figure 16.2. Clicking on **Blank Workbook** icon, gives plain blank workbook. The second method bypass the **New** task pane box creates a new default blank workbook immediately.

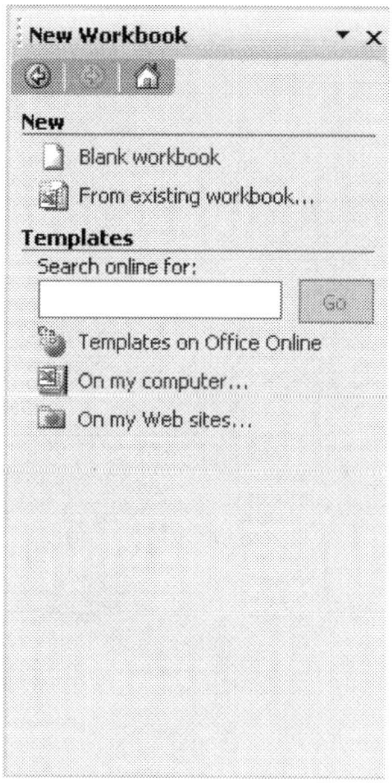

Figure 16.2 : New dialog box

Opening an Existing Workbook

To open a workbook that is already saved to disk, choose any of the following methods:

- Choose File >> Open.
- Press the Ctrl + O shortcut key combination.

The above methods result in the **Open** dialog box, Navigate to and select the desired file, Click on the open button.

Saving Workbooks

After entering the data in the worksheet we need to save the worksheet at the desired location in the computer system. To save a worksheet, perform the following steps:

- Select File > Save As to display the Save As dialog box.
- Select the location from the Save in list where the worksheet is to be saved.
- Enter the name of the file.
- Click the save button to save the file.

Excel automatically adds the file name extension .xls to the filename.

Closing Workbooks

To close an active workbook use one of the following methods:

- Use the File >> Close command.
- Click on the **Close** button in the workbook's title bar.
- Press the Ctrl + F4 shortcut key.

If you've made any changes to your workbook since it was last saved, Excel asks whether you want to save the workbook before closing it.

Deleting a Workbook

First of all, close the workbook that is to be deleted, because workbooks cannot be deleted from inside the Excel environment. Now in the Windows Explorer pane, select the workbook or workbooks to be deleted. Then delete by one of the following ways:

- Right click on the selected workbook and click on delete option.
- Press Del key.

Workspace Files

Workspace means all the workbooks and their screen positions and window sizes — kind of a snapshot of Excel's current state.

To save workspace, use the **File >> Save Workspace** command. Excel proposes the name resume.xlw for the workspace file. Using this name or entering a different name in the **filename** field, the workspace file can be opened. On opening, Excel is set up exactly as it was when the workspace was saved.

Types of Worksheet Data

A worksheet is made up of cells. A cell can hold any of the following three types of data:

Value

Values, written in numbers, represent a quantity of some type: sales, number of employees, test scores, and so on. Values that are entered into cells can be used in formulas or can serve as the data to create a chart. Values can also be dates (such as 7/31/99) or time (such as 11:25 am).

Text

Text can include any combination of letters, numbers, and keyboard symbols. A cell can contain up to 32,000 characters. Text is used to serve as

- labels for values
- headings for columns or
- to provide instruction about the worksheet.

Text that begins with a number (such as 16, Rana Pratap Marg) is also considered a text.

Formulas

Cells in a worksheet can also contain formulas that relate two or more cells. Formulas contain the operators, functions, coordinates of the cells that are used in the formula. The result of the formula appears in the cell in which the formula is written. If the values used by a formula are changed, the formula recalculates and shows new results. Formulas begin with an = sign. Without the = sign, the entry is treated as a text label.

For example, if the cell A10 contains the value 15 and the cell A20 contains the value 5, you can display the result after adding the contents of A10 and A20 in cell A25 by entering the following formula in A25

= A10 + A20

The value 20 is displayed in A25 itself as a result of the formula. Similarly, other mathematical operations can be performed on any two or more cells.

Entering Data into a Cell

To enter data into a cell, select the cell by clicking on it, type numbers, text, or a combination of both then press ↵ (or click on the green check mark that had appeared in the formula bar as you were typing).

Entering Values

Along with the numbers (0-9) the user can include, decimal points and dollar signs. Even the plus signs, minus signs, and commas are also allowed when entering values.

Entering Text

Activate the cell, type the text, and press Enter. If column width prevents a text string from fitting visually in a cell, the display extends over neighbouring cells. However, if the neighbouring cells are occupied, the display is truncated, i.e., the active cell shall contain all the text, even though it may not show and the user may need to scroll inside that cell.

Dates and Time

Excel handles *dates* using a serial number system. The earliest date that Excel understands is January 1, 1900, having a serial number of 1. User can also enter date in a familiar date format. For example, to enter Oct. 14, 1992, simply enter the date by typing Oct. 14, 1992, or 10/14/92 (or any of a number of different date formats).

Excel works with *time* by using fractional days. For example, the date serial number for June 1, 1997, is 35,582. Noon is represented internally as 35582.5. User can simply enter the time into a cell in a recognized format. For example, to enter time 11:30 am, simply type 11:30.

Data Entry Tips

- **Use Ctrl + Enter for repeated information** When multiple cells are required to contain the same data, select all the cells that should contain the data, enter the value, text, or formula, and then press Ctrl+Enter. The same entry will be inserted into each of the selected cells.
- **Use AutoFill feature** Excel uses the **AutoFill** handle to copy the cell or automatically complete a series. In several cases the need may be to write a series of values in contiguous cells. For example, writing the month names starting from January to December. The steps to create a numeric data series are:
  - Enter the first two values of data in adjacent cells. The first two data values determine the increment value and the starting number for the series. For example, in Figure 16.3, the starting value is 10 and the increment value is 1.
  - Select cells B2 through B3.
  - Point to the fill handle with the mouse — the mouse pointer will become crosshairs + .
  - Click and drag through B12 (for example), then release the mouse button. 10 through 20 will be filled into cells B2 through B12.

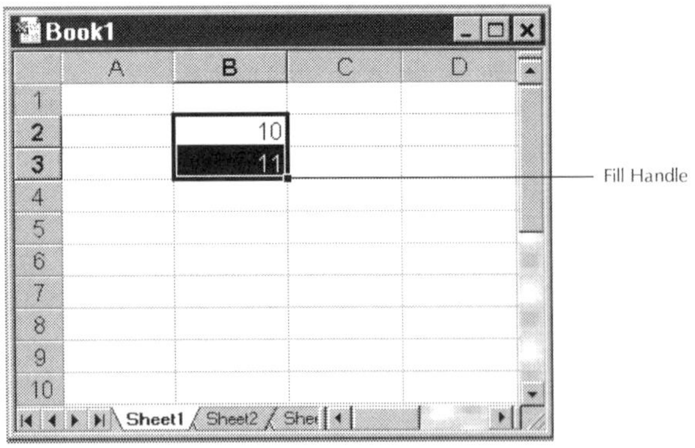

Figure 16.3 : Adjacent selected cells with a fill handle

- **Use AutoComplete feature** User needs to enter a value only once in a column. Subsequently, the **AutoComplete** feature matches the value that user is typing with all the values in that particular column and completes the entry. However, if the user wants to enter a different value, continue typing.
- **Enter the current date** Into a cell using two shortcut keys, Ctrl + ; (semicolon) and current time using Ctrl + Shift + ; (semicolon).

Editing a Worksheet

While working with worksheets you need to edit cell contents, add, or delete cells, rows and columns in worksheets, and so on. Excel provides a number of ways to format a spreadsheet. This includes different items such as the fonts, colours, and borders.

Selecting Cells, Rows and Columns

Whenever you want to make a change to a cell or range of cells, you must first select it. To select a range, click on one cell, hold down the mouse button, and drag across the cells you want to include in the selection. When a range is selected, the cells appear in reverse video. To select a large area of adjacent cells, use the **Shift** key to extend the selection. Click on the first cell of the range you want to select; then, while holding down the shift key, click on the last cell in the range you want to select.

	A	B	C	D	E
1	HARDWARE SALES				
2					
3	PRODUCT	YEAR	SALES	SALESPE	REGION
4	COMPUTER	1997	82760	SWATI	WEST
5	COMPUTER	1996	114400	SWATI	EAST
6	PRINTER	1997	5000	VIKRAM	NORTH
7	COMPUTER	1996	168940	VIKRAM	EAST
8	PRINTER	1997	54820	PREETI	NORTH

Figure 16.4 : A selected range of cells

An entire row or column can be selected by clicking on the desired row or column headings. To select multiple adjacent rows or columns headings. To select multiple adjacent rows and columns, simply click on a row or column heading and drag in the required direction to highlight additional rows and columns. To select multiple (non-adjacent) rows or columns, press **Ctrl** while clicking on the required rows or columns.

A non-contiguous range consists of two or more range (or single cells), not necessarily next to each other. To select a non-contiguous range hold down **Ctrl** while clicking the mouse and drag to highlight the individual cells or ranges at different locations in the worksheet. Use the Edit >>Goto command and enter the range's address manually into the Goto dialog box. Separate the different ranges with comma. Click on OK. For example, F6:F10, H6:H10.

Editing Worksheet Data

If you want to change the contents of the cell then follow any of the steps given below:

- Select the cell containing the data to be edited. Move the insertion point into the text in the formula bar. Make changes in the formula or text.
- Double-click the cell. Press the arrow keys in the selected cell itself to move the I-beam that marks the insertion point to where changes are to be made. Make the required changes to the cell entry. Press Enter to enter the information.

Copying and Moving Cells

When you are working on a worksheet, you may decide to move the contents of one cell or a range of cells to some other part of the spreadsheet. If text is to be moved within the same worksheet or to another worksheet, it should be first cut and then pasted. When you choose cut or copy, the cells are surrounded by a flashing dotted line, and their contents are not actually moved until you click in the cell. Where you want to paste. The contents of the selected cells do not disappear as they do in Word 2003. Copying the text is similar to the cut operation, except that copy retains the text at the original place, but in case of cut, the text is removed from the original cell. To perform the cut, copy and paste operations, follow the steps given below:

- Select the cell or range that is to be copied or moved.
- Choose Edit >> Copy to Copies the selected cells to the clipboard. If you want to move the cell contents, choose Edit >> Cut.
- Activate the cell or range where contents are to be copied or moved.
- Choose Edit >> Paste to paste the clipboard contents to the selected cell or range.

Erasing Cell Contents

If you want to delete the contents of a cell then select the cells and follow any of the methods given below:

- Press the Delete key.
- Use **Edit >> Clear** menu and choose **contents** option from the pop-up menu.

Deleting Cells, Rows and Columns

To delete a row or rows, select an entire row or multiple rows by clicking on the row number in the worksheet border, then use any of the following methods:

- Select **Edit >> Delete** command.
- Right-click on it and choose **Delete** from the shortcut menu.

Deleting columns or cells works in the same way except that you select an entire columns or cells respectively.

Inserting Cells, Rows and Columns

Inserting cells, rows and columns does not change the number of rows or columns. To insert a new row or rows, use any of the following techniques:

- Select an entire row or multiple rows by clicking on the row numbers in the worksheet border. Select the **Insert >> Rows** command.
- Select an entire row or multiple rows by clicking on the row numbers in the worksheet border. Right-click and choose **Insert** from the shortcut menu.
- Move the cell pointer to the row that you want to insert and select the **Insert >> Rows** command.

The procedure to insert a new column(s) or cells is same except that now at every step use **Insert >> Column** or **Insert >> Cell**. The new row is inserted above the selected row while the column is inserted to the left of the selected column.

Changing Column Widths

By default, each column's width is 8.43. Before changing the width, select the column, or multiple columns or all columns, and then do one of the following:

- Drag the **right column border** with the mouse until the column is of the desired width.
- Choose the **Format >> Column >> Width** command and enter a value in the Column Width dialog box.
- Choose the **Format >> Column >> AutoFit** Selection command. This option increases the column width as the content is typed in the cell.
- Double-click on the right border of a column to automatically set the column width to the widest entry in your selection.

Use the **Format >> Column >> Standard Width** command to change the default width of all columns.

Changing Row Heights

Row height is measured in points. As with columns, we can select multiple rows.

- Drag the **lower row border** with the mouse until the row is of the desired height.

- Choose the **Format >> Row >> Height** command and enter a value (in points) in the **Row Height** dialog box.
- Double-click on the button border of a row to automatically set the row height to the tallest entry in the row. Alternatively, use **Format >> Row >> Autofit** command.

The Formatting Toolbar

The Formatting toolbar gives a quick access to frequently used formatting commands. To use a formatting button, select the cell or range that is to be formatted. Then click the appropriate formatting button.

The Formatting toolbar contains many formatting buttons, including Font, Font Size, Bold, Italic, and Underline. Figure 16.5 shows the formatting buttons that are available on the Formatting toolbar.

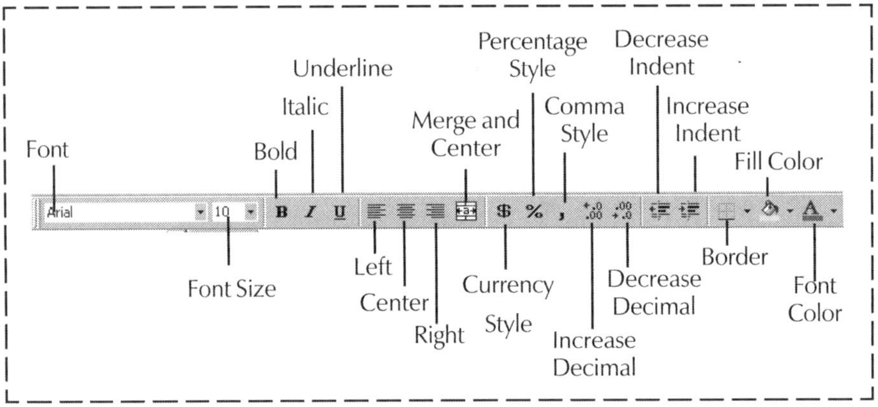

Figure 16.5 : Formatting toolbar

Formatting Number Using the Toolbar

The Formatting toolbar, which is displayed by default, contains several buttons that let the user quickly apply common number formats. On clicking any one of these buttons, the active cell takes on the specified number format. Table 16.2 summarizes number Formatting toolbar buttons.

Tool	Button Name	Formatting Applied
	Currency Style	Adding a dollar sign to the left, separates thousands with comma and displays the value with two digits to the right of decimal point.

	Percentage Style	Displays the value as percentage with no decimal places. Example, if the active cell value is 0.05 and percentage button is clicking, the value changes to 5%.
	Comma Style	Separates thousands with a comma and displays the value with two digits to the right of the decimal place. Example, 700050 will be displayed as 7000,050.
	Increase Decimal	Increases the number of digits to the right of the decimal point by one.
	Decrease Decimal	Decreases the number of digits to the right of the decimal point by one.

Table 16.2 : Number formatting buttons

Alignment

By default, text entries are left-justified in the cell. Values, on the other hand, are displayed right-aligned in the cell. The Table 16.3 contains description to the Alignment tools present on the Formatting toolbar:

Tool	Button Name	Formatting Applied
	Left-align	Aligns the text to the left side of the cell.
	Centre-align	Centres the text in the cell.
	Right-Align	Aligns the text to the right side of the cell.
	Merge and Centre	Centres the text in the selected cells and also merges the cells into one cell.

Table 16.3 : Alignment buttons of Formatting Toolbar

Number Formats

In some cases, accessing the number formats from the Formatting toolbar is easy. More often, however, more control is needed over how the values appear. Excel offers a great deal of control over number formats.

Select the **Format >> Cells** command, a **Format Cells** dialog box appears to format the cell contents. This is a tabbed dialog box as shown in Figure 16.6. To format numbers, use the Number tab.

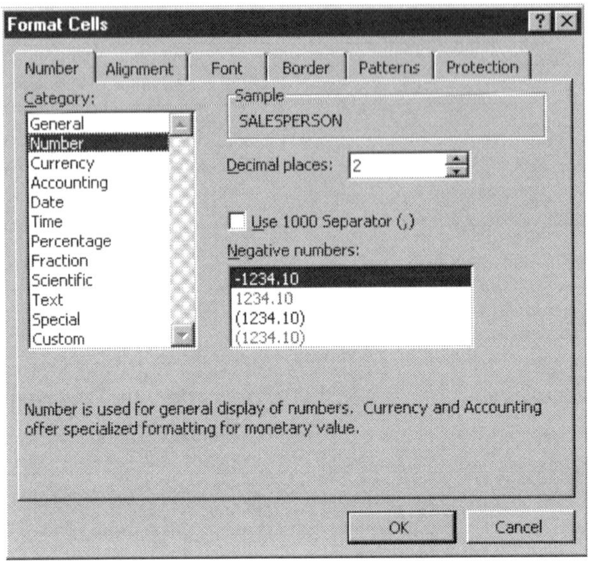

Figure 16.6 : Format Cells dialog box

Table 16.4 displays a list of the number format categories along with the examples from each category.

Number Format Categories	Example
General	86121.8
Number	86,121.80
Currency	$ 38,727.86
Accounting	$ 86,421.80
Date	August 05, 2003
Time	3:20:00 PM
Percentage	9.35%
Fraction	4½
Scientific	3.61214E+14
Text	36121.8
Special	123-45-6789
Custom	Number 0083

Table 16.4 : List of Number Format Categories

Using AutoFormats

Excel has a feature known as **AutoFormat** that can automatically perform many types of formatting. To apply an AutoFormat, move the cell pointer anywhere within a table that is to be formatted. Choose **Format >> AutoFormat** command. Excel responds with the dialog box shown in the Figure 16.7. Choose one of the AutoFormats and click on **OK**. Excel formats the table according to the autoformat selection.

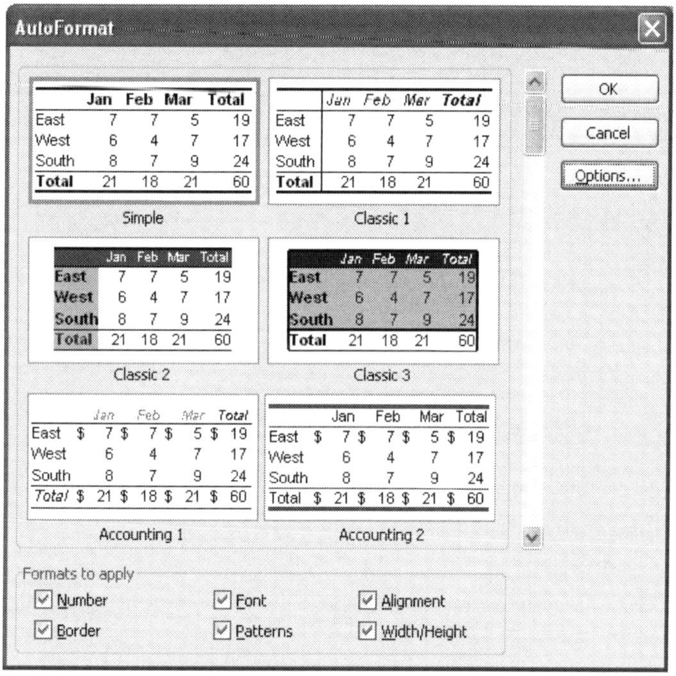

Figure 16.7 : AutoFormat dialog box

Essential Spreadsheet Operations

When a new workbook is opened in Excel, the workbook has some number of worksheets in it. By default, the number of worksheets is three. It may be helpful to think of a workbook as a notebook and worksheets as pages in that notebook. As with a notebook, so with the workbook, the user can activate a particular sheet, add new sheets, remove sheets, copy sheets, and so on.

- **Activating Worksheets** Click on the desired sheet tab.
- **Adding a new Worksheet** Select the **Insert >> Worksheet** command.
- **Deleting a Worksheet** Select the **Edit >> Delete Sheet** command.

- **Renaming a Worksheet** Choose the **Format >> Sheet >> Rename** command.
- **Hiding/Unhiding a Worksheet** Choose **Format >> Sheet >> Hide or Unhide**.
- **Moving/Copying a Worksheet** To Move/Copy a worksheet to either different workbook or its original workbook. Select **Edit >> Move or Copy sheet** command. A dialog box appears as shown in Figure 16.8.

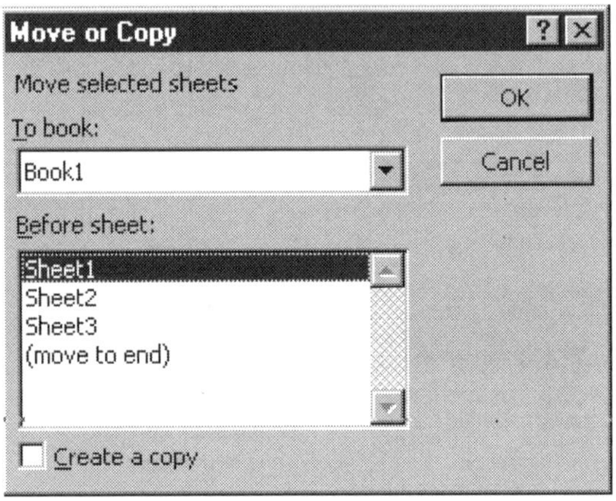

Figure 16.8 : Move or Copy dialog box

Views, Split Sheets, and Frozen Panes

As you add more information to a worksheet, you may find that it gets difficult to navigate and locate what you want. Excel includes a few options that enable you to view your sheet, and sometimes multiple sheets, more efficiently.

Multiple Views

Sometimes you may want to view two different parts of a worksheet simultaneously, or examine more than one sheet in the same workbook simultaneously. To create a new view of the active workbook, choose **Windows >> New Window**. Excel displays a new window with the active workbook.

Splitting Panes

Excel provides another option for viewing multiple parts of the same worksheet. The **Window >> Split** command splits the active worksheet into two or four separate panes, an example of such worksheet is shown in Figure 16.9. The split occurs at the location of the cell pointer. Notice that the row numbers and column letters aren't continuous. In other words, splitting panes enables you to display in a single window widely separated areas of a worksheet. To remove the split panes, choose the **Window >> Remove Split** command.

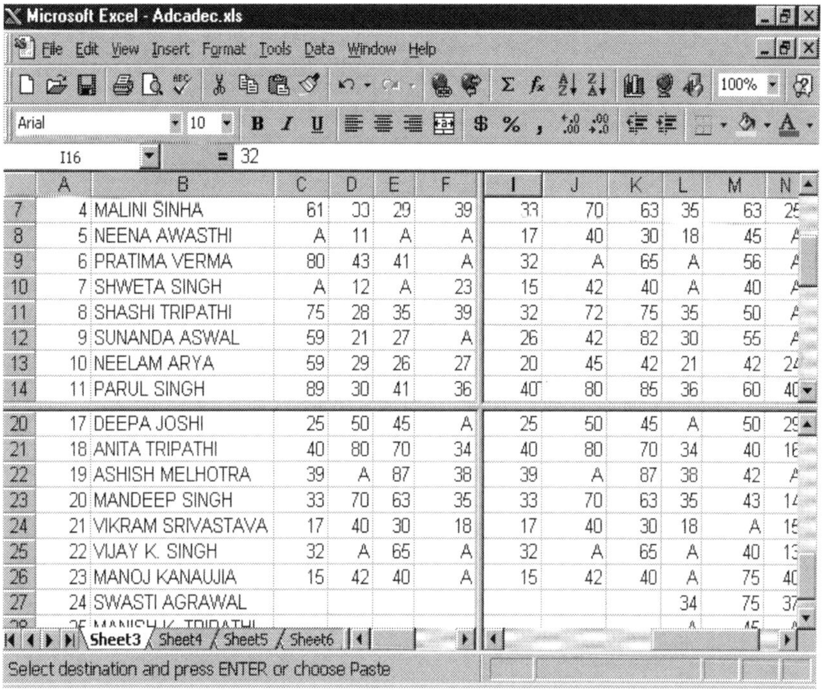

Figure 16.9 : Active worksheet split into four panes

Freezing Panes

Many worksheets are set up with row and column headings. When you scroll through such a worksheet, it is easy to get lost when the row and column headings scroll out of view as shown in Figure 16.10. Excel provides a handy solution to the problem: freezing panes. To freeze panes, start by moving the cell pointer to the cell below the row that you want to freeze and to the right of the column that you want to freeze. Then select **Window >> Freeze Panes**. Excel inserts dark lines to indicate the frozen rows and columns. You will find that the frozen rows and columns remain visible as you scroll throughout the worksheet.

To remove the frozen panes, select **Window >> Unfreeze Panes**.

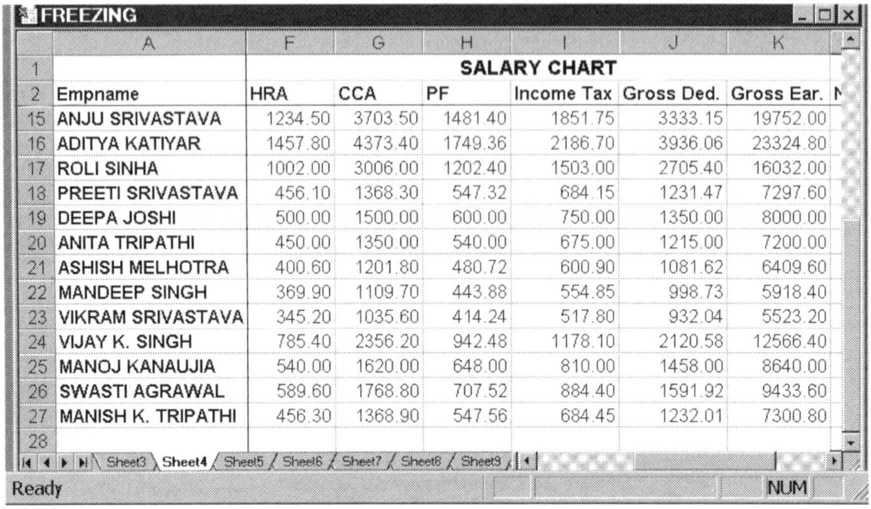

FREEZING

	A	F	G	H	I	J	K
1				SALARY CHART			
2	Empname	HRA	CCA	PF	Income Tax	Gross Ded.	Gross Ear.
15	ANJU SRIVASTAVA	1234.50	3703.50	1481.40	1851.75	3333.15	19752.00
16	ADITYA KATIYAR	1457.80	4373.40	1749.36	2186.70	3936.06	23324.80
17	ROLI SINHA	1002.00	3006.00	1202.40	1503.00	2705.40	16032.00
18	PREETI SRIVASTAVA	456.10	1368.30	547.32	684.15	1231.47	7297.60
19	DEEPA JOSHI	500.00	1500.00	600.00	750.00	1350.00	8000.00
20	ANITA TRIPATHI	450.00	1350.00	540.00	675.00	1215.00	7200.00
21	ASHISH MELHOTRA	400.60	1201.80	480.72	600.90	1081.62	6409.60
22	MANDEEP SINGH	369.90	1109.70	443.88	554.85	998.73	5918.40
23	VIKRAM SRIVASTAVA	345.20	1035.60	414.24	517.80	932.04	5523.20
24	VIJAY K. SINGH	785.40	2356.20	942.48	1178.10	2120.58	12566.40
25	MANOJ KANAUJIA	540.00	1620.00	648.00	810.00	1458.00	8640.00
26	SWASTI AGRAWAL	589.60	1768.80	707.52	884.40	1591.92	9433.60
27	MANISH K. TRIPATHI	456.30	1368.90	547.56	684.45	1232.01	7300.80
28							

Sheet3 Sheet4 Sheet5 Sheet6 Sheet7 Sheet8 Sheet9

Ready NUM

Figure 16.10 : Active Worksheet with Freeze Panes

Hyperlinks

One of the most appealing features of the Web is the convenience to navigate documents using **hyperlinks**. A hyperlink on an Excel worksheet can link to another worksheet range in the same workbook, a different workbook, any file on the local hard drive or network file server, and an Internet/Intranet address or file.

While working, a user may be dealing with documents created in different Microsoft Office applications. By adding hyperlinks to worksheets the user can move between different documents created in Microsoft Office applications with a single click. To create a link in an Excel worksheet to another Office document such as Word, follow these steps:

- Open the Excel worksheet and the document that is to be linked.
- Activate the document to be linked to the Excel sheet - for example, a Word document, and select the text or item that is to be linked.
- Choose **Edit >> Copy**.
- Activate the Excel document and select the cell where the user want the hyperlink.
- Choose **Edit >> Paste as Hyperlink**.
- Click a cell other than the cell in which the hypertext link was pasted.

The selected text appears in the cell containing the hyperlink. It will be colored so that it stands out from other text. After the hyperlink is pasted, the selected text appears in the cell as the hyperlink text.

Another method of creating hyperlinks enable the user to insert hyperlinks to local files or Internet sites. To create a hyperlink to a new file follow these steps:

- Right-click the cell or graphic you want to represent the hyperlink, and then click Hyperlink on the shortcut menu, a insert hyperlinks dialog box appears as shown in figure 16.11.
- Under Link to on the left side of the dialog box, click Create new document.
- Type a name for the new file in the Name of new document box.
- To specify a location other than the one shown under Full Path, type the new location in the Name of new document box or click Change and then select the location you want. Click OK.

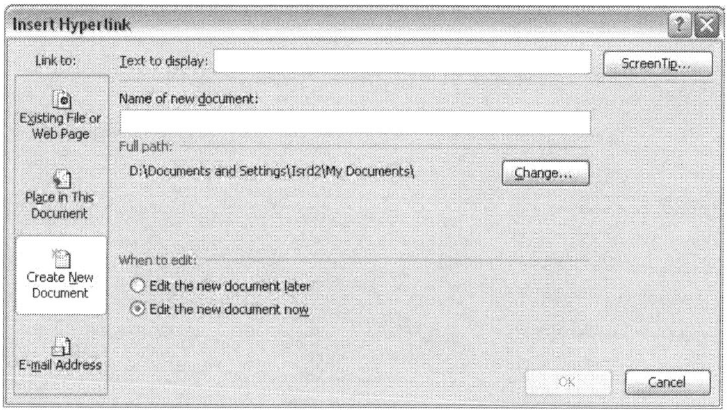

Figure 16.11 : Insert Hyperlink dialog box

- Under When to edit, click an option to specify whether to open the new file for editing now or later.
- To assign a tip to be displayed when you rest the pointer on the hyperlink, click ScreenTip and then type the text you want in the ScreenTip text box. Click OK.

Using Excel with Office Applications

There are essentially three ways to transfer data to and from other Windows applications:

- Copy and paste using the Windows Clipboard.
- Create a link so that changes in the source data are reflected in the destination document.
- Embed an entire object from another application into a document.

Embedding and Linking Objects

There are three different ways of including an object created in one application in a file created in another application:

- Inserting
- Embedding
- Linking

An object can be defined as a component of a file that can be handled separately. For example, charts and ranges in Excel.

Inserting

When an object is inserted in a file, the file contains neither information for editing the object in place nor a link to the object's source file. The object simply appears in the place you specify. Graphics are generally inserted in a file rather than being linked or embedded.

Embedding

When you embed an object in a file, the file contains a full copy of that object. For example, if you embed an Excel chart in a Word Document, the document contains a full copy of the chart. Updation made to the original chart will not be reflected directly in the copy. You must edit the copy separately. Embedding generally increases the size of the file to which the object is embedded.

Linking

Linking is the more complex method of inserting on object created in another application into a file. When an object is linked to a file, the file displays the current information for that object but stores only a link that describes the object. When the information about the link is stored the size of the file is not increased as in the case of embedding the object. Further more when an object is linked you can update the link by issuing the update command. The application reads the latest data from the source of the link and displays it in the file.

Using the Windows Clipboard

The general steps that are required to copy from one application to another are listed below. These steps apply to copying from Excel to another application and to copying from another application to Excel.

- Activate the source document window that contains the information that is to be copied.

- Select the information by using the mouse or the keyboard. If Excel is the source application, this information can be a cell, range or chart.
- Select **Edit >> Copy** That sends the information to the Windows Clipboard.
- Activate the destination application. Move to the appropriate position.
- Select **Edit >> Paste** for the receiving Windows application.

The Excel data is pasted into the receiving application. Figure 16.12 shows a Microsoft Word report having an embedded Excel chart.

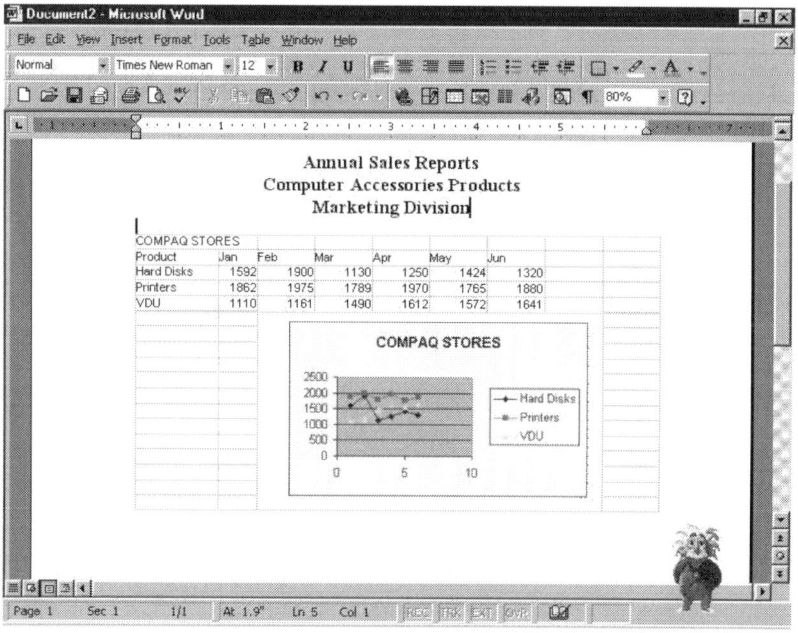

Figure 16.12 : A Microsoft Word report having an embedded Excel chart

Linking Data Between Applications

Linking means to create a dynamic link between the data copied from one Windows application to another. So, if the data changes in the source document, these changes are made automatically in the destination document. Linking takes place in two ways :linking Excel to other application by using a **remote reference formula**--much as linking Excel workbooks together by using external references or by using macros to control the dynamic data Exchanges that produce links. To create a link from one Windows application to another, the general steps are the same as discussed in the above method-- using the **Windows Clipboard**. The only difference is in step 5-select **Paste Special** instead of Paste command and then choose Link option.

Embedding Objects

Another method of sharing information between Window applications is to embed an object in the document. This is known as **Object Linking and Embedding (OLE)**. The user can embed data into an Excel worksheet from any OLE server application. This technique lets the user insert an object from another program and use the other program's editing tools to manipulate it. An object can be embedded into document in two ways:

- Choose **Edit >> Paste Special** and select the "object" choice. Select the **Paste** option rather than the **Paste link** option.
- Select **Insert >> Object**.

Embedding an Excel Range in a Word Document

Let us consider an example. The range shown in Figure 16.13 is embedded in a Word document.

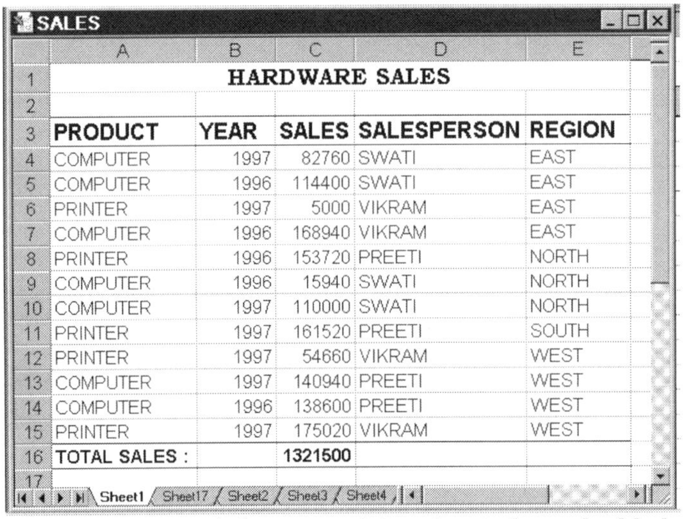

Figure 16.13 : A worksheet containing data to be embedded

To Start

- Select A1 : D15 and copy the range to the Clipboard.
- Activate (or start) Microsoft Word.
- Move the insertion point to the location in the document where the Excel's data is to be embedded.
- Choose Word's **Edit >> Paste Special** command (refer Figure 16.14).
- Select the **Paste** option, and choose the **Microsoft Excel Worksheet** Object format.

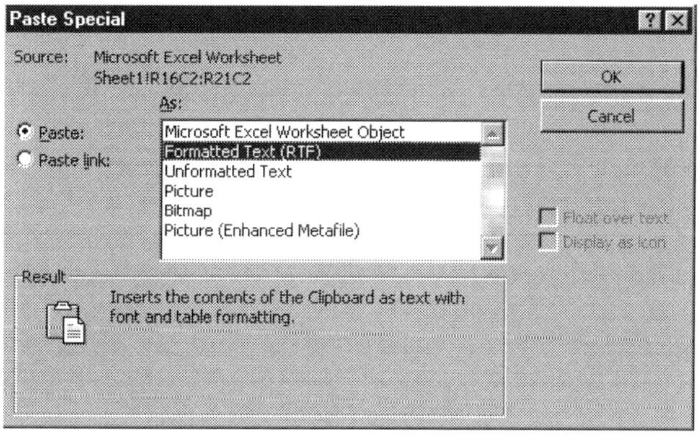

Figure 16.14 : Paste Special dialog box in MS-Word

- Click on OK and the range is pasted to the document.

Printing Your Work

Excel prints only the *active area* of the worksheet. In other words, it will print just those cells that have data in them not all the four million cells.

Choose **File >> Page Setup**, a four tabbed dialog box appears (refer Figure 16.15) that provides access to most print-related settings.

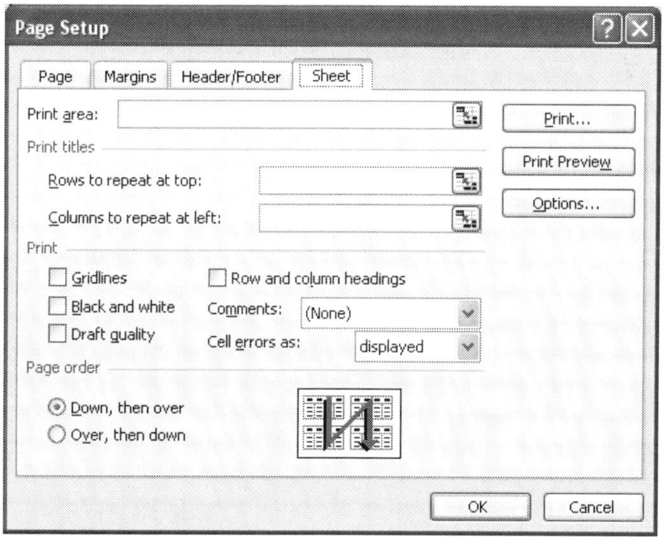

Figure 16.15 : Page Setup dialog box

The **File >> Print** command displays a dialog box (refers to Figure 16.16) that offers the following options:

- **What to Print** The drop-down list offers the following options for printing: Document, Document Properties, Comments, Styles, AutoText entries and Key assignments.
- **Copies** Specify more than one copy of whatever is to be printed.
- **Page Range** To print the entire page range, be sure that the **All** button is darkened. Click on the little radio button next to **All**, if it is not selected.

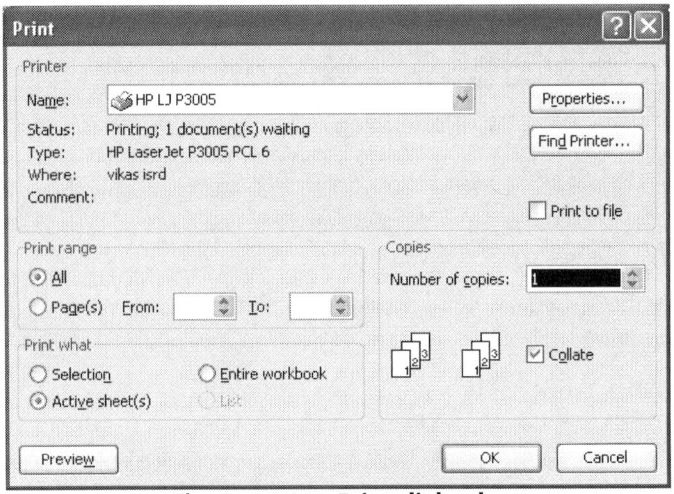

Figure 16.16 : Print dialog box

Summary

- Whatever work is done by user in Excel, gets stored in workbooks.
- A workbook can have any number of worksheets and each sheet has its name displayed in a sheet tab.
- A workbook can contain worksheets, chart sheets, macro sheets, modules, and dialog box sheets.
- The maximum number of cells is upto 4 million.
- The maximum number of rows in a worksheet in 65,536.
- The maximum number of columns in a worksheet can be 255.
- Excel handles dates using a serial number system. A serial number of 1 is given to January 1, 1900.
- Excel's Internet Assistant makes it possible to create new web pages or enhance existing web pages.

- We can save a workbook using HTML as native file format but it will not be interactive when opened in a browser. We can also save a worksheet as an interactive web page.
- The Web toolbar available in Excel is used to move among Excel files and HTML documents.
- Hyperlinks are the most interesting feature of Web which links one piece of data at one place to another piece of data at some other place.
- In Excel, hyperlinks can be inserted or pasted anywhere according to the user's requirements.
- It is also possible to convert data in worksheets into HTML pages to make it accessible to all computers connected through Internet.
- It is also possible to embed an Excel range in a Word document.

Review Exercise

Multiple choice questions

1. The filename extension for an Excel workbook is
   a) .XWB
   b) .XLW
   c) .XLS
   d) .XWL
2. A Workbook consists of a number of
   a) Workspaces
   b) Worksheets
   c) Status Bars
   d) Workbooks
3. The workspace is saved in Excel with an extension
   a) .XWS
   b) .XLS
   c) .XLW
   d) .XWP
4. The formula can start with which of the following
   a) $
   b) =
   c) +

   d) None of the above
5. To automatically complete a series, Excel uses
   a) Autoseries
   b) Sheet tab
   c) Autofill
   d) Split
6. Which of the following ranges is invalid?
   a) A1 : B6
   b) B1 : B2
   c) A1 : V655388
   d) B2 : B50
7. Keyboard shortcut to select a column is
   a) Ctrl + Spacebar
   b) Shift + Spacebar
   c) Alt + Spacebar
   d) None of the above
8. Which of the following is not a way of linking Excel to other application?
   a) Using a Remote Reference Formula
   b) Using Object Linking and Embedding (OLE)
   c) Both of the above
   d) None of the above
9. A hyperlink on an Excel worksheet can link to
   a) Another worksheet range in the same workbook
   b) A different workbook
   c) An Internet Intranet address or file.
   d) All of the above
10. Identify the incorrect statement.
   a) The embedded object is completely independent from the original source.
   b) Not all Windows applications support linking.
   c) You can use Edit >> Break command to break a link.
   d) When you embed a video clip, Excel stores a pointer to the original file

and not the actual video clip file.

State whether true or false

1. To create a new worksheet, select worksheet from the file menu.
2. Workbooks are used in DTP.
3. More than one window can be opened on the screen at a time. However, we can work only in one window at a time.
4. IV65536 is a valid cell address.
5. A non-contiguous range selection is also known as multiple selection.
6. It is possible to clear only the formatting and leave the contents of the cell.
7. A hyperlink on an Excel worksheet can link to an Internet / Intranet address or file.
8. It is possible to create a link in an Excel worksheet to another Word document.
9. In linking, if the data changes in the source document, these changes are not reflected in the destination document.

Fill in the blanks

1. A worksheet contains _______________ columns.
2. A cell can contain up to _________ characters.
3. To delete a worksheet document, select _______________ from the File menu.
4. To clear only the cell's contents and leave the formatting _______________ option must be chosen from Edit >> Clear command.
5. The default column width is _______________.
6. Default alignment for text entries is _______________.
7. ___________ means to create a dynamic link between the data copied from one Windows application to another.
8. ___________ is the technique which enables the users to insert an object from another program and to manipulate it using another program's editing .
9. Excel has the ability to use ______ as a native file format.

Descriptive questions

1. State any three application areas of spreadsheets.
2. How many types of data a worksheet can contain?

3. Describe the way date and time are handled by Excel?
4. What is the difference between a contiguous and a non-contiguous selection?
5. How will you change the column width and row height?
6. What are the buttons available on the Formatting toolbar which can be used to format a number?
7. What is the use of Embedding?
8. How will you embed an Excel range in a Word document?
9. What are the main differences between Linking and Embedding? Explain with the help of a suitable example.

CHAPTER

17 WORKING WITH FORMULAE AND CELL REFERENCING

FEATURING

- Introducing Formulae
- Understanding Cell References
- Excel Error Values
- Linking Workbooks
- Excel Functions

Formulae are the core of an Excel worksheet — they are what make a spreadsheet so useful. Without formulae, a spreadsheet would be nothing more than a word processor with a very powerful table feature. Using formulae lets you perform complete mathematical tasks and calculate results from the data stored in the worksheet. Formulae can also be used to make comparison and to manipulate text. The initial part of this chapter includes working with formulae. The remaining part of the chapter deals with functions. Functions act on data in much the same way as formulae act on numbers. Excel uses prebuilt worksheet functions to perform math, text, or logical calculations or to find information about the worksheet. Functions can speed up calculations compared to writing a formula. They accept information, referred to as arguments, and return a result.

Introducing Formulae

A formula can be defined as a set of instructions for performing a calculation. Formulae provide the real power when doing analysis and **modeling** — creating functioning spreadsheet systems — in Excel. By using formulae, entering a number into a single cell can cause a ripple effect throughout a complex model. A formula entered into a cell can consist of any of the following elements:

- Operators such as + (for addition) and * (for multiplication).
- Cell references such as C5 or P843.
- Values such as 15 or 432.
- Worksheet functions (such as SUM or AVERAGE)

Every Formula in Excel has some basic properties:

- A formula can consist of up to 1,024 characters.
- All formulae begin with an equal sign (=).
- The resulting value is displayed in the cell where formula is entered.
- When a cell containing a formula is selected, the underlying formula is displayed in the formula bar, where the cell contains the value based on that formula.
  - Here are a few examples of formulae

    = 150 * 5.0

    = A1 + B2

    = SUM (A1 : D5)

    = A1 = C1

    = (B1 - B3) * 50
- Formulae can refer to cells in other worksheets. Excel uses a special notation to handle types of references. The three **reference** operators for ranges are listed in the Table 17.1:

Operator	What It Does	Example
: (colon)	Specifies a range	A10 : D10
, (comma)	Specifies the union of two ranges	B1 : B7, AE15 : AE35
(space)	Specifies the intersection of two ranges	B1 : B7 E4 : K4

Table 17.1 : Reference Operators for Ranges

- To use a reference to a cell in another worksheet in the same workbook, use the following format

  = SheetName!CellAddress

  For Example : = B5 * Sheet2 ! A6

  Here is a formula that refers to a cell on a sheet named Departments

  = P15 * 'Departments' ! A18

NOTE Single quotes are used if the name includes one or more spaces.

- To refer to a cell in a different workbook, use the following format

  = [WorkbookName] SheetName ! Cell Address

  For Example : = [Employee.xls] Sheet 5 ! B25

  If the Workbook name in the reference includes one or more spaces, enclose it in single quotation marks.

  For Example : = A2 * '[Employee PF] Sheet1' ! C12

Understanding Cell References

A cell reference is the cell's address and it can be either the absolute location of a specific cell on a specific worksheet, or simply the location of a cell relative to a specific cell. The output of the formula can be varied by changing the value placed in the referenced cells. A cell reference can be relative, absolute, or mixed.

Relative References

Use relative reference to refer to cells **relative to the cell containing the formula**. The formula =A1, when entered into cell B1, actually means "the contents of cell B1 are equal to the contents of the cell that is now one to the left "(A1 being the cell to the left of B1). Since the formula uses a relative reference, the reference automatically adjusts when the cell is copied to another location. Figure 17.1 shows an example worksheet with a formula in cell D2. The formula, which uses the default relative references, is as follows:

= B2 * C2

Excel copies this formula as multiplication of a cell two columns over (B2) with a cell one column over (C2). When this formula is copied to the two cells below it that is, into cells D3 and D4, Excel generates the following formula:

Cell D3 : = B3 * C3

Cell D4 : = B4 * C4

This way, Excel adjusts the cell references to refer to the cells that are relative to the new formula.

D2 = =B2*C2

	A	B	C	D	E
1	Item	Quantity	Price	total	
2	Floppy	20	50	1000	
3	Disks	5	450		
4	Mouse	10	175		
5					
6	Sales Tax	5.50%			
7					
8	Total Tax	25.49			
9					

Figure 17.1 : Formula bar showing relative reference formula

Absolute References

There are times however when you want to copy cell references verbation. Figure 17.2 shows an example worksheet with formula in cell D2 which makes an absolute reference to cells B2 & C2. When the formula in D2 is copied to D3 and D4 the cell address do not change to B3*C3 or B4*C4, as the case might have been if relative referencing is being used, but remains B2*C2. This is because of absolute addressing. Absolute addressing is done by placing a dollar sign, '$', in front of the row & column in context. For example, B2.

D4 = =B2*C2

	A	B	C	D
1	Item	Quantity	Price	Total
2	Floppy	20	50	1000
3	Disks	5	450	1000
4	Mouse	10	175	1000
5				

Figure 17.2 : Formula bar showing absolute reference

Mixed References

Already studied are absolute references (with a dollar sign in front of both the coordinates) and relative references (with no dollar sign). A mixed reference has one absolute coordinate and one relative coordinate.

In some cases, only the row or only the column may be required to be fixed in a formula. In such a case, absolute referencing is used for either the row or the column. All the possible types of cell references are shown in Table 17.2.

Example	Type
A6	Relative reference
A6	Absolute reference
$A6	Mixed reference (column part is absolute)
A$6	Mixed reference (row part is absolute)

Table 17.2 : Possible types of Mixed References

Figure 17.3 shows an example of a situation in which a mixed reference is appropriate. The worksheet contains a table of values in which each cell consists of the value in column A multiplied by the value in row 1. The formula in cell B2 is as follows

= B$1 * $A2

On copying this formula to the range B2 : E5, each cell will contain the correct formula. For example, the formula in cell C4 would be as follows

= C$1 * $A4

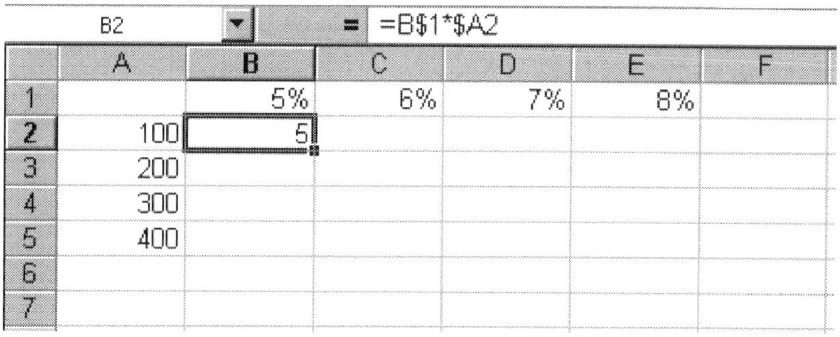

Figure 17.3 : Formula Bar showing Mixed Reference in formula

Excel Error Values

Formulae may return an error value if a cell that they refer to has an error value. In Excel, all the errors begin with a # symbol. Table 17.3 shows possible error values and their explanations that may appear in a cell that has a formula.

Error Value	Explanation
#DIV/0!	The formula is trying to divide by zero. This also occurs when the formula attempts to divide by a cell that is empty.
#NAME?	The formula uses a name that Excel doesn't recognize. This can happen if a deleted name is used in the formula or if there is an unmatched quotation marks when using text. This might also occur when a function name is misspelled.
#N/A	The formula refers to an empty cell range.
#NULL!	The formula uses an intersection of two ranges that do not intersect.
#NUM!	There is a problem with a value. For example, was specified a negative number where a positive number is expected.
#REF!	The formula refers to a cell that is not valid. This can happen if the cell has been deleted from the worksheet.
#VALUE!	The formula includes an argument or operand of the wrong type.
####	The formula is Ok but the cell is too small to display the value.

Table 17.3 : List of various error values

Editing and Deleting Formulas

A formula can be edited or deleted if required. To delete a formula, simply click on the cell that contains the formula and press delete key. If you want to alter the formula, then choose any method given below:

- Double click the cell, which enables you to edit the cell contents directly in the cell.
- Press F2, which enables you to edit the cell contents directly in the cell.
- Select the cell that you want to edit, and then click in the formula bar. This enables you to edit the cell contents in the formula bar.
- Click the Edit Formula button in the formula bar to access the formula palette.

Linking Workbooks

Linking is the process of using references to cells in external workbooks to get data into current worksheet. Linking enables one workbook to share the data in another workbook. Link object can be a single cell, a range of cells, and a named formula or constant, and sheets. The workbook that contains the original data that is the source of the information is the **'source workbook'.** The workbook that receives the linked data is called the "**target workbook'.** The source workbook may or may not be open when working with the target workbook.

Need to Link Workbooks

The linking is most needed when the source workbook is continually being updated. This way the user can always access the most recent information. Linking workbooks also can be helpful if different files need to be consolidated. Linking is also useful as a means to break up a large model into smaller files. Linked data can be formatted by using the same formatting techniques as the ones used on other general cell contents.

Creating External Reference Formulas

There are several ways to create an external reference formula

- Manually typing the cell references.
- Standard pointing techniques, provided the source workbook is open.
- Use the **Edit >> Paste Special** command with the Paste Link button. Source workbook must be open to this option.

Linking Cells by Typing

The general syntax for an external reference formula is as follows:

= ' Path \ [Workbook Name] Sheet Name' ! Cell Address

Some examples are:

= [Salary.xls] Sheet2 ! A10

= SUM ([Salary.xls] Sheet3 ! E6 : E8)

= ' [Salary For August] Sheet2 ' ! A5

= ' I:\Excel \ Account \ [Salary For August] Sheet2 ' ! A15

Linking Cells by Pointing

To create many links that link individual cells within larger formulae, use the pointing method of creating links. To point to a cell or range so that it is included in a formula, just click it as you build the formula, or simply drag across its range. The easier way is to have Excel build the formula for the user. Use the following steps:

- Open the source and target workbooks.
- Activate the target workbook.
- Select the cell that is to contain the link and start typing the formula. The formula may involve many terms and functions or it may be as simple as an equal sign (=) and the single linked cell.

- Activate the source workbook.
- Select the source cell or range that supplies data to the link.
- Continue building the formula by typing another operator (math sign) and continuing to select cells or entering the terms.
- After completing the formula, click the Enter box in the formula bar or press Enter.

Excel Functions

Functions are built-in tools that are used in formulae. Functions accept data through arguments. The user enters the arguments, enclosed in parentheses, after the function name. Each function takes specific types of arguments such as numbers, references, text, or logical values. Excel comes with more than 300 functions. Functions can do the following

- Simplify formulas.
- Allow formulas to perform calculations that are otherwise impossible.
- Speed up some editing tasks.
- Allow "conditional" execution of formulas.

For example, to sum the values in ten cells 'K11 : K20' without using a function, the formula would appear like this

= (K11+K12+K13+K14+K15+K16+K17+K18+K19+K20)

Replace this formula with a much simpler one that uses one of Excel's built-in worksheet functions

=SUM(K11 : K20)

Pasting a Function

Excel has a **Formula Palette** to assist with entering function. The **Formula Palette** ensures that the syntax of the function is correct. It makes sure that the function is spelled correctly and has the proper number of arguments in the correct order. To access the dialog box of **Paste Function** choose any of the following methods:

- Choose the **Insert >> Function** command from the menu.
- Click on the **Insert Function** button on the Standard toolbar.
- Press Shift + F3.

Any of these options displays the **Paste Function** dialog box as in Figure 17.4.

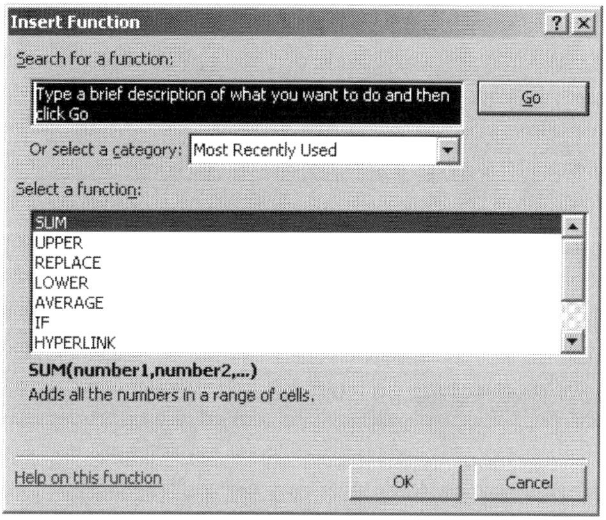

Figure 17.4 : Paste Function dialog box

Inserting a Function: An Example

This example uses the AVERAGE function to computer the average of a range of cell for which the values are entered in the worksheet as in Figure 17.5.

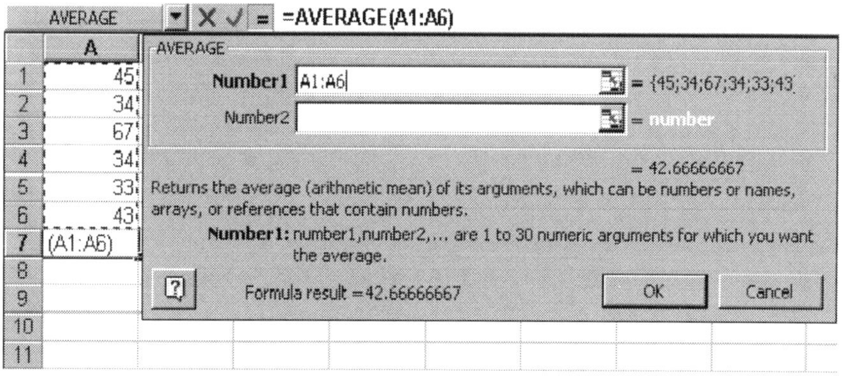

Figure 17.5 : Average function dialog box

- Activate cell A7. This cell will contain the formula.
- Click on the **Insert Function** button on the Standard toolbar. Excel displays its **Paste Function** dialog box.
- Click on **Statistical** in the **Function category** list box. The **Function name** list box displays the statistical functions.
- Click on AVERAGE in the Function name list box.

- Click on OK button. Excel closes the **Paste Function** dialog box and displays the **Formula Palette**.
- Activate the range box labelled Number1.
- Select the range A1: A6 in the worksheet.
- Click on the OK button.

Cell A7 now contains the following formula which returns the average of the values in A1:A6

=AVERAGE (A1:A6)

Date and Time Functions

Working with dates and times is a common worksheet task and Excel includes a rich set of date and time functions. First, it is important to understand how Excel works with date and time values.

- Date and time values are numbers, regardless of how the cells are formatted.
- Dates and time are stored as serial numbers-by default, Excel uses a 1900 date system in which serial numbers range from 1 to 65, 380 corresponding to dates Jan 1, 1900 through Dec 31, 2078.
- In the serial number, digits to the right of the decimal point represent time of day (as fraction of 24 hours); 12:00 p.m. is the equivalent of .5.

TODAY : Returns the serial number of today's date.

Syntax : **TODAY()**

WEEKDAY : Returns the weekday for the specified date as a sequence number between 1 (Sunday) and 7 (Saturday).

Syntax : **WEEKDAY(serial_number)**

Where serial number is the sequential number that represents the data of the day you are trying to find.

DATE : Returns the serial number of a particular date.

Syntax : **DATE(year, month, day)**

Year is the year number, 1900 or larger.

Month is a number representing the month of the year.

Day is a number representing the day of the month.

DAY : Convert a serial number to a day of the month.

Syntax : **DAY(serial_number)**

Serial_number is the date-time code used by Microsoft Excel for date and time calculations.

MONTH : Returns the month of the specified serial data with 1 standing for January to 12 for December.

Syntax : **MONTH (serial_number)**

where serial_number is the sequence number of the date from 1-Jan-1900.

YEAR : Returns the year of the specified serial date.

Syntax : **YEAR (serial_number)**

where serial_number is the sequence_number of the date from 1-Jan1900.

NOW : Returns the serial number of the current date and time.

Syntax : **NOW()**

TIME : Returns the serial number of a particular time.

Syntax : **TIME(hour, minute, second)**

Hour is a number from 1 to 23 that represents the hour.

Minute is a number from 0 to 59 that represents the minute.

Second is a number from 0 to 59 that represents the second.

Example : TIME(13, 50, 27) returns 0.57670389, which is equivalent to 1:50:27 PM.

HOUR : Returns the hour for a time.

Syntax : **HOUR(A1)**

A1 contains the time, for e.g., 7:30:00 AM, then formula returns 7.

MINUTE : Returns the minute for the specified serial time in form of a serial number between 0 & 59.

For example if A1 contains 7:30:00AM then the formula **MINUTE (A1)** will return 30.

SECOND : Returns the second for the specified serial time in form of a serial number between 0 & 59.

For example if A1 contains 7:30:29 AM, then **SECOND (A1)** will return 29.

Financial Functions

Rather than typing financial equations, you can use Excel's financial functions. Excel provides a family of functions that solve annuity problems. An annuity is a series of regular cash flows over a period of time.

FV : Returns the future value of an investment.

Syntax : **FV(rate, npr, pmt, pv, type)**

Rate is the interest rate per period.

Nper is the total number of payment periods in an annuity.

Pmt is the payment made each period.

Pv is the present value, or the lump-sum amount that a series of future payments is worth right now. If pv is omitted, it is assumed to be 0.

Type is the number 0 or 1 and indicates when payments are due. If type is 0, payments are due at the end of the period; if type is 1, payments are due at the beginning of the period.

Examples : FV(0.5%, 10, -200, -500, 1) returns $2581.40.

FV(11%/12, 35, -2000, , 1) returns $82,846.25.

PMT : Returns the periodic payment for an annuity based on constant payments and a constant interest rate.

Syntax : **PMT(rate, nper, pv, fv, type)**

Examples : The following formula returns the monthly payment on a $10,000 loan at an annual rate of 8% that you must pay off in 10 month.

PMT(8%/12, 10, 10000) returns -$1037.03.

For the same loan, if payments are due at the beginning of the period, the payment is PMT(8%/12, 10, 10000, 0, 1) which return -$1030.16.

PV : Returns the present value of an investment (the total amount that series of future payments is worth now). For example, when you borrow money, the loan amount is the present value to the lender.

Syntax : **PV(rate, nper, pmt, fv, type)**

Logical Functions

The logical functions are powerful worksheet functions that enable you to add decision-making and logical preferences to your worksheets results.

IF : Specifies a logical test to perform.

Syntax : **IF(logical_test, value_if_true, value_if_false)**

Logical_test is any value or expression that can be evaluated to true or false.

Value_if_true is the value that is returned if logical_test is true.

Value_if_false is the value that is returned if logical_text is false.

Up to seven IF functions can be nested as *value_if_true* and *value_if_false* arguments to construct more elaborate tests. The result values can display text with an argument such as "Hello", calculate a formula such as B12*6, or display the contents of a cell such as D35. Consider the following formula

= IF(B34>50, B34*2, "Entry tool low!")

In this example, the IF() function produces the answer 110 if B34 is 55. If B34 is 12, however, the cell that contains the function display the text given below.

Entry too low!

AND : The AND function joins test conditions. Returns TRUE if all its logical arguments are TRUE; returns FALSE if one or more logical arguments is FALSE.

Syntax : **AND(logical1, logical2...)**

Examples : AND(TRUE, TRUE) returns TRUE.

AND(TRUE, FALSE) returns FALSE.

AND(2+2=4, 2+3=5) returns TRUE.

OR : Returns TRUE if any argument is TRUE.

Syntax : **OR(logical1, logical2, ...)**

Logical1, logical2, ... are 1 to 30 conditions you want to test that can be either TRUE or FALSE.

Example : OR(1+1=1, 2+2=5) returns FALSE.

If A1:A3 contains the values TRUE, FALSE and TRUE, then OR(A1:A3) returns TRUE.

NOT : Reverses the logic of its argument.

Syntax : **NOT(logical)**

Example : NOT(FALSE) returns TRUE.

NOT(1+1=2) returns FALSE.

Mathematical and Trigonometric Functions

Mathematical and trigonometric functions provide the foundation for the majority of worksheet calculations. Most scientific and engineering functions are found under mathematical functions.

ABS : The ABS function returns the absolute value of a number.

Syntax : **ABS(number)**

Number is the real number for which you want the absolute value.

Examples : ABS(43) returns 43 as 43 is the absolute value of 43.

ABS(-105) returns 105 as 105 is the absolute value of -105.

CEILING : Rounds a number away from zero to the nearest integer or to the nearest multiple of significance.

Syntax : **CEILING(number, significance)**

Number is the numeric value you want to round off.

Significance is the multiple to which you want to round off.

Examples : CEILING (2.5, 1) returns 3.

CEILING(0.234, 0.01) returns 0.24.

FLOOR : Rounds a number down to the level of significance that you specify.

Syntax : **FLOOR(number, significance)**

Number is the numeric value you want to round off.

Significance is the multiple to which you want to round off.

Example : FLOOR(2.5, 1) returns 2.

FLOOR(-2.5, -2) returns -2.

INT : Rounds a number down to the nearest integer.

Syntax : **INT(number)**

Number is the real number you want to round down to an integer.

Examples : INT(8.9) returns 8.

INT(-8.9) returns -9.

ROUND : Rounds a number to a specified number of digits.

Syntax : **ROUND(number, num_digits)**

Number is the number you want to round off.

Num_digits specifies the number of digits to which you want to round off the number.

Example : ROUND(2.149,1) returns 2.1.

ROUND(-1.475, 2) returns -1.48.

ROUND(21.5, -1) returns 20.

SQRT : Returns a positive square root.

Syntax : **SQRT(number)**

Number is the number for which you want the square root.

Example : SQRT(16) returns 4.

SQRT(-16) returns #NUM!

SQRT(ABS(-16)) returns 4.

SUM : Adds its arguments.

Syntax : **SUM(number1, number2, ...)**

Number1, number2, ... are 1 to 30 arguments for which you want the sum.

Example : SUM(3, 2) return 5

SUM (A2:C2) return 50, if cells A2:C2 contain 5, 15 and 30.

MOD : This function returns the remainder left over after a division operation.

Syntax : **MOD (number, divisor)**

Example : MOD (16, 3) will return 1

SIGN : Returns 1 for positive, 0 for 0 and -1 for a negative number.

Syntax : **SIGN (number)**

Example : SIGN (-17) will return -1

TRUNC : Specified number to the specified number of decimal places.

Syntax : **TRUNC (number)**

Example : TRUNC (8.9) will return 8.

TRUNC (-8.9) will return -8.

Statistical Functions

Statistical functions can help you with simple problems such as finding an average or counting items.

AVERAGE : Returns the average of its arguments.

Syntax : **AVERAGE(number1, number2, ...)**

Examples : If A1:A5 is named *Scores* and contains the numbers 10, 7, 9, 27, and 2 then

AVERAGE (A1:A5) returns 11

AVERAGE(Scores) returns 11

COUNT : Counts how many numbers are in the list of arguments.

Syntax : **COUNT(value1, value2, ...)**

Value1, value2, ... are up to 30 arguments that can contain or refer to a variety of data types, but only numbers are counted.

MAX : Returns the maximum value in a list of arguments.

Syntax : **MAX(number1, number2, ...)**

Number1, number2, ... are 1 to 30 numbers for which you want to find the maximum value.

Examples : If A1:A5 contains the numbers 10, 7, 9, 27 and 2, then

MAX(A1:A5) returns 27.

MAX(A1:A5, 30) returns 30.

MIN : Returns the minimum value in a list of arguments.

Syntax : **MIN(number1, number2, ...)**

Number1, number2, ... are up to 30 numbers for which you want to find the minimum value.

Examples : If A1:A5 contains the numbers 10, 7, 9, 27 and 2 then

MIN(A1:A5) returns 2

MIN(A1:A5, 0) returns 0

LARGE : Returns n^{th} largest value in the range.

Syntax : **LARGE(Range, n)**

Range signifies the range of values from which largest number is to be extracted.

n signifies the second, third, fourth or n largest value in the range.

Example: If A1:A5 contains the numbers 5, 12, 16, 10, 30 then LARGE(A1: A5, 3) returns 12.

SMALL : Returns n^{th} smallest value in the range.

Syntax : **SMALL(Range, n)**

Text Functions

Text functions enable you to manipulate text.

CHAR : Returns the corresponding character specified by the code number.

Syntax : **CHAR(number)**

Number is a number between 1 and 255 specifying which character you want.

Example : CHAR(65) returns "A".

CHAR(33) returns "!".

LEFT : Returns the leftmost characters from a text value.

Syntax : **LEFT(text, num_chars)**

Text is the text string containing the character you want to extract.

Num_chars specifies how many characters you want LEFT to return.

RIGHT : Returns the rightmost characters from a text value.

Syntax : **RIGHT(text, num_chars)**

Text is the text string containing the characters you want to extract.

Num_chars specifies how may characters you want to extract.

UPPER : Converts characters to uppercase.

Syntax : **UPPER(text)**

Text is the text string containing the characters you want to convert or reference to some other cell which has the text.

LOWER : Converts characters to lowercase.

Syntax : **LOWER(text)**

Text is the text string containing the characters you want to convert or reference to some other cell which has the text.

REPLACE : Replaces characters with other characters.

Syntax : **REPLACE(text1, start_num, num_chars, text2)**

Text1 is the text containing the string that you're replacing.

Start_num is the character position at which you want to start replacing.

Num_chars is the number of characters to replace.

Text2 is the new text that will replace the existing text.

Example: REPLACE("Albert King", 8, 4, "Collins") returns Albert Collins.

MID : Returns a specific number of characters from a text string starting at the position you specify.

Syntax : **MID(text, start_num, num_chars)**

Text is the text string containing the characters you want to extract.

Start_num is the position of the first character you want to extract in text.

Num_chars specifies how many characters to return from text.

LEN : Returns the number of characters in a text string.

Syntax : **LEN(text)**

Text is the text string whose length you want to find. Spaces count as characters.

PROPER : Capitalizes the first letter in each word of a text value.

Syntax : **PROPER(text)**

Text is text enclosed in quotation marks, a formula that returns text, or a reference to a cell containing the text you want to partially capitalize.

Examples : PROPER ("this is a TITLE") returns "This Is A Title."

CONCATENATE : Text string consisting of the specified text strings joined together.

Example : If A1="Hello" & A2 ="World" then **CONCATENATE (A1,A2)** will give HelloWorld.

Summary

- Formula provides great help when analysis and modelling sort of tasks are performed.
- Formulae can be entered in a cell either manually or by pointing to cell references.
- A cell reference is the cell's address and it can be either the absolute location of a specific cell or simply the location of a cell relative to a particular cell.
- There are three types of cell references : absolute, relative and mixed.
- In Excel whenever a formula evaluates something which is considered as error in Excel, it is represented by an appropriate error value. All the error values begin with a # symbol.
- Functions are built-in tools that can be used in formulae. Functions can be entered into a formula either manually or by using the **Paste Function** dialog box.
- A variety of functions are available to work with numbers, strings, and to perform some logical tests.

Review Exercise

Multiple choice questions

1. Which of the following is correct order of precedence for operators while evaluating an Excel formula?

   a) %, &, *, +

   b) &, *, +, %

   c) %, *, +, &

   d) None of the above

2. To display all formulas in a worksheet use

   a) Ctrl \(Grave Accent)

   b) Ctrl *

   c) Ctrl -

   d) Ctrl %

3. Which of the following is not a reference operator?

   a) : (colon)

   b) , (comma)

c) ; (semicolon)

d) None of the above

4. If the formula in cell B5 reads = \$D\$6/20, what will it be when it is copied to cell E5?

a) = +\$D\$6/20

b) = +\$E\$6/20

c) = +\$O\$6/100

d) None of the above

5. In Excel, Max( ) is one of the

a) Mathematical functions

b) Statistical functions

c) Trigonometric functions

d) Financial functions

6. Which of the following functions calculates the number of days between two dates based on a 300-day year?

a) DATEVALUE

b) DAY

c) DAYS360

d) DATE

7. Function FV( ) takes a total of ________ arguments.

a) 2

b) 6

c) 4

d) 5

State whether true or false

1. You can change the referencing of a cell from absolute to relative by prefixing the cell coordinate with the \$ sign.

2. Absolute referencing implies that if the formula is copied to another location, the cell references change according to the new location of the formula.

3. Every time you change the value in a cell that is used in a formula, the result of the formula is recalculated automatically.

4. ROUND (26.6, -1) will return 26.
5. DATE( ) returns today's date.

Fill in the blanks

1. The default cell referencing method used by a spreadsheet is ____________.
2. A common reference operator is ____________.
3. A formula entry is said to be of ____________ data type.
4. An Excel formula always starts with a __________ sign.
5. A function can begin with a ____________ or ____________.
6. One or more pieces of data, passed to a function are referred to as ____________.
7. ROUND (2.314, 1) will return ____________.
8. CHAR (67) will return ____________.

Descriptive questions

1. Can a formula be removed from the worksheet without removing the calculated value? Explain how?
2. How is relative addressing different from absolute addressing?
3. Discuss the different kinds of errors that could occur while working in Excel.
4. What are functions? Enumerate the different functions.
5. What do you understand by Function Wizard?
6. What is the purpose of using the following functions?
   a) MID
   b) LEFT
   c) LEN
   d) SQRT
   e) TODAY

C H A P T E R

18 CHARTS AND DATA SHARING

FEATURING

- **Overview of Charts**
- **Chart Types**
- **Creating Charts**
- **Formatting Chart Elements**
- **Printing Charts**
- **Hyperlinks**
- **Using Excel with Other Applications**

A chart is a way to present a table of numbers visually. Displaying data in a well conceived chart can make it more understandable. Charts are particularly useful for getting a visual picture of a lengthy series of numbers and their relationships. Making a quick chart helps in spotting trends and patterns that would be nearly impossible to identify in a range of numbers. Excel includes a powerful built-in charting facility that makes it very easy to create a variety of charts for any presentation. The applications in Microsoft Office-2003 — including Excel — have quite a few Internet-related features. A World Wide Web (WWW) is probably the most exciting thing happening these days in the world of computing. Interlinked pages on the Internet enable people with little computer knowledge to move quickly between related information. Excel has the ability to work with other programs and the data created by them. It provides a variety of ways to interact with other programs, import data and utilize a host of new Internet-related features. This chapter explains the details of creating a chart and covers all the basic information needed to start working with charts. You will also study about Internet features of Excel and finally about data-sharing with other Office applications.

Overview of Charts

Charts — also known as **graphs** — are an effective way to present information. They present data in a graphical format and allow the viewer to absorb a lot of information quickly, whereas a traditional column might require considerable study and analysis. Charts are based on numbers that appear in a worksheet. There are two options for placing the chart:

- Insert the chart directly into a worksheet as an object. This is known as an **embedded chart** (refer to Figure 18.1).

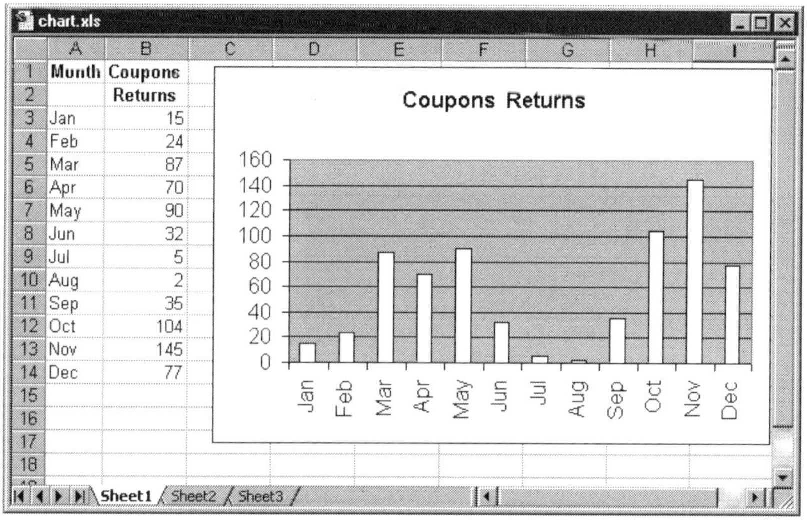

Figure 18.1 : Embedded Chart

- Charts can be created as **chart sheets** in a workbook (refer to Figure 18.2). Chart sheets can hold a single chart and do not have cells.

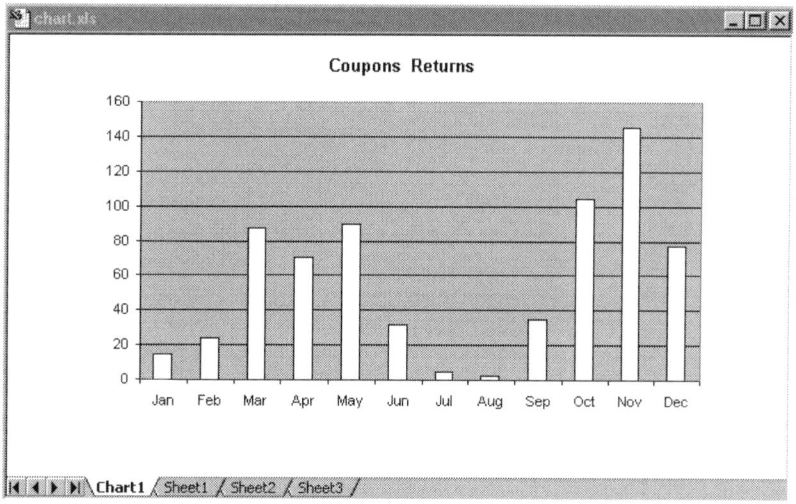

Figure 18.2 : Chart Sheet

Defining Chart Terms

Various terms with reference to charts are listed in Table 18.1.

Object	Description
Axis	The category axis and value axis form the boundaries of a chart and contain the scale against which data is plotted.
Chart Title	The name of the chart.
Axis Title	A little for each of the axes used.
Data Series	A collection of data points, such as sales for the years from 2001 to 2005.
Legend	A guide that explains the symbols, patterns, or colors used to differentiate data series.
Marker	An object that represents a data point in a chart. Bars, pictures, wedges, and symbols are examples of markers.
Plot area	The rectangular area bounded by the two axes.
Text	You can edit and move title (chart, value, and category) and data labels (text associated with data points).
Data labels	Text that appears on or near the data series to identify them.
Grid lines	Reference lines drawn across the chart from the axes so that you can view the values of the data series.
Chart Area	The area occupied by the entire chart, including legend, labels and so on.

Table 18.1 : Terms associated with charts.

Chart Types

Excel offers many built-in chart types. Various distinct advantages and disadvantages should be considered when deciding what type of chart to use. For determining which chart type is best for the user's data there is no standard approach. The best rule of thumb is to use the chart type that gets the message across in the simplest way. Within each chart type there are several subtypes.

Column Charts

These are one of the most common chart types. They are useful for displaying discrete data (as opposed to continuous data). There can be any number of data series and the columns can be stacked on top of each other. Figure 18.3 shows an example of a column chart.

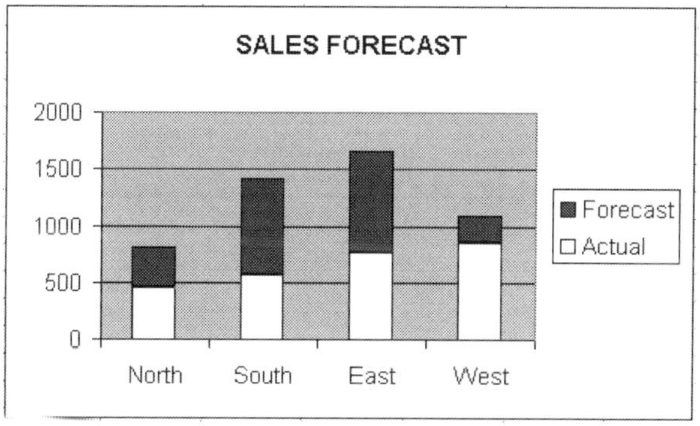

Figure 18.3 : Column Chart

Bar Charts

A **bar chart** is just a column chart that has been rotated 90 degrees to the left. The advantage of using a bar chart is that the category labels may be easier to read (see Figure 18.4). Bar charts can consist of any number of data series. In addition, the bars can be stacked from left to right.

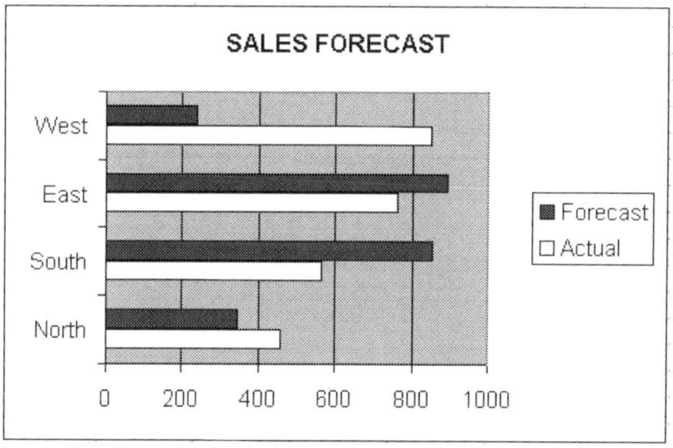

Figure 18.4 : Bar Chart

Line Charts

They are frequently used to plot data that is continuous rather than discrete. They illustrate a trend over even intervals of time . For example, plotting daily sales as a line chart may let you spot trends over time. See Figure 18.5 for an example. There are a number of line styles available too.

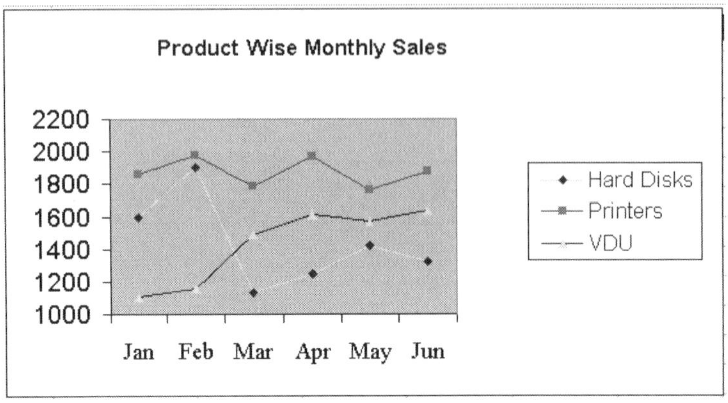

Figure 18.5 : Line Chart

Pie Charts

The uniqueness of a pie chart is that it can only plot one data series. A **pie chart** is useful to show relative proportions or contributions to a whole. Figure 18.6 shows an example of a pie chart. When a pie chart is created too many data points can make the chart illegible, so it is better to keep it simple with few data points.

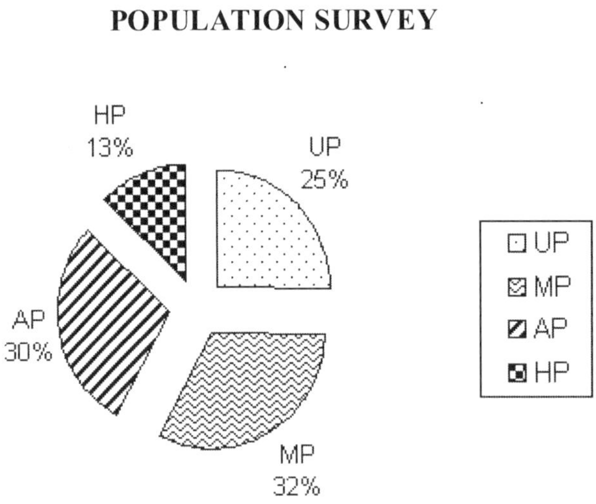

Figure 18.6 : Pie Chart

Creating Charts

The **Chart Wizard** and **Chart menu** have been recognized in Excel. Either the **Chart Wizard** or the **Chart menu** commands can be used to edit a chart once it is created. While creating a chart, however, the easiest way is to use the mouse and the Chart Wizard. Excel creates a chart using the default chart type, that is, **column chart**, if a chart is being created without using the chart wizard. If the **Chart Wizard**, is used, Excel prompts the user for the chart type.

Creating an Embedded Chart Using the Chart Wizard

To create an embedded chart, go by the following steps to invoke the **Chart Wizard**.

- Select the data to be charted (optional).
- Choose the **Insert >> Chart** command (or, click on the **Chart Wizard** tool on the Standard toolbar).
- The first step of **Chart Wizard** dialog box shows up as in Figure 18.7. Select the chart type.

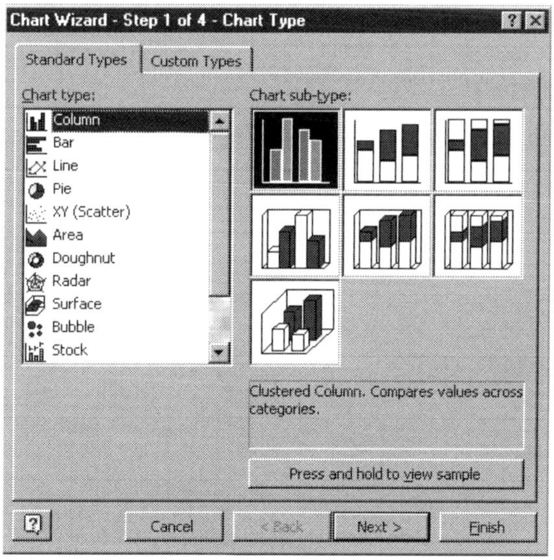

Figure 18.7 : Step 1 of Chart Wizard dialog box

- In the second step of the **Chart Wizard**, verify the data ranges and specify the orientation of the data as in Figure 18.8.

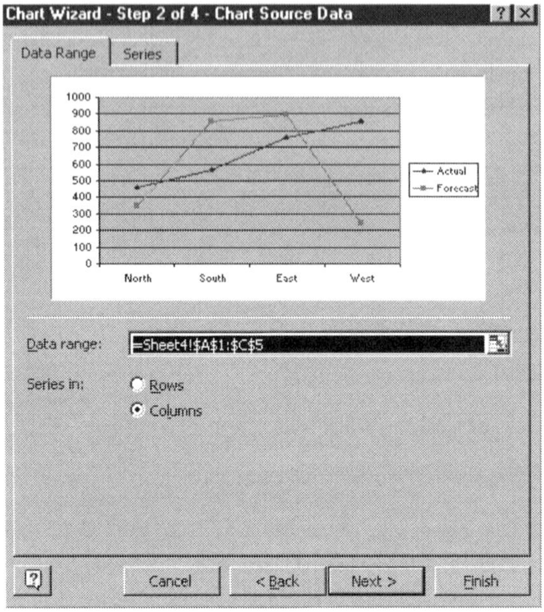

Figure 18.8 : Step 2 of Chart Wizard dialog box

- In the third **Chart Wizard** dialog box as in Figure 18.9, specify most of the options for the chart.

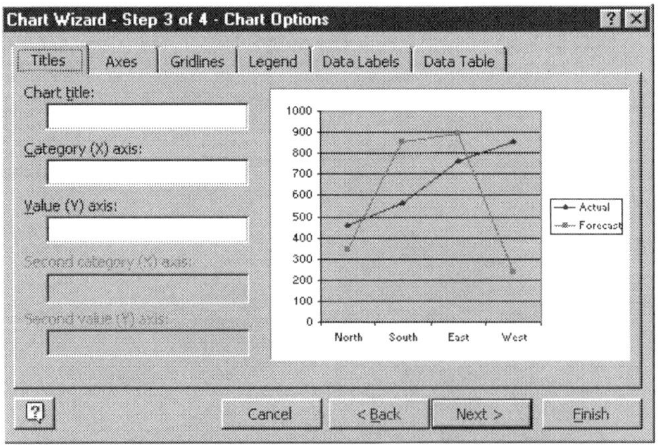

Figure 18.9 : Step 3 of Chart Wizard dialog box

The different tabs of the dialog box in Figure 18.9 are

Titles	:	Add titles to the chart, that is, chart title and category axis.
Axes	:	Turn axes display on or off, and specify the type of axes.
Gridlines	:	Specify gridlines, if any.
Legend	:	Specify whether to include a legend and where to place it.

Data Labels : Specify whether to show data labels and what type of labels.

Data Table : Specify whether to display a table of the data.

- The last step (step 4) of **Chart Wizard** allows the user to specify where to place the chart (refer to Figure 18.10). Select the option button labelled **As object in**. Click on **Finish** button — the specified chart will be embedded on the sheet.

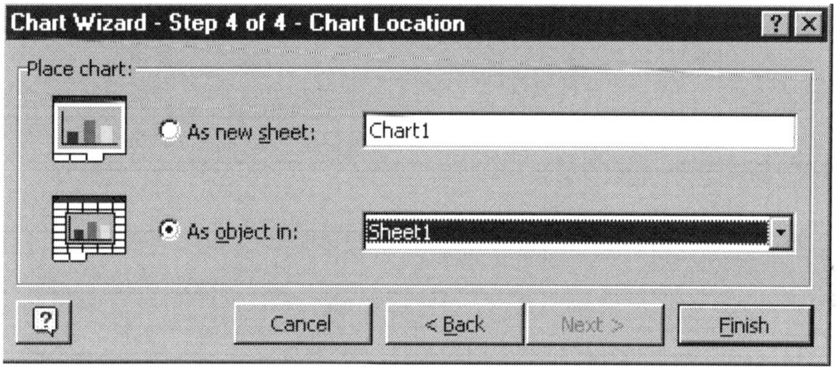

Figure 18.10 : Step 4 of Chart Wizard dialog box

Creating an Embedded Chart Directly

To create an embedded chart without using the **Chart Wizard**

- Display **Chart** toolbar.
- Select the data to be charted.
- Click on the **Chart Type** tool on the Chart toolbar and select a chart type from the displayed icons (refer Figure 18.11).

The chart is added to the worksheet using the default settings. The chart type tool on the **Chart toolbar** displays an icon for the last selected charts (refer to Figure 18.11).

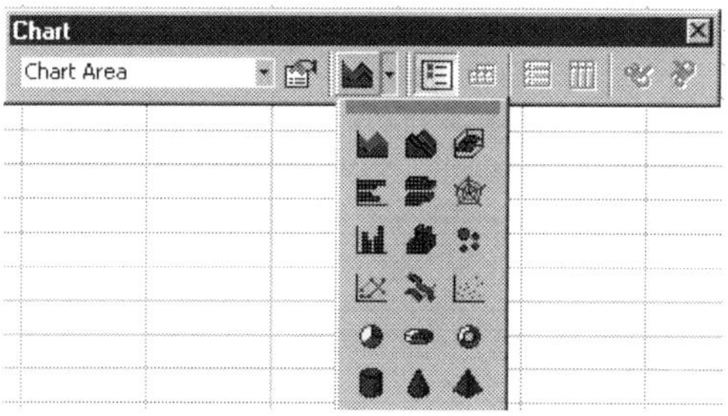

Figure 18.11 : Chart type Tool on Chart toolbar

Creating a Chart on a Chart Sheet Using the Chart Wizard

To invoke the **Chart Wizard** to create a chart on a chart sheet:

- Select the data to be charted.
- Choose the **Insert >> Chart** command (or, click on the **Chart Wizard** tool on the Standard toolbar).
- Make your choices in Step 1 through 3 of the **Chart Wizard**.
- In Step 4 of the **Chart Wizard**, select the option labelled **As New Sheet**. This will insert a new chart sheet in the workbook.

Creating a Chart with One Keystroke

To create a new chart on a chart sheet using the default chart type (column chart), with one keystroke follow steps

- Enter data to be charted into a worksheet.
- Select the range of data entered in Step 1.
- Press F11. Excel inserts a new chart sheet (named Chart1) and displays the chart based on the selected data.

Formatting Chart Elements

There are certain procedures that apply to formatting chart elements regardless of which chart element you are formatting. Figure 18.12 shows various chart elements.

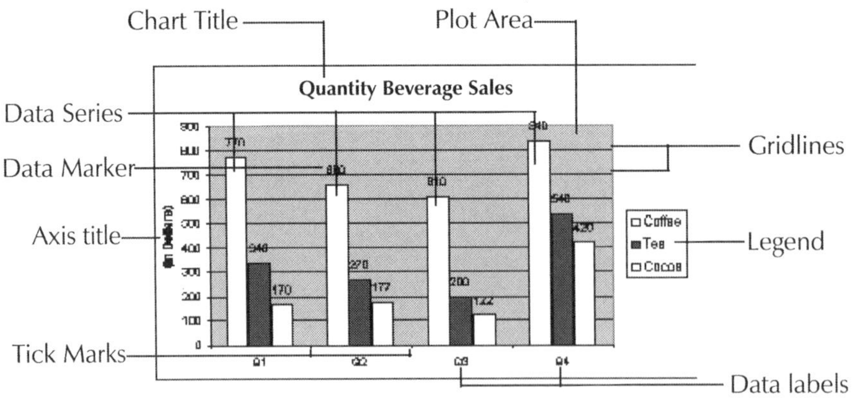

Figure 18.12 : Column Chart showing various chart elements

- The chart elements must be selected in order to format it.
- Double-click on the chart element that is to be formatted to display the **Format dialog** box as in Figure 18.13.

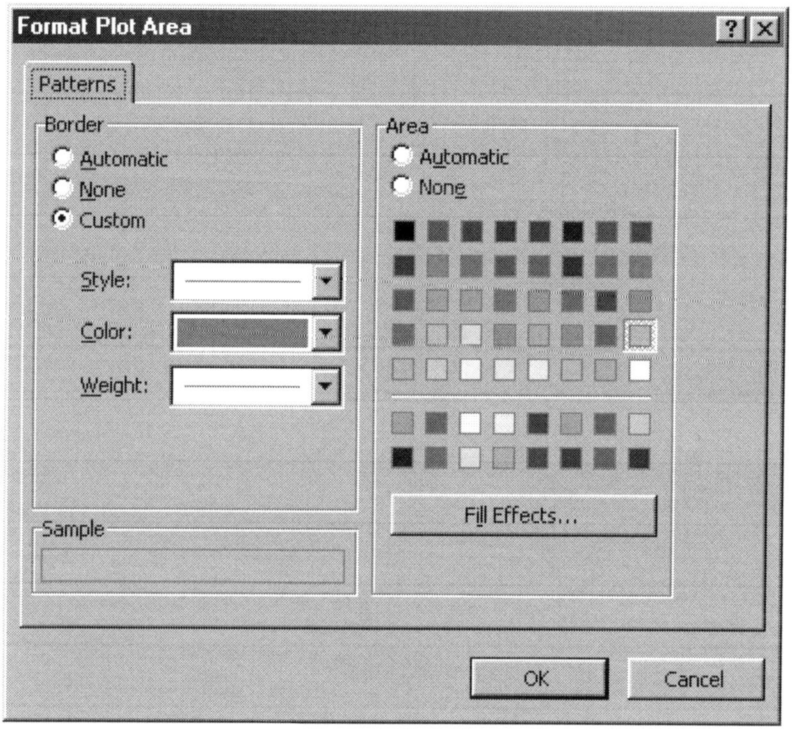

Figure 18.13 : Format dialog box

- Select the formatting options, then click on OK.

Changing the Default Chart Type

Excel's default chart type is a 2-D column chart with a light-gray plot area, a legend on the right, and horizontal gridlines. The default chart type can be easily changed in the following manner:

- Select the **Chart >> Chart Type** command.
- Choose the chart type you want to use as a default chart. This can be a chart from either the Standard Types tab or Custom Types tab.
- Click the button labeled **Set as Default** chart type. You are asked to verify your choice.

Creating Custom Chart Types

To add a custom chart type:

- Create the chart and apply formatting as needed.

- Select the chart.
- Choose **Chart >> Chart type** to display the chart type dialog box.
- Click the Custom Types tab to display it if it's not already displayed, and then select the user-defined option in the Select from area. Excel displays the list of user defined charts as shown on the Figure 18.14. If you have not added any you will see the default chart type.
- Click on **Add** button to display the Add **Custom Chart Type** dialog box as shown in Figure 18.15.
- Type the name (compulsory) and descriptions (optional but recommended) for the chart type & click OK.

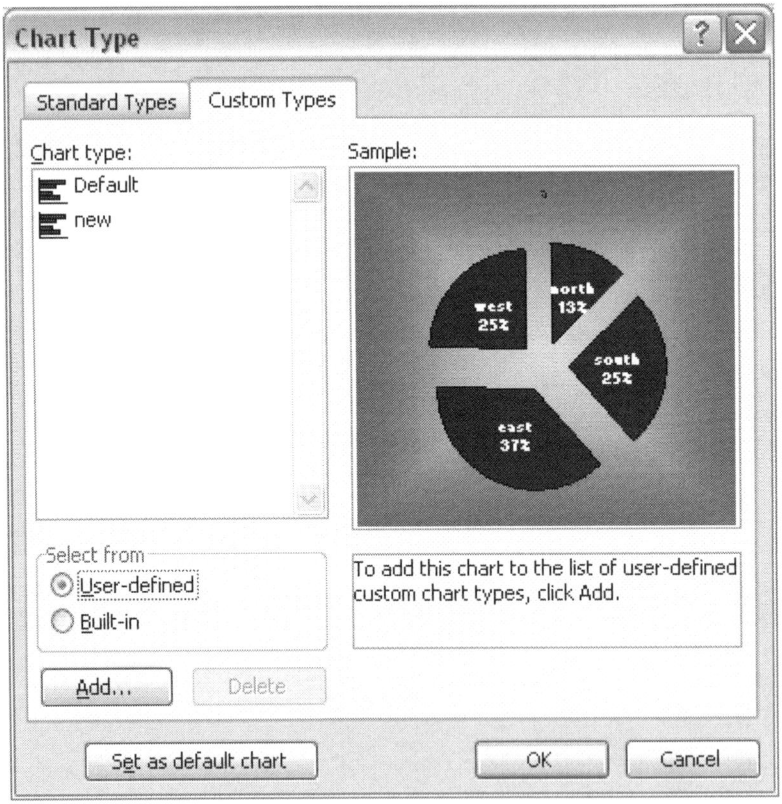

Figure 18.14 : Chart Type dialog box

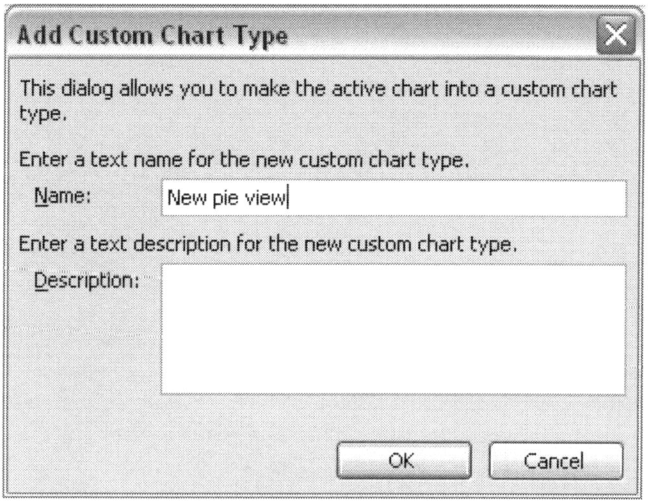

Figure 18.15 : Add Custom Chart Type dialog box

Printing Charts

To print a worksheet without printing a chart embedded in it, select the chart area. Then choose **Format >> Selected Chart Area**, select the Properties tab and clear the **Print Object** check box. Click on OK as in Figure 18.16.

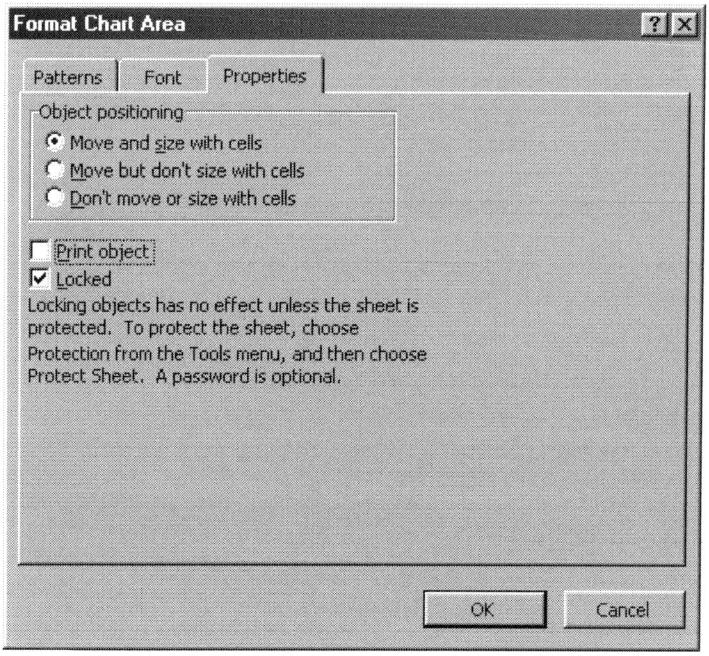

Figure 18.16 : Print Object dialog box

To print an embedded chart without the surrounding worksheet, select it, then choose **File >> Print**.

Hyperlinks

One of the most appealing features of the Web is the convenience to navigate documents using **hyperlinks**. A hyperlink on an Excel worksheet can link to another worksheet range in the same workbook, a different workbook, any file on the local hard drive or network file server, and an Internet/Intranet address or file.

While working, a user may be dealing with documents created in different Microsoft Office applications. By adding hyperlinks to worksheets the user can move between different documents created in Microsoft Office applications with a single click. To create a link in an Excel worksheet to another Office document such as Word, follow these steps:

- Open the Excel worksheet and the document that is to be linked.
- Activate the document to be linked to the Excel sheet - for example, a Word document, and select the text or item that is to be linked.
- Choose **Edit >> Copy**.
- Activate the Excel document and select the cell where the user want the hyperlink.
- Choose **Edit >> Paste as Hyperlink**.
- Click a cell other than the cell in which the hypertext link was pasted.

The selected text appears in the cell containing the hyperlink. It will be colored so that it stands out from other text. After the hyperlink is pasted, the selected text appears in the cell as the hyperlink text.

Another method of creating hyperlinks enable the user to insert hyperlinks to local files or Internet sites. To create a hyperlink to a new file follow these steps:

- Right-click the cell or graphic you want to represent the hyperlink, and then click Hyperlink on the shortcut menu, a insert hyperlinks dialog box appears as shown in figure 18.17.
- Under Link to on the left side of the dialog box, click Create new document.
- Type a name for the new file in the Name of new document box.
- To specify a location other than the one shown under Full Path, type the new location in the Name of new document box or click Change and then select the location you want. Click OK.

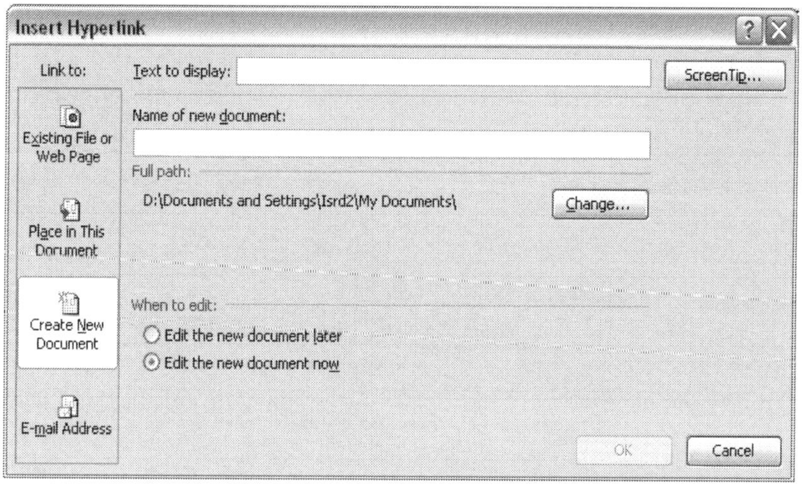

Figure 18.17 : Insert Hyperlink dialog box

- Under When to edit, click an option to specify whether to open the new file for editing now or later.
- To assign a tip to be displayed when you rest the pointer on the hyperlink, click ScreenTip and then type the text you want in the ScreenTip text box. Click OK.

Using Excel with Office Applications

There are essentially three ways to transfer data to and from other Windows applications:

- Copy and paste using the Windows Clipboard.
- Create a link so that changes in the source data are reflected in the destination document.
- Embed an entire object from another application into a document.

Embedding and Linking Objects

There are three different ways of including an object created in one application in a file created in another application:

- Inserting
- Embedding
- Linking

An object can be defined as a component of a file that can be handled separately. For example, charts and ranges in Excel.

Inserting

When an object is inserted in a file, the file contains neither information for editing the object in place nor a link to the object's source file. The object simply appears in the place you specify. Graphics are generally inserted in a file rather than being linked or embedded.

Embedding

When you embed an object in a file, the file contains a full copy of that object. For example, if you embed an Excel chart in a Word Document, the document contains a full copy of the chart. Updation made to the original chart will not be reflected directly in the copy. You must edit the copy separately. Embedding generally increases the size of the file to which the object is embedded.

Linking

Linking is the more complex method of inserting on object created in another application into a file. When an object is linked to a file, the file displays the current information for that object but stores only a link that describes the object. When the information about the link is stored the size of the file is not increased as in the case of embedding the object. Further more when an object is linked you can update the link by issuing the update command. The application reads the latest data from the source of the link and displays it in the file.

Using the Windows Clipboard

The general steps that are required to copy from one application to another are listed below. These steps apply to copying from Excel to another application and to copying from another application to Excel.

- Activate the source document window that contains the information that is to be copied.
- Select the information by using the mouse or the keyboard. If Excel is the source application, this information can be a cell, range or chart.
- Select **Edit >> Copy** That sends the information to the Windows Clipboard.
- Activate the destination application. Move to the appropriate position.
- Select **Edit >> Paste** for the receiving Windows application.

The Excel data is pasted into the receiving application. Figure 18.18 shows a Microsoft Word report having an embedded Excel chart.

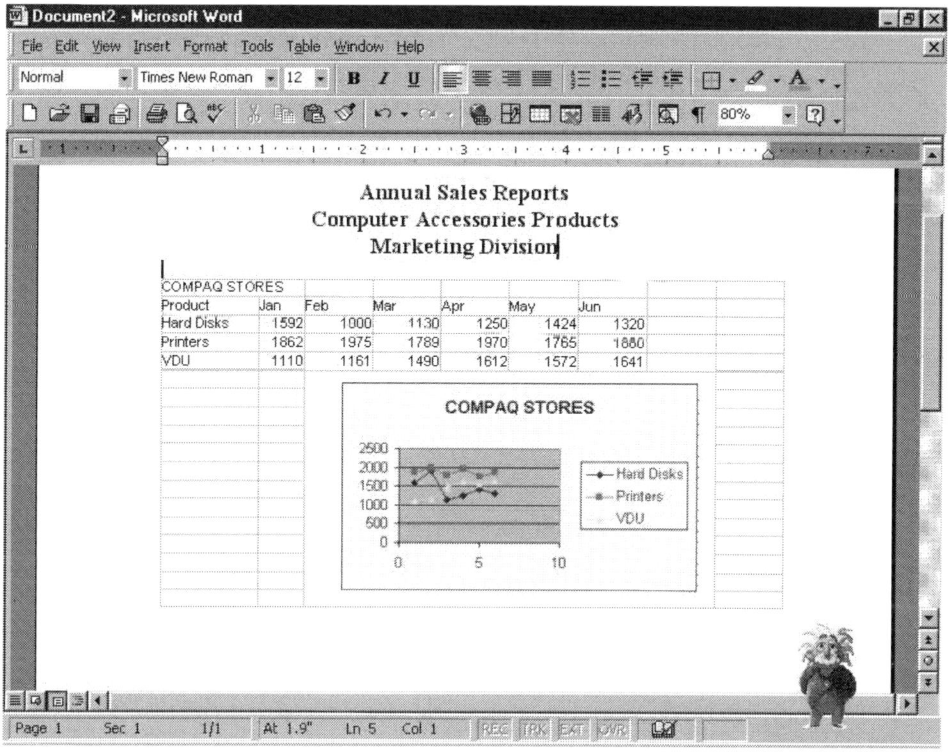

Figure 18.18 : A Microsoft Word report having an embedded Excel chart

Linking Data Between Applications

Linking means to create a dynamic link between the data copied from one Windows application to another. So, if the data changes in the source document, these changes are made automatically in the destination document. Linking takes place in two ways :linking Excel to other application by using a **remote reference formula**--much as linking Excel workbooks together by using external references or by using macros to control the dynamic data Exchanges that produce links. To create a link from one Windows application to another, the general steps are the same as discussed in the above method-- using the **Windows Clipboard**. The only difference is in step 5-select **Paste Special** instead of Paste command and then choose Link option.

Embedding Objects

Another method of sharing information between Window applications is to embed an object in the document. This is known as **Object Linking and Embedding (OLE)**. The user can embed data into an Excel worksheet from any OLE server application. This technique lets the user insert an object from another program and use the other program's editing tools to manipulate it. An object can be embedded into document in two ways:

- Choose **Edit >> Paste Special** and select the "object" choice. Select the **Paste** option rather than the **Paste link** option.
- Select **Insert >> Object**.

Embedding an Excel Range in a Word Document

Let us consider an example. The range shown in figure 18.19 is embedded in a Word document.

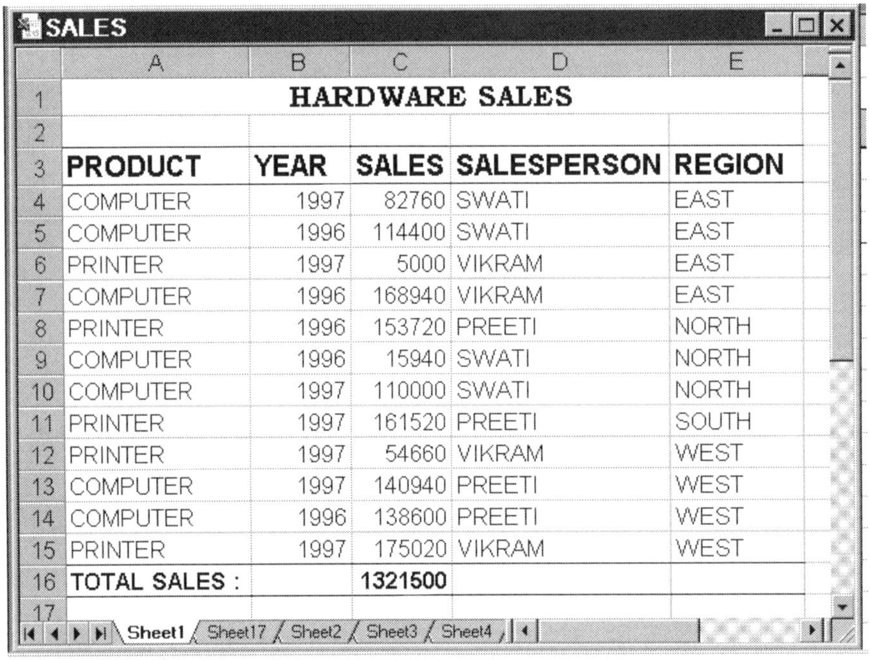

SALES

	A	B	C	D	E
1	HARDWARE SALES				
2					
3	PRODUCT	YEAR	SALES	SALESPERSON	REGION
4	COMPUTER	1997	82760	SWATI	EAST
5	COMPUTER	1996	114400	SWATI	EAST
6	PRINTER	1997	5000	VIKRAM	EAST
7	COMPUTER	1996	168940	VIKRAM	EAST
8	PRINTER	1996	153720	PREETI	NORTH
9	COMPUTER	1996	15940	SWATI	NORTH
10	COMPUTER	1997	110000	SWATI	NORTH
11	PRINTER	1997	161520	PREETI	SOUTH
12	PRINTER	1997	54660	VIKRAM	WEST
13	COMPUTER	1997	140940	PREETI	WEST
14	COMPUTER	1996	138600	PREETI	WEST
15	PRINTER	1997	175020	VIKRAM	WEST
16	TOTAL SALES :		1321500		
17					

Sheet1 / Sheet17 / Sheet2 / Sheet3 / Sheet4

Figure 18.19 : A worksheet containing data to be embedded

To Start

- Select A1 : D15 and copy the range to the Clipboard.
- Activate (or start) Microsoft Word.
- Move the insertion point to the location in the document where the Excel's data is to be embedded.
- Choose Word's **Edit >> Paste Special** command (refer figure 18.20).
- Select the **Paste** option, and choose the **Microsoft Excel Worksheet** Object format.

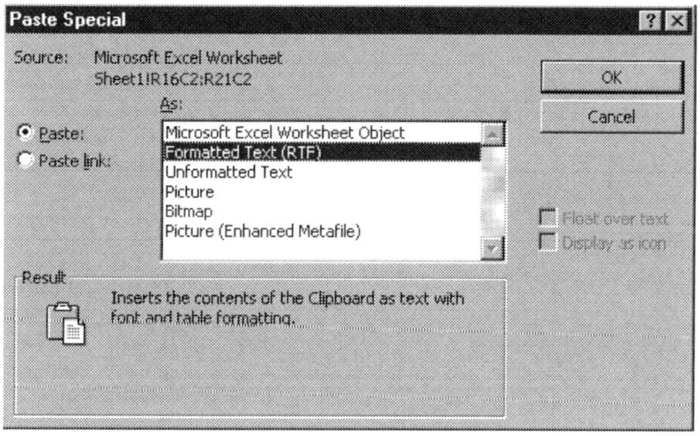

Figure 18.20 : Paste Special dialog box in MS-Word

- Click on OK and the range is pasted to the document.

Summary

- Charts are an effective way to represent information.
- A variety of charts are available in Excel, for example, column charts, bar charts, line charts and pie charts.
- It is possible to create either an embedded chart or an independent chart on a chart sheet.
- Charts can also be printed with and without the other data in a worksheet.
- Hyperlinks are the most interesting feature of Web which links one piece of data at one place to another piece of data at some other place.
- In Excel, hyperlinks can be inserted or pasted anywhere according to the user's requirements.
- It is also possible to convert data in worksheets into HTML pages to make it accessible to all computers connected through Internet.
- It is also possible to embed an Excel range in a Word document.

Review Exercise

Multiple choice questions

1. To change the size of the chart without changing its proportions, which of the following keys should be pressed while dragging the corner handle?

   a) Shift

   b) Ctrl

   c) Alt
   d) None of the above

2. To delete an embedded chart
   a) Select the chart and press Delete
   b) Select the chart and choose Edit >> Clear All
   c) Both of the above
   d) None of the above

3. Select the option that creates a chart automatically on a chart sheet by selecting the data to be plotted.
   a) F11
   b) Alt+F1
   c) Both of the above
   d) None of the above

4. Which of the following statements is incorrect about charts?
   a) The legend can be placed at the desired location.
   b) It is not possible to delete all data series from a chart.
   c) Each axis has two sets of gridlines.
   d) A trendline points out general trends in your data.

5. A pie chart is useful when you want to
   a) Display stock market information.
   b) Show relative properties or contributions to a whole.
   c) Show changing values over time and proportional relationships.
   d) Illustrate differences between each data series and between many data series simultaneously.

6. Which of the following is not a way of linking Excel to other application?
   a) Using a Remote Reference Formula
   b) Using Object Linking and Embedding (OLE)
   c) Both of the above
   d) None of the above

7. A hyperlink on an Excel worksheet can link to
   a) Another worksheet range in the same workbook
   b) A different workbook
   c) An Internet Intranet address or file.
   d) All of the above
8. Identify the incorrect statement.
   a) The embedded object is completely independent from the original source.
   b) Not all Windows applications support linking.
   c) You can use Edit >> Break command to break a link.
   d) When you embed a video clip, Excel stores a pointer to the original file and not the actual video clip file.

State whether true or false

1. The difference between an embedded chart and a chart in a separate sheet is that a chart sheet is not updated automatically when the source data changes.
2. You need to save a chart sheet separately from the main worksheet.
3. The uniqueness about pie chart is that it can only plot one data series.
4. It is not possible to embed a chart from a chart sheet into a worksheet.
5. A hyperlink on an Excel worksheet can link to an Internet / Intranet address or file.
6. It is possible to create a link in an Excel worksheet to another Word document.
7. In linking, if the data changes in the source document, these changes are not reflected in the destination document.

Fill in the blanks

1. A ______________ is just a column chart that has been rotated 90 degrees to the left.
2. A ______________ chart is used for comparing the percentages of a sum that several numbers represent.
3. The ______________ graph is also called a scatter chart and is generally used for plotting the data points within the axis reference.
4. ______________ graph is ideal for presenting trends for continuous data.
5. ______________ charts look like topographical maps.

6. ___________ means to create a dynamic link between the data copied from one Windows application to another.

7. ___________ is the technique which enables the users to insert an object from another program and to manipulate it using another program's editing .

8. Excel has the ability to use ______ as a native file format.

Descriptive questions

1. How many types of charts does Excel support?
2. In any given chart, can two different groups of data have different dimensional views?
3. How will you create an embedded chart using the chart wizard?
4. Explain in brief the following with reference to a chart
   a) Legend
   b) Area chart
   c) Data series
5. You have created a chart based on the data in a worksheet. The chart is displayed in the same worksheet.
   a) How will you change the size of the chart?
   b) If the data that was used to create the chart is changed, what happens to the chart?
   c) It is required to include another data series in the chart. How will you implement this?
6. What is the use of Embedding?
7. How will you embed an Excel range in a Word document?
8. What are the main differences between Linking and Embedding? Explain with the help of a suitable example.

C H A P T E R

19 MICROSOFT POWERPOINT

FEATURING

- Introduction to PowerPoint
- Starting PowerPoint
- The PowerPoint Window
- Creating a Presentation
- Saving a Presentation
- PowerPoint Views
- Outlining the Presentation
- Customizing a Presentation
- Creating Slide Shows
- Printing Presentations

Communication plays a vital role in every business activity. Whether you are addressing a group of potential clients, trying to win management approval for the new product you wish to design, or presenting your viewpoints at seminars, your success depends on how effectively you present your message. PowerPoint is the presentation graphics program of the Microsoft Office suite. This program can be used for creating charts, slides, handouts, overheads, i.e., any conceivable presentation materials. PowerPoint is also capable of creating slide shows, which are electronic presentations that can be run on the computer screen or on a projection device. The look of these presentations can be enhanced by the use of professionally designed templates that come with PowerPoint. This chapter is penned to provide a foundation to harness the power of creating presentation using Microsoft PowerPoint 2003.

Introduction to PowerPoint

PowerPoint is a component of Microsoft Office suite that is used to create professional quality presentations. These presentations can be effectively utilized to inspire, educate, and inform the viewers. Using PowerPoint, you can create attractive slides, organize presentation contents with outlines, and generate speaker's notes. Slides, in a presentation, can contain text, graphics, charts and even sound and video, and can be presented as overheads, as 35 mm slides, or electronically on-screen. Speaker's notes provide the presenter with a page for each slide that contains a small image of the slide with additional notes. PowerPoint makes the creation of any presentation simple by offering a wide variety of built-in professional design elements (called AutoLayouts), presentation templates and galleries of images and sounds.

Other features that make PowerPoint a powerful presentation program include the following:

- An AutoContent Wizard that facilitates in writing the content of your presentation.
- Professionally designed templates, backed with animation, that can be used to quickly create effective presentations.
- A Normal View which displays the slide, the outline, and a notes area.
- An Outline View which can be used to organize the content of your presentation.
- A host of charting features which presents you with a number of ways to display data.
- Full drawing capabilities, which enable you to either add hand-drawn art to your slide show or use any of the clip art files available in PowerPoint.
- Different views — Normal, Slide, Outline, Notes Pages, Slide Sorter, and Slide Show — that enable you to view your presentation in different perspectives.
- The feature of publishing your presentation to the World Wide Web.
- Compatibility with other Microsoft Office programs that makes it easy to fetch data from other programs.

Starting PowerPoint

To start PowerPoint

- Click on the Start button located at the bottom left corner of your screen.
- Select All Programs >> Microsoft Office >> Microsoft Office PowerPoint 2003.
- Instantly, the program window of PowerPoint opens up on the screen (Figure 19.1). Since we have not designed any presentation as yet, let us create a new presentation. But first let us understand the PowerPoint window in detail.

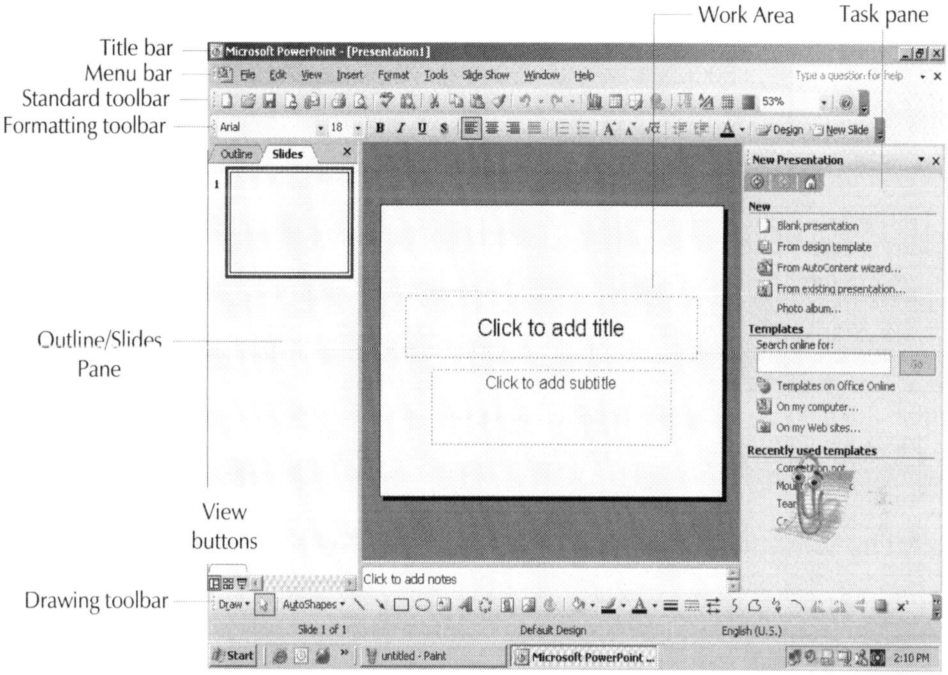

Figure 19.1 : The PowerPoint Window

The PowerPoint Window

The PowerPoint window has many useful tools. The purpose that each of the elements in the PowerPoint window solves is given below:

- **Title bar** The presentation name is displayed here. Dragging the title bar moves the window.
- **Menu bar** It shows a list of commands used in PowerPoint for various tasks.
- **Status bar** Displays the current slide number.
- **Standard toolbar** Houses buttons that can be used for file management, editing, and proofing.
- **Formatting toolbar** Contains buttons for text formatting and create new slides.
- **Drawing toolbar** Houses buttons for adding graphic objects to slides.

- **View buttons** Provide a way for quickly changing the display of the presentation screen.
- **Placeholder** One can click or double-click a placeholder in order to add an element to a slide.
- **Task Pane** It is a specialized toolbar that changes according to what you are doing. its job is to provide common task options so you can easily click and use them.
- **Outline/Slides Pane** The Outline/Slides pane appears on the left side of the PowerPoint interface. This pane allows you to toggle between the slides view and the outlines.

Creating a Presentation

Having discussed the PowerPoint window and its various tools, let us create a presentation. Under the **New** option, there are four methods available for creating a new presentation, in the New Presentation task pane (Figure 19.1).

- From AutoContent Wizard
- From Design Templates
- From Existing Presentation
- Blank Presentation

We will create presentation using all the four methods given above one by one. Let us start with AutoContent Wizard.

Using the AutoContent Wizard

A wizard is an automated utility that walks you through a sequential process and creates a sample outline for your presentation. The AutoContent Wizard will ask you a series of questions, answering which will result in a sample outline of your presentation which can later be altered.

To start a presentation using the AutoContent Wizard follow the steps given below:

- Choose File >> New, the New Presentation taskpane will appear.
- Select AutoContent Wizard from the TaskPane. AutoContent Wizard dialog box shown in Figure 19.2. Click Next.

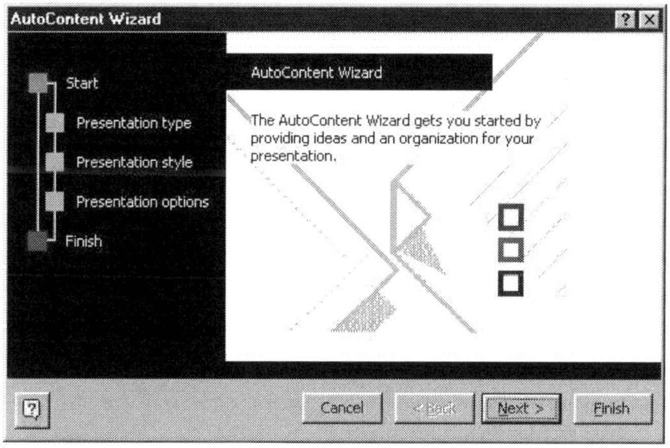

Figure 19.2 : The AutoContent Wizard dialog box

- Select the type of presentation you want to create from the presentation type page, and click Next (refer Figure 19.3).

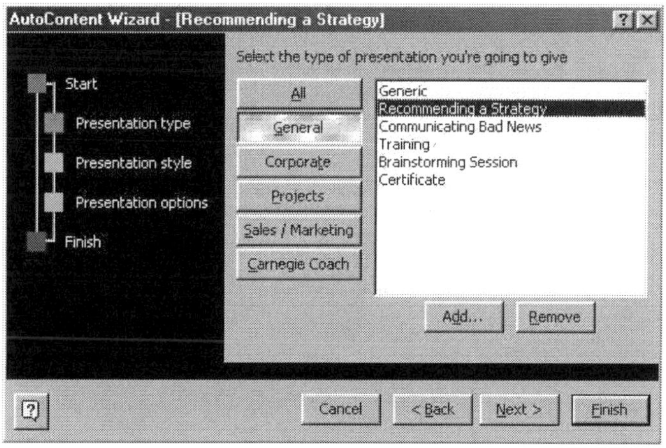

Figure 19.3 : Select a presentation type

- From the output page, presentation style can be selected. Select an option to specify the type of output you intend to have, and Click Next (refer Figure 19.4).

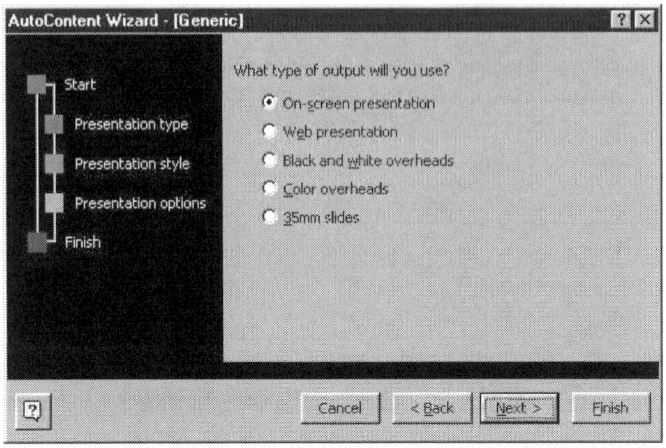

Figure 19.4 : Select the type of output

- The next screen asks you to enter the presentation title, and the footer for each slide. You can even include current date and slide number on each slide by checking the two check boxes present on the screen as shown in Figure 19.5.

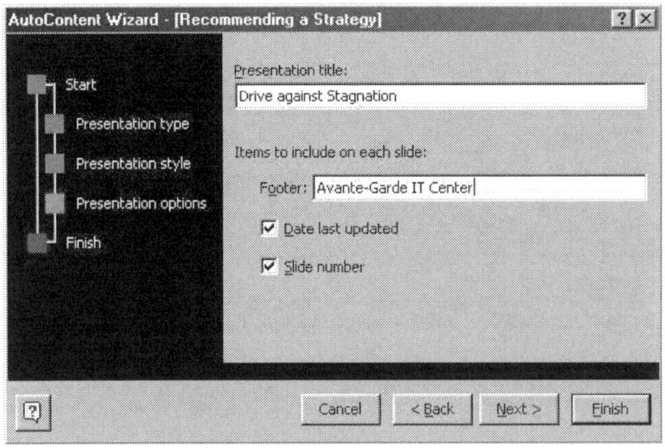

Figure 19.5 : Fill in the Presentation title and footer

- Click the Finish button to see your presentation in the Normal view (refer Figure 19.6).

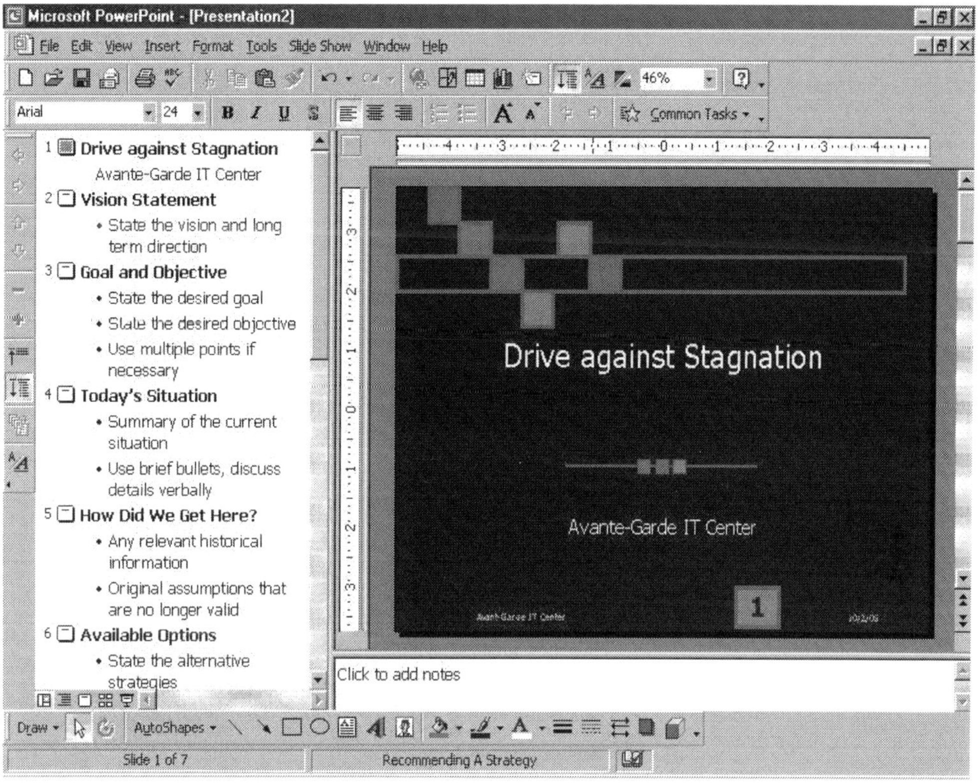

Figure 19.6 : Sample presentation created with AutoContent Wizard

NOTE Each sample presentation outline generates a presentation with a preset look. The look can be changed later by choosing a different design template.

Using Design Templates

PowerPoint offers a number of predefined templates you can put to use for creating effective presentations. The templates of PowerPoint come in two forms, **Design Templates** and **Presentations**. Design templates provide the graphic design and color scheme for your presentation. The presentations available under the Presentations tab suggest content and structure, using a set of slides whose text is editable.

To start with a design template:

- Choose **File >> New**.
- Select '**From design template**' from the taskpane. (refer Figure 19.1). All templates will appears on the pane as shown in Figure 19.7.

- Scroll through the list of templates to locate the one you want.
- Once located click it.

NOTE Notice the drop down arrow control that appears on the right side of the template preview. Click the arrow. A menu appears which gives you the option to apply the template to all slides or only to a selection of slides. (refer Figure 19.7)

Figure 19.7 : Select a template

- The template is applied to your current slide, which is your title slide by default.
- When you insert a new slide you get the option to apply the default layout of the choosen template or select your own template.
- A new presentation opens in Normal view with the design selected through template. It contains one slide.

The design templates provide no suggestions regarding content or organization; but can be effectively employed to enhance the visual appeal of the slides.

Design templates contain color schemes, slide and title masters with custom formatting and styled fonts, all designed to create a particular look (discussed in chapter 31).

Using Sample Presentations

You can create your own template which you can then apply to your presentations. Once you have created a new template, it appears in the slide design task pane the next time you open Microsoft PowerPoint, in alphabetical order under Available for use.

- On the **File** menu, click **New**.
- In the **New Presentation** task pane, under New, click from existing presentation, select the presentation you want, & then click create New.
- Delete any text, slides, or design elements that you don't want to be part of the new template, and apply any changes that you do want in the template.
- On the **File** menu, click **Save As**.
- In the file name box, type a name for your template.
- In the Save As Type box, click Design Template.
- Click Save.

Saving a Presentation

After you finished creating your presentation, you have to save it on the hard disk of the computer. So that you can retrieve it later. For saving the presentation follow the steps given below:

- Choose **File >> Save**, a **Save as** dialog box appears, asking you to specify the file name and the location (i.e. folder), where you like to save the presentation.
- Type the appropriate name, and click on the **Save** button. The file will be saved with the specified name at the specified location.

PowerPoint Views

Microsoft PowerPoint has three main views : Normal View, Slide Sorter View, and Slide Show View. The view buttons are available at the lower left corner of the screen and can be clicked to easily switch between views.

Normal View

Normal view is the main editing view, which you use to write and design your presentation. In all, it contains three panes: the outline pane, the slide pane, and the notes pane. This view is helpful when one has to work on all aspects of the presentation at once; add text in outline and see how it appears on the slide; type the notes that will remain with the current slide (refer Figure 19.8).

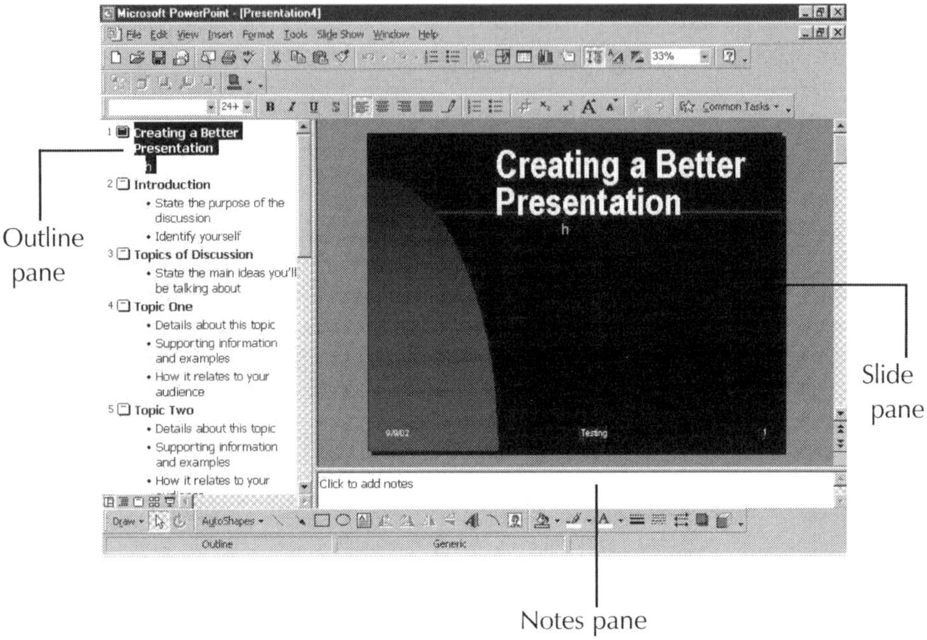

Figure 19.8 : Normal view

The **Outline pane** can be used to organize and develop the contents of your presentation. In the **Slide pane**, you can see how the text appears on each slide. It is through this pane that you can add graphics, movies, and sounds, create hyperlinks, and add animations to slides. The **Notes pane** is used to add speaker notes or information to your presentation, that you can share with the audience.

Outline View

This view displays the presentation text in outline form. It allows you to work easily with the content. It is also helpful in moving, copying or cutting text; spell-checking text; reading through for consistency; or printing a script for your presentation (refer Figure 19.9).

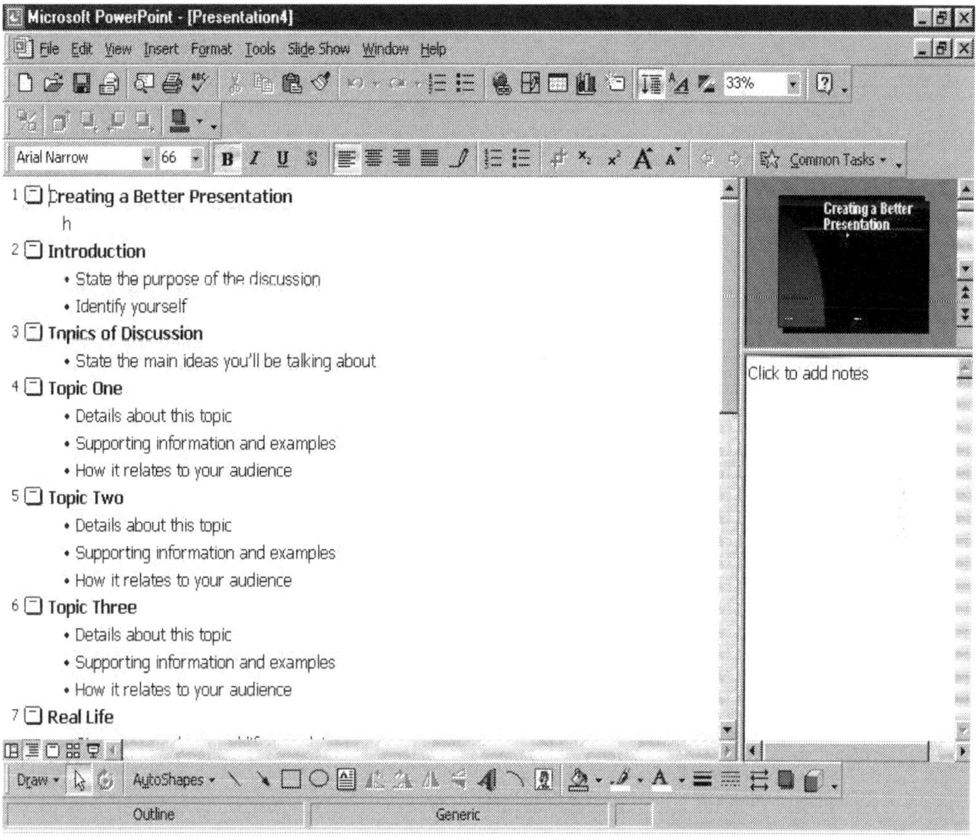

Figure 19.9 : Outline view

Slide View

This view gives you the freedom to work on slides only, one by one, while the outlines are minimized on the smaller left pane. It is comparatively easier to add text or objects to a single slide or format only one slide at a time.

The left pane now contains only the slide numbers, so that you can select any one from them (refer Figure 19.10).

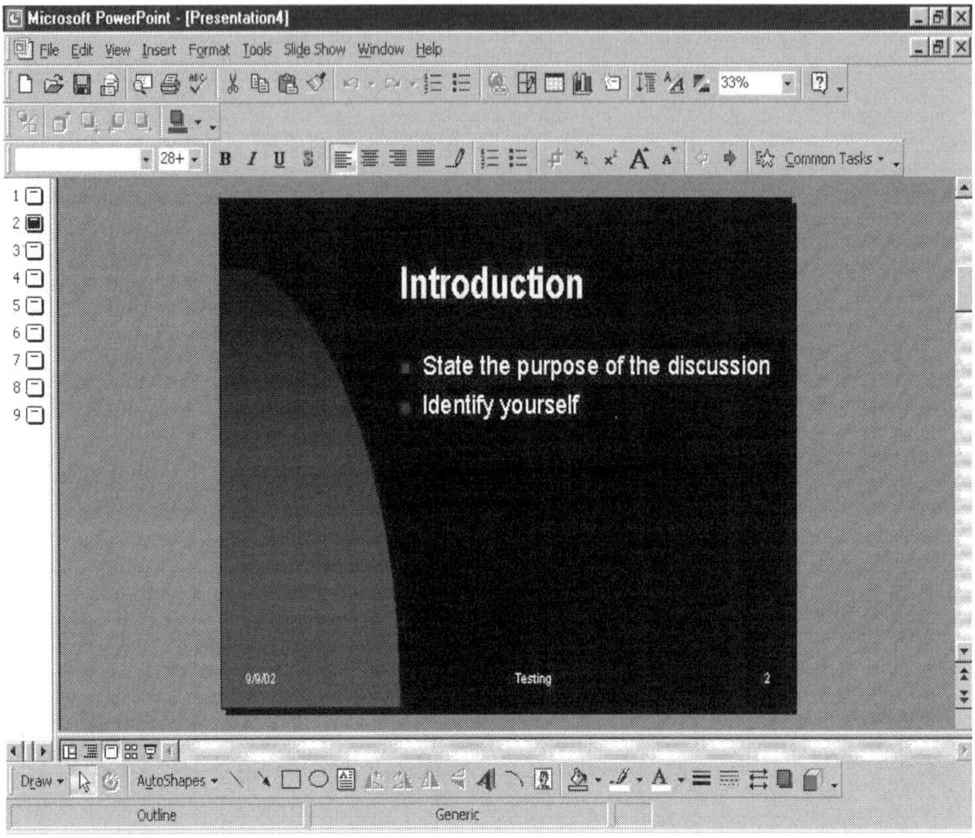

Figure 19.10 : Slide view

Slide Sorter View

It displays miniature versions of all slides in a presentation, complete with text and graphics. In this view, you can reorder slides, add animation, set timings, move or delete slides, insert new slides or check presentation continuity. This view also allows to add and edit the transition effects for the slide show (refer Figure 19.11).

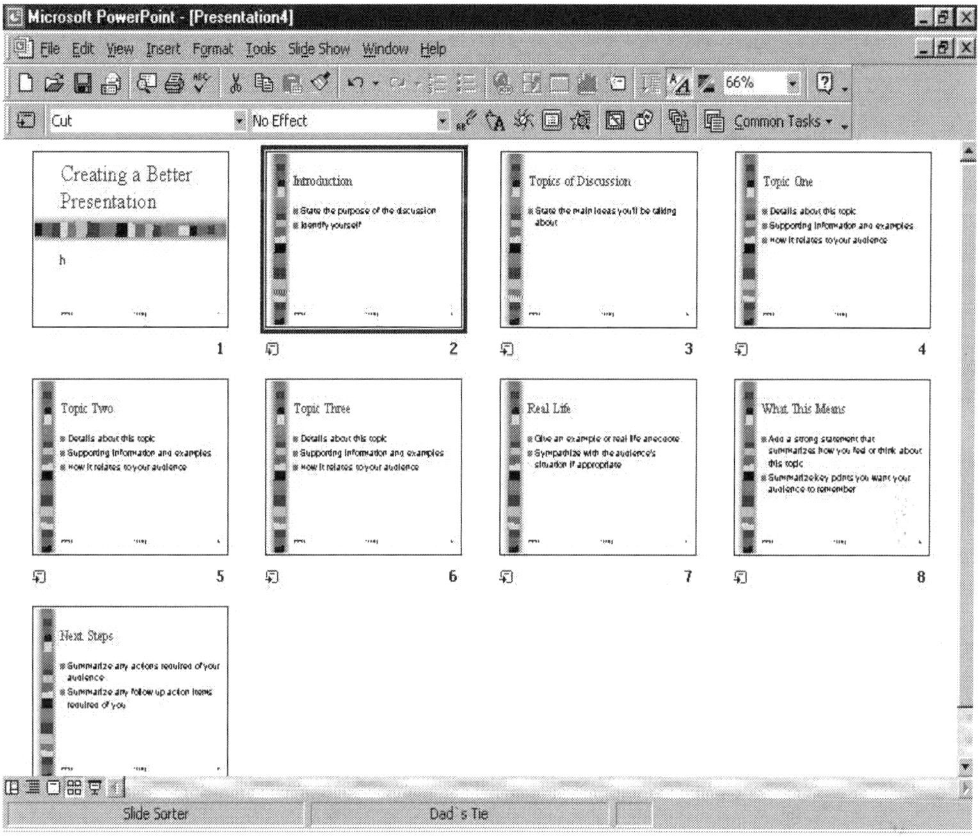

Figure 19.11 : Slide Sorter view

Notes Page View

This view displays the current slide in a reduced size with room for notes at the bottom of the page. It lets you enter and edit speaker's notes for the presenter. It is used for adding a memo, notation or instruction for a slide(s). You can also use this view to design explanatory handouts for your audience. This view is only available from the **View** menu. To change to Notes Page view, choose **Notes Page** from the **View** menu (refer Figure 19.12).

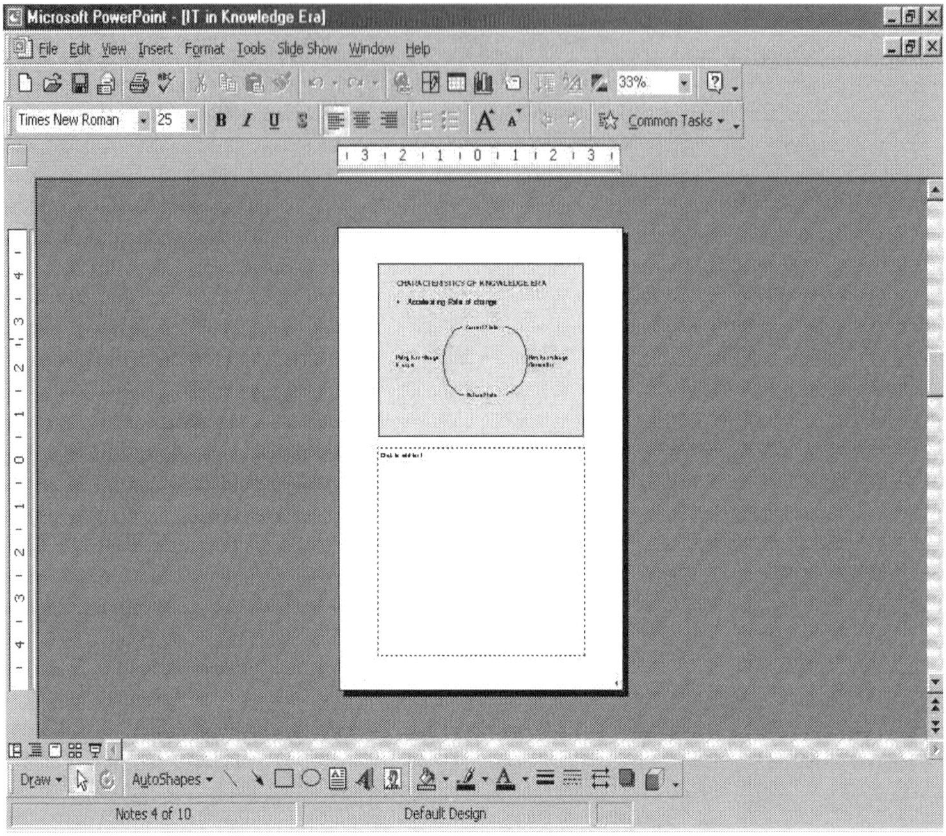

Figure 19.12 : Notes Page view

Slide Show View

This view displays the presentation one slide at a time in sequence as an automatic slide show (refer Figure 19.13).

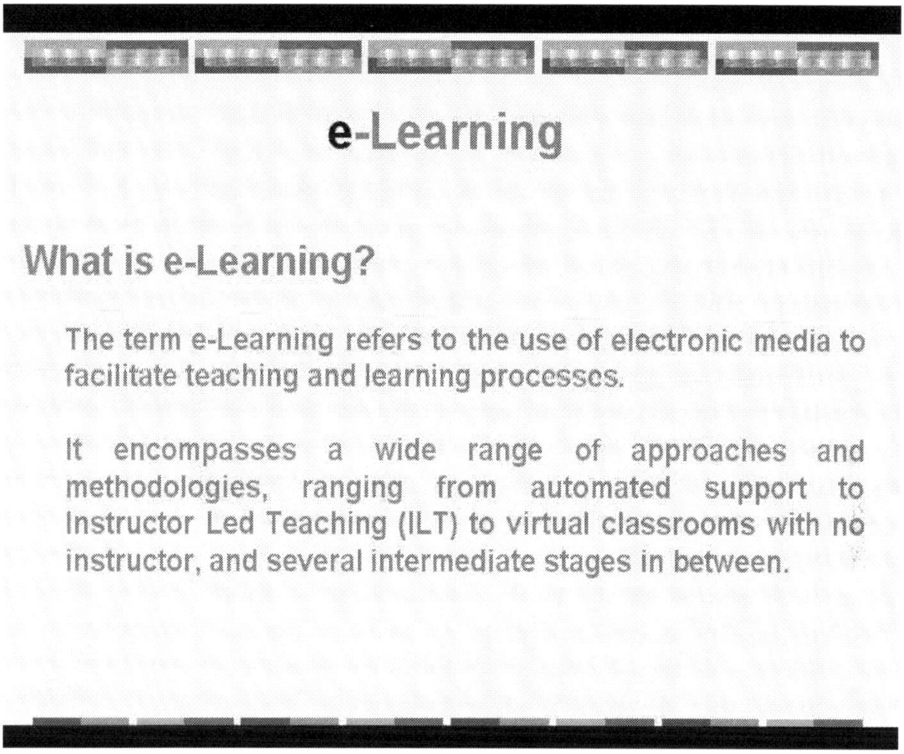

Figure 19.13 : Slide Show view

Outlining the Presentation

Outline view is basically used for textual editing as it only shows the text in outline form and focuses on the content of the presentation rather than the appearance.

Entering the Text

Outline view is one such view in which the text can be entered most conveniently. To enter text, follow the steps given below:

- Type the title for a slide next to the slide icon and press Enter in Figure 19.14.

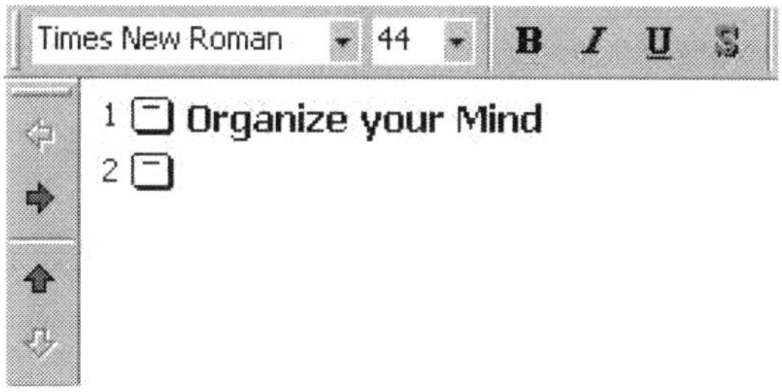

Figure 19.14 : Slide Title

- Type the title of the next slide and press Enter.
- Press Shift + Tab to start a new slide (refer Figure 19.15).

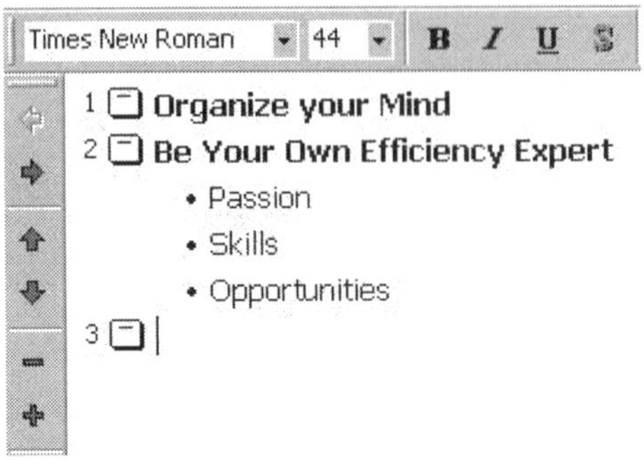

Figure 19.15 : Starting a new slide

- Follow the steps given above to create new slides or add bulleted text points to the current slide.

Replacing Existing Text

To replace text that is provided by the AutoContent Wizard or the sample presentation, follow the steps given below:

- Click a bullet to select a bulleted text line (refer Figure 19.16).

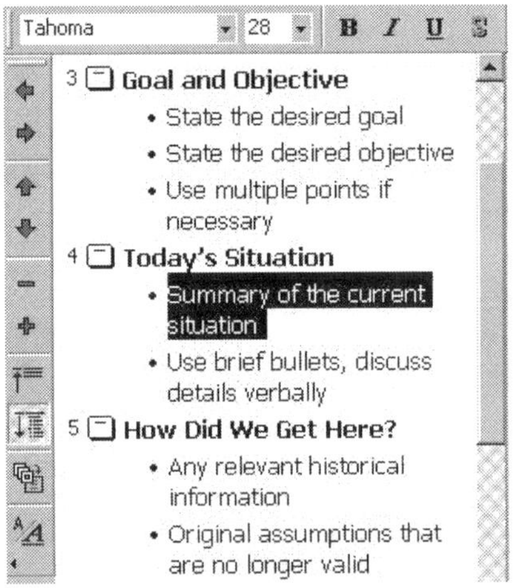

Figure 19.16 : Replacing Text

- Type the new text.

NOTE You can click on the slide icon to select the entire text on a slide and then type the replacement text.

Reorganizing the Slides

Outline view can be used to reorganize the slides either by dragging or by using the buttons on the Outlining toolbar.

For moving a slide follow the steps given below:

- Click and hold a slide icon.
- Drag and release the mouse button to place the slide at its new position.

Deleting Slides

To delete a slide follow the steps given below:

- Click the slide icon to select an entire slide.
- Press the Del key to delete the slide

Rearranging Items in an Outline

After adding text in the slides, sometimes it is required to change the order of occurrence of some items. It is sometimes required to demote or promote some items to create a much more effective presentation.

- To demote any Outline item, select that particular item or line, right click on the outline pane and select Insert Tab.
- Click at the beginning of the line you want to promote and then click on the backspace button.

Customizing a Presentation

Considerable changes can be brought about in a presentation by changing its template. A template contains a color scheme (a combination of colors for various presentation elements like text, etc.) and a slide master design (background color, text fonts and formatting, and background graphic object).

A new design template, colour schemes, and animation schemes can be applied to a presentation by following the steps given below:

- Choose Format >> Slide Design. A Slide Design task pane appears, as shown in Figure 19.17. You can preview and apply a design template to your presentation. The template can be applied to all slides or selected slides, and can apply more than one type of design template in a single presentation.

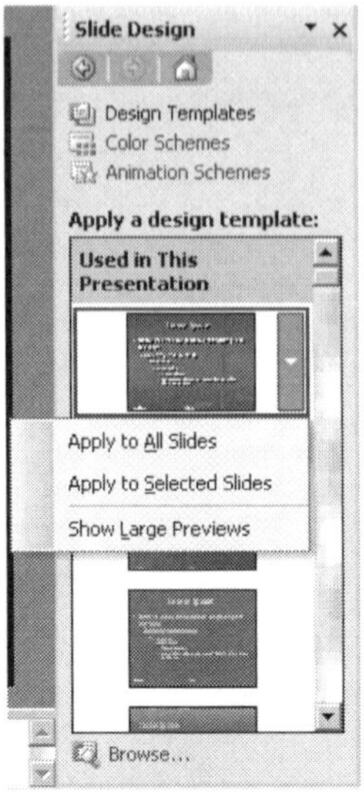

Figure 19.17 : Slide Design task pane Showing Design Templates

- **Applying a New Design** In the Slide Design task pane choose the design template, right click on it and choose Apply to All Slides, or Apply to Selected Slides. (Figure 19.17)
- **Changing the Color Scheme** In the Slide Design task pane choose Color Schemes. Then choose appropriate colour scheme, right click on it and choose either Apply to All Slides or Apply to Selected Slides option. (Figure 19.18)

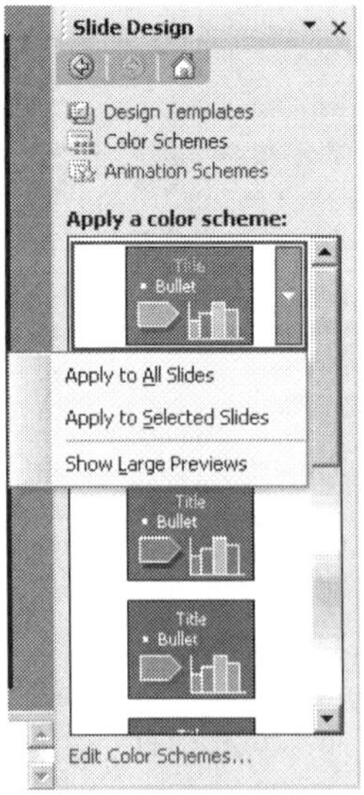

Figure 19.18 : Slide Design task pane Showing Color Schemes

Applying Graphics, Charts and Tables

You can draw shapes, add auto shapes, and insert clipart, pictures, maps and charts, or any other object in your PowerPoint document to enhance the look of your presentation. These graphic elements help us to convey our ideas better in our presentations. In the following section, we will learn to add the various graphics elements such as tables, charts, clipart, images etc. to our presentation.

Tables

Undertakes the following steps to insert a table in a presentation.

- Open the slide on which you want to add table.
- Choose Insert >> Table. Insert table dialog box appears on the screen.

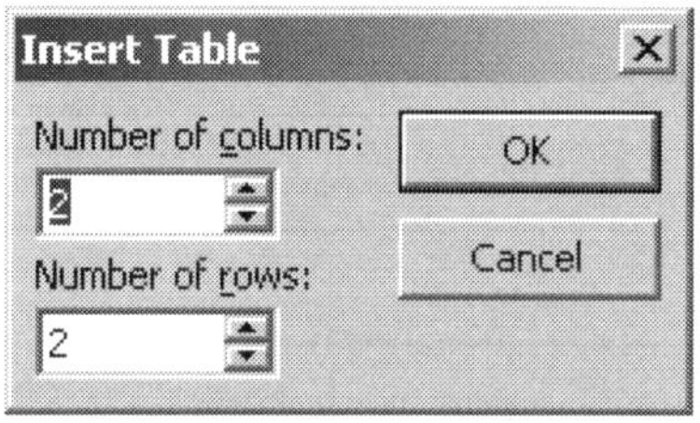

Figure 19.19 : Insert Table dialog box

- Specify the number of columns and rows you need in a table.
- Click on OK, a table appears in the slide pane.

Charts

To insert a chart in your presentation, undertake the following steps:

- Open the slide on which you want to add a chart.
- Choose Insert >> Chart. A sample chart with an excel worksheet appears on the screen over the slide pane area (Figure 19.20). Change the data in excel worksheet (if required), graph will change accordingly.
- If you want to change the style of chart then move the mouse pointer over the chart area, and click the right mouse button. Select **Chart type** option from popup menu. A dialog box appears asking for type of the chart you want. Select the type, click OK. Your chart will appear in the newly selected style.

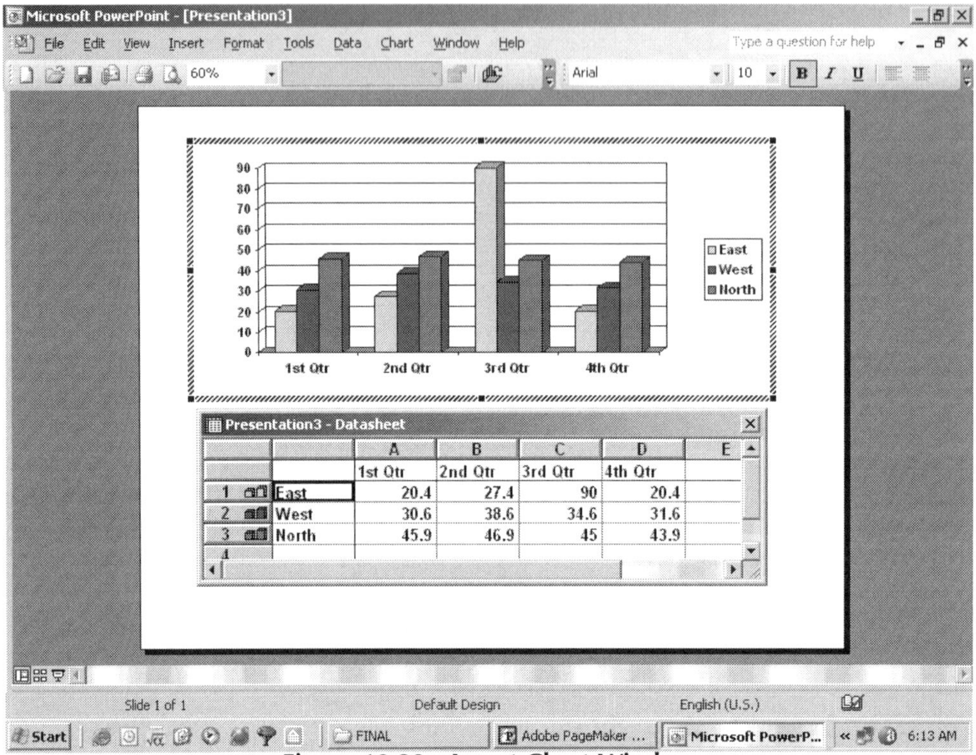

		A	B	C	D	E
		1st Qtr	2nd Qtr	3rd Qtr	4th Qtr	
1	East	20.4	27.4	90	20.4	
2	West	30.6	38.6	34.6	31.6	
3	North	45.9	46.9	45	43.9	
4						

Figure 19.20 : Insert Chart Window

Adding Images

PowerPoint provides many sample images for your use. Adding an image to a slide can enhance its appearance significantly. To add an image from the clipart gallery to your slide, follow these steps:

- Open the slide on which you want to add the clipart. Make sure you are in Normal View.
- Choose Insert >> Picture >> ClipArt option. The Insert ClipArt task pane appears on the right side of the Slide pane (Figure 19.21).
- In the Insert ClipArt task pane, type the keyword that describes the kind of image you are looking for in the box under the **Search Text** option. Click **Search** button.
- Add a desired picture into your presentation by clicking it. The picture will appear in the slide.

Figure 19.21 : Adding Images task pane

Masters

PowerPoint has a built-in feature known as **Masters**. Using Masters one can easily organize, maintain and modify text and animation for creating a slide. Masters can be categorized into three sub heads, the Slide Master, Handout Master, and Notes Master.

The Slide Master

The Slide Master is an element of the design template that stores information about the template, including font styles, placeholder sizes and positions, background design, and color schemes. The Slide Master view get reflected in all slides added through the Slide Layout dialog box, except for the title slide. To switch to Slide Master view:

- Choose **View >> Master >> Slide Master**. The Slide Master view opens up on the screen with the Slide Master View toolbar having many different buttons that allow user to insert, delete, preserve and rename the slides and close the Slide Master View (see Figure 19.22).

- Choose the text, you want to format then choose **Format** menu bar options to change the alignment, background color, add borders, bullets and numbering, and font.

Figure 19.22 : The Slide Master view

NOTE As you format the slide using Slide Master, similarly you can format handouts using Handout Master, and notes (additional information about individual slide) using Notes master.

Animating Art Objects

PowerPoint offers an interesting art feature of animating objects. Animation is the ability to move objects — text, graphics, charts, logos — across, up, or down the slide.

In order to animate any object, select it and click the right mouse button. From the pop-up menu that appears, choose Custom Animation. The Custom Animation task pane appears (refer Figure 19.23).

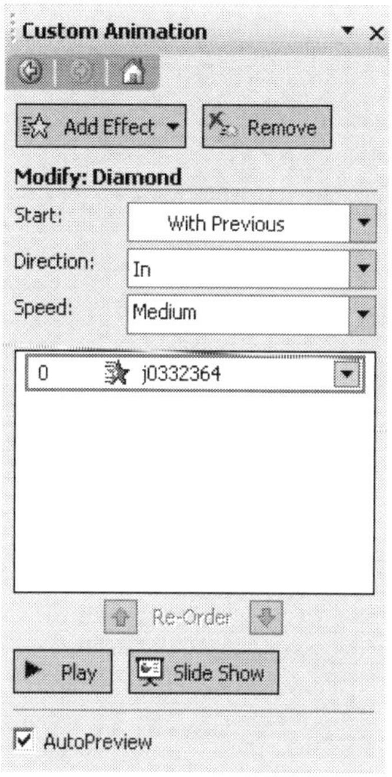

Figure 19.23 : Using Custom Animation to animate art objects

Animation Effects

Click the Add Effect drop down button in the Custom Animation taskpane. Once you have selected this the effect to apply, it will appear in the task pane with some specific name. You can change the way this animation is applied by selecting your choices from the **Direction** drop down box and the **Speed** drop down box. (refer Figure 19.8).

Click on the play button to have a sample preview.

Animation Order and Timing

After applying custom animation on the various objects you can change the order of applying them. To do so:

- Notice the various animation effects that appear in the Custom Animation Task Pane.
- Select the animation you wish to rearrange. (refer Figure 19.24)

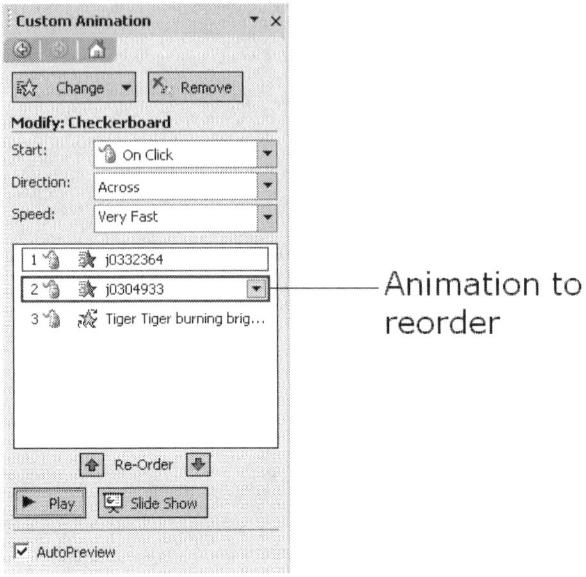

Figure 19.24 : Check to animate slide objects

- Use the up directional or down directional key to move the animation effect up or down.

Creating Slide Shows

A slide show is an animated presentation of slides that you either display on a computer monitor or projection system. When you run the slide show, PowerPoint displays the slides, one at a time, in full screen view. Some of the finishing touches that need to be given before viewing the slide show include adding transition effects between slides, adding animation effects to individual lines of text or charts, adding sound effects, etc. Slide shows can also contain audio or video clips.

Adding Transition Effects

Transition effects are the wipes, fades, dissolves, and other film-like effects that a slide show can use to remove the current slide and bring in a new one. To choose a transition effect for your slide, switch to the Slide Sorter view and follow the steps given below:

- Click the slide to which you want to apply the transition effect.
- Choose Slide Show >> Slide Transition.
- In the Slide Transition taskpane that appears as shown in Figure 19.25, select a transition effect and speed you want.

The Advance Slide Options tell PowerPoint when to advance to the next slide in the slide show. Mark both check boxes if you want the next slide to appear when you click the mouse or automatically after the specified number of seconds.

In the Sound box, click the sound you want to accompany the slide transition effect. The "Loop until next sound" check box, if checked, continues playing the sound until the next sound starts. Clear this check box if you want the sound to play only once.

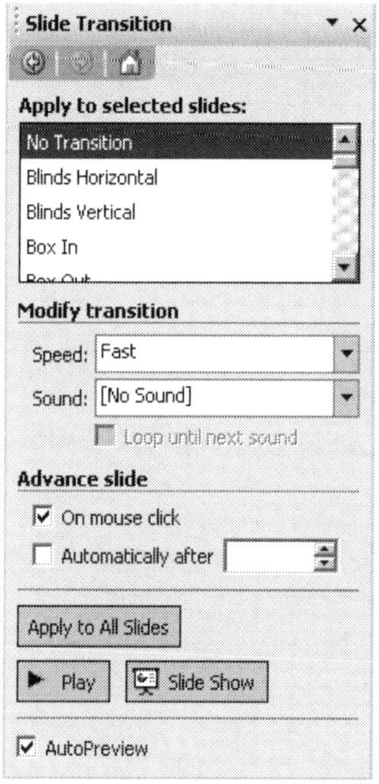

Figure 19.25 : Choose Slide Transition effects

- Click Apply to add the selected transition effect only to the selected slide, or Apply to All to add it to all the slides.

Adding Preset Animation

Preset Animation, if applied, brings slide title and bulleted text into view using a special effect. To choose a preset animation, follow the steps given below:

- Switch to the Slide Sorter view.
- Select the slide that requires preset animation.
- Select an effect from the Preset Animation list on the Slide Sorter toolbar (refer Figure 19.26).

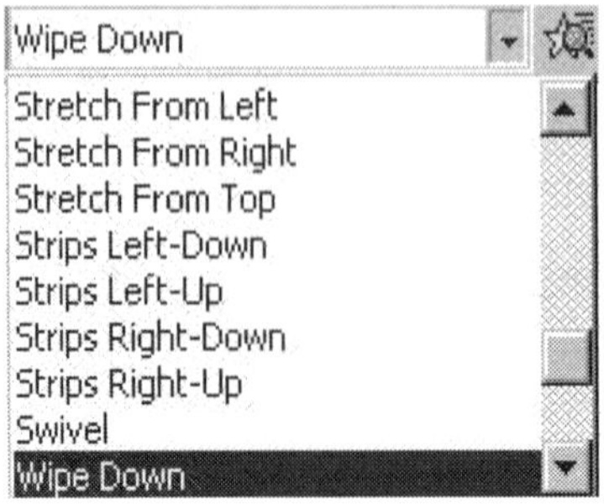

Figure 19.26 : Select a preset animation

Adding Audio and Video

Audio and video can easily be added to the presentation by inserting files from the Clip Gallery or from other folders.

To add on audio or video file, switch to the Slide view and follow the steps given below:

- Display the slide to which you want to add the audio or video file.
- From the Insert menu, choose Movies and Sounds and then choose Sound from File or Movie from File.
- Depending on what you choose, the Insert Sound dialog box or Insert Movie dialog box appears. Type in a filename or browse through the folders to locate the sound/video file.
- Click OK.
- Answer Yes to have the sound/video play automatically or No to have it play when you click it.

Rehearsing Slide Display Timing

Follow the steps given below to rehearse the timing of your presentation:

- Click Slide Show >> Rehearse Timings. The active slide show will begin playing and the automated Rehearsal dialog box is displayed (refer Figure 19.27).

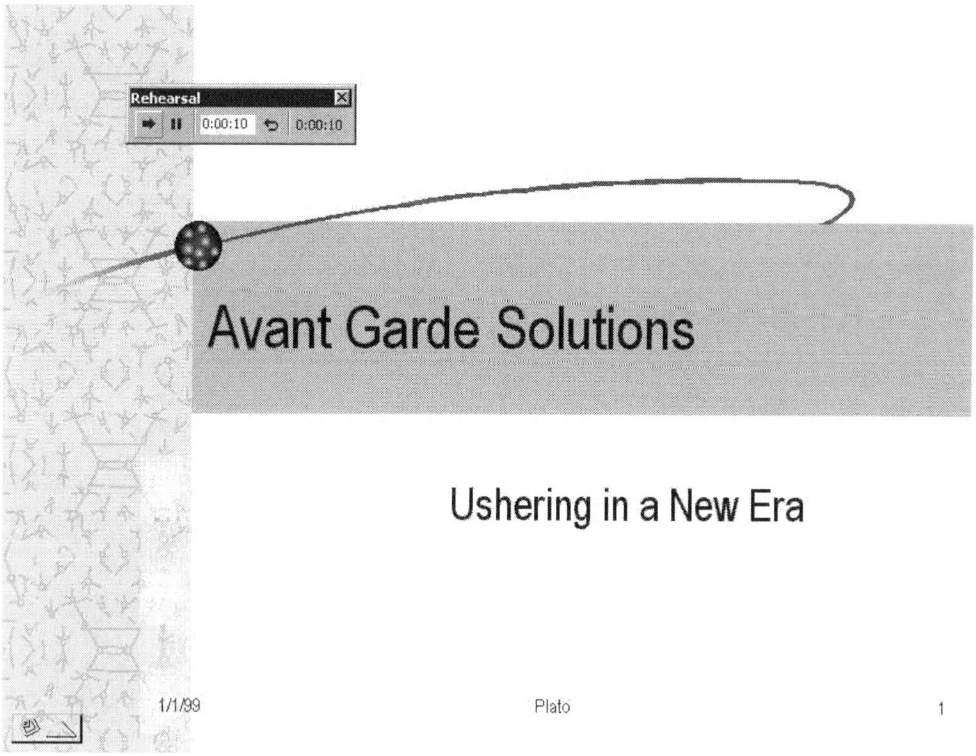

Figure 19.27 : Rehearse slide timing

- After you have timed your delivery for each slide, click the Next button to advance to the next slide.
- Click the Pause button to pause the timing process. Click it again to resume timing.
- Click the Repeat button, if required, to restart the timing for the current slide.
- When the presentation timing is complete, click Yes to accept the set timings (refer Figure 19.28) or Click No to retain the previous timings.

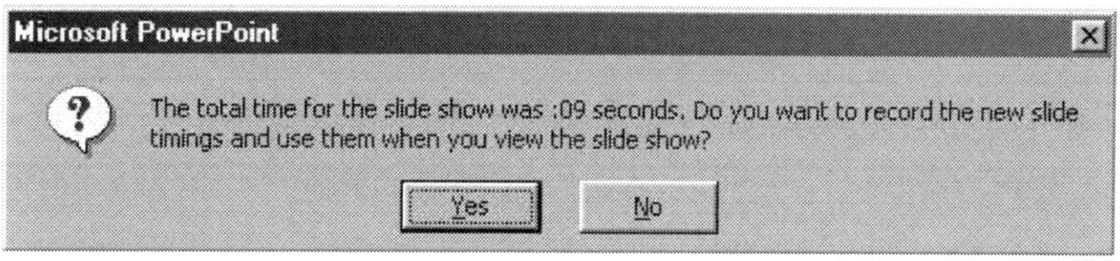

Figure 19.28 : Click Yes to record the new slide timings

If you clicked Yes, Slide Sorter view will get displayed and the new timings will be listed under each slide.

Setting Up the Slide Show

The Slide Show can be set up in Normal, Outline, Slide, or Slide Sorter view. The Set Up Show dialog box controls the way in which a slide show will be run; which slides will be displayed; and whether the show will be presented by a speaker, a viewer, or will automatically run at a kiosk location.

To access the Set Up Show dialog box, click Slide Show >> Set up Show (refer Figure 19.29).

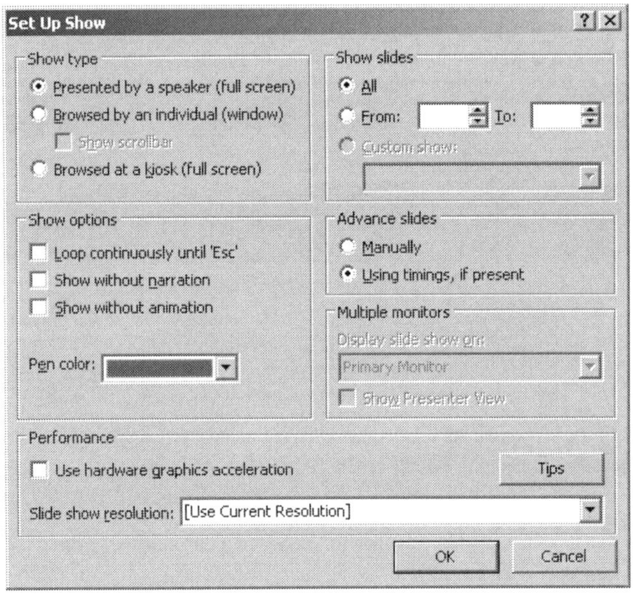

Figure 19.29 : Setting up the slide show

- In the **Show Options** section click "Loop continuously until 'Esc' " if you want to keep the slide show running until the "Esc" key is pressed.
- Click "Show without narration" if you want to eliminate sound during the show. This is useful at trade shows or when system resources are limited.
- Click "Show without animation" when resources are limited.
- In the **Show Slides** section, click "All" if you want to display all slides in the presentation, or Click "From" if you want specific slides to be displayed.
- In the **Advance slides** section click "Manually" to allow the slide show to be advanced using the mouse and the arrow keys on the keyboard, or Click "Using timings, if present" to allow automated preset timings to control the pace of the slide show.

After making the desired settings, click OK to accept the adjustments or Cancel to return to the presentation without making any setup adjustments.

Viewing the Slide Show

After you've finished setting up the slide show, you are ready for the show. Given below are the ways PowerPoint offers to view slide show transitions, animation and other effects.

- **Previewing Individual Slide Effects in Miniature Window** Click Slide Show >> Animation Preview.
- **Previewing Individual Slide Effects on a Full Screen** Click the Slide Show View button at the bottom of the screen.
- **Viewing Entire Slide Show from the beginning** Click Slide Show >> View Show, or Press the F5 function key.

Printing Presentations

After making the slides, you need to print them. For printing the slides, undertake the following steps:

- Choose **File >> Print** option. Print dialog box appears (Figure 19.30)
- Select **All**, if all the slides have to be printed, or mention the slide range to the Print Page range option.
- Finally click on the OK button. Instantly, the slides get printed on the paper.

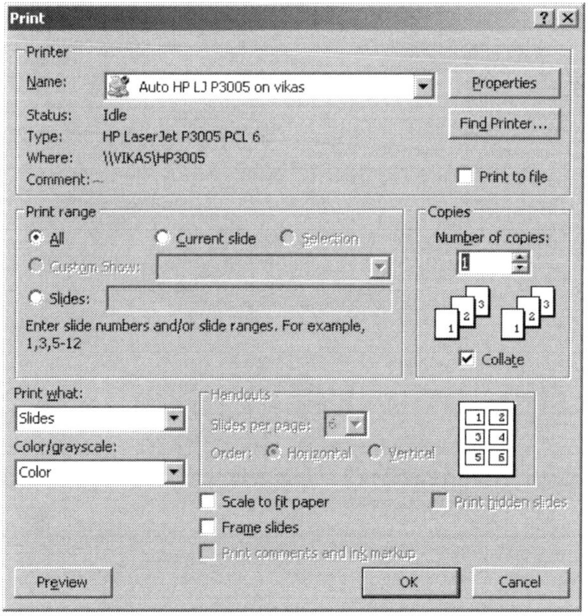

Figure 19.30 : Print dialog box

Summary

- Microsoft PowerPoint is a powerful presentation package.
- The AutoContent Wizard facilitates in writing the content of your presentation and provides an outline based on the answers you provide to the questions.
- PowerPoint offers a number of predefined templates that can be used for creating effective presentations.
- PowerPoint provides several views to look through your presentations.
- The Normal view is the default view of PowerPoint which shows a combination of slide, outline and notes page view.
- The Outline view displays the presentation in outline form making it easy to copy, move or delete slides.
- The Slide view offers one slide at a time for editing. In Slide view, text, charts, graphics, clip art, and other objects can easily be added and you can directly work on the slide.
- The Slide Sorter view displays miniature versions of all slides in a presentation.
- The Notes Page view allows the user to add notes for each slide.
- The Clip Art can easily be added to the slide by selecting the slide with the Clip Art placeholder.
- The Format Picture command can be used to edit images in PowerPoint.
- A slide show is an on-screen presentation of slides.
- A slide transition is the effect PowerPoint uses to remove the current slide and bring in a new one.
- To save your presentation as an HTML file, choose File >> Save as HTML.

Review Exercise

Multiple choice questions

1. After finishing its task, the AutoContent Wizard places you in which view?

   a) Notes Page view

   b) Outline view

   c) Normal view

   d) Slide Sorter view

2. Design templates provide the _________ for your presentation.
   a) Content and organization
   b) Structure and layout
   c) Graphic design and color scheme
   d) All of the above
3. Which view allows you to reorder slides, add animation, set timings, move or delete slides?
   a) Slide view
   b) Notes Page view
   c) Outline view
   d) Slide Sorter view
4. In which view you can add text, charts, graphics, clip art, and other objects with ease?
   a) Notes Page view
   b) Slide view
   c) Slide Sorter view
   d) None of the above
5. One can click or double-click a _________ in order to add an element to a slide.
   a) Placeholder
   b) Office Assistant
   c) Slide view button
   d) Normal view button
6. In which of the views, slide show can be set up?
   a) Normal
   b) Outline
   c) Slide Sorter
   d) All of the above

7. The ________ view displays elements which are common to all the slides, except the title slide.

   a) Slide Sorter

   b) Slide

   c) Slide Master

   d) None of the above

8. Which of the following keys should be pressed to keep the shape of the object precise and symmetrical?

   a) Ctrl

   b) Shift

   c) Alt

   d) Tab

9. You cannot rehearse or view the slide show in ________ view.

   a) Normal

   b) Slide Sorter

   c) Outline

   d) Notes page

10. ___________ are added to grab the audience's attention as well as reinforce the point that needs to be highlighted.

    a) Animation effects

    b) Transition effects

    c) Screen views

    d) Pack and Go

11. If you have an audience of more than 15 people, you need to use ________ to set up and give the broadcast.

    a) Microsoft Outlook Express

    b) Microsoft FrontPage

    c) Microsoft NetShow

    d) None of the above

State whether true or false

1. In Slide view, you can reorder move and delete slides.
2. When a design template is assigned to a slide it is changed in all other slides.
3. Slides in Outline view cannot be printed.
4. In Slide view, only one slide can be formatted at a time.
5. When you apply a design template to your presentation, the slide master, title master, and color scheme of the new template replace the slide master, title master, and color scheme of the original presentation.
6. The Slide Show can be run by pressing the F6 function key.
7. Preset Animation brings slide title and bulleted text into view using a special effect.
8. Any changes made to the elements in the Slide Master view get reflected in all slides added through the Slide Layout dialog box.
9. You cannot add video clips to your presentation.
10. PowerPoint provides many built-in templates with different backgrounds, and text formatting to create a presentation.

Fill in the blanks

1. The normal view simultaneously displays the ______ , ______ , and ______ areas in their own adjustable panes.
2. The templates of PowerPoint come in two forms: ______________ and ________________.
3. PowerPoint files have _________ extension.
4. ________ is the default view of PowerPoint.
5. The keyboard shortcut for starting a new slide in a presentation outline is __________ .
6. You can use the ________ command to edit your images in PowerPoint.
7. A __________ is an on-screen presentation of slides.
8. The _________ dialog box controls the way in which a slide show will be run.
9. The _________ helps you transform your presentations into self-starting ones.
10. A __________ is the effect PowerPoint uses to remove the current slide and bring in a new one.

Descriptive questions

1. Differentiate between a template and a wizard.
2. How can you apply a different color scheme to your presentation?
3. What is an AutoContent wizard?
4. What is the difference between Notes Page and Slide Sorter view?
5. How can you rearrange items in an outline?
6. How can you insert a picture into your slide from any image file?
7. How can you animate art objects?
8. What is the significance of rehearsing the time for each slide?
9. What settings are required to be made for having a self-running presentation?
10. What is the role-played by Masters in PowerPoint? Give the steps involved in adding animations.

CHAPTER 20

DATABASE FUNDAMENTALS

FEATURING

- Database Management Systems
- Data Models
- Database System Architecture
- Relational Database Management System
- Candidate Key and Primary Key in Relation
- Foreign Keys
- Relationships
- Referential Integrity

This chapter provides a basic concepts of Database Management System (DBMS). DBMS is a software, which carry out operations like insertion, deletion, and retrieval, the database needs to be managed. Hence, DBMS can be defined as a collection of interrelated data and a set of programs to access that data. This chapter deals with the basic concepts of data and its organisation, database fundamentals along with its components and architecture.

Database Management Systems

Database management system is a collection of programs that allow you to create and maintain databases. Database is a collection of data stored for a specific purpose. Database management system is a software system that allows you to define, construct and manipulate databases used for various purposes such as to store customer and financial information of an organization.

Features of database management system:

- Prevents data redundancy
- Prevents unauthorized access
- Provides persistent storage for program objects and data structures
- Provides Multiple User interfaces
- Provides Integrity Constraints
- Provides Backup and Recovery

Data Models

A data model in DBMS is defined as the collection of concepts used to describe the structure of a database. Structure of a database refers to the data types, constraints and relationships used on data. In addition, data model also includes basic operations to be used to specify the retrieval of data from a database and performing update on the database. The various data models are:

Relational Data Model

In a relational data model, data is stored in tables. The related tables in the relational data model form a database. The properties of relational data model are:

- Each row in a table is unique from every other row in the table.
- Each row contains atomic data, which implies that data is not repeated and does not contain structures such as arrays.

Hierarchical Data Model

In the hierarchical data model, data is organized in a tree structure. The tree structure consists of hierarchy of parent and child data segments. The hierarchical data model can have repeating information in the child data segments. The advantages of the hierarchical data model are:

- Is simple to construct and operate on data in the hierarchical model.
- Involves hierarchically organised domains such as product information in manufacturing and employee information in organization.

- Uses constructs such as GET, GET UNIQUE and GET NEXT.

Network Data Model

In the network data model, which is also called CODASYL model, data is organised using set construct. A set consists of an owner records type, a set name and a member record type. Unlike hierarchical model, a child segment in a network model can have multiple parent segments. The advantages of the network data model are:

- Enables representing complex relationships and effect of operations such as add and delete on the relationships.
- Uses constructs such as FIND, FIND owner and FIND NEXT within a set that allows the users to navigate through the database.

Object-Oriented Data Model

The object-oriented (OO) data model consists of a collection of entities. Entity refers to the concept or object described in a database.

Database System Architecture

The database system architecture is designed so that the storage details of data in a database are hidden from users. The users accessing a database need to work with data rather than any concern for how the data is physically stored in the database. The database system architecture allows:

- Different user views of the database for users. It provides customized view to each user accessing the same data from the database. Each user view is independent and any change to a view does not affect other views.
- The internal structure of the database to remain unaffected by changes made to the physical storage of data.
- The database administrator to change the structure of a database without the user views of the database being affected.

The architecture of database system is called American National Standards Institute/ Standards planning and Requirements Committee (ANSI/SPARC) model. The (ANSI/SPARC) model is divided into three levels, which are:

- **Internal level** Specifies the way in which the data is physically stored in a database. The internal or physical level of the database system architecture also provides description of the relationship that exists between the data.
- **External level** Specifies the way in which the data stored in a database is viewed by the users.

- **Conceptual level** Specifies the level of interaction between the internal level and external level of system architecture.

Figure 1.1 shows the representation of the different levels of architecture:

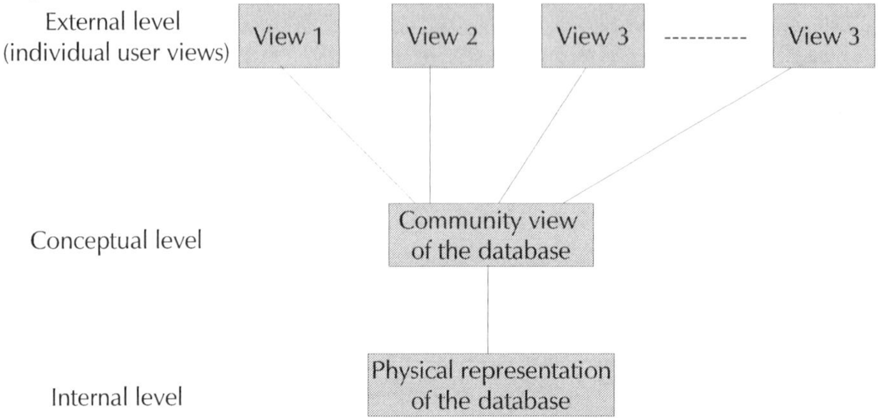

Figure 20.2 : Different Levels of Architecture

Relational Database Management System

Relational database management system (RDBMS) is a type of DBMS in which data is stored in the form of related tables. Some of the common terms used in RDBMS mode are:

- **Relation** Is also known as entity or table.
- **Tuple** Is also known as record or row in a relational table.
- **Attribute** Is also known as field or column in a relational table.

Characteristics of Relational DBMS model are:

- Eliminates all parent-child relationship and represents data in database in tables of data.
- Rows of a table in relational model are referred to as tuples and the columns as attributes. You can create tuples of equal length and place the tuples together to create a table in the Relational model.
- Each table in a Relational model is a separate entity and no relationship exists between the tables.
- The Relational DBMS model provides built-in support for query languages such as ANSI SQL and QBE.
- Relational model supports built-in query language, which can be used to manipulate data.

- The Relational model provides a non-procedural interface in which you need to specify the operations such as addition and deletion to the database to be performed and do not need to specify how the operations are to be performed.

Candidate Key and Primary Key in Relation

Each relational table consists of an attribute, which is unique in a relational table and enables you to identify the tuples of the relational table. Primary key in a relational table refers to one or more attributes that uniquely identify a tuple. If a relational table consists of more than one attribute that is unique for the table, then the attributes are referred to as candidate keys for the relational table. You can arbitrarily select a key from the set of candidate keys as primary key for the relational table. For example, consider an employee table that lists the values of various attributes such as employee id and project id of each employee. Table 20.1 lists the information details of employees in an organisation.

Emp_id	First_name	Last_name	Dept_name	Proj_id
010	Sachin	Verma	Sales	01
011	Kapil	Singh	Sales	12
012	Rohit	Agarwal	Accounts	33
013	Kapil	Singh	Accounts	24

Table 20.1 : The Employee Table (department wise)

In the above table, the attributes Emp_id and Proj_id uniquely identify each tuple in the table. Therefore, Emp_id and Proj_id are the candidate keys for the Employee table. We can select one of the candidate keys, say Emp_id to uniquely identify the rows or tuples in the table. Then Emp_id is called as the primary key and Proj_id as the alternate key in the Employee relational table.

Foreign Keys

A foreign key refers to one or more attributes in a table that must also appear in another table. The table, which the foreign key refers, is called as parent table and the table, in which the foreign key exists, is called the child table. The foreign key in a child table references a primary key in the parent table. Foreign keys provide a method for maintaining integrity in the data called as referential integrity. For example, consider the employees and jobs table stored in a database of an organisation. Table 20.2 lists the employee information.

emp_id	emp_name	emp_lastname	job_id
010	Rohit	Agarwal	01
011	Kapil	Singh	02
012	Sachin	Verma	03

Table 20.2 : The Employee table with Job_id as the foreign key

job_id	job_desc
01	Sales Manager
02	Accounts Manager
03	Technical Personnel

Table 20.3 : The Jobs table

In the employee table, job_id attribute is a foreign key that relates the employee table and the jobs table. The foreign key job_id refers to the primary key emp_id of the employee table and therefore, links the employee and jobs table. The rows of the primary key, which are referenced by the foreign key, cannot be deleted to preserve referential integrity. Also, you cannot add a value in a foreign key column that does not refer to an existing value in a primary key column.

Relationships

Relationship is an association, dependency or link between two or more entities. A relationship works by matching data in key-fields — usually a field with the same name in both tables. In most cases, these matching fields are the primary key from one table, which provides a unique identifier for each record, and a foreign key in the other table.

A One-to-Many Relationship

A one-to-many relationship is the most common type of relationship. In a one-to-many relationship, a record in first table (parent) can have many matching records in second Table (child), but a record in second Table has only one matching record in first Table. For example, a department may have more than one employee but an employee has only one department.

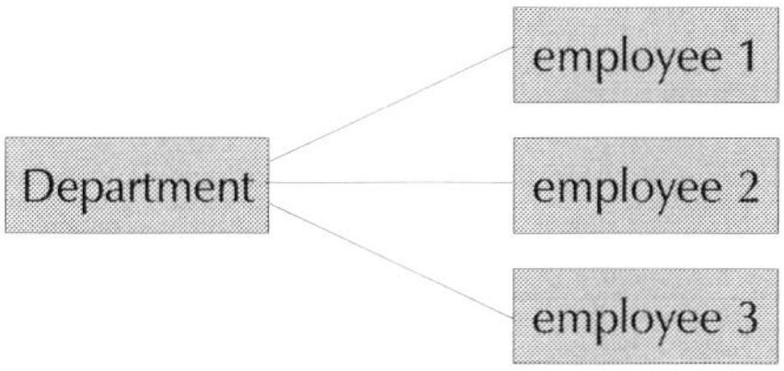

Figure 20.3 : One-to-Many Relationship

A Many-to-Many Relationship

In many-to-many relationship, a record in first Table can have many matching records in second Table, and a record in second Table can have many matching records in first Table. This type of relationship is only possible by defining a third table (called a junction table) whose primary key consists of two fields — the foreign key from both tables. A many-to-many relationship is really two one-to-Many relationships with a third table.

For example, a customer can buy many goods and many customers can buy the same good.

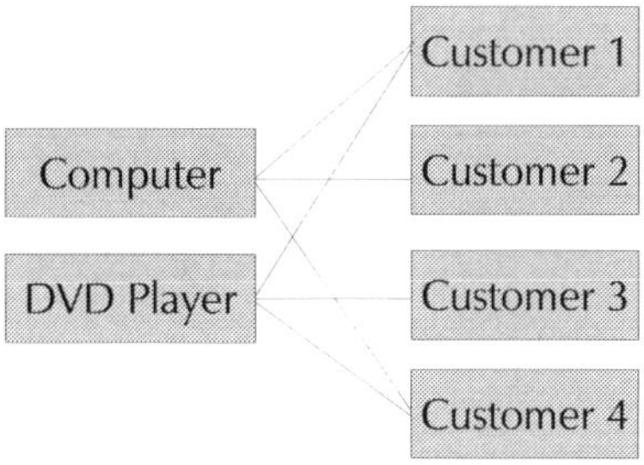

Figure 20.4 : Many-to-Many Relationship

A one-to-one Relationship

In a one-to-one relationship, each record in first table can have only one matching record in second Table, and each record in second Table can have only one matching record in first Table. For example, an employee has only one employee code.

Figure 20.5 : One-to-One Relationship

Referential Integrity

Referential Integrity is a system of rules that RDBMS uses to ensure that relationships between records in related tables are valid, and that you don't accidentally delete or change related data. You can set referential integrity when all of the following conditions are met:

- The matching field from the primary table is a primary key or has a unique index.
- The related fields have the same data type.
- Both tables belong to the same database. Referential integrity can't be enforced for linked tables from databases in other formats.

The following rules apply when you use referential integrity:

- You can't enter a value in the foreign key field of the related table that doesn't exist in the primary key of the primary table.
- You can't delete a record from a primary table if matching records exists in a related table.
- You can't change a primary key value in the primary table, if that record has related records.

Summary

- Data is a collection or raw items.
- When data, is processed and converted into a meaningful and useful form, it is known as information.
- A field is the smallest unit of data, which possesses meaning to its users.
- Primary key denotes a key that is choose by the database designer as the principal means of identifying records within a table.
- Relationship in which one record in a table is related to only one record in another table is known as 1:1.

Review Exercise

Multiple choice questions

1. In which data model, data is stored in tables.

   a) Relational data model

   b) Network data model

   c) Hierarchical data model

   d) None of the above

2. In a one-to-many relationship
   a) a record in Table A can have many matching records in Table B
   b) many records in Table A can have many matching records in Table B
   c) a record in Table A can have one matching record in Table B
   d) None of the above
3. Father and Son share __________ type of relationship.
   a) 1:M
   b) M:M
   c) 1:1
   d) None of the above

State whether true or false

1. MS-Access is a true relational database management system.
2. In a table, columns represents fields and rows represents records of data.
3. The process data is called information.
4. Conceptual level specifies interaction between the internal and external level of system architecture.
5. A many-to-many relationship is really two one-to-many relationships with a third table.

Fill in the blanks

1. A ____________ key refers to one or more attributes in a table that must also appear in another table.
2. __________ is a system of rules to ensure the relationships between records in related tables are valid.
3. A ____________ is used to extract information from a database.
4. Network data model also called ___________ model.
5. ____________ ensure that relationships between records in related tables are valid.

Descriptive questions

1. What do you mean by DBMS? Explain with suitable examples.
2. Define database, table, record, field and values.
3. Why we use more than one table in a database?
4. What do you mean by relationships regarding database?
5. Explain all types of relationships with suitable example.
6. Write a short note on referential integrity.

CHAPTER 21

MICROSOFT ACCESS BASICS

FEATURING

- **Introduction**
- **Creating a New Table**
- **Creating Relationships**
- **Editing a Table Structure**
- **Add or Edit Data**
- **Move between Records or Fields**
- **About Finding or Replacing Data**
- **Deleting Records**
- **Sorting Records**

Access is one of the world's most popular relational database systems. Using Access, you can create sophisticated and powerful databases to store and analyze information on any number of topics. Access provides you with a set of powerful tools for collecting, retrieving , and presenting data. The most important concept is that the data is stored in a "Black box" known as a table and that by using the tools of the database, you can retrieve, display and report the data in any format. In this chapter, we will take you on a whirlwind tour of Access. You learn to start the process of database and table creation. Later in this chapter you also learn, how to use a datasheet to put data into a table. This method enables you to see multiple records as well as fields simultaneously. You learn to add, change, and delete data, and you learn about features for display data in a datasheet.

Introduction

Microsoft Access is a Relational Database Management System (RDBMS) that allows the user to create a database and then access, retrieve and present the data in it. MS-Access stores the data in the form of rows and columns i.e. in the form of tables. MS-Access comprises of a database engine known as Microsoft Jet Database Engine and a GUI. One can store all kind of information in an Access database, use queries to analyse the data, and create professional reports. Access can be used by almost any user. Beginners can learn to use the wizards and the easy-to-understand interface. MS-Access is used by business organizations and programmers for creating an organized database system.

Access Database Files

Using Microsoft Access, you can manage all your information from a single database file. Within the file, you can use:

- **Tables** to store your data.
- **Queries** to find and retrieve just the data you want.
- **Forms** to view, add, and update data in tables.
- **Reports** to analyze or print data in specific layout.
- **Data access pages** to view, update, or analyze the database's data from the Internet or an Intranet.

Starting Access

You can start Microsoft Access by one of the following methods:

- Click on **Start** button and choose Microsoft Access from the **Programs** menu.
- Click the **Start** menu button, choose Microsoft office from the **Programs** menu and then select MS-Access.
- Choose **Start >> Run**, enter the path and program name (MS Access) in the open text box and then click the **OK** button to start Access.

The Access Window

The Access window is the center of activity for everything that is done in Access. From this window, many windows can be opened simultaneously, each of which displays a different view of your data. Figure below shows the Access window.

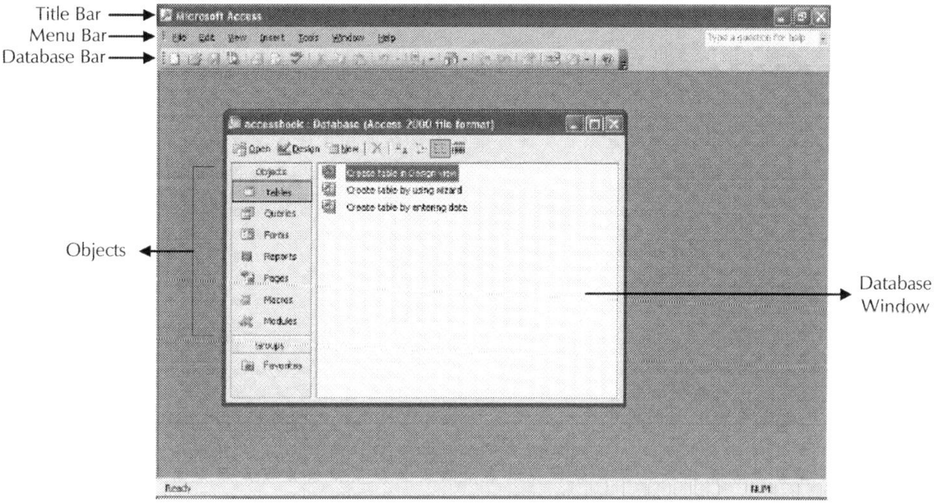

Figure 21.1 : Access Window

Some Access window features that you should be familiar with are:

Title bar	:	Displays the program name, Microsoft Access, the control menu, Minimize, Restore/Maximize, and Close buttons.
Menu bar	:	Most of the menu commands are dimmed and not available in the empty Database Window. The File menu offers options to create a new database or open an existing one. All the Help menu options are also available.
Tool bar	:	The toolbar is a group of picture buttons just below the menu bar; it provides shortcuts for running commands. The buttons on the toolbar vary, depending on what you are working on.
Status bar	:	It is located at the bottom of the Access window and provides a running commentary about the ongoing task and the Access working environment. It also indicate the presence of a filter and the status of various toggle keys such as INSERT, CAPS LOCK, SCROLL LOCK; and NUM LOCK.
Task Pane	:	In Access, whenever you open a new document a task pane appears at right side from which you can select the task you want to perform.
Database Window	:	This window appears whenever a database is open, it is the control center of your database. This window is used to open the database objects like tables, queries, forms, reports, macros, and modules.

Creating an Access Database

The Database window displays all the various object files from your database that you may create while using Access. Actually, a database is a single file. As you create new *object files*, they are stored within the database file.

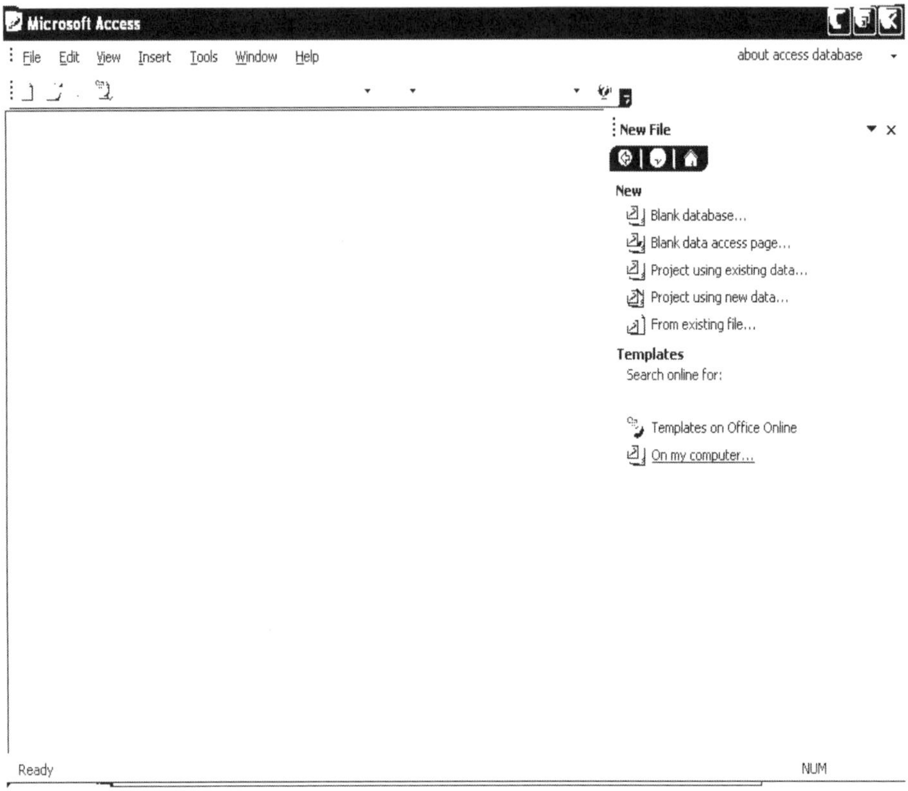

You can create a blank database and then add the tables, forms, reports, and other objects later. This is the most flexible method, but it requires you to define each database element separately. Either way, you can modify and extend your database at any time after it has been created.

1. Click **New** on the toolbar.
2. In the **New File** task pane, under **New**, click **Blank Database**.
3. In the **File New Databases** dialog box, specify a name and location for the database, and then click **Create**.

The Database window appears, and you can create the objects that you want in your database.

Creating a New Table

A table is a collection of data about a specific topic, such as products or suppliers. Using a separate table for each topic means that you store that data only once. This results in a more efficient database and fewer data-entry errors. Tables organize data into columns (called fields) and rows (called records).

The Table Design Process

A table design is like the design of a house: It determines how the table (house) will look, and what kind of data (possessions) will belong inside it. By following the steps in order, your table design can be created readily and with minimal effort:

1. Create a new table.
2. Enter each field name, data type, and description.
3. Enter properties for each defined field.
4. Set a primary key.
5. Create indexes for necessary fields.
6. Save the design.

One of the methods to create a new table design is to first select the **Tables** object under **Objects** and then click the **New** command button in the Database window.

The New Table Dialog Box

Figure 21.3 is the new table dialog box as Access displays it.

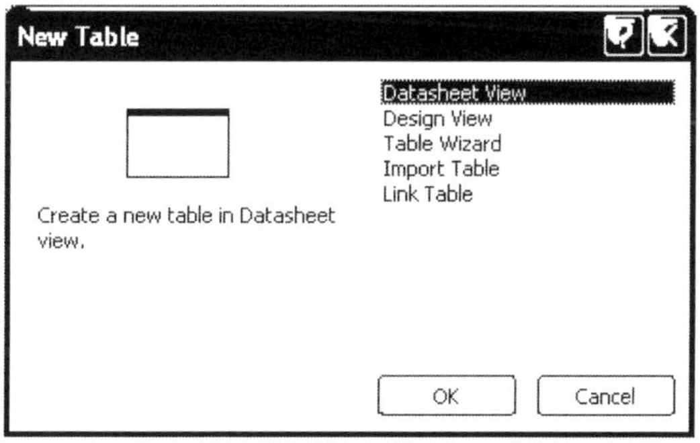

Figure 21.3 : The New Table dialog box

Use this dialog box to select one of these five ways to create a new table.

To create a blank (empty) table for entering your own data, you can:

- Use the **Table Wizard** to choose the fields for your table from a variety of predefined tables such as business contacts, household inventory, or medical records.

- Create a table in **Design view**, where you can add fields, define how each field appears or handles data, and create a primary key.
- Enter data directly into a blank datasheet using **Datasheet view**. When you save the new datasheet, Microsoft Access will analyze your data and automatically assign the appropriate data type and format for each field.

To create a table from existing data, you can:

- **Import or link** data from another Access database or data in a variety of file formats from other programs.
- Perform a make-table query to create a table based on data in a current table.

A Sample Database

Most of this part will use an example of Access techniques, a simple system to help a newsagent keep track of newspaper deliveries and customer accounts. Details will be held on customers and newspapers, and which newspapers the customers have delivered to them each day. For this, designs of customer, newspaper, and delivery tables are depicted in table 21.1, 21.2, 21.3 respectively, which are used throughout in next chapters for explaining queries, forms, and reports.

CUSTOMER : Table name : tblCustomer

Attribute Name	Data Type	Description/Validation
CustomerID	AutoNumber	Key field, automatically incremented for each new customer
Surname	Text (20)	
Initial	Text (1)	
Title	Text (4)	Lookup from list – Mr, Mrs., Miss, Ms,Dr
Address 1	Text (20)	1st line of address
Address 2	Text (20)	2nd line of address
Round	Integer	1-3
CurrentDue	Currency	This week's amount due
PostDue	Currency	Past amount due
HolBegin	Date	Date holiday starts
HolEnd	Date	Date holiday ends

Table 21.1 : Design for the table CUSTOMER

NEWSPAPER : Table name : tblNewspaper

Attribute Name	Data Type	Description
NewspaperID	Text (4)	Key field
NewspaperName	Text (25)	
Price	Text (Currency)	
Morning/Evening	Text (1)	M or E

Table 21.2 : Design for the table NEWSPAPER

DELIVERY : Table name : tblDelivery

Attribute Name	Data Type	Description/Validation
Customer ID	Long Integer	Part of the key field – must exist on CUSTOMER table
NewspaperID	Text (4)	Part of the key field – must exist on NEWSPAPER table
Monday	Yes/No	Y/N indicates whether paper delivered on Monday
Tuesday	Yes/No	As for Monday
Wednesday	Yes/No	"
Thursday	Yes/No	"
Friday	Yes/No	"
Saturday	Yes/No	"
Sunday	Yes/No	"

Table 21.3 : Design for the table DELIVERY

Creating a New Table from Scratch

The easiest way to start a new table from a blank table design is to double-click the "**Create table from Design view**" item in the Tables page of the Database window. An empty table appears in the Table Design window, ready to add fields. Figure 21.4 shows Table Design window after specified field names, data types, description, and properties of Customer table.

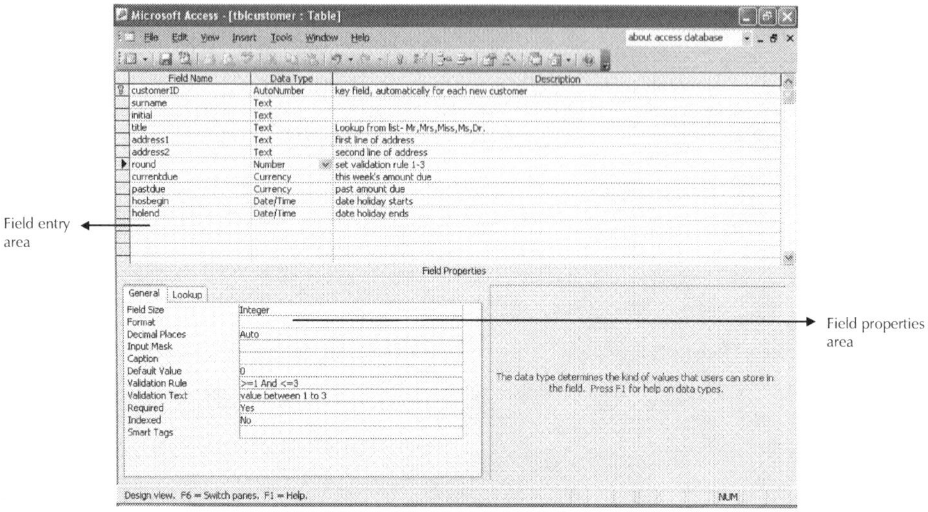

Figure 21.4 : The Table Design Window

The Table Design window is divided horizontally into two panes. The upper pane is the field entry area where you enter the field name, data types and an optional description. The lower pane is devoted to specifying the individual field properties such as size, display appearance, validity rules and many more.

Working with Fields

Fields are created by entering a *field name* and a *field data type* in each row of the field entry area of the Table window. The *field description* is an option to identity the field's purpose; it appears in the status bar during data entry.

Naming a Field

To enter a field name, position the pointer in the first row of the Table window under the Field Name column. Then type a valid field name, observing these rules:

- Field names can be from 1 to 64 characters.
- Field names can include letters, numbers and many special characters.
- Field names cannot include a period (.), exclamation point(!), brackets ([ ]), or accent grave(`).
- You cannot use low-order ASCII characters for example Ctrl+J or Ctrl+L (ASCII values 0 to 31)
- You cannot start with a blank space.

Specifying a Data Type

When you move the pointer into the Data Type column, a down arrow (↓) appears in the text entry box. To open this menu, move the cursor into the Data Type column and click on the down arrow (↓), the dropdown box appears as shown in Figure 21.5.

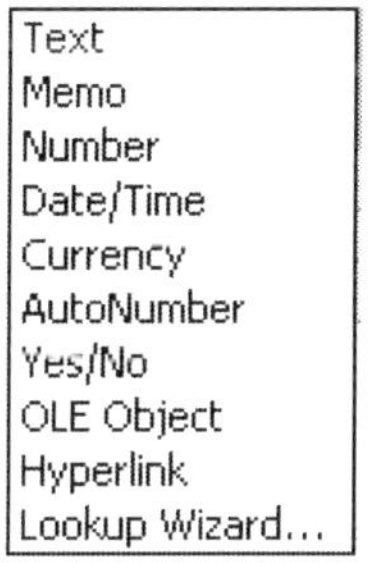

Figure 21.5 : The Data Type dropdown box

The following list summarizes all the field data types available in Microsoft Access, their uses, and their storage sizes.

- **Text** Use for text or combinations of text and numbers, such as addresses, or for numbers that do not require calculations, such as phone numbers, part numbers, or postal codes.

  Stores up to 255 characters. The **Field size** property controls the maximum number of characters that can be entered.

- **Memo** Use for lengthy text and numbers, such as notes or descriptions.

  Stores up to 65,536 characters.

- **Number** Use for data to be included in mathematical calculations, except calculations involving money (use Currency type).

  Stores 1,2,4 or 8 bytes; stores 16 bytes for Replication ID (GUID), The **Fieldsize** property defines the specific Number type.

- **Date/Time** Use for dates and times.

  Stores 8 bytes.

- **Currency** Use for currency values and to prevent rounding off during calculations.

  Stores 8 bytes.

- **AutoNumber** Use for unique sequential (incrementing by 1) or random numbers that are automatically inserted when a record is added.

  Stores 4 bytes; stores 16 bytes for Replication ID (GUID).

- **Yes/No** Use for data that can be only one of two possible values, such as Yes/No, True/False, On/Off. Null values are not allowed.

  Stores 1 bit.

- **OLE Object** Use for OLE objects (such as Microsoft Word documents, Microsoft Excel spreadsheets, pictures, sounds, or other binary data) that were created in other programs using the OLE protocol.

  Stores up to 1 gigabyte (limited by disk space).

- **Hyperlink** Use for hyperlink can be a UNC path or a URL.

  Stores up to 64,000 characters.

- **Lookup Wizard** Use to create a field that allows you to choose a value from another table or from a list of values using a combo box — choosing this option in the data type list starts a wizard to define this for you.

  Requires the same storage size as the primary key that corresponds to the lookup field - typically 4 bytes.

Setting Field Properties

After you enter the field names, data types, and field descriptions, define properties for each field. Field properties determine how the values in the field are stored and displayed. Each type has a particular set of properties.

Here is a list of all the general properties (note that they may not all be displayed, depending on which data type you choose):

Field size	:	Text : limits size of the field to the specified number of characters (1-255); default is 50
Numeric	:	Allows specification of numeric type
Format	:	Changes the way data appears after you enter it (uppercase, dates, and so on)
Input Mask	:	Used to create a 'field template', that uses literal display characters to control how data is entered in a field or control
Decimal Places	:	Specifies number of decimal places (Numeric /Currency)
Caption	:	Optional label for form and report fields
Default value	:	Used to specify a value that will be automatically entered when you add a new record
Validation Rule	:	Validates data based on rules created through expressions or macros
Validation Text	:	Displays a message when data fails validation
Required	:	Specifies whether you must enter a value into a field

Allow zero length	:	Determines whether you may enter the value " " into a text field type to distinguish it from a null value
Indexed	:	Speeds up data access and (if desired) limits data to unique values
Unicode Compression	:	Allows string data which is now stored in Unicode format to be compressed to save storage space.

Choosing a Field Size

Field size specifies the storage and display size. You should enter the size for each field with a Text data type. Number fields are sized a little differently, specifying the name of the number layout rather than the number of characters. The options are described in Table 21.4.

Field Size Setting	Range	Decimal Places	Storage Size
Byte	0-255	None	1 byte
Integer	-32,768 to 32,767	None	2 bytes
Long Integer	-2,147,483,648 to 2,147,483,647	None	4 bytes
Double	-1.797×10^{308} to 1.797×10^{308}	15	8 bytes
Single	-3.4×10^{38} to 3.4×10^{38}	7	4 bytes
Replication ID	N/A	N/A	16 bytes

Table 21.4 : Numeric Field Settings

Input Mask Characters

Microsoft Access interprets characters in the **InputMask** property definition as shown in Table 21.5:

Character	Description
0	Digit (0 through 9, entry required; plus [+] and minus [-] signs not allowed).
9	Digit or space (entry not required; plus and minus signs not allowed).
#	Digit or space (entry not required; blank positions converted to spaces, plus and minus signs allowed).
L	Letter (A through Z, entry required).
?	Letter (A through Z, entry optional).
A	Letter or digit (entry required).

a	Letter or digit (entry optional).
&	Any character or a space (entry required).
C	Any character or a space (entry optional).
. , : ; - /	Decimal placeholder and thousands, date, and time separators. (The actual character used depends on the regional settings specified in Microsoft Windows Control Panel).
<	Causes all characters that follow to be converted to lowercase.
>	Causes all characters that follow to be converted to uppercase.
!	Causes the input mask to display from right to left, rather than from left to right. Characters typed into the mask always fill it from left to right. You can include the exclamation point anywhere in the input mask.
\	Causes the character that follows to be displayed as a literal character. Used to display any of the characters listed in this table as literal characters (for example, \A is displayed as just A).
Password	Setting the **InputMask** property to the word **Password** creates a password entry text box. Any character typed in the text box is stored as the character but is displayed as an asterisk (*).

Table 21.5 : Input Mask Characters

Set the Primary Key

The field or fields that contain the unique value is the *primary key*. In the Table Design view, click in the field row that you want to use as the primary key, then you have three ways to designate the field as primary key:

- Click the primary key toolbar button.
- Choose Edit >> Primary key.
- Right click the field row in the upper pane and choose primary key from the shortcut menu.

NOTE : Save the table without creating a primary key and Access automatically creates an AutoNumber field.

Saving the Completed Table

The table design does not have to be complete before you save it. To save the table design, click the **Save** button or choose **File >> Save**. The first time you save a new table, Access prompts you for a name.

Creating Relationships

As we have already discussed about different keys and relationships in previous chapter, it is the time to implement them. To set relations between tables, you must establish a link between fields that contain common information. The fields themselves do not need to have the same name. The field's data type and lengths must be the same. Generally, a relationship is established by linking these key fields between tables — the primary key in one table to a foreign key in another table.

Open the Relationships window using any one of three methods:

- Right click anywhere in the Database window and select Relationships;
- Press the Relationships button on the toolbar;
- Select Tools>>Relationships from the menu bar.

The following window (Figure 21.6) appears, showing that Access has already recognized that relationships exist between the tables, which are linked by common fields.

NOTE : If the tables that you want to relate are not visible in the Relationships window, click the Show Table button on the toolbar, and double-click the name of each of the tables you are relating.

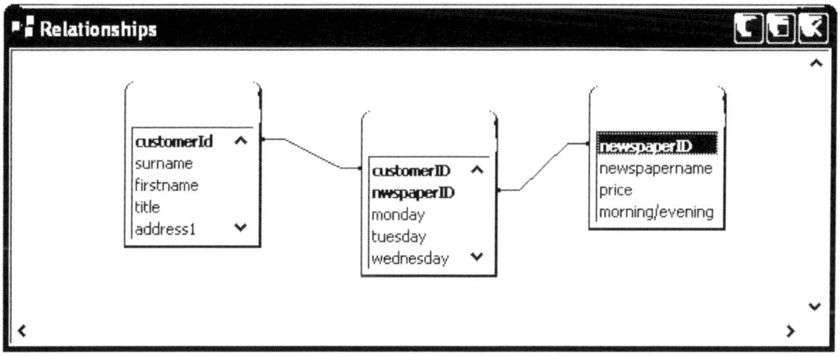

Figure 21.6 : The Relationships Window

Lets relate tblCustomer, tblDelivery, and tblNewspaper tables:

- To set the degree of the relationship (one-to-many) between tblcustomer and tbldelivery, drag the key field customerID from tblcustomer (the one side of the relationship) to customerID in tblDelivery (the many side of the relationship).
- A message appears warning you that a relationship already exists, and asking if you want to edit it, click Yes.
- The Edit Relationships window appears as shown in Figure 21.7. Check **Enforce Referential Integrity** to select it. Click OK.

- Enforcing referential integrity means that Access will not allow the user to enter a delivery record for a customer who has not already been entered on the tblcustomer table, or specify a newspaper delivery for a newspaper which is not in tblnewspaper.

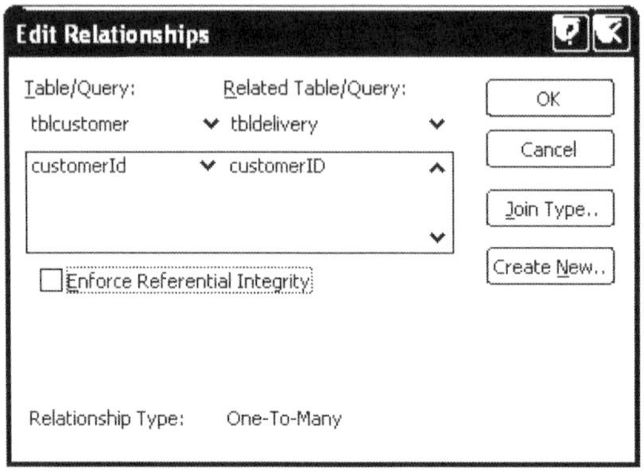

Figure 21.7 : The Edit Relationships Window

- Similarly, drag NewspaperID from tblNewspaper to NewspaperID in tblDelivery. Click yes in the warning message box. Check **Enforce Referential Integrity** to select it. Click OK.
- The Relationships window now looks slightly different, showing the one-to-many relationship as shown in Figure 21.8.

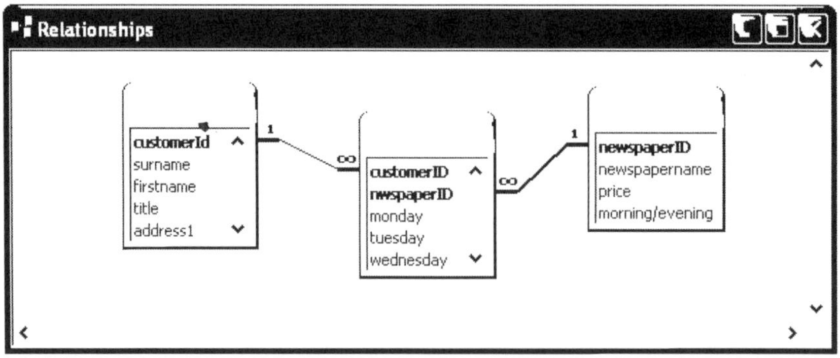

Figure 21.8 : One-to-many Relationships with Referential Integrity

- Save the relationships by closing window and choosing Yes when asked if you want to save.

Editing a Table Structure

As you create your table, you should be following a well-planned design. Yet, changes are sometimes necessary, even with a plan.

- In the Database window you will see that your new table is now listed.
- Select the table name, click the **Design view** button and you are returned to **Design view.**

Inserting a Field

To insert a new field follow the steps:

- Place your cursor on an existing field.
- Select **Insert> >Row** or click on the **Insert Row** icon in the toolbar. A new row is added to the table and any existing fields are pushed down. You can then enter a new field definition.

Deleting a Field

There are three ways to delete a field:

- Select the field by clicking the row selector and pressing Delete.
- Select the field and choose **Edit> >Delete Row**.
- Select the field and click the Delete Row icon in the toolbar.

Moving a Field

- Click the row selector to the left of the field's name to select the field.
- Click again and drag to where you want the field to be. You will see a line appear between fields as you drag over them to indicate where the field will be placed.

Modifying or Deleting the Primary Key

To change the primary key, select the row you want as the primary key and click the Primary key button. The key icon is removed from the old key field and appears in the new one. To remove the primary key designation, select the primary key field and click the Primary key button. If the key is used in a relationship, you must delete the relationship before you can remove the key.

Add or Edit Data

When you open a datasheet, all the records in your table are visible; if you just created your table design, there isn't any data in the new datasheet yet. Figure 21.9 show datasheet with one record.

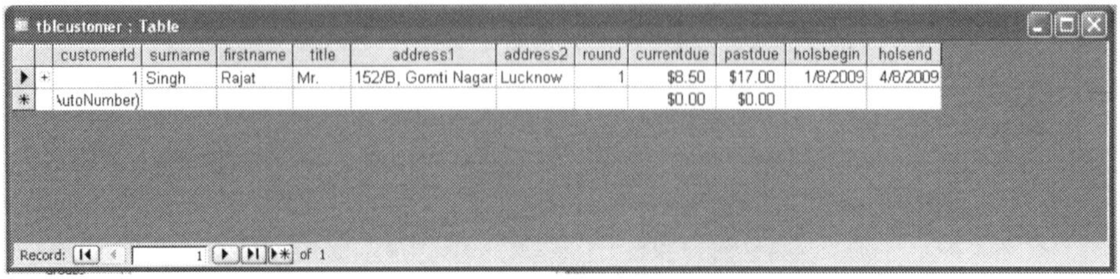

Figure 21.9 : Entering a record into the Datasheet

To add or edit data in a datasheet follow the steps:

- Open a datasheet
- Do one of the following:
  - To add a new record, click **New Record** on the toolbar, type the data, and then press TAB to go to the next field. At the end of the record, press Tab to go to the next record.
  - To edit data within a field, click in the field you want to edit, and then type the data.
  - To replace the entire value, move the pointer to the left most part of the field until it changes into the plus pointer (+), and then click. Type the data.

NOTE :

- To correct a typing mistake, press BackSpace. To cancel your changes in the current field, press Esc. To cancel your changes in the entire record, press Esc again before you move out of the field.
- When you move to another record, Microsoft Access saves your changes.

Move between Records or Fields

Move between records by using navigation buttons in a datasheet (see Figure 21.10). The navigation buttons are located at the bottom of the window in datasheet. You can use these buttons to move quickly between records.

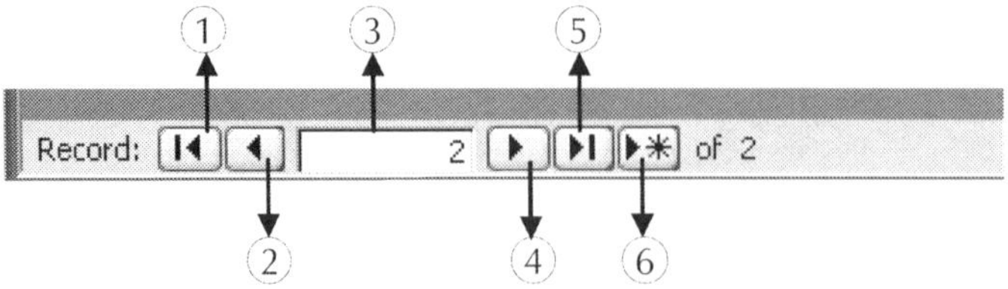

Figure 21.10 : Navigation buttons in a datasheet

The description of numbers indicated in Figure 21.10 is given below:

1. First record
2. Previous record
3. Record number
4. Next record
5. Last record
6. New record

Adding the **GoTo Field** box makes it easier to move between fields in long records in datasheet view. To add this box, steps are:

- Open a table in Datasheet view.
- Click **Toolbars** on the **View** menu.
- Select **Formatting** (Datasheet).
- Click Close.

The **GoTo field** box is the leftmost item on the **Formatting (Datasheet)** toolbar. Use it to click the name of the field that you want to move to in the current record.

About Finding or Replacing Data

There are many ways that Microsoft Access can find or replace just the data you need, whether you're looking for a particular value, one record, or a group of records.

- You can find a record by scrolling in a datasheet, or by typing its record number in the record number box.
- With a filter, you can temporarily isolate and view a specific set of records to work with while you have a form or datasheet.
- With the Find dialog box, you can locate specific records or find certain values within fields. You can navigate through records as Access finds each occurrence of the item you're looking for. If you want to replace certain values that you find, use the Replace dialog box instead.

Choose last method by selecting **Edit>Find**. The Find and Replace dialog box appears as shown in Figure 21.11. To limit the search to a specific field, make sure your cursor is on the field that you want to use in the search before you open the dialog box.

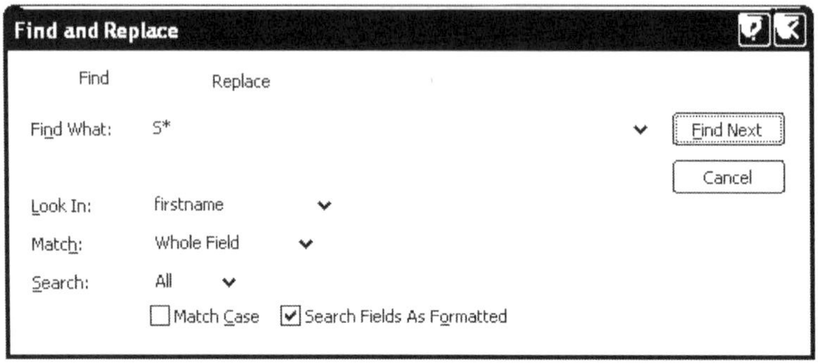

Figure 21.11 : The Find and Replace Dialog Box

In the Find What text box, you enter the value to be searched for. You can enter the value just as it appears in the field, or you can use three types of wildcards:

*	Any number of characters
?	Any one character
#	Any one number

Examples of using these wildcard characters :

AB*	This will search any value beginning with AB.
*001	This will search any value ending with 001.
AB??001	This will search for any value that begins with AB, ends with 001, and contains any two characters in between.

The Match drop-down list contains three choices:

- Any part of field : This search finds the value anywhere in the field.
- Whole field : This finds only the whole value you enter.
- Start of field : Searches value from the beginning of the field.

You can click one or more of three choices (up, down, all) in the Search combo box.

Match case determines whether the search is case-sensitive. The default is not case-sensitive. Using Search Fields As Formatted may slow the search process.

Replacing Values

Click on the Replace tab of Find and Replace dialog box as shown in Figure 21.12.

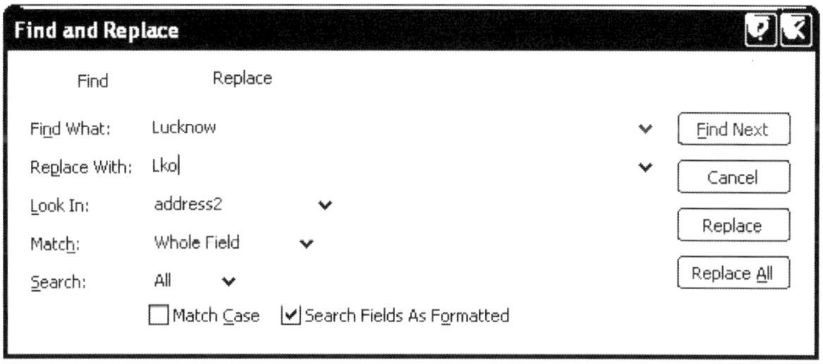

Figure 21.12 : Find and Replace Dialog box with the Replace tab showing

You can select your search options in the Replace tab. Enter what you want to replace the existing value with. Now select one of command buttons on the side.

Find next	:	Finds the next field that contains the value in the Find What field.
Cancel	:	Close the form and performs no find and replace.
Replace	:	Must use the Find Next button first. When you click on Replace, it replaces the value in the current field only.
Replace all	:	Finds all the fields with the Find What value and automatically replaces them with the Replace With value.
More/Less	:	Displays the search options/hides the search options.

Deleting Records

You can delete any number of records by selecting the record(s) and then choosing any of the following method:

1. Press the Delete key.
2. Choose Edit >> Delete.
3. Click Delete Record on the toolbar.

Choosing any option, a dialog box (see Figure 21.13) asks you to confirm the deletion. If you select Yes, the records are deleted. If you select No, no changes are made.

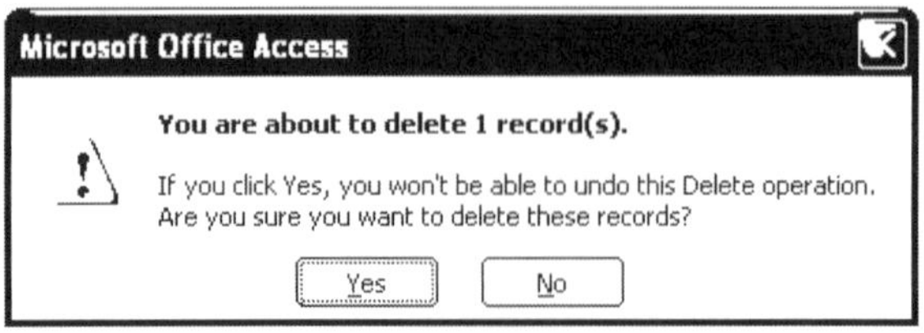

Figure 21.13 : The Delete Record Dialog Box

NOTE : When you delete data, you might want to delete related data in other tables. For example, if you delete a supplier, you probably want to delete the products that the supplier supplies. In some cases, you can make sure the proper data is deleted by enforcing referential integrity and turning on cascade deletions.

Sorting Records

Access automatically sorts records by the value in the primary key field. During data retrieval and presentation, there will be times when you want the records to be arranged in a different order. For example, you may want to lookup all the work orders sorted by the employee who is acting as the supervisor so you can keep tabs on the workload.

There are two types of sorts you can do, simple and complex.

Simple Sorts

To sort by a single field in a datasheet click in the field you want to sort by and then do one of the following:

- Click Sort Ascending (A to Z). 
- Click Sort Descending (Z to A) 
- Choose Records >>Sort>>Sort Ascending.
- Choose Records >>Sort>>Sort Descending.
- Right click in the field and choose Sort Ascending from the shortcut menu.
- Right click in the field and choose Sort Descending from the shortcut menu.

Complex Sorts

To sort by more than one field, the fields must be adjacent into the datasheet. In addition, Access uses a sort precedence from left to right so the records are sorted first by the values in the left column. If duplicate values appear in that column, a secondary sort is performed on those records by the values in the next column to the right. If the columns involved in the sort are not adjacent or are in the wrong relative position in the datasheet, move the columns before sorting the records. When all are in position, select the columns you want to sort on and click one of the sort buttons as before or choose from the records or the shortcut menu.

NOTE : You can't sort on OLE object under any circumstances. You can sort memo or hyperlink field in a table, query, form or report. Memo fields will only be sorted based on the first 255 characters.

Summary

- Access is a Database Management System (DBMS).
- Database contains objects such as tables, queries, forms, reports, pages, macros, and modules.
- You can create a table by using a Datasheet view, Design view, or Table wizard.
- Table designs consist of field names, data types, and descriptions.
- You can choose from ten basic data types : Text, Number, Currency, AutoNumber, Date/Time, Yes/No, Memo, OLE, Hyperlink, and Lookup wizard.
- Each field has properties. Each table has a primary key field.
- Data is entered into a datasheet at the new record indicator.
- The navigation buttons enables you to move quickly between records.
- Using Filter by Selection or Filter by Form, you can specify sort orders or filters to limit the record display of a datasheet.
- File >>Print prints your datasheet.

Review Exercise

Multiple choice questions

1. Field name can be upto how many characters?
   - a) 64
   - b) 68
   - c) 60
   - d) None of these
2. Memo data type stores upto how many characters?
   - a) 65,356
   - b) 65,536
   - c) 65,653
   - d) None of these

3. The key which contains the unique value in a field is
   a) Foreign
   b) Primary
   c) Unique
   d) None of these

State whether true or false

1. The default extension of database files are .mdb.
2. There are eight objects available in Access.
3. The property area of Table Design window sets the properties of a table.
4. The entry in field description of Table design window is not optional.
5. Date/Time data type occupy 8 bytes in memory.
6. In Yes/No data type -1 is expressed for no and 0 for yes.
7. Field properties are same for each data type.

Fill in the blanks

1. You can create table using ____________ view, using ____________ , or by ____________ data.
2. You can create table, by selecting ____________ option from menu.
3. The table design window consists of two areas ____________ and ____________.
4. ____________ data type displays data from another table.
5. The ___________ data type stores an integer the Access increments it automatically as you add a new record.

Descriptive questions

1. Write in steps the process of designing tables.
2. What do you mean by creating structure of a table? Explain.
3. Define field. Write the rules you have to follow while naming a field.
4. Explain various data types available in Access.
5. What is the significance of lookup wizard data type? Explain.
6. Why we need to set the field properties? Explain.
7. What is the difference between primary key and foreign key.

C H A P T E R

22 ACCESS OBJECTS

FEATURING

- Forms
- Creating a Form using Form Wizard
- Queries
- Creating a Query
- Setting Special Criteria
- Relating Multiple Tables in a Query
- Creating a Total Query
- Summary Query
- Reports
- Creating a Report using Report Wizard

As we already discussed that MS-Access manages all your information from a single database file. Within the file, you can use tables, forms, queries and reports. In this hands-on chapter, you will learn to create and manipulate the above said objects.

Forms

Once you've created tables for all the entities in your database and created relationships between them, you can turn your attention to how the user will enter data. There are two ways of entering data into an Access database, known respectively as Datasheet View and Form View. A form provides the best flexibility for viewing and entering data. A form lets you view one or more records at a time while viewing all of the fields. Forms are useful for viewing data in a formatted display, as well as for entering, changing , or deleting data. The six types of forms available in Access are as follows:

The columnar Form

In columnar form, the fields are arranged as columns onscreen. The form can occupy one or more screen pages. Generally, this type of form is used to simulate the hard-copy entry of data; the fields can be arranged any way that you want.

Tabular Form

A tabular form is one, where you see several records at one time. You can format any part of a tabular form. Tabular forms can also have multiple lines per record, and you can add special effects to the fields.

Main/SubForm

A subform is a form that is inserted in another form. The primary form is called the main form (main form : A form that contains one or more subforms), and the form within the form is called the subform. Subforms are especially effective when you want to show data from tables or queries with a one-to-many relationship. The main form shows data from the "one" side of relationship and the subform shows data from the "many" side of the relationship.

Pivot Table Forms

You can view detail or summarized data by arranging fields in the filter, row, column, and detail areas. Through these forms, you can dynamically change the layout of a form to analyze data in different ways. You can rearrange row headings, column headings, and filter fields until you achieve the desired layout. Each time you change the layout, the form immediately recalculates the data based on the new arrangement.

Pivot Chart Forms

You can display data visually by selecting a chart type and viewing data by arranging fields in the filter, series, category, and data areas.

Datasheet Vs Forms

With a datasheet, you have very little control over the display of data. By using forms, you can place each field in an exact specified location, add colour and shading to each field, and add text control to make data entry more efficient. A form has more flexibility in data entry than a datasheet. You can add calculated fields as well as enhanced data-validation and editing controls to a form. OLE objects (such as pictures or graphs) are visible *only* in a form or report. Managing memo fields in forms are flexible than datasheet.

Creating a Form using Form Wizard

The easiest way to build a form is by using the Form Wizard.

The wizard asks you detailed questions about the record sources, fields, layout, and format you want and creates a form based on your answers.

1. In the Database window, click **Forms** under **Objects**.
2. Click the **New** button on the Database window toolbar. The New Form dialog box appears as shown in Figure 22.1.

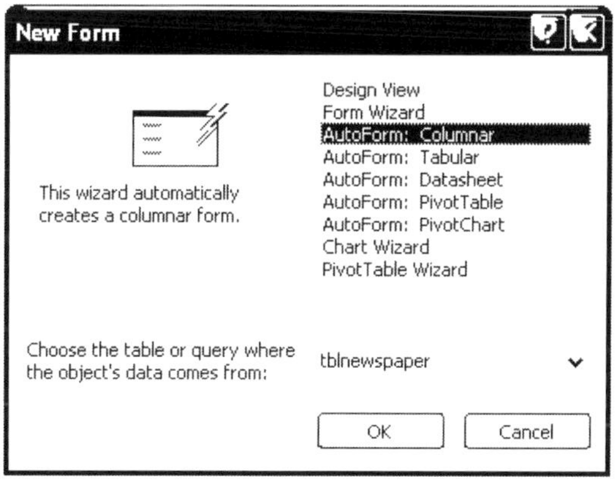

Figure 22.1 : The New Form Dialog Box

3. In the **New Form** dialog box, click the wizard that you want to use. (For this example, choose the Form Wizard option).
4. Click the name of the table or other related source that includes the data you want to base your form on.
5. Click **OK**.
6. After selecting Form Wizard, the field selection box appears as shown in Figure 22.2. The **Available Fields** list box on the left displays all fields from the selected table/query used to create a form.

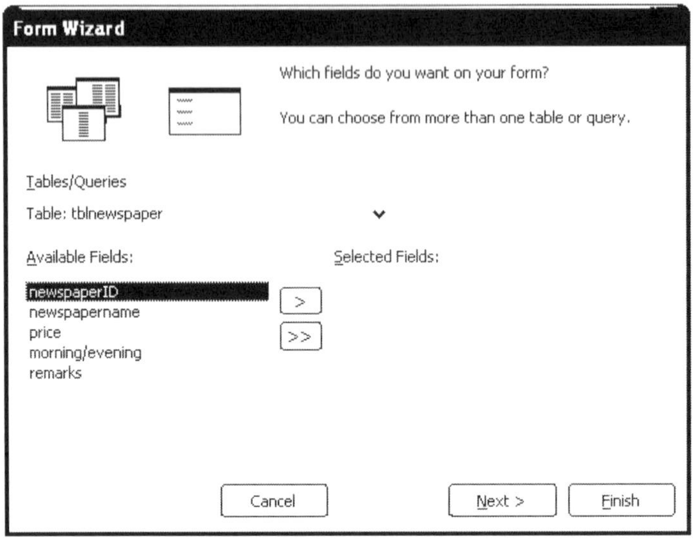

Figure 22.2 : Choosing the Fields for the Form

7. Select all the fields by clicking the **>>** button. When you are finished, click the **Next >** button to display the layout dialog box as shown in Figure 22.3, from which to choose a form layout.

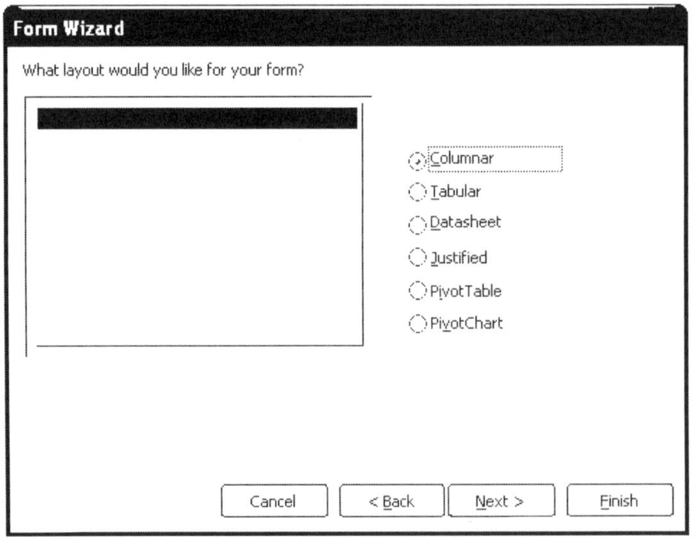

Figure 22.3 : Choosing the type of layout for the Form

8. As you click the option button choices, the display changes to show how the form will look. Select the option button, (eg., Columnar) then click the **Next>** button to display the style of the form. (see Figure 22.4)

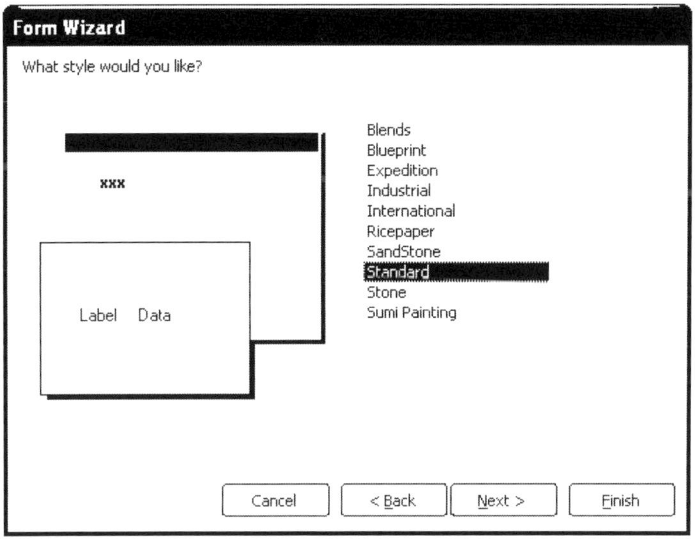

Figure 22.4 : Choosing the Style of your Form

9. Choose the style (eg., Standard) for the form's look from the dialog box shown in Figure 22.4, then click the **Next>** button to display the dialog box (see Figure 22.5), which offers you to add title to your form.

10. The form title dialog box is usually the last dialog box in a Form Wizard. Type the appropriate title for the form.

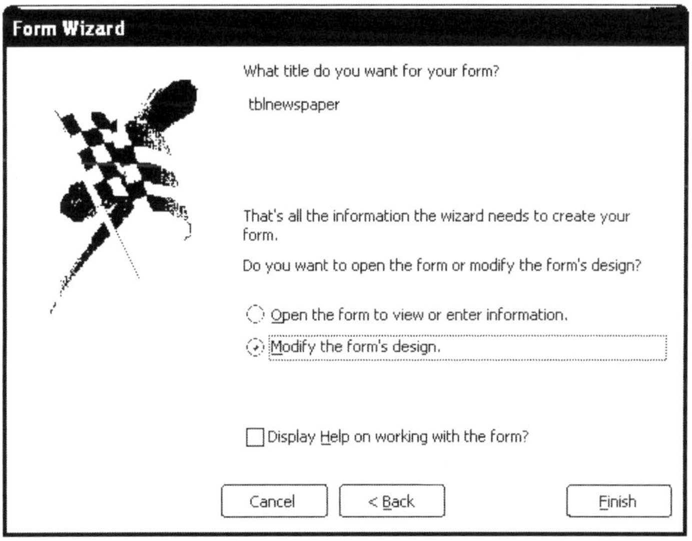

Figure 22.5 : Choosing a Form Title

11. After you complete all the steps to design your form, you open the new form by selecting one of these two options:

- Open the form to view or enter information
- Modify the form's design

For this example, select the former and then click the **Finish** button. Once you click the Finish button, the form appears in the Form View window (as shown in Figure 22.6)

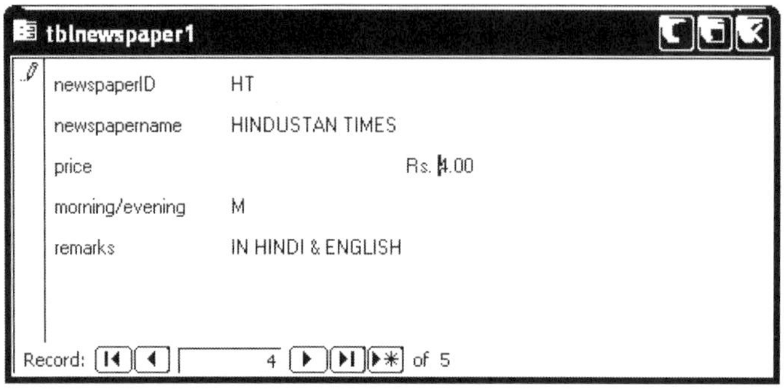

Figure 22.6 : A form design created with a Form Wizard

Changing the Appearance of the Form

We will just make some minor changes to this form, altering the size of the fields and inserting a space in the field label or caption.

- Click the Design View icon on the toolbar.
- The form appears in Design View. Increase the size of the window so that all the fields are visible as shown in Figure 22.7.

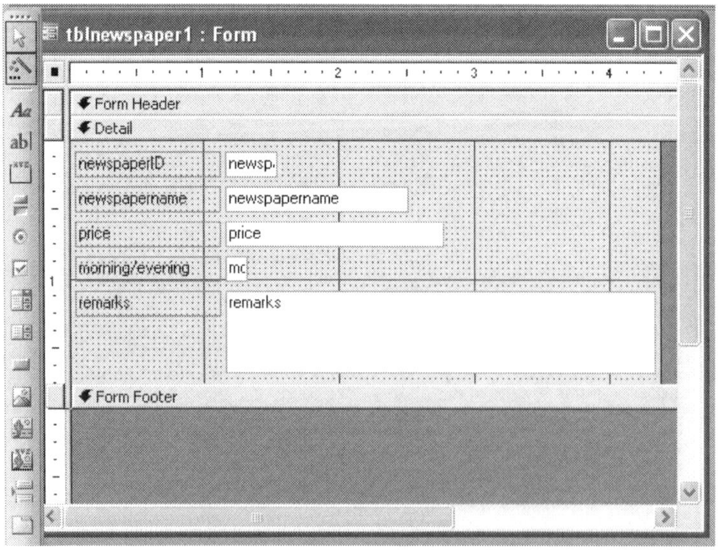

Figure 22.7 : The Form in Design View

- Click in any field (not the label). Make the field smaller or larger by dragging the middle handle on the right hand side of the field.
- Click any label. Click again in the label name and insert a space or change name so that the label becomes more understable.

Adding a form heading and arranging fields

- Press the view button again to return to Form View. The form still looks very small and cramped. It needs more space and a heading at the top. Return to Design View.
- Enlarge the window, and drag the top edge of the **Form Footer** down to enlarge the **Detail** section of the form.
- Select all the fields and labels in the **Detail** section.
- Drag the fields down and to the right to leave space at the top for a heading.
- Click the toolbox on the toolbar. (see Figure 22.8)

Figure 22.8 : The Form Design Toolbox

- Click the Label tool on this toolbox and drag out an area in the upper center of the **Detail** section of the form. Type the heading.
- Using the Formatting toolbar, format the heading.
- Click the View button to return to Form View. Now the form will looks like as shown in Figure 22.9.
- Press the **Save** icon and save the form. Close the form.

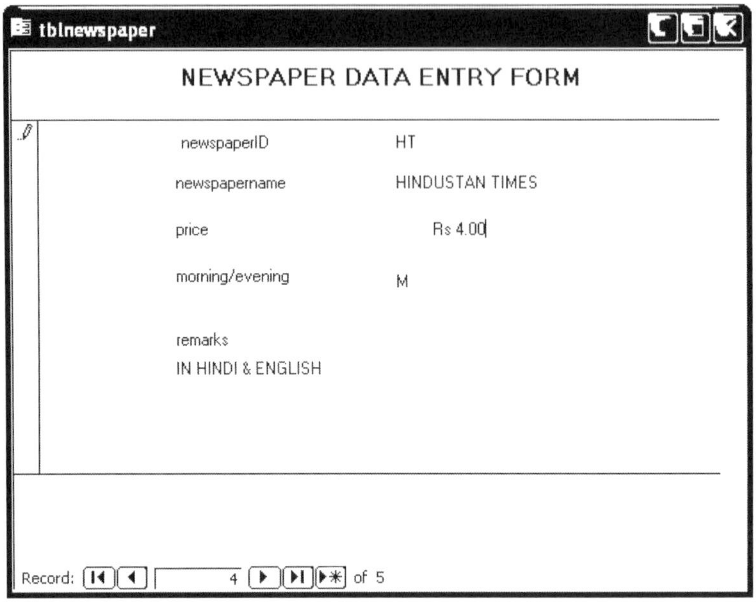

Figure 22.9 : The edited Newspaper Form

Creating a Subform

If the subform is to be linked to the main form, make sure the underlying record sources are related before using this procedure.

Create a form and subform at the same time

1. In the Database window, click **Forms** under **Objects**.
2. Click the **New** button on the Database window toolbar.
3. In the **New Form** dialog box, double click **Form Wizard**.
4. In the Form Wizard dialog box, select a table or query from the Tables/Queries drop-down list box. For example, it would be useful to be able to see all the details about each customer and which newspaper they have delivered, on the same form, select the *tblcustomer* table (the "one" side of the one-to-many relationship).
5. Double-click the fields you want to include from this table (for this example, select all fields).
6. In the same Wizard dialog box, select another table or query from the list. Using the same example, select the *tbldelivery* table. (the "many" side of the one-to-many relationship), (refer to Figure 22.10).

7. Double-click the fields you want to include from this table (for this example, except customerID, select all fields). Click on **Next>**.

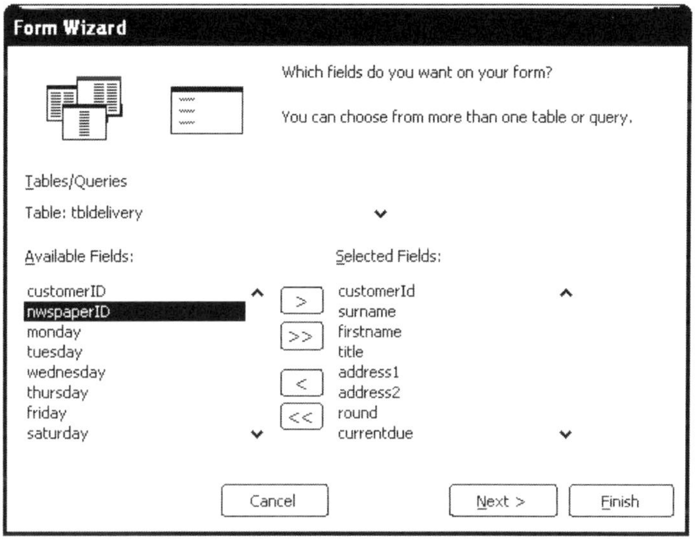

Figure 22.10 : Selecting Fields for the Subform

8. If you set up the relationships correctly before starting the wizard, the wizard asks which table or query you want to view by. Using the same example, to create the tblcustomers form, click **By tblcustomer** as shown in Figure 22.11.

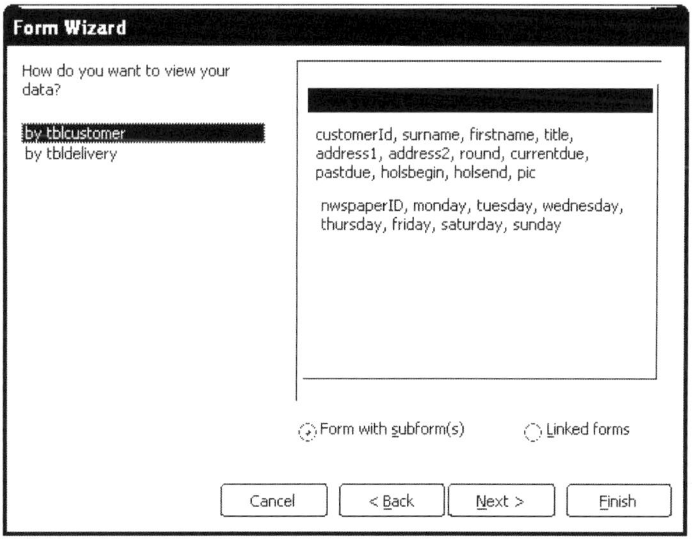

Figure 22.11 : Selecting the Form with Subform Option

9. In the same wizard dialog box, select the **Form with Subform(s)** option and click on **Next >** button.

10. Follow the directions in the remaining wizard dialog boxes. When you click **Finish**, Access creates two forms, one for the main form and subform control, and one for the subform.

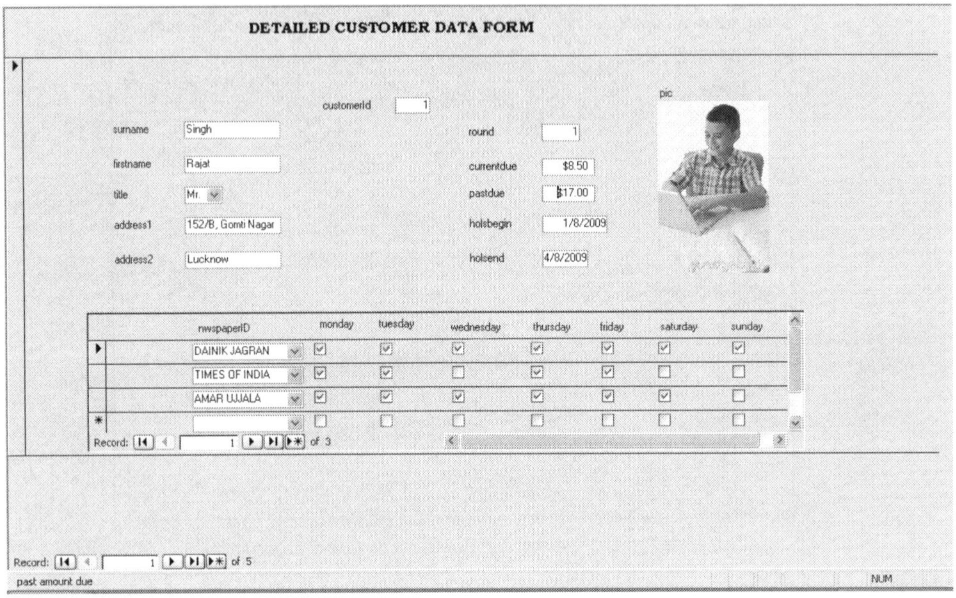

Figure 22.12 : Form with Subform

Queries

Queries are one of the most important tools in a database for converting raw data into useful information. A query can be thought of as a request to find all records satisfying certain criteria so that they can be displayed in a form or record. Your query can be a simple question about information stored in a single table, or it can be a complex question about information stored in several tables. After you create and run a query MS-Access can return and display the set of records you asked for in a datasheet. This set of records is called a *dynaset*, which is the set of records selected by a query. You use queries to view, change, and analyze data in different ways. You can also use them as a source of records for forms, and reports. There are several types of queries in Microsoft Access.

Select Queries

A select query is the most common type of query. It retrieves data from one or more tables and displays the results in a datasheet where you can update the records (with some restrictions). You can also use a select query to group records and calculate sums, counts, averages, and other types of totals.

Parameter Queries

A parameter query is a query that on running displays its own dialog box prompting you for information, such as criteria for retrieving records or a value you want to insert in a field.

Crosstab Queries

You use crosstab queries to calculate and restructure data for easier analysis of your data. Crosstab queries calculate a sum, average, count, or other type of total for data that is grouped by two types of information — one down the left side of the datasheet and another across the top.

SQL Queries

An SQL query is a query which you create by using an SQL statement. You can use Structured Query Language (SQL) to query, update and manage relational databases such as Access.

Action Queries

An action query is a query that makes changes to or moves many records in just one operation. There are four types of action queries:

- **Delete Queries** A delete query deletes a group of records from one or more tables. With delete queries, you always delete entire records, not just selected fields within records.
- **Update Queries** An update query makes global changes to a group of records in one or more tables. With an update query, you can change data in existing tables.
- **Append Queries** An append query adds a group of records from one or more tables to the end of one or more tables.
- **Make Table Queries** A make-table query creates a new table from all or part of the data in one or more tables. Make-table queries are helpful for creating a table to export to other Microsoft Access databases or a history table that contains old records.

About Dynaset

Access takes the records that result from a query and displays them in a datasheet, in which the actual records are called a dynaset. Physically a dynaset looks like a table; in fact, it is not a table. The dynaset is a dynamic (or virtual) set of records. This dynamic set of records is not stored in the database. When you close a query, the query dynaset is gone; it no longer exists. When you run a query, Access places the resultant records in the dynaset. When you save the query, the information is not saved; only the structure of the query is saved.

Creating a Query

After you create your tables and place data in them, you are ready to work with queries. We will start with the simplest, the select query. We'll create a query that displays all the fields of all customers on Round 1. To begin a query, follow these steps:

- From the Database window, click the **Queries** object button.
- Click the **New** button. The New Query dialog box appears as shown in Figure 22.13. You select from the five choices. The first choice displays the Query Design window.

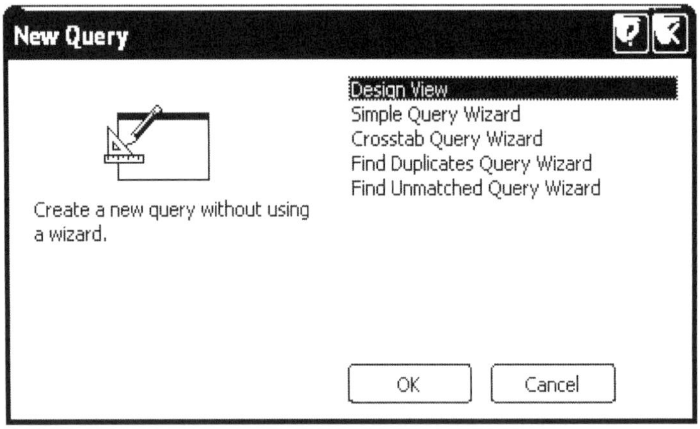

Figure 22.13 : The New Query Dialog Box

- Double click **Design View** to open a query window. A query window appears with the **Show Table** dialog box floating on top of it as shown in Figure 22.14.

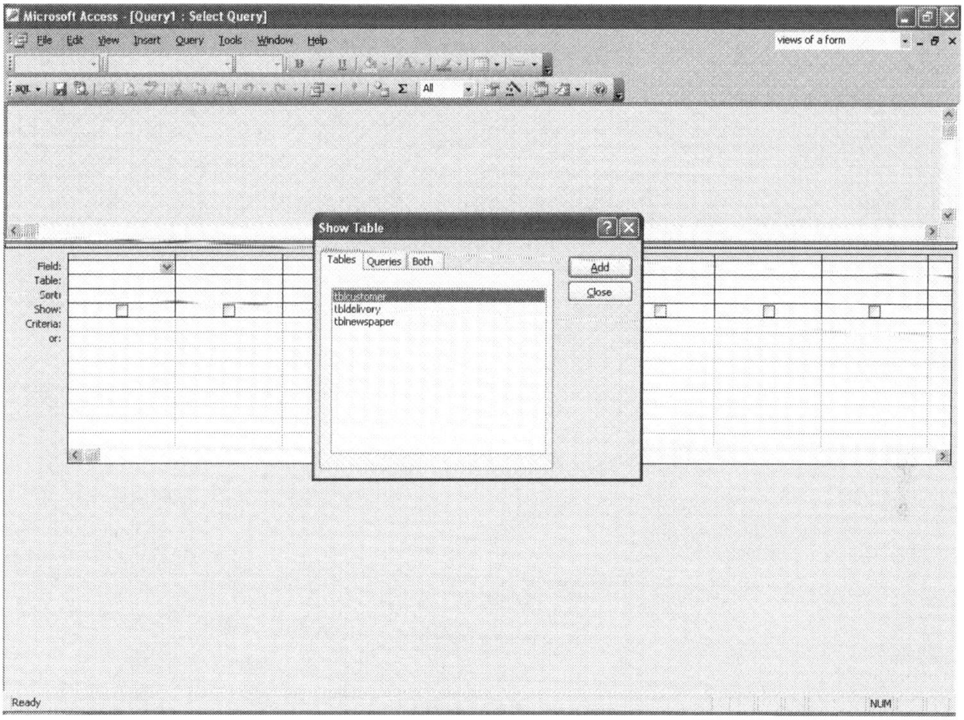

Figure 22.14 : The Show Table dialog box in the Query Design Window

- Select the desired table from the Show Table box. (for this example select tblcustomer table).
- Click on the Add button to add the table to the Query Design window.
- Click on the Close button. A table pops up on the query window.

The query window has two modes, the design mode and the datasheet mode. The design mode is where you create the query, and the datasheet mode is where you display the query's dynaset. The query design window consists of two panes:

- The upper pane is the table pane, which displays the field lists for all the tables in the query.
- The lower pane is the QBE (Query By Example) design grid, which shows the elements of the query design. Each column in the QBE design pane contains information about a single field from a table or query in the upper pane.
- The next step is to select the fields that you want to see in the query. To placed the fields on the query grid just double click the field name.
- Now set the criteria. This is where you enter the first line of criteria to limit the record selection. For example if we only want to see the customers for round 1.

- In the **criteria** row type 1 in the column for **round**.
- The query grid now appears as shown in Figure 22.15.

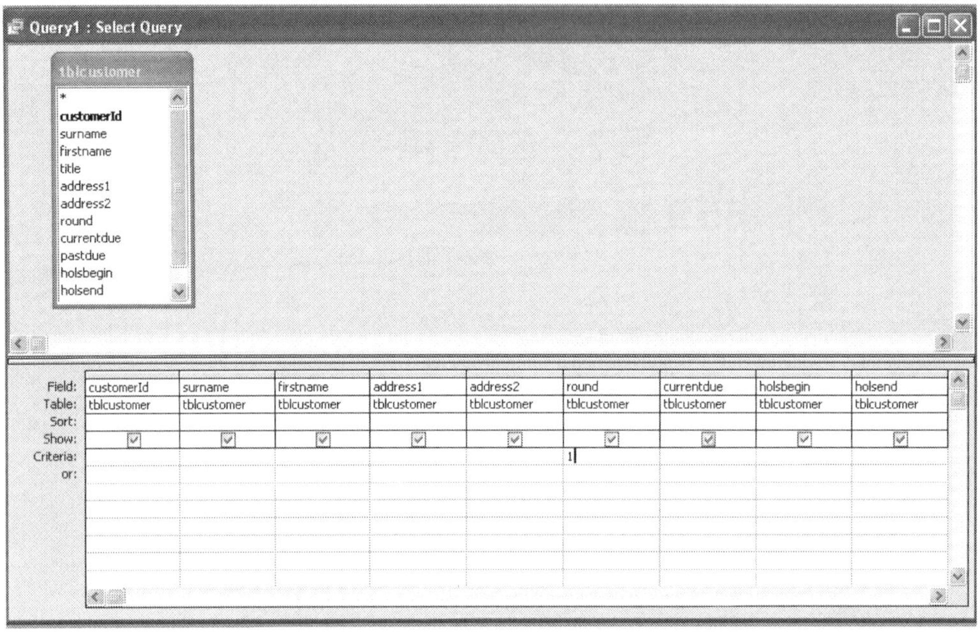

Figure 22.15 : Selecting Fields and Criteria

- Click the **Run** button on the toolbar to execute the query. The query results appear like below:

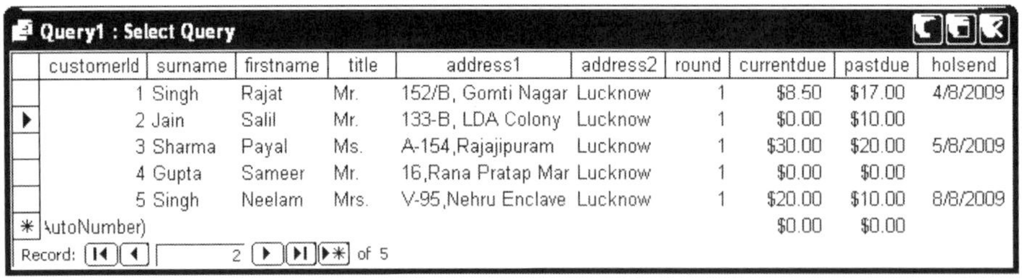
Query1 : Select Query

customerId	surname	firstname	title	address1	address2	round	currentdue	pastdue	holsend
1	Singh	Rajat	Mr.	152/B, Gomti Nagar	Lucknow	1	$8.50	$17.00	4/8/2009
2	Jain	Salil	Mr.	133-B, LDA Colony	Lucknow	1	$0.00	$10.00	
3	Sharma	Payal	Ms.	A-154,Rajajipuram	Lucknow	1	$30.00	$20.00	5/8/2009
4	Gupta	Sameer	Mr.	16,Rana Pratap Mar	Lucknow	1	$0.00	$0.00	
5	Singh	Neelam	Mrs.	V-95,Nehru Enclave	Lucknow	1	$20.00	$10.00	8/8/2009
\utoNumber)							$0.00	$0.00	

Record: 2 of 5

Figure 22.16 : Query Results

Setting Special Criteria

Criteria are limits you place on a query or an advanced filter to identify the specific records you want to work with. To specify criteria for a field in the design grid, enter an expression in the **Criteria** cell for that field.

Looking for Non-blanks

Suppose you want to look for all customers who have entries in the **holsbegin** field.

- Return to Design View.
- Delete the criteria from the round field so that we have a few more records to choose from, and check its Show box to select it.
- In the criteria for **HolsBegin**, type **Is Not Null** as shown in Figure 22.17.
- Run the query.

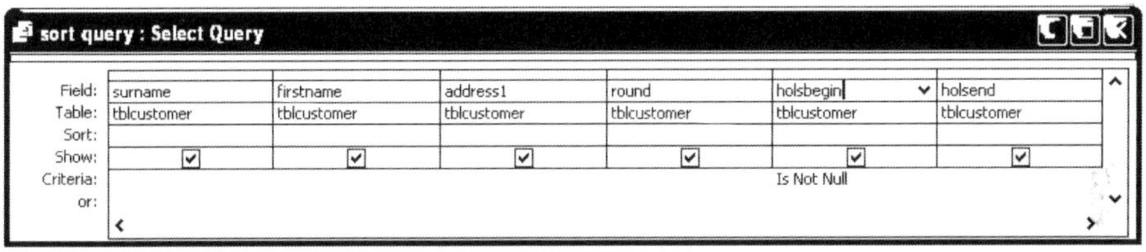

Figure 22.17 : Searching for records with non-blank *HolsBegin* field

Looking for a Range of Values

Now supposing you want to find all customers whose holidays begin on or after April 27th 2009. Return to Design View, Delete the criteria Is Not Null in the holsBegin field and type >= 27/04/09 instead, Run the query.

Combining Criteria with the AND or the OR operator

You can enter additional criteria for the same field or different fields. When you type expressions in more than one **criteria** cell, Access combines them using either the **AND** or the **OR** operator. If the expressions are in different cells in the same row, Access uses the **AND** operator, which means only the records that meet the criteria in all the cells will be returned. If the expressions are in different rows of the design grid, Access uses the **OR** operator, which means records that meet criteria in any of the cells will be returned. The following examples shows different ways to combine criteria with the **AND** operator or the **OR** operator.

One field using the OR operator

The query design in Figure 22.18, finds all customers who live in Gomtinagar or Dalibagh. The Criteria are entered on two separate rows as Like "*Gomtinagar*", Like "*Dalibagh*". Note that the use of the wildcard * allows you to find all records containing the word "**Gomtinagar**" or "**Dalibagh**".

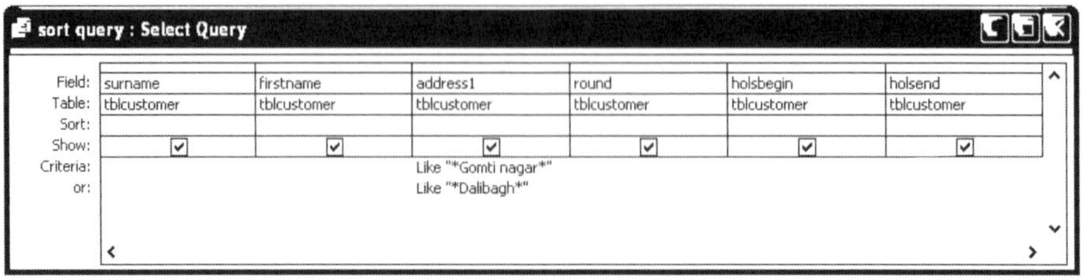

Figure 22.18 : Using OR in Query Criteria

One field using the AND Operator

You can also include the word "AND' in your query criteria. For example if you want to find all customers whose Pastdue amount is between Rs. 10 and Rs. 20 inclusive, type >=10 and <=20 in the **Pastdue** field, as shown in Figure 22.19.

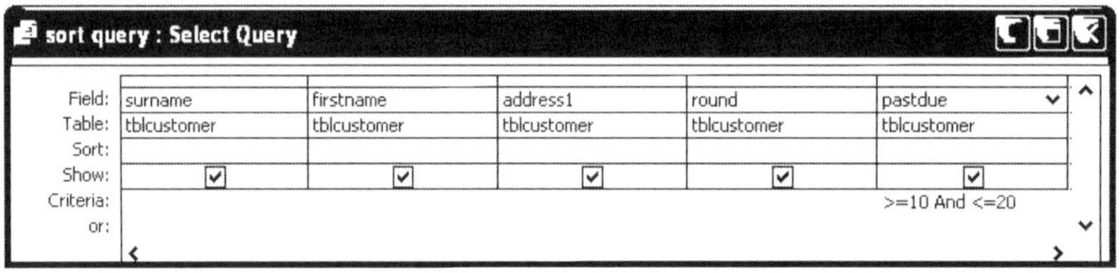

Figure 22.19 : Looking for a range of values in a field

Two Fields using the OR Operator

Figure 22.20 shows a query design by setting up criteria in two fields, to retrieve those records only in which **address1** is either **Gomtinagar** or **round** is 2.

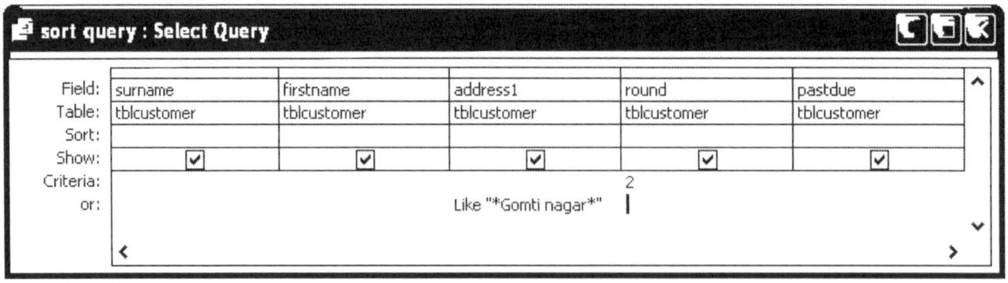

Figure 22.20 : Using OR in two fields

Two Fields using the AND Operator

Figure 22.21 shows a query, where the criteria is setup in two different fields in such a manner, so that only those records will be displayed in which **address 1** = Gomtinagar and **round** =2.

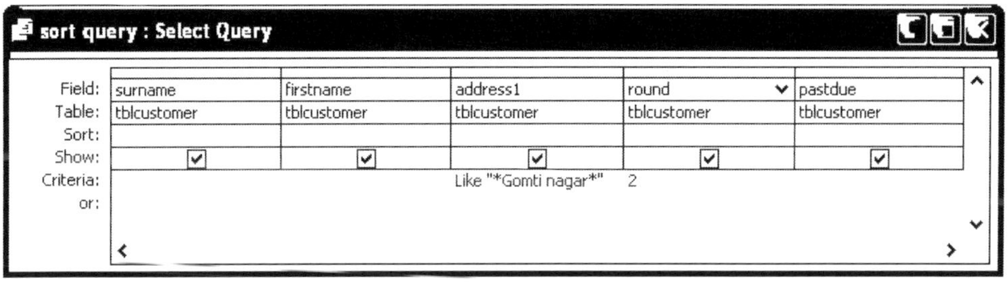

Figure 22.21 : Using OR in two fields

Parameter Query

It is often useful when you are developing a customized application to be able to save a query but let the user type in the criteria when the query is run. For example, you could allow the user to specify the round number in the original query instead of having the query always find customers in round 1. To create this query, follow these steps:

- In Design view, click the **Criteria** row of the **round** column and type [*Please enter round number:*]. Make sure the prompt must be enclosed in square brackets.
- Press the Run button to run the query. The message you typed in displayed asking the user to enter the round number. (refer to Figure 22.22).
- Enter 2 and press OK. The query finds all customers on round 2.

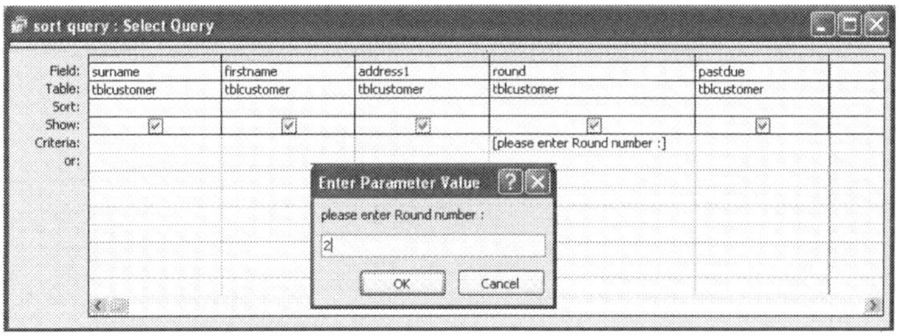

Figure 22.22 : Parameterised Query

Relating Multiple Tables in a Query

You really begin to see the power of a relational database system when you build a query using more than one table. As you add tables, the query has access to more and more information. As an example, suppose we want to display for a particular customer, their surname, and customerID for each newspaper they have been delivered, the newspaper name and whether it is a morning or evening paper.

For this data, you need to get the information from three separate tables: Customer, newspapers and delivery. The relationship between the customer and delivery tables, and relationship between newspaper and delivery tables gives access to the complete information. The following steps shows how to create query with multiple tables.

1. Click the Query object in the Database window.

2. Click the New toolbar button to create a new query.

3. Select Design View and click the **OK** button in the New Query dialog box.

4. In the Show Table dialog box, select and add each table in turn.

5. Click Close in the Show Table dialog box.

6. Select the desired fields from all the three tables one-by-one as shown in Figure 22.23.

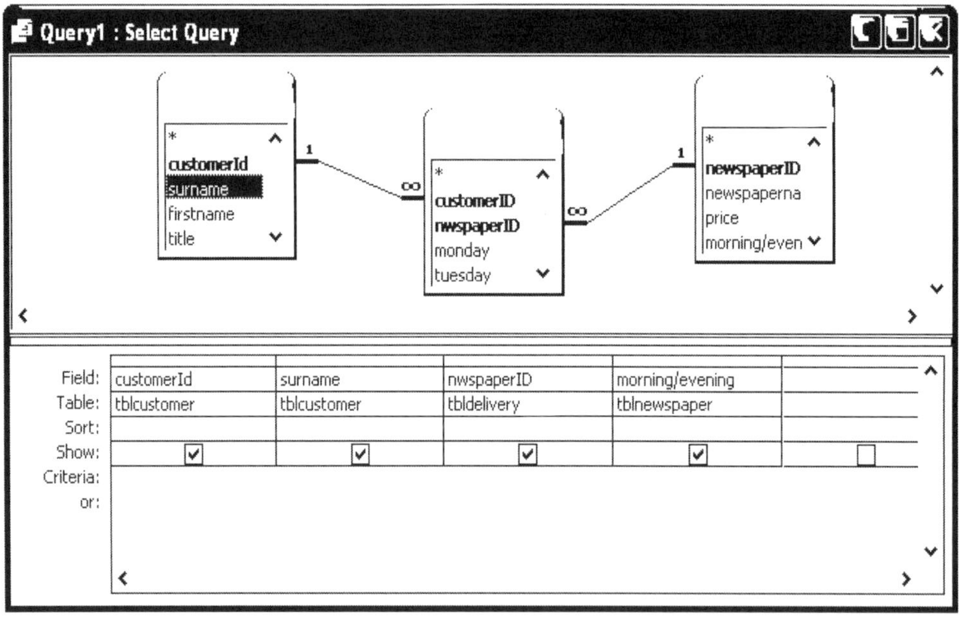

Figure 22.23 : Query Combining Fields from Different Tables

7. Run the query, results are displayed as shown in Figure 22.24.

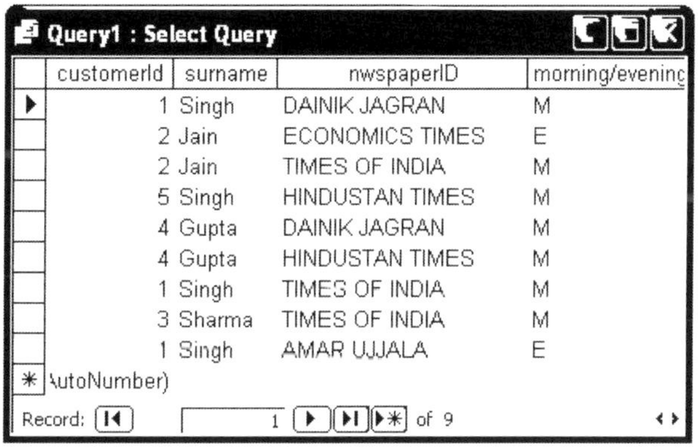
Query1 : Select Query

	customerId	surname	nwspaperID	morning/evening
▶	1	Singh	DAINIK JAGRAN	M
	2	Jain	ECONOMICS TIMES	E
	2	Jain	TIMES OF INDIA	M
	5	Singh	HINDUSTAN TIMES	M
	4	Gupta	DAINIK JAGRAN	M
	4	Gupta	HINDUSTAN TIMES	M
	1	Singh	TIMES OF INDIA	M
	3	Sharma	TIMES OF INDIA	M
	1	Singh	AMAR UJJALA	E
*	AutoNumber)			

Record: 1 of 9

8. Save the query and close it to return to the database window.

Creating a Totals Query

Calculate totals on all the records in a query.

1. Create a select query in Design view and add the tables whose records you want to use in the calculations.
2. Add the fields on which you want to perform calculation and specify criteria.
3. Click **Total** ($\sum$) on the toolbar. Microsoft Access displays the **Total** row in the design grid.
4. For each field in the design grid, click its cell in the **Total** row, and then click one of the following aggregate functions : **Sum, Avg, Min, Max, Count, StDev, Or Var**, or click the other functions, **First** and **Last**.
5. If you want, enter criteria to affect the results of the calculation.
6. If you want, sort the results.
7. Click **View** on the toolbar to view the results.

Summary Query

We will use a calculation and a summary operator **Sum** in a query to calculate this week's payment.

- From the database window start a new query, select Design as the query type and add **tblcustomer**, **tbldelivery** and **tblnewspaper** tables to the query window. Close the Show Table dialog box.
- Place customerID from **tbldelivery** and surname from **tblcustomer** tables on the query grid.

- Place NewspaperID from **tbldelivery** on the query grid.
- In the next field type the following expression:

  DueThisWeek : -([Monday]+[Tuesday]+[Wednesday]+[Thursday]+[Friday]+[Saturday]+[Sunday])*[Price]

- With the pointer in the column which you have named **DueThisWeek**, click the **Totals** button on the toolbar.
- Select **Sum** in the **Group by** drop-down list (refer to Figure 22.25).

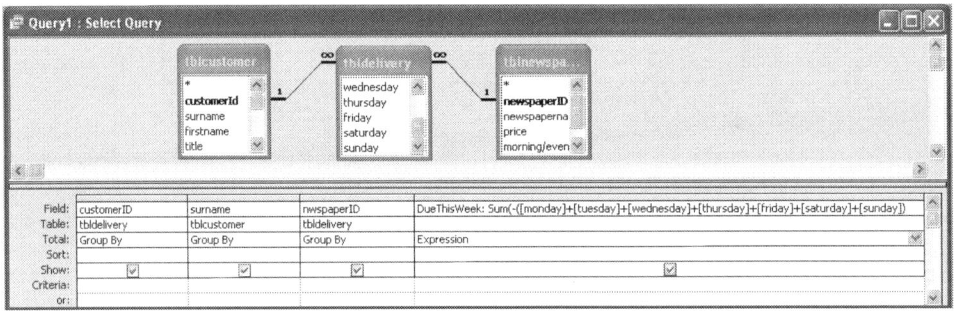

Figure 22.25 : Calculating the weekly amount due

- Run the query, the result is shown in Figure 22.26.

Query1 : Select Query

customerID	nwspaperID	surname	DueThisWeek
Singh	AMAR UJJALA	Singh	$18.00
Singh	DAINIK JAGRAN	Singh	$21.00
Singh	TIMES OF INDIA	Singh	$20.00
Jain	ECONOMICS TIMES	Jain	$36.00
Jain	TIMES OF INDIA	Jain	$30.00
Sharma	TIMES OF INDIA	Sharma	$20.00
Gupta	DAINIK JAGRAN	Gupta	$18.00
Gupta	HINDUSTAN TIMES	Gupta	$20.00
Singh	HINDUSTAN TIMES	Singh	$28.00

Record: 6 of 9

Figure 22.26 : Query Results

In order to get the totals for each customer, the field NewsPaperID must be removed from the query grid.

- Return to Design View and delete the NewspaperID column.
- Run the query again. This time the results should be what you want.

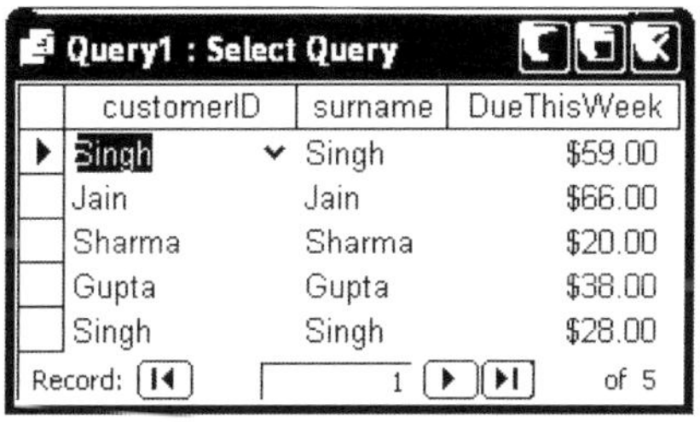

Figure 22.27 : Totals for each Customer

- Save the query and close it.

Reports

Although you can print your data directly form tables, query dynasets, forms, but reports give you greater control over how that data is printed. Among other things, reports enables you to specify which fields you want printed, sort records, group records, calculate summary information, control the overall layout and appearance of your report. You can print pictures and other graphics as well as Memo fields in a report. If you can think of a report you want, Access can probably create it. Four basic types of reports are used generally:

Tabular reports	These print data in rows and columns with groupings and totals. Variations include summary and group/total reports.
Columnar reports	These print data as a form and can include totals and graphs.
Mail-Merge reports	These create form letters.
Mailing labels	These create multicolumn labels or snaked-column reports.

Reports Vs Forms

Although you create Access reports using the same techniques as for creating forms, there are major differences between forms and reports with respect to the design concepts. Forms deal with data and the processes of data management, such as data entry, validation, and retrieval. Reports, on the other hand deal with information derived from the data. For example, the numbers 563345892 are simply data and mean nothing to you until you turn the sequence into information : 563-34-5892.

Forms are used primarily by people who are acquainted with computers and database management systems, so forms can be somewhat abbreviated, assuming that the user understands the process at hand. Reports are much more widely distributed, sometimes to people who may never have seen a computer. Reports must, therefore, be self-explanatory and focus on the purpose of the report in plain language.

Creating a Report using Report Wizard

Report wizards simplify the layout process of your fields by visually stepping you through a series of questions about the type of report that you want to create and then automatically creating the report for you. We'll start by creating a simple customer report.

1. In the Database Window, click **Reports** under **Objects**.
2. Click the **New** button on the Database window toolbar.
3. In the **New Report** dialog box, click the wizard that you want to use. (Here we are choosing Report Wizard).
4. Select the query or table that contains the data you want to base your report on (for this example, select tblcustomer).
5. Click OK, a field selection box appears, as shown in Figure 22.28.

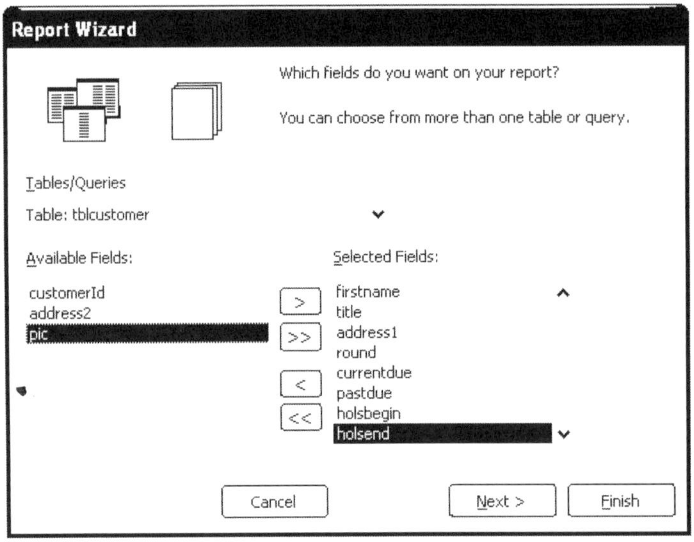

Figure 22.28 : Selecting fields for the Report

6. Select the fields to place them in the **Selected Fields** area, then click **Next** button (for this example, select all fields except customerID, address2, and pic).
7. The next dialog box lets you choose which field(s) you want to use for a grouping. Using the Report Wizard, you can select up to four different group fields for your report. Select round field as the grouping field as shown in Figure 22.29.

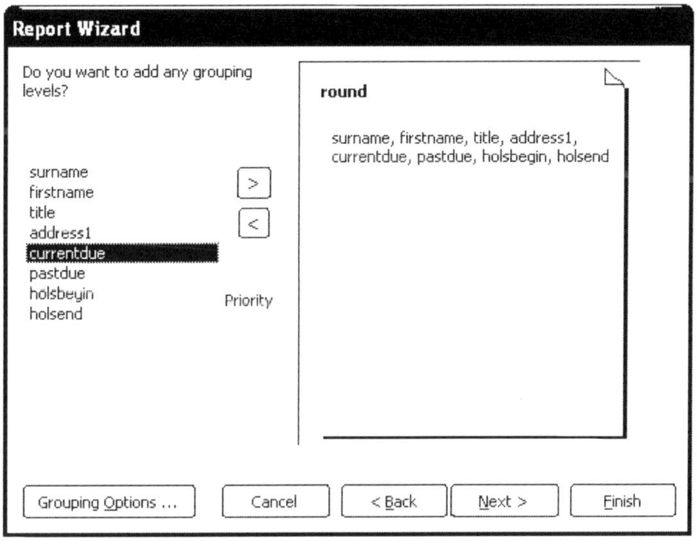

Figure 22.29 : Grouping on Round

8. After you select the group field(s), click the **Grouping Options** button at the bottom of the dialog box to display **Grouping Intervals** dialog box as shown in Figure 22.30, which lets you further define how your report will use the group field.

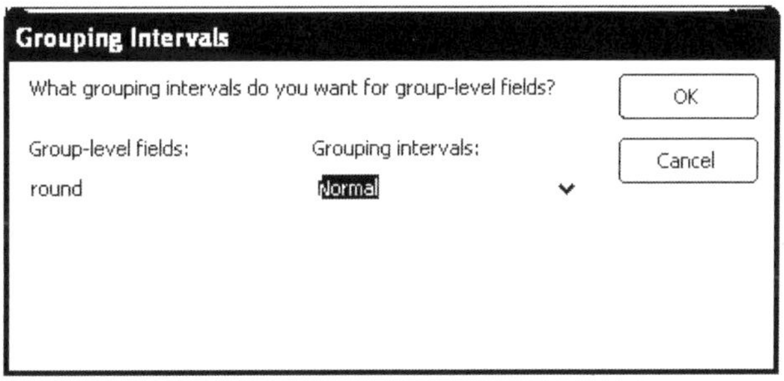

Figure 22.30 : Grouping Interval Dialog Box

9. Choose the default text-field grouping option if Normal is acceptable. Click the OK button to return to the Grouping Levels dialog box, and then click the **Next** button to move to the Sort order dialog box as shown in Figure 22.31.

10. Access sorts the group record fields automatically in an order that helps the grouping make sense. You can select fields that you have not already chosen to group and use these as sorting fields. Choose first name here.

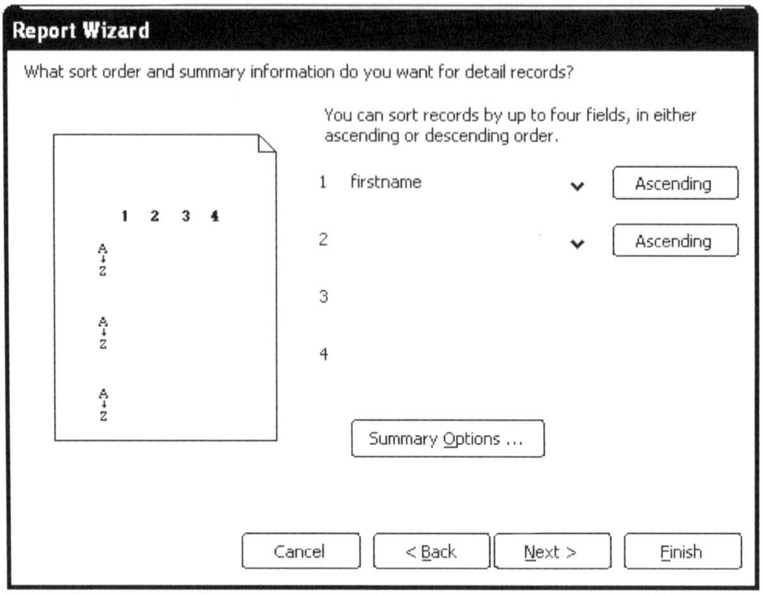

Figure 22.31 : Selecting a Sort Order

11. Click the Summary Options button in this window, a Summary Options dialog box appears as shown in Figure 22.32. This dialog box provides additional options for numeric fields. As you can see, the field currentdue and pastdue are to be summed. Additionally, you can display averages, minimums and maximums.

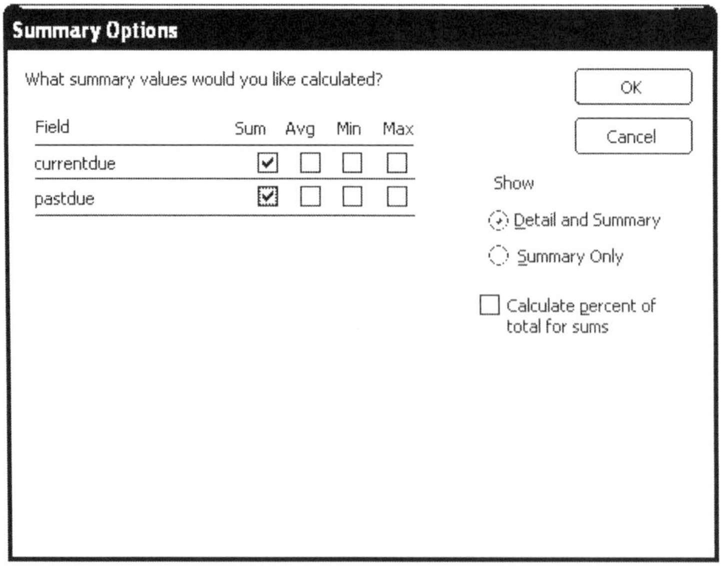

Figure 22.32 : Selecting Summary Options

12. By selecting Detail and Summary option, the report will show the detail data; selecting Summary Only hides the detail section showing only totals in the report. Clicking the OK button in this dialog box returns you to the sorting dialog box. There you can click the **Next** button to move on to the layout wizard dialog box (refer Figure 22.33).

13. This wizard gives you options to choose layout and orientation of your report. Choose Align Left1 option, then click on Next.

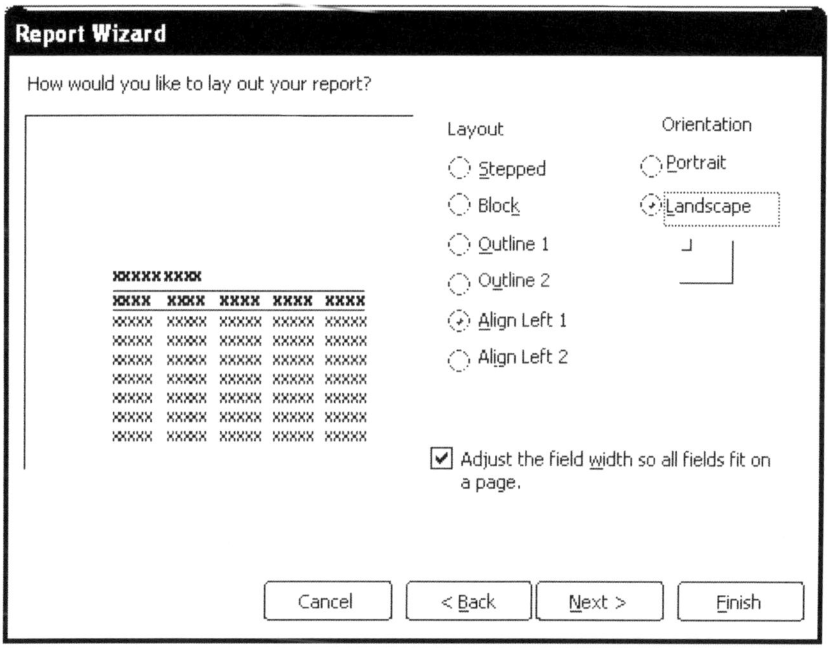

Figure 22.33 : Selecting a Report Layout

14. Now you have to select a report style from the dialog box shown in Figure 22.34. Each style has different background shadings, font size, typeface, and other formatting. For this example, choose corporate. Finally, click the **Next** button to move to the last dialog box.

NOTE : You can customize any of the style, or add your own, by using the AutoFormat menu option from the Format menu of the Report Design window and choosing customize.

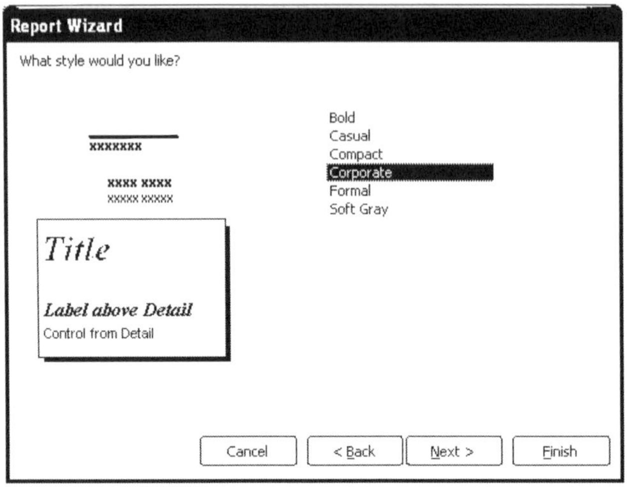

Figure 22.34 : Choosing the Style of your Report

15. Figure 22.35 is the final Report Wizard dialog box. Type the title of your report which will appear once at the beginning of the report. Next you can choose one of the option buttons at the bottom of the dialog box to either Preview the report or to Modify the report's design. For this example, leave the default selection intact to preview the report.

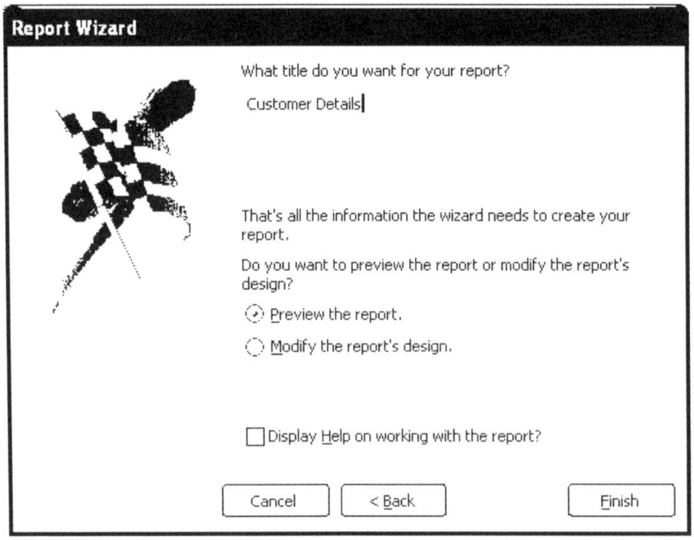

Figure 22.35 : Choosing the Title of your Report

16. Click Finish to complete the Report wizard and view the report.

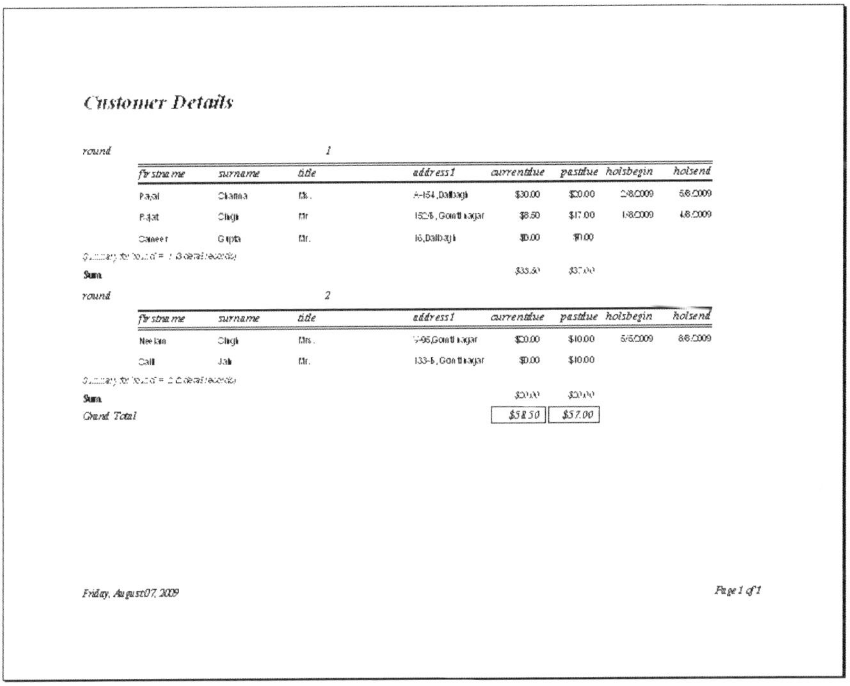

Figure 22.36 : The report in Print Preview Mode

Sections of a Report

The information in a report can be divided into sections. All reports have a detail section, but a report can also include a report header a page header, a page footer, and a report footer section. Each section has a specific purpose and prints in a predictable order in the report. Five sections of a report are:

- The **report header** appears once at the beginning of a report. You can use it for items such as a logo, report title, or print date. The report header is printed before the page header on the first page of the report.
- The **page header** appears at the top of every page in the report. You use it to display items such as column headings.
- The **detail section** contains the main body of a report's data. This section is repeated for each record in the report's underlying record source.
- The **page footer** appears at the bottom of every page in the report. You use it to display items such as page numbers.
- The **report footer** appears once at the end of the report. You use it to display items such as report totals. The report footer is the last section in the report design but appears before the page footer on the last page of the printed report.

You can add a header and footer to each group in a report. The header displays the value on which the records are grouped, and the footer displays a subtotal for the group.

- A **group header** appears at the beginning of a new group of records. You use it to display information that applies to the group as a whole, such as a group name.
- A **group footer** appears at the end of a group of records. You use it to display items such as group totals.

You can hide or resize a section, add a picture, or set the background color of a section. You can also set section properties to customize how the contents of a section print.

Summary

- Data entry forms provide the most flexible format for viewing your data.
- Form Wizards simplify form creation by giving you a starting point for form design and stepping you through the process.
- There are five basic types of forms : Full-screen (columnar), tabular, main/subforms, PivotTables, and graphs.
- Queries let you ask questions about your data and return the answer in the form of information.
- Types of queries include select, total, crosstab, action and SQL.
- Queries create a virtual view of the data, known as a dynaset. The data is displayed in a datasheet.
- The query window has two panes. Design view, and QBE.
- You can limit records being displayed with record criteria, specifying character, numeric, date/time, and yes/no.
- The Access report writer lets you create tabular reports, columnar reports, business graphs, and mailing labels.
- Report Wizards let you create reports by filling in a series of dialog boxes.
- Reports can be printed or viewed onscreen in Print Preview mode.

Review Exercise

Multiple choice questions

1. The type of form, which allows you to see several records at one time is
   a) Columnar
   b) PivotTable
   c) Tabular
   d) None of these
2. In Main/Subform view how many navigational bars you have:
   a) Two
   b) Three
   c) Any number
   d) None of these
3. The query which provides the capability to sum or produce totals in a select query is
   a) Select
   b) Total
   c) SQL
   d) None of these
4. A row in QBE grid to provide checkbox
   a) Sort
   b) Criteria
   c) Show
   d) All of these
5. An operator which returns the value true if all conditions are true is
   a) OR
   b) AND
   c) NOT
   d) None of these

6. With Access Report you can
   a) Create mailing labels
   b) Show totals in a chart
   c) Group records into categories
   d) All of these

State whether true or false

1. Forms only provide the way for adding your data.
2. A main/subform is commonly used to display many-to-one relationships.
3. Form can only be created using tables.
4. Total queries provide the capability to sum or produce total in a select query.
5. The Query Design window consists of two panes, the table/query entry pane and QBE design pane.
6. Columnar reports are also known as form reports.
7. Using Report Wizard method, you can only create tabular reports.
8. Reports can only be viewed onscreen in Print Preview mode.

Fill in the blanks

1. You can customize the style of form by changing a form and then using the ____________ function in the form design screen.
2. After completing all the steps to design your form, through wizard, you can open the new form by selecting ____________ or ____________ options.
3. ____________ objects are visible only in a form or report.
4. The query window has two modes, the ____________ mode and the ____________ mode.
5. ____________ are simply some rule or rules that you supply for Access.
6. You can use the ____________ operator to determine whether an object is within a specific range of values.
7. You can automate the process of changing criteria for queries, that you run on a regular basis by creating ____________ queries.
8. Reports are used for presenting a ____________ view of your data.
9. Tabular reports are also known as ____________ reports.

Descriptive questions

1. What are the basic types of forms available in Access?
2. How form are different from datasheet?
3. What is a query? Explain.
4. How many types of queries are available in Access? Explain each with example.
5. What are action queries? How many types of action queries you can make in Access?
6. What is dynaset? How is it will helpful in making query?
7. Explain Access Report? How it will be useful for presenting information to the user?
8. How many types of reports can be created in Access? Explain each with suitable example.
9. What is the difference between reports and forms?

C H A P T E R

23 INFORMATION TECHNOLOGY AND SOCIETY

FEATURING

- Introduction
- Indian IT Act
- Intellectual Property Rights - Issues
- Applications of Information Technology

Information Technology has penetrated in every sector of modern society, be it for commercial purposes or in economic matters. The impact of IT is all pervasive in modern society. Companies and countries are leveraging IT to gain significant competitive advantage in the international trade arena. In this chapter we are going to explore the use of IT in various areas such as business, education, kiosks, banking, *telephone exchanges , and many more.*

Introduction

Information technology is the combination of information and technology. IT comprises telecommunications and computers for obtaining, processing, storing and communicating information in various forms to different persons and places. Today the world is changing at a very fast pace. One of the most important factors of change is technology. For the development of the technology, information is essential. IT involves the processing of information by a computer. For that we require hardware, software, services and the supporting infrastructure to manage and deliver information. IT is used in every walk of our life for example, the use of mobile phones to make calls, to send text messages, use of ATM machines for banking and so on.

Indian IT Act

The IT Act, 2000 is an act to provide legal recognition for transactions carried out by means of electronic data interchange and other means of electronic communication, which is commonly referred to as "electronic commerce". It involve the use of alternatives to paper-based methods of communication and storage of information, to facilitate electronic filing of documents with the Government agencies and further to amend the Indian Penal Code, the Indian Evidence Act, 1872, the Banker's Books Evidence Act, 1891 and the Reserve Bank of India Act, 1934 and for matters connected therewith or incidental thereto.

Intellectual Property Rights - Issues

Intellectual Property (IP) refers to creations of the mind : inventions, literacy and artistic works, and symbols, names, images, and designs used in commerce. IP is divide into two categories : Industrial property, which includes inventions (patents), trademarks, industrial designs, and geographic indications of source; and Copyright, which includes literary and artistic works such as novels, poems and plays, films, musical works, artistic works such as drawings, paintings, photographs and sculptures, and architectural designs.

Intellectual property plays an important role in an increasingly broad range of areas, ranging from the Internet to health care to nearly all aspects of science and technology and literature and the arts. Understanding the role of intellectual property in these areas - many of them still emerging - often requires significant new research and study. In an effort to promote informed discussion of the intellectual property issues involved in these fields, WIPO regularly produces various explanatory publications on current issues of interest.

In modern societies the sharing of knowledge in the public domain is challenged by the Internet and the protection of knowledge through Intellectual Property Rights (IPR).

What Information Technology is Protected by Copyright?

Copyright is currently a primary source of protection for software programs, user manuals, databases, websites and other information technology works in Canada, provided that they meet the requirements of the federal copyright act.

To be the subject - matter of copyright, the work be "original", meaning that it originate from the author and was not copied. Further, for a work to garnet copyright protection in Canada it must be fixed. Fixation is not always clear, especially with respect to information technology.

Applications of Information Technology

IT plays an important role in today's global economy. It has made a significant impact in science, research and development. Business is changing as every organization adopts IT in some form or the other to perform the tasks in effective manner. The major areas impacted by the advent of information technology includes business, education, banking, railways, and so forth. Below are some applications of information technology that changes every aspect of life, be it politics, society, or economy.

Electronic Commerce

Electronic Commerce (EC or E-Commerce) denotes the use of computer networks — intranets, extranets, private networks, and the Internet, to execute complete business transactions. Prior to 1997, EC was mainly identified with Electronic Data Interchange (EDI), and older, less flexible technology using proprietary networks which were not very convenient and useful. EC is now implemented on the Internet using a variety of sophisticated, web-based tools. The scope of EC includes the customer interactions of advertising, product selection, contract negotiation to the product and services delivery and payment settlement.

Due to the differences in the nature of transactions involved, two distinct categories of EC are recognized:

- **Business-to-Business EC** The use of the Internet or private networks to automate business transactions between companies or organizations.
- **Business-to-Consumer EC** The use of the Internet to sell merchandise or provide services to customers in much the same way as a shopkeeper.

The term Electric Business (e-biz) has also been introduced which includes not only EC, but all the web-enabled core business processes, extensive customer integration and connectivity, and strategic transformation of business processes to exploit the full capabilities of emerging IT tools.

Educational Applications

The learning process can be enriched in many subjects because of the volume and range of information which a computer databank can provide. Learning process can be further facilitated because of the flexible mode (multimedia) and speed of presentation of learning material. Computers can be used as a resource in teaching and learning at all levels of education.

Using the computer to provide intelligent tutoring is gaining popularity in both high schools and colleges. An intelligent tutoring program can adapt itself based on student responses to review areas where the student is weak and to skip areas where the student has already mastered the material. CBTs are helpful to students no matter what their level of subject mastery is. Advanced students are not bored by questions that seem repetitive and simplistic. Students finding the subject problematic will be asked more questions in order to reinforce concepts. A student will receive immediate feedback from the computer, enabling him or her to see the correct answers while the question is still fresh in the student's mind.

When a computer is used as a teaching aid, it is referred to as Computer-Assisted-Instruction or Computer-Aided-Instruction (CAI). Software for CAI can be prepared by class teachers or can be purchased. The subject material is displayed on the CRT screen. The CAI programs can be prepared in a variety of modes such as tutorial, discovery and problem solving —modelling and drill and practice.

Virtual Classrooms

This new technology helps captivate the student's interest. Virtual class rooms involves a student with software that reacts and interacts, unlike a book. With the help of virtual learning, students can listen to pre-recorded audio comments to enhance knowledge, search the databases for their views and of other students, students can get immediate feedback on their actions, students can get on-line education from remote places using virtual classrooms. Virtual classrooms are beneficial to those students who are unable to attend the physical classrooms due to some problems such as distant location of institutes or universities.

Question papers (objective type) are kept in computer database. In a designed screen the questions are displayed for a fix period of time. Students indicates their answer by pressing an option like a, b, c, d. Computer immediately assesses the answer. Marks are displayed instantly to declare the students result.

Hotel Management

The business of hotel management involves utilizing a large inventory of rooms and large number of employees per hotel, and providing best services to customers. Hotel management has associated components like reservation, check-in, billing for room and services, checkout and bill settlement.

All the functions are carried out through integrated IT applications. When customer requests for reservation, the operator checks for room availability and enters arrival date and time, estimated departure date, name, etc. The program can also be made to check if the customer is eligible to avail some discount. If the customer accepts the rate sent by the operator, the system creates necessary records in the reservation database and the system mails the confirmation of the reservation to the customer.

Various lists can be printed and sent to concerned departments. At any stage, the system lets the management check the hotel occupancy rate.

The services ordered by the customers are billed to the room account. The hotel telephone exchange automatically bills all telephone calls dialed from the room to the linked room account. The food bills, car rents, etc., are entered into the billing system and charged to the customer account.

When the customer checks-out, the checkout system retrieves bills for all the services availed by the customer and prints a single consolidated bill. It automatically adjusts any payments that the customer might have made earlier. To facilitate payment by a credit card, billing system may be linked to the credit card company's computer system to automatically validate the credit card payment.

Multimedia

Multimedia represents the convergence of computers, digital video, digital audio, and sound synthesis technologies. It can be referred to as a means of entertainment because of its applications in interactive games and leisure programs. Its popular applications include video player, television video, telecommunication, audio CD Player and CD-ROM player.

- **Games for Young Children** Games often provide young children an early introduction to computers. Children enjoy using the computer to play games and in turn learn something as they play. Many computer games build some of the same skills that reading does — maintaining focus, problem-solving, and developing imagination.
- **Advertising Applications** Advertisement is an important activity in the marketing department. In some firms, advertising department exists separately. Advertising departments create ads and other promotional materials . Various computerized tools are available for marketing, advertising and sales. Organizations trying to bring their products and services to people's notice are using the Internet in a big way. Companies pay to put the details of their products and services on web sites to maximize out reach. Once the companies grow big and the volume of business increases, companies can opt for creating their own web sites.
- **Home Delivery Service** Home shopping is a growing area of Internet use. Through electronic commerce it has become very easy to order the items through the web site and pay electronically. The goods are delivered at home, hence the entire transaction is electronic.

This can be achieved in the following steps:

- Visit the merchant's web site, select the items, and enter shipping instructions. The merchant's server returns a summary of item, price and transaction ID.
- Click the pay buttons which launches the cybercash wallet. Choose a credit card from your wallet and click OK to forward the order and encrypted payment information to the merchant.
- Merchant receives the packet, strips-off the order and forwards the encrypted payment information to cybercash server.
- Cybercash server receives the packet, takes the transaction behind its firewall, reformats the transaction and forwards it to the merchant's bank over dedicated lines.
- The merchant's bank forwards the authorization request to the issuing bank via the card association.
- Cybercash returns the approval to the merchant who then dispatches the goods to the customer.

Railways

Before the introduction of computerised Ticket Reservation System, the booking system was very slow and did not offer any way of booking in trains originating from other cities.

The Indian Railway's Computerised Ticket Reservation System works around central computers located in major cities and terminals placed in other cities. The reservation system is a complex Database Management System (DBMS) application. The application takes care of number of trains. The details maintained by the application regarding trains in the database, are:

- The list of trains, having information regarding train number, name, type of train, etc.
- Train schedule i.e., place and time of departure, days of week the train travels , etc.
- Route of train.
- Types of accommodation, e.g., first, second, third, first AC, second AC, etc.
- Number of seats, and coaches available, and number of reserved seats.
- Quota of seats for Railway or Government employees.
- Discounts for special category of passengers, e.g., handicapped, senior citizens, etc.
- How many days in advance can booking be done?

These reservation details are kept in several related files. An RDBMS is used to maintain data in these linked files.

When a person requests for ticket reservation, the operator feeds train number and date of journey. The program checks whether the train runs on that day or not. If yes, the operator feeds additional details, e.g., number of seats, class, name of traveller, etc., Now, the program checks the database to find the total number of seats in that class. Next, it checks the database to find the number of reservations done. If seats are available, the reservation is done and the program stores the necessary details. If seats are not available, the program still records the reservation request and allots waiting list number. Later, if some passenger wants to cancel the reservation, the program updates the database, calculates amount to be refunded, and allots the cancelled seats to wait-listed passengers.

The database information can be used to print various lists, queries on the database can be answered, and the data can also be linked to a web program that can provide this information on Internet. A web application can fetch the information regarding arrival and departure to provide real time information through Internet.

Airlines

Information technology is widely used in airlines. Main areas of application in airlines are flight tracking system, flight scheduling and controls, on-line reservation/cancellation, and infodesk for travellers

This system keeps track of the flight on a long route. This includes the timestamp for each halt, take-off and total time taken to reach each point of halt. System also keeps a track of the route followed by a particular airbus. Some airlines provide this information on-line through Internet or infodesk for the convenience of passengers.

Flight scheduler system schedules the flight time, engineer, pilot and other manpower required for the journey.

This service allows the airline customers to reserve or cancel their seats on-line through Internet. Computer controlled seat reservation/cancellation brings benefits to the airlines and customers. To avoid over booking, a complete list of all bookings needs to be maintained. Whenever a seat is reserved the information system is automatically updated.

The flight control system relays traffic control instructions to the pilot as well as information about factors like variations in atmospheric pressure, wind speed, and directions. Small computers installed as a part of the aeroplane's equipment, provide the information needed to control the flight and other navigational calculations. These computers are programmed to continuously analyze data, which is relayed direct from the various instruments.

Banking

Banks were among the first to invest heavily in computing and today banking is almost totally dependent on the computers. In most banks a server computer is installed centrally which keeps the record of all accounts, account holders and other details required for banking. Under computer control, customer statements are prepared and printed out onto specially designed or preprinted stationary.

Leading national and international banks provide Automatic Teller Machine (ATMs) points on different locations where transactions are done 24 hours a day. Automatic teller machines are popularly known as ATMs. Besides ATM facilities, banks are making full use of Internet technologies to provide on-line transactions and information 24 hours. One can transfer funds and purchase items on-line.

Insurance

Many consumers view insurance as a necessary evil and insurance companies as slow-moving behemoths, but IT in these organizations is just the opposite. Insurance being an information-dependent product, the best insurance companies view IT as a strategic business partner and key contributor to gaining and servicing customers, controlling costs, determining risk, and processing claims. Insurance companies usually support large, thriving IT organizations and tend to be early adopters of new technologies. For example, they were among the first companies to adopt imaging technologies as a core application for claims adjustment and processing.

As insurance companies continue to diversify into financial planning and investment services in addition to personal and corporate insurance packages, the activities in IT are increasingly diversified as well. Customer extranets are a growing trend as insurance companies rely more on customer self-service to lower costs and speed up claims processing. Similarly, extranets to service independent agents and claims adjusters are also a key application. While insurance may not be a glamorous industry, the array of hardware, software, and networking technologies required in insurance IT today means endless challenges, change, and opportunity for IT professionals who want exposure to myriad technologies and business problems.

Telephone Exchanges

Computerized telephone exchanges handle an ever-increasing volume of calls. Such telephone exchanges can be easily linked to other network exchanges for wider use. Through satellites, a call can be transmitted at faster speed than through conventional networks. The computer can maintain a call log for subsequent billing. Computer controlled telephone exchanges make use of ISDN (Integrated Services Digital Network). ISDN integrate telephone, data, text and video. ISDN services allow - Digital transmission and switching with synchronization protocols, Digital link-up to the subscriber's premises.

Mobile Phones

Generally, mobile device applications include mobile phones, PDAs, handled PC, digital cameras and video cameras. Mobile phones and PDAs are representative products of the mobile device market. Mobile communications has seen changes in the past decade as first generation analog technology has been phased out and second generation digital wireless communications has emerged as the dominant technology. At present, most people in the US connect to the Internet through wires. Much of the growth in Internet connections, however, is expected to be through wireless connections. Currently, more people around the world have mobile phones than Internet access. Over the next few years, most mobile phones will obtain Internet access. By 2005, the penetration level of mobile devices (including phones) with data capabilities is expected to approach mobile phones user penetration levels in the US, Western Europe, and Japan. It is expected that, by then, all mobile terminals will be data enabled and subscribers will be able to access data and Internet services via mobile phones. As a result, it is likely that in many areas of the world where there are more mobile phone users than personal computer users, more people will have access to the Internet through mobile phones than through computers.

Internet access through mobile phones is qualitatively different from access through computers because of the relatively small screen size, limited memory, and weak data entry capabilities of mobile phones. Efforts are under way to determine what applications will work effectively for mobile phones. Successful mobile applications are likely to differ from typical computer-based applications. In addition to limited e-mail and web browsing capabilities, mobile phones may also offer various location-based services, such as information on restaurants, shops, and services in the vicinity of the phone's current location.

Information technology has been applied in mobile phones industry from establishing the network to handsets. Computer controlled systems at transponding stations are used to connect mobile phone calls, maintain records and other operations. With the deployment of CDMA (Code Division Multiple Access) in India, major telecom equipment manufacturers are manufacturing CDMA handsets. GSM (Global System for Mobile communications), another technology which has automatic roaming as a key feature allows use of GSM handsets right across Asia and Europe. WLL (Wireless in Local Loop) is in use in India for effective voice communication and better voice quality at a lower cost.

Kiosks

Multimedia kiosks, which provide details of products and services, have already been installed in shops, museums and public places. Typically they combine text and graphics; some also provide image, audio, animation and video. Information can be accessed by touch screen (the most popular method), mouse or keyboard. Most incorporate some elements of hypermedia to enable the user to move around the system.

Kiosks are used to inform the public about the facilities offered by organizations such as art galleries, museums, parks, hotels and airports. They use interactive multimedia to arouse the visitor's natural sense of curiosity. Once involved, users touch buttons and pictures to find out information.

Point-Of-Sale (POS) systems are used to support sales staff, disseminate information, encourage brand awareness, boost sales and promote new products. Point-of-sale kiosks allow a retailer to reach a wide range of customers through the use of third party locations and 24-hour availability. They can extend the range of products offered, and provide faster and more convenient service. Retailers can ensure that the information provided will be consistent and accurate. During quiet periods, kiosks can be used for staff training.

Kiosks can also be used to capture statistical data on usage that enables in-depth market research to be carried out on consumer trends. This enables retailers to respond to rapidly changing market conditions and customer demands.

Kiosks can also be used to inform the general public about local government services. In the UK, for example, Nottinghamshire County Council has installed County Contact, a system that covers a range of general and specific information about the County Council's organization and services. Almost each kiosk contains features like - touch screen activation, audio, full motion video, color graphics, still pictures/photographs, laser printer, information pages, e-services, telephone, frequently asked questions, and index.

For example:

- Home, a leading Danish real-estate chain, has developed a successful information kiosk to provide potential property buyers with "candidate" information, based on the criteria set by the buyers.
- Florsheim Shoes in the US uses a multimedia POS to promote and sell shoes in shops and department stores. Customers can order direct from the system, with delivery to their homes within hours.
- In the UK a public information system called Micro Gallery provides visitors with information about each painting. Based on Apple Macintoshes with touch screens, this uses text, image and graphics to describe every painting in the gallery, as well as a wide range of additional information by topic. Users can plan a tour and print out a map at the end of the session before they enter the main gallery.

Careful supervision is required to ensure that information held in kiosks is up-to-date and that all Point-of-Information systems contain the same material. Linking the kiosks by a network is the obvious solution to this problem.

Summary

- IT refers to the scientific, technological, and engineering disciplies as well as management technologies used in information handling.
- IT comprises hardware, software, people, and data.

- Virtual classroom is a chat facility with in blackboard, which allows staff and students to conduct synchronous communication online.
- Two distinct categories of Electronic Commerce are Business to Business and Business to Consumer.
- Computers have entered not only in business organizations but they are doing wonders even in scientific and education systems.
- Moreover, computers have brought a new revolution in the field of entertainment and advertisement.
- Information Technology can be applied in railways, airlines, banking, insurance, etc.

Review Exercise

Multiple choice questions

1. Organizations use computers for
   a) Transaction Processing
   b) Management Control Operations
   c) Decision Making
   d) All of the above.
2. One of the latest technologies in mobile computing is:
   a) PSTN
   b) Multimedia
   c) GPRS
   d) News-Pad
3. Information is needed for
   a) Communication
   b) Decision-making
   c) Both (a) and (b)
   d) None of these
4. Which of the following option is included in E-learning
   a) Computer-based training
   b) Web
   c) Both (a) and (b)

d) None of the above.

5. Entertainment applications does not include

a) Audio and Video CD Player

b) Games and animation packages

c) Computer Based Tutorials

d) None of the above.

State whether true or false

1. Information is the collection of facts gathered by various means of communication.
2. Computer based learning is done using multimedia, email, and virtual classrooms.
3. In this digital age, using paper mode as print media is wastage of paper.
4. Kiosks cannot be used to capture statistical data.
5. Internet based training is a kind of e-learning.

Fill in the blanks

1. Through ____________ it has become very easy to order the items through web site and pay electronically.
2. Applications involving mathematical, statistical, and model processing are called ____________.
3. Inventory means ____________ which a firm maintains for future requirements.
4. ____________ is not an example of print media.
5. Computer based training is delivered with the help of ____________.

Descriptive questions

1. Briefly explain the Financial Information System. How computers are useful in accounts?
2. Explain the need of information in our times.
3. Elaborate how a computer can be utilized in our education system?
4. Write short notes on:

    a) IT in Electronic learning

    b) Virtual classroom

5. What is Kiosk and describe some of its features.

INDEX

Made in United States
Orlando, FL
04 November 2026

90201482R00247